SCRIPTURE, CANON, AND COMMENTARY

SCRIPTURE, CANON, AND COMMENTARY

A COMPARISON OF CONFUCIAN AND WESTERN EXEGESIS

JOHN B. HENDERSON

PRINCETON UNIVERSITY PRESS

PRINCETON, NEW JERSEY

Copyright © 1991 by Princeton University Press
Published by Princeton University Press, 41 William Street,
Princeton, New Jersey 08540
In the United Kingdom: Princeton University Press, Oxford

Library of Congress Cataloging-in-Publication Data

Henderson, John B., 1948–
Scripture, canon, and commentary : A comparison of
Confucian and western exegesis / John B. Henderson.
p. cm.
Includes bibliographical references and index.
ISBN 0-691-06832-1 (alk. paper)
1. Chinese classics—History and criticism.   2. Philosophy,
Confucian.   I. Title.

PL2461.Z7H46   1991   895.1′09—dc20   90–42121

This book has been composed in Linotron Baskerville

Princeton University Press books are printed
on acid-free paper, and meet the guidelines for
permanence and durability of the Committee on
Production Guidelines for Book Longevity
of the Council on Library Resources

Printed in the United States of America by
Princeton University Press, Princeton, New Jersey

19 9 8 7 6 5 4 3 2 1

CONTENTS

ACKNOWLEDGMENTS   vii

PERIODS OF CHINESE HISTORY   ix

ABBREVIATIONS AND SHORT FORMS USED IN THE NOTES   xi

INTRODUCTION   3

CHAPTER 1
Origins and Antecedents of the Classics   21

CHAPTER 2
Integration, Development, and Closure of Canons   38

CHAPTER 3
Origins, Dimensions, and Apotheosis of Commentaries   62

CHAPTER 4
Commentarial Assumptions   89

CHAPTER 5
Commentarial Strategies   139

CHAPTER 6
Death and Transfiguration of Commentarial World Views   200

GLOSSARY OF CHINESE NAMES, TERMS, AND TITLES IN THE TEXT   225

SELECTED BIBLIOGRAPHY   229

INDEX   237

ACKNOWLEDGMENTS

I WISH first of all to thank Professor Tu Wei-ming of Harvard University and Professor Kidder Smith of Bowdoin College for their many valuable comments and helpful suggestions on earlier versions of this study. Their expert and careful readings of these earlier versions resulted in a much improved book, although I alone am responsible for the deficiencies that remain. Thanks are also due to my former colleague at LSU, Stephen Farmer, for having widened my world-historical perspective on scriptures, canons, and commentaries and for having shared his ideas on these and related topics. My home institution, Louisiana State University, contributed much to the completion of this book by supporting me during a year's leave of absence during which I composed the first draft.

To my colleagues and students in the History Department and Honors Program at LSU, and to my friends in Baton Rouge, I wish to express an especially heartfelt thanks for sustaining me during a serious illness that interrupted my work on this project in its later stages. Several of my colleagues, particularly Kevin Cope, Ward Parks, Paul Paskoff, and Deborah Jacobs, helped teach me to use a word processor at a time when I could not easily use a typewriter; and Peggy Seale and Keuren Pinkney deserve credit for printing out the final manuscript. I wish also to thank members of my family, especially my brother Joseph Henderson, my stepmother Thelma Henderson, as well as Ward and Karin Parks, for the love and support they have given me throughout the research and composition of this book. To Margaret Case of Princeton University Press, I wish to express my gratitude for her understanding and patience throughout the review process, and to Charles Purrenhage, my appreciation for his meticulous and conscientious copyediting.

Finally, I dedicate this book to the memory of my grandmother, Mrs. Hugh Henderson, in whose company I spent the happiest times of my life.

PERIODS OF CHINESE HISTORY

Shang dynasty 1766–1122 B.C. (traditional dates)

Chou dynasty 1122–256 B.C.
    Spring and Autumn era, 722–481 B.C.
    Warring States era, 403–221 B.C.

Ch'in dynasty 221–206 B.C.

Han dynasty 202 B.C.–A.D. 220
    Former Han era, 202 B.C.–A.D. 9
    Latter Han era, A.D. 25–220

Period of Disunion 220–581

Sui dynasty 581–618

T'ang dynasty 618–906

Sung dynasty 960–1279
    Northern Sung, 960–1126
    Southern Sung, 1126–1279

Yüan dynasty 1279–1368

Ming dynasty 1368–1644

Ch'ing dynasty 1644–1912

ABBREVIATIONS AND SHORT FORMS
USED IN THE NOTES

Ching-i k'ao

Ching-i k'ao (Investigations of Meanings in the Classics), 8 vols., comp. Chu I-tsun, *Ssu-pu pei-yao* edition (see SPPY, below).

Ch'ing-ju hsüeh-an

Ch'ing-ju hsüeh-an (Scholarly Records of Ch'ing Confucians), 8 vols., comp. Hsü Shih-ch'ang (Taipei: Shih-chieh shu-chü, 1979 reprint).

Chung-kuo tzu-hsüeh ming-chu chi-ch'eng

Chung-kuo tzu-hsüeh ming-chu chi-ch'eng, Ju-chia tzu pu (A Collection of Distinguished Works of Chinese Philosophy, Section on Philosophers of the Confucian School), comps. Huang Chieh et al. (Taipei: Chung-kuo tzu-hsüeh ming-chu chi-ch'eng pien yin-chi chin-hui, 1977).

Huang-Ch'ing ching-chieh

Huang-Ch'ing ching-chieh (Explications of the Classics from the Brilliant Ch'ing Era), 21 vols., comps. Juan Yüan et al. (Taipei: Fu-hsin shu-chü, 1972 reprint).

Ku-shih pien

Ku-shih pien (Critiques on Ancient History), 7 vols., comp. Ku Chieh-kang (Shanghai: Ku-chi ch'u-pan she, 1982 reprint).

SPPY

Ssu-pu pei-yao editions (Taipei: Chung-hua shu-chü, 1965).

Ssu-shu wu-ching

Ssu-shu wu-ching, Sung-Yüan jen chu (The Four Books and Five Classics with Sung and Yüan Commentaries), 3 vols. (Beijing: Chung-kuo shu-tien, n.d.).

Sung-Yüan hsüeh-an

Tseng-pu Sung-Yüan hsüeh-an (Scholarly Records of Sung and Yüan [Confucians] with Supple-

ments), 6 vols., comps. Huang
Tsung-hsi and Ch'üan Tsu-
wang, *Ssu-pu pei-yao* edition (see
SPPY, above).

T'u-shu chi-ch'eng   *Ku-chin t'u-shu chi-ch'eng* (Complete
Collection of Illustrations and
Books, Past and Present), 79
vols., comps. Ch'en Meng-lei et
al. (Taipei: Ting-wen shu-chü,
1977 reprint).

SCRIPTURE, CANON, AND COMMENTARY

INTRODUCTION

COMMENTARIES and commentarial modes of thinking dominated the intellectual history of most premodern civilizations, a fact often obscured by the "great ideas" approach to the history of thought and by modern scholars' denigration of the works of mere exegetes and annotators. Until the seventeenth century in Europe, and even later in China, India, and the Near East, thought, especially within high intellectual traditions, was primarily exegetical in character and expression. As José Faur has observed, "The most peculiar aspect of the medieval thinker is that he developed his ideas around a text and expressed them as a commentary."[1] Even those identified as the greatest philosophers in various medieval civilizations, such as Shankara (788–820), Ch'eng I (1033–1107), and al-Ghāzalī (d. 1111), framed their cogitations in the form of commentaries on classical or scriptural texts. Small wonder that in most premodern cultures "the most important thoughts emerge in Hermeneutics," and that "not system but commentary is the legitimate form through which truth is approached."[2]

With respect to China, the modern scholar Chou Yü-t'ung has remarked that "classical studies were the mainstay of China's feudal culture."[3] They structured and at times dominated key aspects of literature, philosophy, science, and even politics. Hence, a study of the relationships between classics and their commentaries is central to an understanding of premodern Chinese intellectual history, as of that of most traditional civilizations.

Just what these relationships were has not been the focus of many modern studies, although there exist several standard histories of classical scholarship, especially Chinese and Western. The present study does not aim to recapitulate or update these histories; it does not cover the same ground as P'i Hsi-jui's *History of Classical Studies*

---

[1] José Faur, *Golden Doves with Silver Dots: Semiotics and Textuality in Rabbinic Tradition* (Bloomington: Indiana University Press, 1986), p. 59.

[2] Wolfgang Bauer, *China and the Search for Happiness: Recurring Themes in Four Thousand Years of Chinese Cultural History*, trans. Michael Shaw (New York: Seabury Press, 1976), p. xiii; Gershom Scholem, "Revelation and Tradition as Religious Categories in Judaism," in Scholem, *The Messianic Idea in Judaism* (New York: Schocken Books, 1971), p. 289. Scholem makes this statement with particular reference to rabbinic Judaism.

[3] Chou Yü-t'ung, " 'Ching,' 'ching-hsüeh,' ching-hsüeh shih" ("The Classics," "Classical Studies," and the History of Classical Studies), in *Chou Yü-t'ung ching-hsüeh shih lun-chu hsüan-chi* (Selected Treatises by Chou Yü-t'ung on the History of Classical Studies), comp. Chu Wei-cheng (Shanghai: Jen-min ch'u-pan she, 1983), p. 660.

(Ching-hsüeh li-shih) or Honda Shigeyuki's *History of Chinese Classical Studies* (Chūgoku keigaku shi). I do not include a comprehensive account of the historical development of classical studies in the Confucian tradition from antiquity to the twentieth century. Still less do I set out to analyze the history of interpretations of the individual Confucian classics, such as the various cosmological, divinatory, political, moral, and philosophical readings of the *Classic of Change* (I-ching). Instead, my main object is to relate how commentators approached the classics, especially what assumptions they made regarding the character of these classics—for example, that they are consistent with one another—and how they dealt with problems in canonical texts that seemed to challenge or contravene such assumptions—for example, that they apparently contain contradictions. Hence the heart of the present book, chapters 4 and 5, analyzes these assumptions or presuppositions (chapter 4) and the strategies and arguments that commentators devised to support them (chapter 5). In order to set this analysis in a proper historical and cultural context, however, it is necessary to discuss first the antecedents and origins of the Confucian canon (or canons) in the Chou era (chapter 1), its integration and development under the Han dynasty (chapter 2), and the origins, dimensions, and apotheosis of commentaries on the classics and scriptures (chapter 3). I conclude with an account in chapter 6 of the unraveling in the late-traditional era of the classical-commentarial nexus that bound much of Chinese intellectual history and with a description of some modern rewindings of this nexus in the realms of both literature and ideology.

Much of this study, especially the last three chapters, follows a comparative approach. Specifically, it adduces examples from at least five other major commentarial traditions besides the Chinese Confucian: namely, Vedānta, Qur'ānic exegesis, rabbinic Judaism, ancient and medieval Christian biblical exegesis, and the classical epic (mainly Homer). To compare such diverse traditions with a view toward identifying and explaining what is universal in them may seem unjustifiable, especially in view of their widely divergent classical or textual bases. From a literary standpoint, what could be more different from an epic poem (such as the *Iliad*) than a divinatory manual (such as the early strata of the *Classic of Change*)?[4] Drawing any meaningful com-

---

[4] William A. Graham has also noted the "radical diversity in form and content among the notable scriptures of world religion and, indeed, often within the same scriptural text or corpus. Myth and legend, historical narratives, ritual books, legal codes, ecstatic or mystical poetry, apocalyptic visions, utterances of prophets and teachers, divine revelations, and hymns and prayers to a deity have all found a place in one

parisons between the two might seem as hopeless as relating Attila the Hun to a computer.[5]

But if these classical or scriptural texts indisputably differ widely from one another, it is just as indisputable that the commentarial traditions which evolved from attempts to interpret these texts have much in common. As the modern critic Jan Gorak has observed, "the classics sound much alike in critical commentary, however much they differ at the time of reading."[6] In fact, it may be stated as a general rule that the further commentarial traditions developed away from their canonical sources, both chronologically and conceptually, the more similar they became to one another, both with respect to the assumptions they made about the nature of the canon and the strategies they devised for supporting these assumptions. The very act of canonization had systematic consequences that were in part independent of the peculiarities of the canonical text. One may thus contrast the great variety among the classics or scriptures in various premodern traditions with the increasing uniformity of the commentarial presuppositions and procedures that grew out of attempts to interpret these texts. This is not to say that commentarial activities in their developed phases were unaffected by the literary and intellectual character of their classical textual bases. But it should be clear (at least by the end of chapter 5) that the Neo-Confucian Chu Hsi (1130–1200) has more in common with the Vedantist Shankara than does Confucius with the anonymous authors of the Veda. These resemblances exist, moreover, despite the fact that later commentators in various traditions harbored a great variety of attitudes toward their respective canons, ranging from worshipful reverence (as in Islam, the prime example of a "Book religion") to playfulness (as in much Jewish midrash).[7] Whether or not a canon is, strictly speaking, "scrip-

---

or another scripture." Graham, *Beyond the Written Word: Oral Aspects of Scripture in the History of Religion* (Cambridge: Cambridge University Press, 1987), p. 3.

[5] I owe this memorable trope to my colleague Ward Parks.

[6] Jan Gorak, *Critic of Crisis: A Study of Frank Kermode* (Columbia: University of Missouri Press, 1987), p. 54. Gorak adds that "Sainte-Beuve testifies to the unanimity among interpreters of the classic, who repeatedly find in their chosen texts a treasure house of order, urbanity, and design" (p. 54).

[7] Graham, *Beyond*, p. 79; Geo Widengren, "Holy Book and Holy Tradition in Islam," in *Holy Book and Holy Tradition*, eds. F. F. Bruce and E. G. Rupp (Grand Rapids, Mich.: William B. Eerdmans, 1968), p. 210. On the playfulness of types of rabbinic midrash ("exegesis" or "interpretation"), see Susan A. Handelman, *The Slayers of Moses: The Emergence of Rabbinic Interpretation in Modern Literary Theory* (Albany: State University of New York Press, 1982), p. 75; and Harold Fisch, "The Hermeneutic Quest in Robinson Crusoe," in *Midrash and Literature*, eds. Geoffrey H. Hartman and Sanford Budick (New Haven: Yale University Press, 1986), p. 230.

ture" or held to be divinely inspired, appears not to have greatly affected the exegetical devices employed in the commentarial traditions to which it is related.

Strangely, in view of the wide divergence among canonical texts in various traditions and the progressive convergence of commentarial presuppositions and procedures in these same traditions, there have been more attempts to compare the classics and their purported authors than there have been efforts to relate commentaries and commentators cross-culturally. Jonathan Z. Smith's call for "the study of comparative systematics and exegesis" and Hans-Georg Gadamer's vision of "a critical history of hermeneutics, the study of its basic principles and strategies" remain largely unheeded or unfulfilled.[8] Indeed, historians of scholastic and commentarial traditions in both East and West often display a strange myopia concerning possible parallels in the intellectual history of premodern civilizations. They sometimes speak of their subjects' "propensity to classification, specification and categorizing" or of their delight in "distinction, definition, tabulation" as if these traits were practically unique to a particular medieval culture.[9] One of the aims of this book is to establish that some such propensities and delights were not peculiar to any premodern intellectual tradition, but were largely systematic consequences of attempts to solve problems raised by the interpretation of canonical texts. In brief, similar assumptions about the nature of the canon in various commentarial traditions gave rise to similar strategies and methods for supporting these assumptions. These strategies and methods, moreover, were not mere techniques, but developed into the exegetical modes of thought that dominated the medieval mental world in both East and West and that were common to many otherwise quite diverse traditions.

Granted that there may be some basis for comparing commentarial assumptions and strategies in various premodern classical or scriptural traditions, why select the five particular ones named above for special consideration? In the first place, most seem to be obvious choices inasmuch as four of them—Christian biblical exegesis,

[8] Jonathan Z. Smith, "Sacred Persistence: Towards a Redescription of Canon," in *Approaches to Ancient Judaism: Theory and Practice*, ed. William Scott Green (Missoula, Mont.: Scholars Press, 1978), p. 18; Kurt Mueller-Vollmer, "Introduction. Language, Mind, and Artifact: An Outline of Hermeneutic Theory since the Enlightenment," in *The Hermeneutics Reader: Texts of the German Tradition from the Enlightenment to the Present*, ed. Mueller-Vollmer (New York: Continuum, 1988), p. 45. Mueller-Vollmer is here presenting Gadamer's viewpoint.

[9] Jan Gonda, *Medieval Religious Literature in Sanskrit*, vol. 2 of *A History of Indian Literature*, ed. Gonda (Wiesbaden: Otto Harrassowitz, 1977), p. 131; C. S. Lewis, *The Discarded Image: An Introduction to Medieval and Renaissance Literature* (Cambridge: Cambridge University Press, 1976), p. 10.

Qur'ānic exegesis, rabbinic Judaism, and Vedānta—are associated with the most prominent of the living world religions.[10] The focus on Vedānta within the rather broad and amorphous Hindu tradition as well as the peculiarities of rabbinic Judaism may require a little explanation.

Although Vedānta was not the only commentarial tradition to have developed from attempts to interpret the classic Veda, particularly the Upanishads, it was by far the most prominent. It was not only "the leading and principal tradition in the history of Indian philosophy," but may even be said to have swallowed up its rivals among the other five orthodox Hindu philosophical systems.[11] Even today, according to Romila Thapar, "most Indian philosophers claim either to be Vedantists or to be deeply influenced by Vedānta."[12]

Vedānta, moreover, is the only orthodox Hindu philosophical system that not only draws upon the Upanishads but treats them as a canon, as "absolutely authoritative sacred texts."[13] Its chief concern, even its raison d'être, is the explanation and reconciliation of the various metaphysical portions of the Upanishads.[14] Despite its philosophical reputation, Vedānta is "first and foremost a kind of Mīmāmsā or exegesis."[15]

The dominance of rabbinic Judaism in the postexilic Jewish tradition is even more complete than that of Vedānta in the Hindu philosophical tradition, so complete as to obscure the fact that it had serious rivals in antiquity.[16] Although the term "rabbi" ("my master" or

[10] I have not included much discussion on major religious traditions that were prominent in East Asia; instead, my focus is on those commentarial traditions with which Confucianism has had relatively little interaction. The most conspicuous and troubling omission from my survey may be Buddhism, which Donald Lopez, however, has characterized by its "relative dearth of hermeneutical strategies," which he attributes in part to the "size and plastic nature of the Mahāyāna canon." Donald S. Lopez, Jr., "Introduction to Buddhist Hermeneutics," *The Ten Directions* (published by Zen Center of Los Angeles and the Kuroda Institute) 9, no. 1 (Spring/Summer 1988): 8.

[11] Hajime Nakamura, *A History of Early Vedānta Philosophy*, trans. Trevor Leggett et al. (Delhi: Motilal Banarsidass, 1983), pt. 1, p. 2; Eliot Deutsch and J.A.B. van Buitenen, eds., *A Source Book of Advaita Vedānta* (Honolulu: University Press of Hawaii, 1971), p. 77.

[12] Romila Thapar, *A History of India* (Harmondsworth, Eng.: Penguin Books, 1983), vol. 1, p. 163.

[13] Nakamura, *Early Vedānta*, p. 115.

[14] V. S. Ghate, *The Vedānta: A Study of the Brahma-Sūtras with the Bhāsyas of S'amkara, Rāmānuja, Nimbārka, Madhva, and Vallabha*, Government Oriental Series, class c, no. 1 (Poona: Bhandarkar Oriental Research Institute, 1960), p. 12.

[15] Karl H. Potter, ed., *Encyclopedia of Indian Philosophies: Advaita Vedānta up to Śamkara and His Pupils* (Princeton: Princeton University Press, 1981), p. 46.

[16] For a clear and concise statement of the ways in which rabbinic Judaism dominated Judaism "from third-century Babylonia to nineteenth-century Europe," see Jacob Neusner, *The Wonder-Working Lawyers of Talmudic Babylonia: The Theory and Practice*

"teacher") did not appear until the first century A.D., the literature and attitudes of rabbinic Judaism may be traced back to about the fourth century B.C.[17] After the destruction of the Second Temple in A.D. 70, the rabbis eclipsed their Jewish rivals, founding a "religion of interpretation"[18] that sanctified exegetical enterprises to an extent unparalleled in world intellectual history. The rabbis even presented God as a rabbi whose chief activity was interpreting his own Torah. In the words of Susan Handelman, "interpretation—as opposed to incarnation—was the central divine act."[19] Moreover, were the study and interpretation of the Torah ever to cease, the world would come to an end. According to Simeon ben Zemah Duran (1361–1444), "This round world is suspended in space and has nothing to rest on except the breath of Torah study from the mouths of students—just as a man may keep something up in the air by the blowing of his breath."[20]

The inclusion in this study of the commentarial traditions that developed from Homer and, to a lesser extent, Vergil may also require some explanation or justification. Although moderns tend to regard the *Iliad*, *Odyssey*, and *Aeneid* primarily as literary works, this was not so true of the ancients for many of whom Homer, in particular, was scripture.[21] The epic poems attributed to him were the subjects of extensive commentary, literary imitations, and even school exercises throughout most of classical antiquity. The *Iliad* and *Odyssey* were not only the chief subjects of Hellenistic scholarship, but were also "the center of education, the source of mythology, the model of literature, the inspiration of artists; known and quoted by all."[22] According to

of Judaism in Its Formative Age (Lanham, Md.: University Press of America, 1987), pp. 43–44.

[17] James L. Kugel, "Part One. Early Interpretation: The Common Background of Late Forms of Biblical Exegesis," in James L. Kugel and Rowan A. Greer, *Early Biblical Interpretation* (Philadelphia: Westminster Press, 1986), pp. 63–64; Handelman, *Slayers of Moses*, p. 31.

[18] Kugel, "Early Interpretation," p. 72.

[19] Handelman, *Slayers of Moses*, p. XIV.

[20] Simeon ben Zemah Duran, quoted in *The Living Talmud: The Wisdom of the Fathers and Its Classical Commentaries*, selected and trans. with essay by Judah Goldin (New York: New American Library, Mentor Books, 1959), p. 47.

[21] Robert Drummond Lamberton, "Homer the Theologian: The *Iliad* and *Odyssey* as Read by the Neoplatonists of Late Antiquity" (Ph.D. diss., Yale University, 1979), pp. 29–30. Birger Pearson adds that "in ancient Greece, and in the Hellenistic world until the end of paganism, the chief sacred text of Greek culture and paideia was Homer's *Iliad* and *Odyssey*." Pearson, "Some Observations on Gnostic Hermeneutics," in *The Critical Study of Sacred Texts*, ed. Wendy Doniger O'Flaherty (Berkeley: Graduate Theological Union, 1979), p. 243.

[22] John A. Scott, *The Unity of Homer* (New York: Biblo and Tannen, 1965), p. 1.

Moses Finley, "Few works—and probably none which are not scriptural—have ever had such a hold on a nation for so many centuries."[23] Even in the Middle Ages, when his works were largely unavailable and unread in the Latin West, Homer retained much influence through the tradition of allegorical commentary mediated by the encyclopedists of late antiquity.[24] The commentarial tradition on Homer, in the absence of the texts it interpreted, assumed a life of its own.[25]

Vergil, unlike Homer, was widely read as well as the subject of extensive commentary throughout most of the Middle Ages and Renaissance. His *Aeneid* was the inexhaustible master text of the Latin West, its "greatest literary classic and the subject of countless imitations."[26] Vergil's epic, too, became a kind of scripture, the more so because its author was generally regarded as a prophet of the evangel and an oracular source of wisdom. But even the pagan commentator Macrobius (c. 400) regarded him as "an infallible sage of enormous and deep learning."[27]

Epics and epic poets do not enjoy such favor and fame in all premodern civilizations, a fact that is often obscured by their importance in the West. The *Epic of Gilgamesh*, for example, had no special place in Akkadian literature and was never canonized in any sense of the word. It was apparently little known and even unappealing to the ancient Mesopotamians.[28] So it is not surprising that this epic, like others in various ancient civilizations, did not become the focus of commentarial traditions within the culture that generated it.

But there is one other major epic tradition, that of India, in which epics, specifically the *Mahābhārata* (The Great Descendants of Bharata) and the *Rāmāyana*, did become the subjects of extensive commentaries, and even assumed the aura of a canon, a "fifth Veda." While the "texts" of these epics were never as fixed or compact as

[23] M. I. Finley, *The Ancient Greeks* (Harmondsworth, Eng.: Penguin Books, 1979), p. 26.

[24] Robert Lamberton, "Introduction" to *Porphyry: On the Cave of the Nymphs*, trans. and intro. Lamberton (Barrytown, N.Y.: Station Hill Press, 1983), pp. 13–14.

[25] Robert Lamberton, *Homer the Theologian: Neoplatonist Allegorical Reading and the Growth of the Epic Tradition* (Berkeley: University of California Press, 1986), pp. 261, 272, and 282.

[26] Barbara J. Bono, *Literary Transvaluation: From Vergilian Epic to Shakespearean Tragicomedy* (Berkeley: University of California Press, 1984), p. 2.

[27] Leslie George Whitbread, "Introduction" to Fulgentius, "The Exposition of the Content of Virgil According to Moral Philosophy," in Whitbread, *Fulgentius the Mythographer* (Columbus: Ohio State University Press, 1971), p. 110.

[28] A. Leo Oppenheim, *Ancient Mesopotamia: Portrait of a Dead Civilization*, rev. ed. completed by Erica Reiner (Chicago: University of Chicago Press), p. 256.

those of most canons or scriptures, they were related to their commentaries in ways similar to those in the great religious or scriptural traditions mentioned above. Moreover, one of these epics, the *Mahābhārata*, contains the most famous and revered classical text in the Hindu tradition, the *Bhagavad Gītā*, which could hardly be ignored in any comparative study of major exegetical traditions. Even the great Vedantist Shankara described the *Gītā* as "the quintessence of all the Upanisadic (Vedic) teachings."[29] The *Rāmāyana*, too, was not just an epic poem but a type of canon or scripture. In fact, one of its later renditions, that by the sixteenth-century Hindi poet Tulsīdās, has been described as the "Bible of Northern India."[30] Hence, this study also includes some discussion of the relationships between classic and commentary in the Indian epic tradition.

· · · · ·

The attempt to provide a comparative perspective notwithstanding, the emphasis in this study is on commentarial approaches to the canon in the Chinese Confucian tradition. But does it make any sense to speak of this commentarial tradition as a whole? Did there not exist a number of quite distinct approaches to the classics among Confucian commentators of later centuries, including statecraft studies (*ching-shih chih hsüeh*), moral-philosophical studies (*i-li chih hsüeh*), textual studies (*k'ao-chü chih hsüeh*), and literary studies (*ts'u-chang chih hsüeh*)? Is there not, moreover, supposed to be a sharp divergence between Han-era commentators on the classics, many of whom are typed as mere annotators and glossators, and the more philosophically inclined Sung and Ming Neo-Confucians? Indeed, the most prominent of these Neo-Confucians, Chu Hsi, worked to establish such a dichotomy in remarking that "from the Ch'in and Han eras sagely learning was not transmitted; and Confucian scholars knew only how to arrange and annotate [texts], and were ignorant of how to recover the ideas of the sages."[31] They were concerned only with glossing the meanings of particular words and phrases, taking little

[29] Shankara, quoted in John G. Arapura, *Gnosis and the Question of Thought in Vedānta: Dialogue with the Foundations* (Dordrecht: Martinus Nijhoff, 1986), p. 94.

[30] H. Daniel Smith, *Reading the Rāmāyana: A Bibliographic Guide for Students and College Teachers; Indian Variants on the Rāma-Theme in English Translations*, Foreign and Comparative Studies, South Asian Special Publications, no. 4 (Syracuse: Maxwell School of Citizenship and Public Affairs, Syracuse University, 1983), p. 32.

[31] Chu Hsi, "Hsü" (Preface) to Shih Tun, *Chung-yung chi-chieh* (Collected Explications of the *Doctrine of the Mean*), in *Chu-tzu ta-ch'üan* (Complete Writings of Master Chu), SPPY ed., 75.27a (vol. 9).

note of the great moral and metaphysical principles contained in the classics. According to Chu Hsi, the Sung Neo-Confucians restored the philosophical teachings of the ancient Confucian sages, resumed the "transmission of the Way" (*Tao-t'ung*) after a hiatus of about fourteen hundred years.

The extent to which the Sung Neo-Confucians reoriented Confucianism in their time should not go unrecognized. And indeed it has not, especially by modern historians of Neo-Confucian thought who, like Burckhardtian historians of the Renaissance, sometimes take their subjects' reformationist rhetoric a little too uncritically. For such classical revivals, renaissances, and reformations, which are a common feature of most premodern intellectual or scholastic traditions, often obscure significant continuities in these traditions. The Han-era commentators, Cheng Hsüan (127–200) and Chao Ch'i (d. 201), may not have articulated the more sublime doctrines of Neo-Confucian moral metaphysics; but some historians have not sufficiently appreciated the extent to which even these later doctrines are based on developments of the same exegetical modes of thought and procedures followed by commentators in the pre-Sung era. At the other extreme, few if any commentators in the Confucian or any other intellectual tradition have been mere glossators, naively and simply. All, or almost all, harbor a set of largely unproven assumptions regarding the text that they are glossing, assumptions that cannot but influence their approach to the text. One of the aims of the present study is to demonstrate (mainly in chapter 4) that Confucian commentators of various eras and schools entertained similar sets of such presuppositions, most of which they, moreover, shared with commentators in other major premodern intellectual traditions.

To accomplish this aim fully would perhaps require a comprehensive historical survey of the major commentaries stemming from each of the Confucian classics, as well as of all the principal schools in the history of Confucian and Neo-Confucian discourse. But such a procedure is hardly feasible for a lone scholar writing a single book. Hence, I have found it necessary, especially in chapters 4 and 5, to focus on a few particular books in the Confucian canon (or "canons," for there were several enumerations of the Confucian classics). Specifically, I emphasize the commentarial traditions stemming from two of the Confucian Five (or Six) Classics (*wu-ching*)[32]—namely, the *Classic of Change* and the *Spring and Autumn Annals* (Ch'un-ch'iu)—and

[32] This numerical discrepancy arises from the controversy over whether or not to include the "lost" *Record of Music* (Yüeh-chi), or *Music Classic* (Yüeh-ching), or alternatively the *Rites of Chou* (Chou-li) in the standard enumeration of the classics.

two of the Four Books (*ssu-shu*) canonized by the Sung Neo-Confucians—the *Analects* (Lun-yü) of Confucius and the *Mencius* (Meng-tzu). Inasmuch as this selection may seem arbitrary, I will attempt to justify it.

Why, in the first place, focus on commentaries on the *Classic of Change* and the *Spring and Autumn Annals* at the expense of the more venerable *Documents Classic* (Shu-ching) and *Songs Classic* (Shih-ching) and the more compendious *Record of Rites* (Li-chi)? One reason is that these were the only two of the five Confucian classics supposed to have been composed (at least in part) by the Sage, Confucius. Whereas Confucius was believed only to have edited or expurgated the other three of the Five Classics, the *Change* and the *Spring and Autumn Annals* "were really written by Confucius' own hand. Thus they preserve the Sage's spirit and design."[33] Of course, Confucius was supposed to have composed only the canonical appendices to the *Change*, the so-called Ten Wings, not the whole classic, the earliest strata of which were generally attributed to certain legendary sage rulers of high antiquity, particularly Fu Hsi and King Wen. But in so doing, Confucius was widely believed to have transformed that classic from a manual used for divination into a philosophical and cosmological exposition.[34]

Confucius' alleged authorship was not the only basis for commentators' having paired the *Change* with the *Annals*. Traditional and modern scholars alike have remarked that these two classics are the most difficult, enigmatic, and profound of all the books in the Confucian canon.[35] Hence, they were allegedly placed last in the standard

[33] Chin Chü-ching, "Tsung-hsü" (General Preface) to Chao Fang, *Ch'un-ch'iu shih-shuo* (My Teacher's Explanations on the *Spring and Autumn Annals*), in *Ching-i k'ao* 198.8b (vol. 6).

[34] Chou Yü-t'ung, " 'Liu-ching' yü K'ung-tzu ti kuan-hsi wen-t'i" (On the Question of the Relationships between the "Six Classics" and Confucius), in Chu, comp., *Chou Yü-t'ung ching-hsüeh shih lun-chu hsüan-chi*, pp. 796–797; P'i Hsi-jui, *Ching-hsüeh t'ung-lun* (Comprehensive Discussions of Classical Studies) (Taipei: Ho-Lo t'u-shu ch'u-pan she, 1974 reprint), 1.10–11. As early as the Sung era, however, scholars called into question Confucius' alleged authorship of the appendices to the *Change*, especially the "Great Commentary." The most prominent of these scholars was Ou-yang Hsiu (1007–1072), whose views on the composition of the "Ten Wings" are recounted in Iulian K. Shchutskii, *Researches on the I Ching*, trans. William L. MacDonald and Tsuyoshi Hasegawa with Hellmut Wilhelm (Princeton: Princeton University Press, 1979), pp. 65–71. As Willard Peterson has pointed out, the earliest statement that connects Confucius with some of the "Ten Wings" appears in the *Records of the Historian* (c. 100 B.C.). See Peterson, "Making Connections: 'Commentary on the Attached Verbalizations' of the *Book of Change*," *Harvard Journal of Asiatic Studies* 42, no. 1 (1982): 73–74.

[35] See, for example, Chu Hsi, "Ta Chao Tso-ch'ing" (Reply to Chao Tso-ch'ing), in *Chu-tzu ta-ch'üan* 43.16a (vol. 5); Chao Fang, "Lun hsüeh Ch'un-ch'iu chih yao" (A Dis-

educational curriculum of antiquity and, by some accounts, were even excluded from it altogether as too advanced for ordinary students.[36] Partly for the same reasons, the *Change* and the *Annals* gave rise to the most extensive and vigorous commentarial traditions and controversies in the history of Confucian scholarship. Indeed, the earliest recognized commentaries on one of the Confucian classics, principally the *Kung-yang Commentary* (Kung-yang chuan), the *Ku-liang Commentary* (Ku-liang chuan), and the *Tso Commentary* (Tso-chuan), were associated with the *Spring and Autumn Annals*.[37] According to Hiraoka Takeo, studies of the *Spring and Autumn Annals* became the pivot of classical studies in the Han era, although few Han commentaries on this classic survive.[38] During the Sung period, more commentaries were composed on the *Annals* than on any of the other classics, leading one modern historian, Sung Ting-tsung, to remark that studies of the *Annals* were the main current of classical scholarship in that era.[39] A voluminous commentary literature, "an entire library of rather impressive size," also developed around the *Classic of Change*.[40]

Despite the evident literary dissimilarities between these two clas-

---

cussion of the Essentials for Studying the *Spring and Autumn Annals*), from *Ch'un-ch'iu shih-shuo* (My Teacher's Explanations on the *Spring and Autumn Annals*), in *T'u-shu chi-ch'eng* 56:1920; Chou Yü-t'ung, " 'Ch'un-ch'iu' yü 'Ch'un-ch'iu' hsüeh" (The *Spring and Autumn Annals* and the Study of the *Spring and Autumn Annals*), in Chu, comp., *Chou Yü-t'ung ching-hsüeh shih lun-chu hsüan-chi*, p. 492; Hsiung Shih-li, *Lun liu-ching* (Discussions of the Six Classics) (Taipei: Ming-wen shu-chü, 1988), p. 2; Honda Shigeyuki, "Shun-shū kei seiritsu ni tsuite no kōsatsu" (On the Genesis of the Canon Ch'un Ch'iu), *Shinagaku* (Sinology) 5, no. 3 (October 1929): 175. In this case, as in all others, I have retained the English translation of the title of the article given in the Japanese journal in which it appears.

[36] Chu Hsi, "Tso-I" (On the Composition of the *Change*), from *Chu-tzu ta-ch'üan chi*, in *T'u-shu chi-ch'eng* 55:872; Wu K'ang, "K'ung-tzu yü Ch'un-ch'iu" (Confucius and the *Spring and Autumn Annals*), in Tai Chün-jen et al., *Ch'un-ch'iu san-chuan lun-wen chi* (A Collection of Articles on the *Spring and Autumn Annals* and Its Three [Primary] Commentaries) (Taipei: Li-ming wen-hua shih-yeh, 1981), p. 25; P'i Hsi-jui, *Ching-hsüeh li-shih* (History of Classical Studies) (Taipei: I-wen yin-shu kuan, 1966 reprint), p. 25.

[37] Honda Shigeyuki dates the *Tso-chuan* from just after the time of Mencius, probably the first half of the third century B.C. See Honda, *Chung-kuo ching-hsüeh shih* (History of Chinese Classical Studies) (Taipei: Ku-t'ing shu-wu, 1975 reprint), pp. 72–73. According to Hsü Fu-kuan, the *Ku-liang chuan* dates from just after the middle of the Warring States era. Hsü, *Liang-Han ssu-hsiang shih* (Intellectual History of the Han Eras) (Taipei: Hsüeh-sheng shu-chü, 1979), 3:251.

[38] Hiraoka Takeo, *Keisho no seiritsu* (The Formation of the Classics) (Osaka: Zenkoku shobō, 1946), p. 37.

[39] Sung Ting-tsung, *Ch'un-ch'iu Sung-hsüeh fa-wei* (A Disclosure of the Subtleties of Sung Studies on the *Spring and Autumn Annals*) (Taipei: Wen-shih-che ch'u-pan she, 1986), pp. 4 and 36.

[40] Shchutskii, *Researches*, pp. 196–197.

sics—the one a sort of manual of divination and collection of omens and anecdotes with moral and cosmological appendices, the other a very terse historical chronicle of the state of Lu from 722 to 481 B.C.—Confucian commentators found other ways of associating them. One of these was by pairing them symmetrically as complementary opposites. Chu Hsi, for example, remarked that "the *Change* goes from the hidden to the manifest, while the *Spring and Autumn Annals* proceeds from the perceptible to the hidden. . . . The *Change* explains what is within form [or the corporeal] by what is above form [or the incorporeal]; and the *Spring and Autumn Annals* explains what is above form by what is within form."[41] The great philosophical historian Chang Hsüeh-ch'eng (1738–1801) wrote less cryptically but just as symmetrically that "the *Change* delves into human affairs through the ways of heaven; and the *Spring and Autumn Annals* harmonizes with the ways of heaven through human affairs."[42] The late-Ch'ing scholar-adventurer K'ang Yu-wei (1858–1927) paired these classics symmetrically with the two most important heterodox philosophical schools of antiquity, the *Change* with the Taoist and the *Annals* with the Mohist, the one associated with anarchic individualism and the other with communitarian universalism.[43]

Commentators sometimes devised such dualities between other books of the Confucian canon, though not nearly so frequently as with the *Change* and the *Annals*. The two historical classics, the *Documents Classic* and the *Annals*, were often associated along such lines. According to the *Han History* "Treatise on Bibliography" (Han-shu, I-wen chih), "the historian of the left recorded words and the historian of the right recorded events. The [record of] events became the *Spring and Autumn Annals* and the [record of] words became the *Documents of Antiquity* [= Documents Classic]."[44] The prominent Sung-era scholar-official Su Ch'e (d. 1112) associated the *Songs Classic* with

---

[41] Chu Hsi, quoted in "Kang-ling" (Outline) to *Ch'un-ch'iu san-chuan* (The *Spring and Autumn Annals* with the Three [Primary] Commentaries), in *Ssu-shu wu-ching*, vol. 3; this quotation from the *Chu-tzu ta-ch'üan chi* also appears in *T'u-shu chi-ch'eng* 55:871.

[42] Chang Hsüeh-ch'eng, *Wen-shih t'ung-i* (The Comprehensive Meaning of Literature and History) (Taipei: Kuang-wen shu-chü, 1967 reprint), 1.10.

[43] K'ang Yu-wei, *Nan-hai K'ang hsien-sheng k'ou-shuo* (Oral Sayings of Mr. K'ang of Nan-hai) (Chung-shan ta-hsüeh ch'u-pan she, 1985), p. 13.

[44] *Han-shu, I-wen-chih chu-shih hui-pien* (*Han History* "Treatise on Bibliography" with Collected Annotations), comp. Chen Kuo-ch'ing (Beijing: Chung-hua shu-chü, 1983), p. 73. The "Yü-tsao" (Jade Elegance) chapter of the *Record of Rites* presents a similar schema, but reverses the terms as follows: "The historian of the left writes about actions, and the historian of the right writes about words." *Li-chi chi-shuo* (The *Record of Rites* with Collected Explanations), annot. Ch'en Hao, p. 165, in *Ssu-shu wu-ching*, vol. 2.

the *Annals*, proposing that "if one does not observe the *Songs*, one will have no way of knowing the easiness of the kingly way; if one does not observe the *Spring and Autumn Annals*, one will have no way of knowing the difficulty of kingly government."[45] Wang Ying-lin (1223–1296) also connected these two classics, remarking that "the *Songs* and the *Spring and Autumn Annals* are related to one another as inner and outer. What the *Songs* reprimands, the *Annals* censures."[46] But the links that Confucian commentators forged between these other classics are far less frequently joined, and are less elaborate and symmetrical, than those which paired the *Annals* with the *Change*. For many of these commentators, these two classics formed an independent and even comprehensive unit within the larger Confucian canon, even though they were not formally designated as such.[47] Indeed, the famous Han scholar Liu Hsin (d. A.D. 23) allegedly even sought to combine them into one book.[48]

The *Change* and the *Annals*, taken singly, were also regarded as outstanding among the Confucian classics. That the *Change* is the object of extensive praise and self-praise is so well known to students of Chinese intellectual history as to hardly require extensive documentation. Nevertheless, a few expressions of the place accorded the *Change* in traditional commentarial literature should serve to illustrate the special position of this classic among the books in the Confucian canon.

The idea that the *Change* comprehends the Confucian canon as a whole may be traced at least as far back as the Han historian Pan Ku (32–92), who remarked that the *Classic of Change* was the source or

[45] Su Ch'e, quoted in *Ching-i k'ao* 231.2a (vol. 7).

[46] Wang Ying-lin, *Weng-chu K'un-hsüeh chi-wen* (A Record of What I Have Learned in Difficult Studies, with Weng's Commentary), SPPY ed., 6.1a (vol. 3). As Honda Shigeyuki has noted, the *Songs* and the *Annals* were originally unrelated to one another, but came to be connected through their both being used as texts in the Confucian educational curriculum. Honda, "Shun-shū kei," p. 176.

[47] Aside from the points mentioned above, there did exist an early semicanonical authority for linking these two classics. This appears in the *Tso-chuan* under the second year of Duke Chao (540 B.C.): "The marquis of Ch'in sent Hsüan-tzu of Han [to the state of Lu] to pay his respects. Observing the documents in the care of the grand historian [of Lu], he saw the emblems of the *Change* and the *Spring and Autumn Annals* of the state of Lu. He remarked that 'the traditions of the Chou are all [preserved] in the state of Lu. I indeed now understand the virtue of the Duke of Chou and how the house of Chou attained the kingship.' " For another English translation of this passage, see James Legge, *The Chinese Classics*, vol. 5: *The Ch'un Ts'ew with the Tso Chuen*, 2nd ed. (Taipei: Wen-shih-che ch'u-pan she, 1971 reprint), p. 583.

[48] According to the Sung scholar Yeh Shih, as quoted in *Sung-Yüan hsüeh-an* 54.22b (vol. 4).

origin of the Way expressed in the other classics.[49] The premier Sung Neo-Confucian cosmologist, Chou Tun-i (1017–1073), added that the *Change* was not only the source of the Five Classics, but was the secret repository of heaven and earth and spiritual forces as well.[50] The eighteenth-century editors of the general catalog to the *Complete Library in Four Treasuries* (Ssu-k'u ch'üan-shu) proposed that "among the Six Classics, only the *Change* encompasses the multitudinous patterns."[51] A modern historian of classical studies, Ch'u Po-ssu, has similarly remarked that although explanations of the Confucian Way may be dispersed among the Six Classics, they are all summed up in the *Change*.[52] The *Change*, in brief, comprehends both the classics and the cosmos.

Apart from the *Change*, the Confucian classic that commentators most frequently singled out, or more particularly counterposed to the other classics as a whole, was the *Spring and Autumn Annals*. According to the Ch'ing commentator Liu Feng-lu (1776–1829), the *Annals* was the master key to the Five Classics: "One who does not understand the *Annals* cannot discuss the Five Classics."[53] And K'ang Yu-wei remarked that although the Six Classics are very voluminous and divergent, their guiding principles can all be found in the *Spring and Autumn Annals*.[54]

In the view of most earlier commentators, however, the *Annals* merited a special place among the Confucian classics not so much because of its comprehensiveness and alleged Confucian authorship as for its practical illustrations of Confucian principles in particular historical events and human affairs. As the Sung Neo-Confucian cosmologist Shao Yung (1011–1077) explained, "the Six Classics of the sages are traceless and trackless like the ways of heaven. Therefore, the *Spring and Autumn Annals* records real affairs, and thus good and evil take concrete form in it."[55] The philosopher Ch'eng I expressed

[49] Chen, comp., *Han-shu, I-wen-chih*, p. 96.

[50] Chou Tun-i, *Chou-tzu T'ung-shu* (Master Chou's Comprehensive Book [on the *Change*]), SPPY ed., p. 6b.

[51] *Ssu-k'u ch'üan-shu tsung mu* (General Catalog to the Complete Library in Four Treasuries), comp. Chi Yün et al. (Taipei: I-wen yin-shu-kuan, 1974 reprint), 1:536 (*chüan* 26.1b).

[52] Ch'u Po-ssu, *Liu-ching tao lun* (A Discussion of the Way of the Six Classics) (Taipei: K'ai-ming shu-tien, 1971), p. 114.

[53] Liu Feng-lu, *Ch'un-ch'iu Kung-yang ching Ho-shih shih-li* (The *Kung-yang* Version of the *Spring and Autumn Classic* with Mr. Ho's Explanatory Examples), in *Huang-Ch'ing ching-chieh* 1,280.9a (vol. 19, p. 14,034).

[54] Kung-chuan Hsiao, *A Modern China and a New World: K'ang Yu-wei, Reformer and Utopian, 1858–1927* (Seattle: University of Washington Press, 1975), p. 73.

[55] Shao Yung, *Huang-chi ching-shih shu* (Book of the Supreme Polarities Governing the World), "Kuan-wu wai-p'ien" (Outer Chapters on Observing Things), in *T'u-shu*

a more widely quoted analogy between the position of the *Annals* among the classics and the place of judgments in law, remarking that "the Five Classics' having the *Spring and Autumn Annals* is like the law's having judgments. Laws only discuss rules of conduct. Not until judgments are made can one begin to see their application."[56] Alternatively, but also analogically, "the Five Classics resemble medical prescriptions, while the *Spring and Autumn Annals* is like using the medicine to cure a disease. The practices of the Sage are complete in this book. If the scholar will only inspect the *Annals*, he can also exhaustively comprehend the Way."[57] A later Neo-Confucian scholar, Cheng Yü (1298–1358), drew a similar distinction, asserting that while the other classics, principally "the *Change*, the *Songs*, and the *Documents*, discuss principles, the *Annals* records affairs. If one had only the *Change*, the *Songs*, and the *Documents* without the *Annals*, they would all be only empty words," something that Confucius particularly wished to avoid.[58]

It is of course true that scholars and commentators in almost any tradition, especially the Confucian with its diverse multibook canon, tend to single out for special praise the classical texts to which they devote their primary attention. But such expressions as those noted above of why a particular classic is the master key or necessary complement to all of the others are somewhat more rare. In the Confucian commentarial tradition, such expressions seldom appear with respect to any of the Five (or Six) Classics apart from the *Change* and the *Annals*. Hence, these two books are set apart from the other classics not only as a complementary pair, but also singly for their special relationships to the canon as a whole.

Unlike the Five Classics, which were integrated into a Confucian canon in the Former Han era, the Four Books—the *Analects*, *Mencius*, *Doctrine of the Mean* (Chung-yung), and *Great Learning* (Ta-hsüeh)—

chi-ch'eng 56:1851; a slightly different rendering of Shao Yung's words on this point may be found in *Ching-i k'ao* 194.1b (vol. 6).

[56] Ch'eng I, in *Chin-ssu lu* (Reflections on Things at Hand), comps. Chu Hsi and Lü Tsu-ch'ien; annot. Chiang Yung (Taipei: Kuang-wen shu-chü, 1972 reprint), 3.20. Hu An-kuo is the apparent source for this analogy. See Conrad Shirokauer, "Chu Hsi and Hu Hung," in *Chu Hsi and Neo-Confucianism*, ed. Wing-tsit Chan (Honolulu: University Press of Hawaii, 1986), p. 481; and Hu An-kuo, *Ch'un-ch'iu chuan* (Commentary on the *Spring and Autumn Annals*), in *Ching-i k'ao* 185.1b (vol. 6).

[57] Ch'eng I, quoted in *T'u-shu chi-ch'eng* 56:1849.

[58] Cheng Yü, "Tzu-hsü" (Author's Preface) to *Ch'un-ch'iu chuan ch'üeh-i* (A Commentary on the *Spring and Autumn Annals* That Sets Aside Doubtful Points), in *Ching-i k'ao* 197.1a (vol. 6). On Confucius' alleged composition of the *Annals* as a means of avoiding the expression of his teachings in the form of empty words, see Ssu-ma Ch'ien, "T'ai-shih-kung tzu-hsü" (Author's Preface by the Grand Historian), in *Shih-chi* (Records of the Historian), 10 vols. (Beijing: Chung-hua shu-chü, 1975), 10:3297 (*chüan* 70).

were not identified as a unit before Sung times. However, these books together with the *Classic of Change* formed the main classical basis of the Neo-Confucian philosophy of the Sung, Yüan, Ming, and early Ch'ing eras. Since Neo-Confucianism includes the most important and highly developed commentarial tradition in the history of Confucian thought, it is appropriate to devote special attention in this study to the classical texts that the Neo-Confucians particularly emphasized.

Among the Four Books, the *Analects* and the *Mencius* are especially distinguished by virtue of their being the chief repositories of the words of the two greatest Confucian sages, Confucius and Mencius. Although the other classics, said the Northern Sung scholar Tsou Hao (1060–1111), "all emanated from the sages, they are not purely the words of the sages."[59] Thus, Chu Hsi maintained that "if one wishes to get directly the basic ideas of the sages without mistake, it is not necessary to understand the other classics. One must first concentrate one's thought on the *Analects* and the *Mencius*."[60] Chu Hsi here echoed an idea expressed by Ch'eng I, who argued that "scholars ought to take the *Analects* and the *Mencius* as the basis [of their studies]. Once the *Analects* and *Mencius* are studied, then the Six Classics can be clarified without being studied."[61]

Later commentators found in the *Analects* in particular the essence of the Sage's teaching and a master key to the classics as a whole. According to the prominent Ch'ing historian of the classics Ch'en Li (1810–1882), "the essentials of classical studies are all in the *Analects*."[62] Liu Feng-lu remarked that "the *Analects* sums up the great meanings of the Six Classics."[63] A similar view is expressed in an introduction to the earliest extant commentary on the *Mencius*, that by Chao Ch'i, which characterizes the *Analects* as the linchpin of the Five Classics. The *Mencius* only orders and illustrates the *Analects*.[64]

---

[59] Tsou Hao, "Tzu-hsü" (Author's Preface) to *Lun-yü chieh-i* (Explications of the Meanings of the *Analects*), in *Ching-i k'ao* 213.7b (vol. 6). The *Analects* does not, of course, consist solely of Confucius' sayings, but includes many utterances by his disciples as well. Moreover, a number of chapters in the *Analects* were not compiled until long after Confucius' death.

[60] Chu Hsi, "Tu-I" (Studies on the *Change*), from *Chu-tzu yü-lu* (Recorded Conversations of Master Chu), in *T'u-shu chi-ch'eng* 55:874.

[61] Ch'eng I, quoted in Chu Hsi, "Lun Meng ching-i kang-ling" (An Outline of the Essential Meanings of the *Analects* and *Mencius*), from *Chu-tzu i-shu* (Surviving Works of Master Chu), in *T'u-shu chi-ch'eng* 57:2877.

[62] Ch'en Li, *Tung-shu tu-shu chi* (Reading Notes of [Ch'en] Tung-shu) (Taipei: Shang-wu yin-shu-kuan, 1970 reprint), 2.14.

[63] Liu Feng-lu, "Hsü" (Preface) to *Lun-yü shu Ho* (The *Analects* Following Ho [Yen's Commentary]), in *Huang-Ch'ing ching-chieh* 1,298.10a (vol. 19, p. 14,221).

[64] Chao Ch'i, "Ch'i t'i-tzu" ([Chao] Ch'i's Laudatory Introductory Words) to *Meng-tzu*

Confucian commentators customarily linked the *Mencius* not only with the *Analects*, but sometimes with the *Change* and *Annals* as well. Thus, Ch'eng I remarked that both of these classics are best approached through the *Mencius*.[65] A later scholar of the Ch'eng-Chu school, Hao Ching (1223–1275), lamented that Mencius did not spell out his profound understanding of the *Annals* in particular in the proper form of a commentary, thus leaving later generations of scholars confused on the meanings of that classic.[66]

While the other two of the Four Books, the more concentrated and philosophical *Doctrine of the Mean* and *Great Learning*, were also the subjects of intensive study and extravagant praise by Neo-Confucian commentators, seldom were they systematically related to one another or to the Five Classics as a whole in the ways described above.[67] These two short texts, moreover, originally comprised chapters in the canonical *Record of Rites*, from which they were extracted and established as classics in their own right only in the Sung period. Hence, they did not become the subjects of extensive commentary until relatively late in Chinese intellectual history. Even in the post-Sung era, some scholars challenged the independent canonical position of these two texts, and proposed to study them only as parts of the compendious *Record of Rites*.[68] Finally, both the *Doctrine of the Mean* and the *Great Learning* are much shorter and more homogeneous than either the *Analects* or the *Mencius*. Thus, they do not present quite the range of exegetical issues and problems as these other two of the Four Books.

. . . . .

While focusing on two of the Five Classics and two of the Four Books in this study of commentarial approaches to the classics in the Chi-

---

chu (The *Mencius* with Annotations), in *Ching-i k'ao* 232.2a (vol. 7). This introduction does not appear in the SPPY edition of the *Meng-tzu Chao-chu*.

[65] Ch'eng I, "Ch'un-ch'iu" (The *Spring and Autumn Annals*), from *Ch'eng-tzu i-shu*, in *T'u-shu chi-ch'eng* 56:1849.

[66] Hao Ching, "Tzu-hsü" (Author's Preface) to *Ch'un-ch'iu wai-chuan* (Outer Commentary on the *Spring and Autumn Annals*), in *Ching-i k'ao* 193.5a (vol. 6).

[67] Some later scholars did, however, pair these two classics as complementary opposites, remarking that the *Great Learning* discusses mind (*hsin*) but not human nature (*hsing*), and the *Mean* human nature but not mind, and that while the former concentrates exclusively on the Way of man, the latter also talks about the Way of heaven. Ch'en Jung-chieh [Wing-tsit Chan], "Ch'u-ch'i ju-chia" (Confucianists in the Early Period), *Chung-yang yen-chiu-yüan, li-shih yü-yen yen-chiu-suo chi-k'an* (Bulletin of the Institute of History and Philology of the Academia Sinica) 47, no. 4 (December 1976): 750.

[68] Benjamin A. Elman, *From Philosophy to Philology: Intellectual and Social Aspects of Change in Late Imperial China* (Cambridge: Harvard University Press, 1984), p. 47.

nese Confucian tradition, I have not ignored other Confucian canonical texts. Chapter 1, for example, discusses the venerable *Documents Classic*, which records the purported words and deeds of the legendary sage-kings of high antiquity, as well as the *Songs Classic*, a collection that includes types of verse ranging from royal court odes to peasant work songs. I have also drawn heavily on literature that is not cast in the form of direct or running commentary on particular classical texts: for example, prefaces to works of classical scholarship reproduced in such monumental anthologies as the *Ching-i k'ao* (Investigations of Meanings in the Classics) and the *Ku-chin t'u-shu chi-ch'eng* (Complete Collection of Illustrations and Books, Past and Present). Through use of these more varied sources, I hope to escape the suspicion of having attempted to reform the Confucian canon by devising my own version of the Four Books.[69]

[69] My four-book schema, however, does come close to one attributed to Ch'eng I by Kuo Yung, who remarked that what Ch'eng "studied, practiced, and taught for the most part appears in the *Change*, the *Annals*, the *Doctrine of the Mean*, the *Analects*, and the book of *Mencius*." Kuo, "Kuo-shih ch'uan-chia I-shuo tzu-hsü" (Author's Preface to Mr. Kuo's Explanations on the *Change* Transmitted to His Heirs), in *Sung-Yüan hsüeh-an* 28.3a (vol. 2).

Chapter 1

ORIGINS AND ANTECEDENTS OF THE CLASSICS

THE CONFUCIAN canon (or canons) is as diverse in its origins and complicated in its development as that of almost any major classical or scriptural tradition.[1] Its antecedents may plausibly be traced back to such variegated sources as the oracle-bone divination of the second millennium B.C. and to folk songs and sayings by early inhabitants of the North China Plain. Although standard versions of the canon were fixed under the Han dynasty, with a major reformation coming more than a millennium later in the Sung era, classical scholars continued to propose revisions and re-enumerations of the classics in the centuries that followed. The relatively amorphous and permeable character of the Confucian canon was, in fact, a source of perplexity for at least one famous scholar of the Han era, the grand historian Ssu-ma T'an (d. 110 B.C.), who once commented that "the Confucians are too broad and lack a vital center."[2]

This complaint notwithstanding, the heterogeneity of the books in the Confucian canon, particularly the Five Classics established under the Han, is not at all atypical when compared with that of canons in other major classical or scriptural traditions. Few if any of these are unified works composed by a single hand or even like-minded hands. Almost all canons are complex anthologies assembled by "schools" and even whole civilizations over long periods of time. The Bible, for

[1] The relative diversity of the books in the Confucian canon may be related to the nontheocentric orientation of Confucianism. As William A. Graham has remarked, "In theocentric traditions, scripture is preeminently 'the place where God speaks to men,' and the historical tendency for this speech to be conceived of as a unitary whole, as a single text or 'book,' is especially strong in these contexts. On the other hand, in nontheistic or semitheistic traditions, scripture tends to be more readily conceived of as the cumulative record of the teachings of sages or holy persons, however unitary the truth of these teachings is ultimately perceived to be." Graham, *Beyond the Written Word: Oral Aspects of Scripture in the History of Religion* (Cambridge: Cambridge University Press, 1987), p. 68.

[2] Ssu-ma Ch'ien, "T'ai-shih-kung tzu-hsü" (Author's Preface by the Grand Historian) to *Shih-chi* (Records of the Historian), 10 vols. (Beijing: Chung-hua shu-chü, 1975), 10:3289 (*chüan* 70). Ssu-ma T'an's Taoist proclivities, especially his high regard for simplicity, may account in part for his perception of the Confucian classics as too complex and centerless. Whether or not the Confucian canon or canons does in fact contain a vital center or comprise a holistic vision is a cosmological issue that I would prefer to leave for others to solve.

example, comprises what remains of the library of an articulate culture assembled over many hundreds of years. It presents such a mosaic of literary forms, including "commandments, aphorisms, epigrams, proverbs, parables, riddles, pericopes, parallel couplets, formulaic phrases, folktales, oracles, epiphanies, *Gattungen, Logia*, bits of occasional verse, marginal glosses, legends, snippets from historical documents, laws, letters, sermons, hymns, ecstatic visions, rituals, fables, genealogical lists, and so on almost indefinitely," that Northrop Frye speculates: "In no language but Biblical Hebrew, perhaps, would it have been possible to put together so miscellaneous a mass of material."[3] This miscellaneousness was, in fact, better recognized by medieval commentators, who customarily spoke not of the "Bible" but of the "holy books" (*sacri libri*) and "divine books" (*divini libri*), than it is by moderns.[4] But for sheer miscellaneousness, the Indian epic, the *Mahābhārata*, outstrips even the Bible and the Hebrew scriptures. According to J.A.B. van Buitenen, an analogical work in Western culture might include something like the following: "an *Iliad*, rather less tightly structured than it is now, incorporating an abbreviated version of *The Odyssey*, quite a bit of Hesiod, some adapted sequences from Herodotus, assimilated and distorted pre-Socratic fragments, Socrates by way of Plato by way of Plotinus, a fair proportion of the Gospels by way of moralizing stories, with the whole complex of 200,000 lines worked over, edited, polished by successive waves of anonymous church fathers."[5] Even relatively homogeneous Indian canonical texts such as the Upanishads contain "all sorts of miscellaneous ideas, injunctions, incantations, theological interpretations, conversations, traditions, and so forth . . . assembled and set down without any sequence."[6]

Other major scriptures, particularly the Qur'ān, are more homogeneous and unified. But even that book "represents an arbitrary ar-

---

[3] Northrop Frye, *The Great Code: The Bible and Literature* (San Diego: Harcourt Brace Jovanovich, Harvest/HBJ Books, 1983), pp. 206 and 208. The miscellaneousness of the material included in the Bible may stem more from its early use in educational curricula than from the special qualities of the Hebrew language. For a discussion of the possible use of the biblical proto-canon in early Jewish education, see James L. Kugel, "Part One. Early Interpretation: The Common Background of Late Forms of Biblical Exegesis," in James L. Kugel and Rowan A. Greer, *Early Biblical Interpretation* (Philadelphia: Westminster Press, 1986), pp. 55–57.

[4] Jean Châtillon, "Les Écoles du XIIᵉ siècle," in *Le Moyen Age et la Bible*, eds. Pierre Riché and Guy Lobrichon (Paris: Editions Beauchesne, 1984), pp. 164–165.

[5] J.A.B. van Buitenen, "The Indian Epic," in Edward C. Dimock, Jr., et al., *The Literatures of India: An Introduction* (Chicago: University of Chicago Press, 1978), p. 53.

[6] Hajime Nakamura, *A History of Early Vedānta Philosophy*, trans. Trevor Leggett et al. (Delhi: Motilal Banarsidass, 1983), pt. 1, p. 109.

rangement of short passages which had been uttered by the Prophet at various times and in various places throughout his lifetime."[7] Finally, the *Iliad* and *Odyssey*, which owing to their finer literary qualities as well as their having been edited by Alexandrian scholars should present more of a united front, have been characterized as containing "a motley collection of tales, traditions, legends, and even forms from different times and places."[8] In sum, although the classics or scriptures in various traditions differ widely from one another in their literary character and intellectual orientation, they are at least alike in their *différance*, in their heterogeneity and internal dissonance. The characterization of the *Classic of Change* by the great nineteenth-century *I-ching* scholar Matsui Rashu, as "an incredible conglomeration of very diverse elements,"[9] could well be applied to almost any of the non-Chinese classics or scriptures mentioned above.

Even some traditional commentators recognized the anthological character and disparate sources of canonical works. The T'ang-era classicist Lu Te-ming (556–648), for example, characterized one of the five Confucian classics, the *Record of Rites*, as an anthology of assorted leftovers from the other two classics on ritual, the *Deportment and Rites* (I-li) and the *Rites of Chou* (Chou-li).[10] The Neo-Confucian scholar Wu Ch'eng (1247–1331) also regarded this classic as a heterogeneous collection of fragments with many gaps, and even went so far as to rearrange the received text to make the chapters follow one another in a more logical order.[11] Few classical scholars and commentators, however, expressed such views regarding most of the books in their canon. For such ideas contravened some of their basic assumptions (discussed in chapter 4, below) regarding the character of the canon, particularly that it is self-consistent and well ordered.

While they generally rejected or failed to consider the notion that the classics originated as anthologies that redactors assembled from disparate sources, classicists and commentators in traditional civiliza-

---

[7] N. J. Coulson, *A History of Islamic Law* (Edinburgh: Edinburgh University Press, 1964), p. 13.

[8] D. Gary Miller, *Improvisation, Typology, Culture, and "The New Orthodoxy"* (Lanham, Md.: University Press of America, 1982), p. xi.

[9] Iulian K. Shchutskii, *Researches on the I Ching*, trans. William L. MacDonald and Tsuyoshi Hasegawa with Hellmut Wilhelm (Princeton: Princeton University Press, 1979), p. 157.

[10] Li Yüeh-kang, "Li-chi ming-shih k'ao-shu" (An Investigation and Explanation of the Name and Substance of the *Record of Rites*), in Li Yüeh-kang et al., *San-Li yen-chiu lun-chi* (A Collection of Articles on the Study of the Three Ritual Classics) (Taipei: Li-ming wen-hua shih-yeh, 1981), p. 2.

[11] P'i Hsi-jui, *Ching-hsüeh li-shih* (History of Classical Studies) (Taipei: I-wen yin-shu-kuan, 1966 reprint), p. 255.

tions could hardly have ignored such an important and obvious question as that of the provenance of their canons. Although divine revelation and inspiration is perhaps the most commonly recognized answer to this question in Western and Middle Eastern scriptural traditions,[12] other explanations are possible, including those proposed by early Confucians. Since these explanations considerably influenced Confucian commentators' approaches to their canon, it is appropriate to include an account of them here.

．　．　．　．　．

One of the most peculiar of these theories traced each of the classics to a particular department or office in the legendary exemplary bureaucracy of high antiquity. Specifically, the Office of Music issued the *Songs Classic*, the Office of Records the *Documents Classic* and the *Spring and Autumn Annals*, the Office of Divination the *Classic of Change*, and the Office of Ritual the *Rites*.[13] This theory at least had the merit of presenting the classics as an ordered whole, congruent with the organization of the ideal bureaucracy, while implicitly acknowledging their heterogeneous character. It also explained the apparent orientation of a number of these Confucian classics toward matters of statecraft.

A related conception of the origins of the Confucian classics saw them as products of the decline and fall of the ancient bureaucracy and of the exemplary political and moral order it represented. Some traditional scholars expressed this idea with regard to the canon as a whole. According to the *Sui History* "Treatise on the Classics" (Sui-shu, Ching-chi chih), Confucius' expounding and editing of the classics was his response to the decline of the Chou dynasty and its attendant political and moral order.[14] The Sung-era encyclopedist Cheng Ch'iao (1104–1162) viewed this development from a more cosmic

[12] For a discussion of the relationships between inspiration and canon in modern Christian theology, see David G. Meade, *Pseudonymity and Canon: An Investigation into the Relationship of Authorship and Authority in Jewish and Earliest Christian Tradition* (Tübingen: J.C.B. Mohr [Paul Siebeck], 1986), pp. 208–219.

[13] Chou Yü-t'ung, "Yu kuan Chung-kuo ching-hsüeh shih ti chi-ko wen-t'i" (On Several Questions Concerning the History of Chinese Classical Studies), in *Chou Yü-t'ung ching-hsüeh shih lun-chu hsüan-chi* (Selected Treatises by Chou Yü-t'ung on the History of Classical Studies), comp. Chu Wei-cheng (Shanghai: Jen-min ch'u-pan she, 1983), p. 694. For an account of a similar arrangement by the Ch'ing-era scholar Wang Chung (1745–1794), see Honda Shigeyuki, *Chung-kuo ching-hsüeh shih* (History of Chinese Classical Studies) (Taipei: Ku-t'ing shu-wu, 1975 reprint), p. 292.

[14] *Sui-shu* 32, "Ching-chi chih" 1 (*Sui History* "Treatise on the Classics"), 6 vols. (Beijing: Chung-hua shu-chü, 1975), 4:904.

perspective, remarking that when heaven ceased to give birth to sage-rulers as a means of instituting proper political order and human relationships, it did the next best thing by giving birth to the Sage, Confucius, who established the Six Classics as a substitute.[15]

But Confucian commentators more frequently advanced the theory that the classics are products of an era of decline by reference to two particular classics, the *Songs Classic* and the *Spring and Autumn Annals*, which are linked in the saying in *Mencius* that "when the traces of the [ancient] kings were extinguished the *Songs* was lost; and when the *Songs* was lost the *Annals* was composed."[16] A statement in the important Han-era compendium *Huai-nan-tzu* ([Book of the] Master of Huai-nan) explains the meaning of this rather cryptic utterance by asserting that "when the kingly Way deteriorated, the *Songs Classic* was composed; when the house of Chou was abandoned and rites and rightness decayed, the *Spring and Autumn Annals* was composed. The *Songs* and *Annals* are epitomes of learning. [But] they are both products of an era of decline."[17] The most important and influential such characterization of the origins of the *Songs Classic* appears in its "Great Preface" (Ta-hsü), a work traditionally attributed to one of Confucius' disciples, Tzu-hsia, but actually composed by a scholar in the Han era. A famous passage in this preface relates that "when the kingly Way declined and rites and rightness were abandoned, and government by moral instruction lost with each state having a different government and each family different customs, then the 'Changed Airs' and 'Changed Odes' [sections of the *Songs*] were composed."[18] The *Shuo-yüan* (Garden of Discourses), a work by the famous Han-era scholar and imperial librarian Liu Hsiang (77–6 B.C.), sets the *Annals* in a similar context of cultural decline when it attributes to Confucius the following words: "If the virtue of the Chou had not been lost, the *Spring and Autumn Annals* would not have been composed. As soon as the *Annals* was composed, gentlemen knew that the Way of the Chou was lost."[19] A more elaborate expres-

[15] Cheng Ch'iao, "Fu-tzu tso Liu-ching" (On the Master's [Confucius'] Composition of the Six Classics), from *Liu-ching ao-lun* (Subtle Discussions of the Classics), in *T'u-shu chi-ch'eng* 57:3159.

[16] *Mencius* 4A, 21:1.

[17] *Huai-nan-tzu* ([Book of the] Master of Huai-nan), "Fan lun hsün" (Extensive Lessons and Discussions), SPPY ed., 13.3b.

[18] This passage from the "Great Preface" to the *Songs* may be found in *Mao-Shih Cheng chien* (The *Songs* [According to the] Mao [Recension] with the Commentary by Cheng [Hsüan]), SPPY ed., 1.2a.

[19] *Shuo-yüan* (Garden of Discourses), "Chün-tao p'ien" (On the Way of the Prince) (Taipei: Shih-chieh shu-chü, 1966 reprint), 1.1.

sion of this idea appears in a nineteenth-century subcommentary by Ch'en Li (1809–1869) on the *Kung-yang Commentary* to the *Annals*:

> When the house of Chou [was forced to] move eastward [in 771 B.C., thus marking the end of its effective power], the order and writings of the [ancient] three dynasties were spent. With respect to what is above, none investigated the Way; and with respect to what is below, no one defended the law. Thus the Sage [Confucius] was constrained to compose the *Annals* to elucidate the system of kingship.[20]

Thus, the one classic that was widely believed to be the product of Confucius' own hand, the *Annals*, was supposedly his answer to the decline of the ancient political and moral order.

.   .   .   .   .

But what of Confucius' relationship to the other classics, specifically the *Documents*, *Songs*, *Rites*, and *Change*? The *Analects* does contain a couple of brief and enigmatic statements that apparently link Confucius to some of the classics, or preclassics. For example: "The Master frequently talked about the *Songs*, the *Documents*, and upholding the Rites."[21] Confucius was also said to have wished that he had fifty more years to devote to the study of the *Change*.[22] These classical texts, however, evidently do not record Confucius' own teachings. The Master is said only to have studied and perhaps taught these texts, or the arts or disciplines associated with them. But is this a sufficiently strong link between the revered founder of a tradition and its canon? Must not Confucius have had a hand in the formation or formulation of the classics and not just in their teaching and transmission?

Scholars of the Han era devised a number of rather intricate formulae that ascribed to Confucius a more active and exalted role in the development of the classics. According to the *School Sayings of Confucius* (K'ung-tzu chia-yü), "Confucius was born in [the era of] the declining Chou [dynasty] when the records of the former kings were in chaos and disorder. . . . He expurgated the *Songs*, expounded the *Documents*, fixed the *Rites*, arranged the *Music*, composed the *Spring and Autumn Annals*, and exalted and clarified the Way of the *Change*. Thus he handed down the teachings to later ages as a model."[23]

---

[20] Ch'en Li, *Kung-yang i shu* (Subcommentary on the Meanings of the *Kung-yang Commentary*), SPPY ed., 1.7a.

[21] *Analects* 7:17.

[22] Ibid. 7:16.

[23] *K'ung-tzu chia-yü* (School Sayings of Confucius), quoted in Hua Chung-lin, "Liu-

One might interpret the last sentence in this account to mean that Confucius' primary role was that of a transmitter of the sagely wisdom embodied in the classics. This conception is, moreover, supported by the influential remark attributed to Confucius in the *Analects* that "I expound but do not innovate, trusting and loving antiquity."[24] But few later commentators took Confucius at his word on this point, identifying him simply as a transmitter. As the Han Confucianist Yang Hsiung (53 B.C.–A.D. 18) remarked regarding the *Documents*, *Songs*, *Rites*, and *Annals*, Confucius "in some cases followed [existing works] and in some cases composed [new works]."[25] "How," queried the T'ang-era Confucian philosopher Li Ao (fl. 798), "could he like Lao P'eng have confined himself to expounding on ancient affairs?"[26]

Further, even with respect to those classical texts that he was not supposed to have actually composed (principally the *Documents*, the *Songs*, and the *Rites*), Confucius, by most traditional accounts, did not merely transmit. Nor did he limit himself simply to editing or compiling the records of the ancient sage-rulers. Rather, his chief contribution, many scholars of the Han and later eras argued, was in his having expurgated these precanonical writings in the course of transmitting them. The Chinese classics, in other words, became classics, were transformed from collections of ancient records on matters related to politics and ritual into a set of canonical texts by a process of excision or expurgation. And Confucius himself was the grand expurgator of the tradition. Although such a characterization might seem to portray Confucius as a singular figure as nefarious as the proverbial Grand Inquisitor, expurgation and excision are among the main devices employed by commentators in classical or scriptural traditions in general. They are strategies by which later commenta-

---

ching t'ao-yüan yü K'ung-tzu shu-tso" (An Examination of the Sources of the Six Classics and of Confucius' Expounding or Composing [These Classics]), in Wang Ching-chih et al., *Ching-hsüeh yen-chiu lun-chi* (A Collection of Articles on Research in Classical Studies) (Taipei: Li-ming wen-hua shih-yeh, 1981), p. 23. This theory of Confucius' editorial activities regarding the Six Classics did not appear full-blown, but emerged gradually from such disparate sources as the *Mencius* (which says that Confucius composed the *Spring and Autumn Annals*) and the *Records of the Historian* of Ssu-ma Ch'ien. See Ku Chieh-kang, "Lun K'ung-tzu shan shu Liu-ching shuo chi chan-kuo chu-tso wei-shu shu" (A Letter Discussing the Theory That Confucius Expurgated and Expounded the Six Classics and the Writing of the Counterfeit Books of the Warring States Era), in *Ku-shih pien* 1:42.

[24] *Analects* 7:1.

[25] Yang Hsiung, quoted in Ma Tsung-huo, *Chung-kuo ching-hsüeh shih* (History of Chinese Classical Studies) (Taipei: Shang-wu yin-shu-kuan, 1976), p. 9.

[26] Li Ao, quoted in Han Yü, *Lun-yü pi-chieh* (Notes Explaining the *Analects*), A.13b, in *Chung-kuo tzu-hsüeh ming-chu chi-ch'eng* 3:28.

tors and redactors deal with such problems in canonical texts as impropriety, superfluities, and internal contradictions (as we shall see).

Not all Confucian commentators of later centuries shared this conception of Confucius as grand expurgator or exciser, but most did agree that Confucius' primary contribution to the *Songs* was his having deleted those which were superfluous or inappropriate for ethical instruction.[27] In the words of Chu Hsi, Confucius "deleted what was superfluous and corrected what was disordered. As to what was good yet not fit to be taken as a model, and evil yet not fit to be taken as a warning, he cut and deleted it in order to conform with succinctness and to make [the *Songs*] known perpetually."[28] In so doing, Chu Hsi indicated, Confucius transformed a book of its own age, the *Songs*, into a book for all the ages, one that might teach the good and reform the wicked. In short, through his judicious exercise of excision, Confucius supposedly transformed a precanonical anthology of songs into a classic.[29]

Some scholars of the Han era maintained that Confucius expurgated not only the *Songs* but the *Documents* as well, particularly those portions which were confused and irrelevant to the practice of statecraft.[30] The Ming Neo-Confucian philosopher Wang Yang-ming (1472–1529), whose only apparent link with Han exegetes is that both have been characterized as "Confucian," also argued that Confucius abridged the *Documents*. In so doing, said Wang, he "[retained] only a few chapters concerning the four or five odd centuries of the T'ang, Yü, and Hsia periods."[31] The *Record of Rites*, the third of the three

[27] The claim that Confucius expurgated the *Songs* appears first in Ssu-ma Ch'ien's *Records of the Historian*. Chang Shou-lin, "*Shih-ching* shih pu-shih K'ung-tzu suo shan-ting-ti?" (Was the *Songs* Classic Expurgated by Confucius?), in *Ku-shih-pien* 3:376–377. For an English translation of Ssu-ma Ch'ien's account on this subject, see James Legge, *The Chinese Classics*, vol. 4: *The She King; or, The Book of Poetry*, 2nd ed. (Taipei: Wen-shih-che ch'u-pan she, 1971 reprint), p. 1 of "Prolegomena."

[28] Chu Hsi, "Shih-ching chuan hsü" (Preface to the Commentary on the *Songs* Classic), p. 1, in *Ssu-shu wu-ching*, vol. 2.

[29] Confucius' alleged expurgation of the *Songs* set a sort of precedent in Confucian scholarship. Thus Wang Po, a second-generation disciple of Chu Hsi, further expurgated the *Songs*, and also patched up the *Documents*, according to his understanding of the ideas of Chu Hsi. Honda, *Chung-kuo ching-hsüeh shih*, p. 251; P'i, *Ching-hsüeh li-shih*, p. 11.

[30] For an account of this theory and its sources, see Chao Chen-hsin, " 'Shu-hsü pien' hsü" (A Preface to My "Critique on the Preface to the *Documents*"), in *Ku-shih pien* 5:319–325; and Hiraoka Takeo, *Keisho no seiritsu* (The Formation of the Classics) (Osaka: Zenkoku shobō, 1946), p. 53. For an English translation of K'ung An-kuo's account of Confucius' alleged abridgment of the *Documents*, see Legge, *The Chinese Classics*, vol. 3: *The Shoo King; or, The Book of Historical Documents*, p. 4 of "Prolegomena."

[31] Wang Yang-ming, *Ch'uan-hsi lu* (Instructions for Practical Living), annot. Yeh Chün-tien (Taipei: Shang-wu yin-shu-kuan, 1971 reprint), p. 23. I have based this translation on that of Wing-tsit Chan in *Instructions for Practical Living and Other Neo-*

classics that Confucius was said to have only transmitted, not composed, was also supposed to have been formed through a process of excision, although not necessarily by Confucius. According to a scholar of the third century, Ch'en Shao, the *Rites* as we have it is the product of a succession of parings, from 204 chapters to 85 chapters to 49 chapters.[32] Even in composing the *Spring and Autumn Annals*, Confucius by some later accounts judiciously culled material from existing historical chronicles, principally that for the state of Lu, in order to form his classic. In so doing, said the late-Ch'ing historian of the classics P'i Hsi-jui (1850–1908), Confucius "selected only one-tenth [of the original chronicle of Lu]. In general he selected [for inclusion] those affairs which could clarify his meaning and stand as a model for later ages. The rest he excised and did not record."[33] Confucius' having followed this procedure, P'i argued, accounted for most of the apparent lacunae and other anomalies in the classic.

P'i contended that Confucius' approach to the books of antiquity in general was to expurgate or abridge them. These books, in fact, were transformed into classics through Confucius' astute exercise of excision.[34] This strategy, said P'i, was intended not only to highlight those principles which Confucius particularly wished to convey, but also to avoid confusing the mass of people with masses of nonessential books and words.[35] Wang Yang-ming concurred, remarking that "when Confucius expounded the Six Classics, he feared that superfluous writing was creating a chaos in the world; so he lost no time in simplifying them to cause the [people of the] world to strive to eliminate [superfluous] writing and seek the real substance."[36] Wang extended his ideas on the virtues of expurgation by arguing that the notorious first emperor of the Ch'in dynasty should not be condemned for burning books, only for burning the wrong ones and for harboring a selfish intention in doing so.[37]

There is little reliable evidence that the historical Confucius actu-

---

Confucian Writings by Wang Yang-ming, trans. and annot. Chan (New York: Columbia University Press, n.d.), p. 21.

[32] Ch'en Shao, "Chou-li lun hsü" (Preface to Discussions of the *Rites of Chou*), quoted in Chiang Po-ch'ien, *Shih-san ching kai-lun* (General Discussions of the Thirteen Classics) (Shanghai: Ku-chi ch'u-pan she, 1983), p. 333. For a critical discussion of Ch'en Shao's theory regarding the composition of the *Record of Rites*, see Jeffrey Kenneth Riegel, "The Four 'Tzu Ssu' Chapters of the *Li Chi*: An Analysis of the *Fang Chi*, Chung Yung, *Piao Chi*, and *Tzu I*" (Ph.D. diss., Stanford University, 1978), pp. 37–39.

[33] P'i Hsi-jui, *Ching-hsüeh t'ung-lun* (Comprehensive Discussions of Classical Studies) (Taipei: Ho-Lo t'u-shu ch'u-pan she, 1974 reprint), 4.22.

[34] Ibid., 1.102–103; P'i, *Ching-hsüeh li-shih*, pp. 1–2.

[35] P'i, *Ching-hsüeh t'ung-lun* 3.86.

[36] Wang, *Ch'uan-hsi lu*, p. 20; also translated in Chan, *Instructions*, p. 19.

[37] Wang, *Ch'uan-hsi lu*, pp. 20–21.

ally did edit or expurgate the texts or collections, particularly the *Documents* and *Songs*, that may have fallen into his hands (or ears), although he may well have transmitted them in some fashion. But in attributing such a role to Confucius, scholars of the Han period and later established the Sage as the first great commentator in Chinese history. For expurgation and excision, to say nothing of editing and compiling, are essential commentarial activities in almost any tradition or civilization. Thus, Confucius as portrayed by Confucian classicists resembles the Alexandrian scholars of Hellenistic antiquity more than he does the founders of other great religious or scriptural traditions. Just as some of these Alexandrians took as their primary task the expurgation of Homer, the elimination of literary and moral improprieties,[38] so Confucius was said to have taken a similar approach to the *Songs* and, by some accounts, to others of the classics as well. But while the Alexandrian scholars, in contrast to Homer, cut obscure figures in Western intellectual history, Confucius, the great commentator, was exalted in China as the "Great Sage and Teacher of Ten Thousand Generations."

On the other hand, even Homer (not to mention Jesus and Muhammad) was a commentator of a sort.[39] Jesus, as presented in the Gospels, apparently used rabbinic rules like those of Hillel and Ishmael to interpret passages from the Jewish scriptures.[40] His discourse on the Bread of Life in John 6:25–59 has been characterized as "a midrashic treatment of Exodus 16:4."[41] According to James A. Sanders, "Christ's major contribution to the Gospels, and to the gospel," may have been "the way he understood and applied Scripture—his hermeneutics."[42] But it was also Jesus' hermeneutics, his reinterpretations of favorite passages in Scripture, that most offended his contemporaries.[43]

[38] Rudolf Pfeiffer, *History of Classical Scholarship from the Beginnings to the End of the Hellenistic Age* (Oxford: Clarendon Press, 1968), pp. 230–231. Most Homeric scholars, however, did not actually delete such improprieties, but only marked offending passages with a special sign in the margin. See N. G. Wilson, *Scholars of Byzantium* (London: Duckworth, 1983), p. 16.

[39] "Homer," John L. Myres remarks, was "an editor or compiler himself." Myres, *Homer and His Critics* (London: Routledge and Kegan Paul, 1958), p. 59.

[40] Karlfried Froehlich, *Biblical Interpretation in the Early Church* (Philadelphia: Fortress Press, 1984), p. 8; Frederic W. Farrar, *History of Interpretation* [1886] (Grand Rapids, Mich.: Baker Book House, 1979 reprint), p. 19.

[41] Raymond F. Collins, *Introduction to the New Testament* (Garden City, N.Y.: Doubleday, Image Books, 1987), p. 5.

[42] James A. Sanders, *Canon as Paradigm: From Sacred Story to Sacred Text* (Philadelphia: Fortress Press, 1987), p. 61.

[43] James A. Sanders, "Isaiah in Luke," in *Interpreting the Prophets*, eds. James Luther Mays and Paul J. Achtemeier (Philadelphia: Fortress Press, 1987), p. 61.

The prophet Muhammad, too, may be characterized as a hermeneute, not only of the Jewish and Christian scriptures and stories
known to him, but also of the Qur'ān. In fact, "The Qur'ān itself an-
nounces the role of Muhammad as the interpreter of the revealed
text in Q 16/44: 'We have revealed to you the message (*dhikr*) so that
you might explain to people that which has been revealed to
them.' "[44] Thus, Muslim tradition records many instances in which
Muhammad interprets the meaning and implications of passages in
the Qur'ān.[45] In carrying out this hermeneutical enterprise, however,
Muhammad is supposed to have had a little help from his friends,
particularly the angel Gabriel.[46]

The presentation of great sages, prophets, and even angels as exegetes may, however, reflect later commentators' attempts to recast
these august figures in their own image. Such a transfiguration evidently occurred in the Hindu tradition in which Vyāsa ("compiler" or
"editor") is identified as the creator of the great epic, the *Mahābhārata*, as well as of the *Brāhma Sūtra*. By virtue of his great ascetic
power, Vyāsa was also credited with the stupendous redactional feat
of dividing the classic Veda into four parts.[47] The earliest commentators in the Homeric tradition, rhapsodes or the Homeridae, also
exalted their kind by portraying both Achilles (*Iliad* 9) and Odysseus
(*Odyssey* 11) as singers of tales. But the commentarial transfiguration
of epic characters appears most clearly in rabbinic Judaism in what
Jacob Neusner has called "the rabbinization of scriptural heroes"
such as Moses and David, whose military exploits are often interpreted as exegetical exercises.[48] Indeed, rabbinical commentators
went so far as to interpret a verse in one of the most stirring and
martial anthems in the entire Hebrew Bible, the Song of Deborah
(Judges 5:10), as "a description of the triumph of the Lord in the
'wars of the Torah.' "[49]

[44] R. Marston Speight, "The Function of *Hadīth* as Commentary on the Qur'ān, as
Seen in the Six Authoritative Collections," in *Approaches to the History of the Interpretation
of the Qur'ān*, ed. Andrew Rippin (Oxford: Clarendon Press, 1988), p. 64.

[45] Fred Leemhuis, "Origins and Early Development of the *Tafsīr* Tradition," in Rippin, ed., *Approaches*, p. 13.

[46] Harold Coward, *Sacred Word and Sacred Text: Scripture in World Religions* (Maryknoll, N.Y.: Orbis Books, 1988), pp. 95–96.

[47] Chakravarthi V. Narasimhan, *The Mahābhārata: An English Version Based on Selected
Verses* (New York: Columbia University Press, 1965), p. 14.

[48] Jacob Neusner, *Midrash in Context: Exegesis in Formative Judaism* (Philadelphia: Fortress Press, 1983), p. 122.

[49] Jacob Neusner, *Formative Judaism, Second Series: Religious, Historical, and Literary
Studies* (Chico, Calif.: Scholars Press, 1983), pp. 49–50. For other examples of the rabbinization of scriptural heroes, including Adam, Noah, and Jacob, see Shmuel Safrai,

If one can speak of the "rabbinization of scriptural heroes," might one also speak of the commentatorization of Confucius and of other sages and worthies in the Confucian tradition? That one can so speak is indicated by the Ch'ing commentator Liu Feng-lu's interpretation of a term in the first line of the Confucian *Analects*: "The Master said: 'Is it not a pleasure to learn and to practice frequently what one has learned?'" The character "to learn," says Liu, "refers to the expurgation and establishment of the Six Classics" by Confucius.[50] Moreover, the Ming Neo-Confucian scholar Chou Ju-teng presented not only Confucius but also some of the sage-rulers of high antiquity, such as Fu Hsi, as commentators who "expounded but did not innovate."[51]

If later scholars' accounts of Confucius' editing and expurgating of the classics cannot be confirmed, there is more substantial support for the portrayal of the Sage as commentator in the chief record of his words and deeds, the *Analects*. According to one modern scholar, Lu

---

"Oral Tora," in *The Literature of the Sages, First Part: Oral Tora, Halakha, Mishna, Tosefta, Talmud, External Tractates*, ed. Safrai (Assen/Maastricht: Van Gorcum; Philadelphia: Fortress Press, 1987), p. 102; and Rashi, *Commentaries on the Pentateuch*, selected and trans. by Chaim Pearl (New York: Viking Press, 1973), pp. 36 and 59. The reverse of this phenomenon of the rabbinization of scriptural heroes—what might be called the "athleticization of exegetes"—occurred in several traditions as well. Saint Ambrose, for example, used "the Pauline metaphor of the nude athlete in the stadium, his limbs rubbed with oil, . . . to express the noble combats of the exegete in deciphering the meanings of the scriptures." Gérard Nauroy, "L'Écriture dans la pastorale d'Ambrose de Milan," in *Le Monde latin antique et la Bible*, eds. Jacques Fontaine and Charles Pietri (Paris: Editions Beauchesne, 1985), p. 387. The great *Rāmāyana* poet-redactor Vālmīki is athleticized in more than a metaphorical sense, inasmuch as he is credited with teaching archery to Rāma's twin sons and "giving them powerful astra-mantras to direct their weapons unfailingly." H. Daniel Smith, *Reading the Rāmāyana: A Bibliographic Guide for Students and College Teachers; Indian Variants on the Rāma-Theme in English Translations*, Foreign and Comparative Studies, South Asian Special Publications, no. 4 (Syracuse: Maxwell School of Citizenship and Public Affairs, Syracuse University, 1983), p. 52. Even Confucius, who by his own modest admission simply expounded and did not create, or at least portrayed as a more vigorous type, in Mencius' comparison of his world-ordering achievement in composing the *Spring and Autumn Annals* to that of Yü the Great in taming the flood waters and of the Duke of Chou in quelling barbarians and expelling wild beasts from the land (*Mencius* 3B, 9:11).

[50] Liu Feng-lu, *Lun-yü shu Ho* (The *Analects* Following Ho [Yen's Commentary]), in *Huang-Ch'ing ching-chieh* 1,297.1a (vol. 19, p. 14,209). Many other instances of the unlikely interpretation of phrases from the *Analects* as referring to Confucius' exegetical activities may be found in this commentary by Liu; see, for example, pp. 3a, 3b, and 11a.

[51] Chou Ju-teng, *Ssu-shu tsung-chih* (The General Purport of the Four Books), from *Shang-Lun* (First Part of the *Analects*), p. 43a, in *Chung-kuo tzu-hsüeh ming-chu chi-ch'eng* 20:363.

Yüan-chün, this work as a whole may be typed as a commentary (*chuan*), not as a classic (*ching*), and may be considered the first example of the *chuan* genre in Chinese history.[52] The text includes quotations from and references to both the *Documents* and the *Songs*, though sometimes without attribution, leading Jun Sekiguchi to conclude that "classical studies" already existed with Confucius and his circle.[53] Indeed, the famous Ch'ing scholar-official Juan Yüan (1764–1849) observed that "Confucius' and Mencius' drawing lessons from the *Songs* and *Documents* is like our contemporaries' drawing lessons from the *Analects* and *Mencius*."[54] Confucius in the *Analects* particularly recommended the study of the *Songs*, which "can be used to inspire, to observe, to make you fit for company, to express grievances; near at hand, [it will teach you how] to serve your father and, [looking] further, [how] to serve your sovereign; [it also enables you] to learn more of the names of birds, beasts, plants, and trees."[55] In brief, Confucius advocated the study of the *Songs* for rhetorical purposes, to teach morality and proper conduct, and to learn biological nomenclature.

In so doing, Confucius may seem to have approached the *Songs* more as an encyclopedia of useful information and instruction than as a classic.[56] But as we shall see in chapter 4, below, one of the basic assumptions that commentators in every major classical or scriptural tradition made regarding the canon was that it was comprehensive or encyclopedic, even that one of its primary functions was to serve as an encyclopedia. Thus, scholars and students alike in classical Greek and Hellenistic antiquity generally valued the *Iliad* and *Odyssey* more as encyclopedic sources of knowledge than as models of literary excellence or founts of religious truth. Even canons in those traditions which were more strictly speaking "scriptural," such as the Bible and

[52] Lu Yüan-chün, "Ching-hsüeh chih fa-chan yü chin-ku-wen chih fen-ho" (The Development of Classical Studies and the Division and Union of the Old and New Text [Schools]), in Wang et al., *Ching-hsüeh yen-chiu lun-chi*, p. 88.

[53] Jun Sekiguchi, "Keigakuteki shi-i kōzō no bunseki" (A Study of the Way of Thinking Observed in the Course of Formation of the Confucian Classics), *Tōhōgaku* (Eastern Studies), no. 51 (January 1976): 15.

[54] Juan Yüan, "Shih Shu ku-hsün hsü" (Preface to Ancient Lessons on the *Songs* and *Documents*), in *Yen-ching wu hsü-chi* (Supplementary Writings from the Hall for the Study of the Classics) (Taipei: Shang-wu yin-shu-kuan, 1966 reprint), 1.37.

[55] *Analects* 17:9. The translation given here is by James J. Y. Liu, slightly modified, and appears in Liu's *Chinese Theories of Literature* (Chicago: University of Chicago Press, 1975), p. 109.

[56] Chiang, *Shih-san ching*, p. 246, remarks that the *Songs* may really have served as a sort of encyclopedia in Confucius' era, there not being other such reference works at the time.

the Qur'ān, were frequently regarded as encyclopedic, even as containing all significant knowledge.

Classical Confucians were not alone among their contemporaries in approaching ancient precanonical collections of documents as sources of useful information, rhetorical examples, and guides to political practice and moral conduct. Various versions of the *Documents*, in particular, were quoted in several diverse philosophical and historical works of the classical era, including the *Mencius*, *Hsün-tzu*, *Mo-tzu*, *Tso-chuan* (Tso Commentary), *Kuo-yü* (Conversations of the States), *Chan-kuo ts'e* (Intrigues of the Warring States), and *Lü-shih ch'un-ch'iu* (Master Lü's Spring and Autumn Annals).[57] Among the major schools of classical philosophy, the Mohist apparently had its own version of the *Documents* which, however, differs from the extant version much more than those drawn upon by the classical Confucians, Mencius and Hsün-tzu.[58] According to Matsumoto Masaaki, the Legalists too may have compiled their own version of the *Documents*.[59] Even among those identified as Confucians, there existed different recensions of the *Documents*. Not only did the Confucianists of the states of Lu and Ch'i each have their own separate versions, but the *Documents* was apparently revised and enlarged in the time of Mencius as well, in order to deal with new historical concerns.[60] Not until the time of Hsün-tzu was the text of the *Documents* apparently fixed, at least in the Confucian school. For the quotations in the *Hsün-tzu* from the *Documents* almost all appear in the extant version of the latter, in contrast to those which figure in the earlier Confucian classics, the *Analects* and the *Mencius*.[61]

In sum, the inchoate collections of ancient writings from which Confucian scholars eventually extracted their canon, particularly the *Documents* and the *Songs*, apparently served as a *bonum commune* to

[57] Li Chen-hsing, "Shang-shu liu-yen shu-yao" (An Account of Important Points in the Development of the *Documents of Antiquity*), *K'ung-Meng hsüeh-pao* (Journal of the Confucius and Mencius Society), no. 41 (April 30, 1981): 71.

[58] Lo Ken-tse, "Yu *Mo-tzu* yin ching t'ui-tse Ju Mo liang-chia yü ching-shu chih kuan-hsi" (An Estimation of the Relationships between the Confucian and Mohist Schools and the Classics, Based on the Quotations from the Classics in the *Mo-tzu*), in *Ku-shih pien* 4:278 279.

[59] Matsumoto Masaaki, "The *Fa-chia* and the *Shang-Shu*," in *Memoirs of the Research Department of the Tōyō Bunkō* (The Oriental Library), no. 26 (1968), pp. 15–16 and 38.

[60] Matsumoto Masaaki, "Sengoku zenki ni okeru Shōsho no tenkai" (The Revision of the *Shang-shu* in the Early Chan Kuo Period), *Tōyō Gakuhō* (Reports of the Oriental Society) 43, no. 1 (June 1960): 62.

[61] Nomura Shigeo, "SenShin ni okeru Shōsho no ryōden ni tsuite no jakkan no kōsatsu" (Some Considerations of the Inheritance of *Shang-shu* in the Period of Pre-Ch'in), in *Nippon Chūgoku Gakkai-Hō* (Bulletin of the Sinological Society of Japan), no. 17 (1965), pp. 14–15; Hiraoka, *Keisho*, pp. 54 and 57.

several schools and strands of classical philosophy.[62] Throughout most of the Chou era, the "texts" of these collections were in quite a fluid state and existed in diverse forms.[63] According to the renowned modern scholar Fu Ssu-nien, even the concept of the book did not exist in the Chou era, only *p'ien* (roughly "chapters"), most of which were written on silk rolls or bamboo strips. These *p'ien* were combined and recombined in diverse ways for various reasons to form collections, but not books in the modern sense. The *Lü-shih ch'un-ch'iu* (c. 239 B.C.), Fu argues, was the first book written in Chinese history.[64] But even the Ma Wang Tui manuscripts, which date from 168 B.C., have only chapter headings and not book titles.

If the fluid agglomerations of *p'ien* that eventually coagulated into the Confucian classics served as a *bonum commune* for several different classical schools, the Confucians turned them to the best account. In fact, one of the main reasons for the political and intellectual triumph of Confucians in the Han dynasty was their having successfully linked these ancient collections, this broad stream of tradition, with their own school. In the words of R. P. Kramers, "the Confucians were valued as the preservers and transmitters of earlier royal traditions, and not simply as representatives of one school among others."[65]

The Confucian appropriation of common traditions and the texts that embodied them was no mean achievement, although Vedantic and rabbinic commentators accomplished similar feats in their respective cultures. The *Documents*, as noted above, was not throughout

[62] In this respect, these collections might be compared with the Upanishads, which served as a sort of canon for all six of the orthodox systems of Hindu philosophy.

[63] Nikkilä Pertti remarks in this connection that "the *Book of Songs* in the Lu state was not necessarily the same book which was used in other states." Pertti, *Early Confucianism and Inherited Thought in the Light of Some Key Terms of the Confucian Analects: I. The Terms in Shu Ching and Shih Ching* (Helsinki: The Finnish Oriental Society, 1982), pp. 22–23.

[64] Jung Chao-tsu, " 'Yüeh-ling' ti lai-yüan k'ao" (An Investigation of the Origins of the "Monthly Ordinances" [Chapter of the *Record of Rites*]), *Yen-ching hsüeh-pao* (Yen-ching Journal of Chinese Studies), no. 18 (December 1935): 104. The reference to Fu Ssu-nien is from his "Chan-kuo wen-chi chung chih p'ien-shih shu-t'i" (The Divisions and Calligraphic Styles of Books of the Warring States Era), *Kuo-li chung-yang yen-chiu-yüan li-shih yü-yen yen-chiu-suo chi-k'an* (Bulletin of the Institute of History and Philology of the Academia Sinica), vol. 1, pt. 2. On the fluidity of these collections of *p'ien* in pre-Han times, see also Ch'en Meng-chia, *Shang-shu t'ung-lun* (Comprehensive Discussions of the *Documents of Antiquity*) (Beijing: Chung-hua shu-chü, 1985), p. 176.

[65] R. P. Kramers, "The Development of the Confucian Schools," in *The Cambridge History of China*, vol. 1: *The Ch'in and Han Empires, 221 B.C.–A.D. 220*, eds. Denis Twitchett and Michael Loewe (Cambridge: Cambridge University Press, 1986), p. 765. Other reasons for the triumph of Confucianism at the Han court are discussed in Homer H. Dubs, "The Victory of Han Confucianism," in Pan Ku, *The History of the Former Han Dynasty*, 3 vols., trans. and annot. Dubs (American Council of Learned Societies, 1944), vol. 2, 351–352.

the Chou era the exclusive preserve of the Confucians. Nor was the *Songs*, which at least one modern scholar has traced to a rival school of classical philosophy, the "diplomatists" or "political scientists" (*Tsung-heng chia*).[66] The early strata of the *Change*, those concerned primarily with divination, apparently had little relation to Confucius or classical Confucianism. Even as late as the 210s B.C., the *Change* was regarded as a book of divination not connected with any particular philosophical school, and thus escaped destruction at the hands of the Ch'in.[67] Most of the cosmologically oriented "Confucian" appendices to that classic were apparently not added until the Han era. Even these appendices, the "Ten Wings," evidently bear little relationship with the teachings of Confucius as presented in the *Analects* and other classical sources.[68] Finally, there is little if any convincing evidence that Confucius, or even Confucians, had a hand in the composition of the *Spring and Autumn Annals*. The earliest and most authoritative statement that Confucius composed the *Annals* appears only in the *Mencius*.[69]

In appropriating these texts, in attempting to monopolize what had been a common tradition, Confucian scholars of the late-classical and Han eras focused on defining and redefining Confucius' own role in the transmission and development of this tradition. Thus, there emerged the image of Confucius as editor and expurgator of texts that were generally believed to have predated him. As "law" in the Hebrew tradition was by Moses, "psalms" by David, and "wisdom" by Solomon; and "epic" in the ancient West was by Homer; and "compilation" in India was by Vyāsa; so in Han Confucianism was "expurgation and commentary" by Confucius. According to one Han Confucian source, the *K'ung-tzu shih-chia* (House of Confucius) as interpreted by Jeffrey Riegel, even Confucius' life, or important episodes in it, was a sort of commentary on a classical text, the *Songs*. Specifically, figures of speech in the *Songs* are transformed into literal prose anecdotes in the *K'ung-tzu shih-chia* account of Confucius' life.[70]

[66] Chiang, *Shih-san ching*, p. 248.

[67] Honda, *Chung-kuo ching-hsüeh shih*, p. 90.

[68] Willard Peterson points out that "no reference or allusion can be cited from pre-Han times to connect Confucius with the Ten Wings. The earliest statement which associates some of them with Confucius is in the *Records of the Historian*, completed in about 100 B.C." Peterson, "Making Connections: 'Commentary on the Attached Verbalizations' of the *Book of Change*," *Harvard Journal of Asiatic Studies* 42, no. 1 (1982): 73–74.

[69] *Mencius* 3A, 8:8, 11.

[70] Such a transformation of figures of speech from earlier canonical works into literal prose anecdotes appears in the Christian Gospels as well. For example, the statement in Hosea 11:1, "Out of Egypt I have called my son," is said to be fulfilled in the Holy

In Riegel's words, "the life of Confucius is made the summation of the *Shih ching* lessons he so revered."[71]

The attribution to Confucius of such a reverential attitude toward a text, or even of the lessons allegedly contained in such a text, is probably anachronistic. Precanonical man was seldom infected by what Renaissance scholars called "book madness." But Confucius, at least on the evidence of the accounts preserved in the *Analects*, had reached the point of extracting the *Songs* (or Songs) from their earlier oral performance context, of treating it (or them) as a source of useful information and moral instruction, if not yet, like Mencius, of timeless principles.[72] In so doing, the Great Sage and Teacher of Ten Thousand Generations took an important step toward the formulation of a canon. For insofar as a canon is generally supposed to express truths and beauties that transcend particular times and places, it is usually convenient, if not absolutely necessary, to remove it from the limiting historical and cultural context that nurtured it. In China, a series of historical events, especially the political upheavals of the late third century B.C., facilitated such a removal, creating an essential historical distance between canon (or precanon) and canonizers.

Family's flight to and return from Egypt; and the oracular words of Zechariah 13:7, "Smite the shepherd and scatter the sheep," are applied to the passion narratives. See F. F. Bruce, "Scripture and Tradition in the New Testament," in *Holy Book and Holy Tradition*, eds. F. F. Bruce and E. G. Rupp (Grand Rapids, Mich.: William B. Eerdmans, 1968), pp. 80 and 83.

[71] Jeffrey K. Riegel, "Poetry and the Legend of Confucius' Exile," *Journal of the American Oriental Society* 106, no. 1 (January–March 1986): 21. Wilfred Cantwell Smith remarks that in the Islamic tradition, too, "the life of the Prophet has been regarded as essentially a commentary on and exposition of the Qur'ān." Smith, "The True Meaning of Scripture: An Empirical Historian's Nonreductionist Interpretation of the Qur'ān," *International Journal of Middle East Studies* 11, no. 4 (July 1980): 491.

[72] For an account of this difference between Confucius' and Mencius' approaches to the *Songs*, see Ku Chieh-kang, "*Shih-ching* tsai ch'un-ch'iu chan-kuo chien ti ti-wei" (The Position of the *Songs Classic* in the Spring and Autumn and Warring States Eras), in *Ku-shih pien* 3:358.

Chapter 2

INTEGRATION, DEVELOPMENT, AND CLOSURE OF CANONS

CANONIZATION, the identification and stabilization of a body of classical or sacred texts that is declared to be authoritative, frequently proceeds by political, ecclesiastical, or literary fiat.[1] Such fiats are often confirmed by high-powered councils and supported by such forceful political figures as the Emperor Wu (Han Wu-ti) in Han China and the Emperor Constantine in the late-Roman West.

Councils and kings certainly played a significant role in the establishment of Confucian canons in the Han era. As early as 136 B.C., the Emperor Wu, acting on the advice of Tung Chung-shu (c.179– c.104 B.C.) and other Confucian scholars, limited the orthodox program of study in the Imperial Academy to the five Confucian classics and established erudites or academicians (*po-shih*) to teach each of these classics.[2] Later Han emperors convened conferences of eminent Confucian scholars to discuss and resolve questions regarding the de-

---

[1] S.G.F. Brandon has particularly emphasized the degree to which "the status of the sacred literature of the great religions of mankind has originally derived from what we may fairly term 'ecclesiastical authority' " which, he argues, has "played the decisive role in determining the status of the Holy Book, and in selecting its contents." To support these assertions, Brandon cites examples from the Vedic, rabbinic, Islamic, and Buddhist traditions. See Brandon, "Holy Book, Tradition, and Ikon," in *Holy Book and Holy Tradition*, eds. F. F. Bruce and E. G. Rupp (Grand Rapids, Mich.: William B. Eerdmans, 1968), pp. 14–15.

[2] Ch'en Ch'i-yun, "Confucian, Legalist, and Taoist Thought in Later Han," in *The Cambridge History of China*, vol. 1: *The Ch'in and Han Empires, 221 B.C.–A.D. 220*, eds. Denis Twitchett and Michael Loewe (Cambridge: Cambridge University Press, 1986), p. 769; R. P. Kramers, "The Development of the Confucian Schools," ibid., pp. 751 and 756. Homer H. Dubs, however, has pointed out that "the victory of Confucianism" was a gradual process, extending over two centuries of Former Han history. See Dubs, "The Victory of Han Confucianism," in Pan Ku, *The History of the Former Han Dynasty*, 3 vols., trans. and annot. Dubs (American Council of Learned Societies, 1944), vol. 2, p. 351. Benjamin Wallacker adds that Tung Chung-shu's contribution to the establishment of Confucianism was not so great as some have supposed: "He held no high position in the government, nor was he an intimate of the emperor." Wallacker, "Han Confucianism and Confucius in Han," in *Ancient China: Studies in Early Civilization*, eds. David T. Roy and Tsuen-hsiun Tsien (Hong Kong: Chinese University Press, 1978), p. 216.

limitation and interpretation of the Confucian classics. These conclaves bound the canon even more closely to the fortunes of the Chinese imperial state.[3] But focusing too narrowly on this political or institutional aspect of canonization obscures prior intellectual developments that made it possible, or even conceivable. It also obstructs a comparative approach to the study of canonization by making it seem to depend on the acts of remarkable rulers and scholars, such as the Emperor Wu and Tung Chung-shu in China of the Former Han era.

A comparative perspective reveals that the fixing of a canon occurred in several major traditions following a sharp break with the classical past in which canonical writings were first composed or revealed. In the Jewish tradition, for example, early attempts at delimiting a canon proceeded in part from a belief that the Age of Prophecy, specifically the era from the death of Moses to the reign of Artaxerxes (465–424 B.C.), had ended.[4] The Jews of the Second Temple period, which postdated this Age of Prophecy, sensed that they were living in a postclassical or silver age in which it was no longer possible to compose canonical works.[5] The political catastrophes of the first century A.D., culminating in the destruction of the Temple in Jerusalem in A.D. 70, set the background for a more formal and final definition of a Jewish canon at the Council of Jabne (Jamnia) around A.D. 90 and for the use of midrash to interpret that canon.[6] In Islam as well, the codification of jurisprudence in the early tenth century of our era followed "the closing of the door of *ijithad*," the end of the prophetic or creative age.[7] Finally, Homer was acknowl-

---

[3] Riegel proposes that one of the Confucian classics, the *Record of Rites*, may actually have emerged from these conclaves or conferences—indeed, that it "is a record of these very discussions and councils as well as other lesser known activities of the Han scholars" who were "primarily charged with discussing and advising the court on ritual and propriety." Jeffrey Kenneth Riegel, "The Four 'Tzu Ssu' Chapters of the *Li Chi*: An Analysis of the *Fang Chi*, Chung Yung, *Piao Chi*, and *Tzu I*" (Ph.D. diss., Stanford University, 1978), p. 43.

[4] G. W. Anderson, "Canonical and Non-Canonical," in *The Cambridge History of the Bible*, vol. 1: *From the Beginnings to Jerome*, eds. P. R. Ackroyd and C. F. Evans (Cambridge: Cambridge University Press, 1970), pp. 114, 116, and 127–128.

[5] Shaye J. D. Cohen, *From the Maccabees to the Mishnah* (Philadelphia: Westminster Press, 1987), pp. 192 and 194.

[6] Karlfried Froehlich, trans. and ed., *Biblical Interpretation in the Early Church* (Philadelphia: Fortress Press, 1984), p. 2; Gary G. Porton, *Understanding Rabbinic Midrash: Texts and Commentary* (Hoboken, N.J.: KTAV Publishing, 1985), pp. 10–11. Porton remarks that at this juncture, "just as the Torah replaced the Temple as the locus for meeting God, so also the midrashist replaced the priest as the intermediary between God's work and humanity" (p. 10).

[7] N. J. Coulson, *A History of Islamic Law* (Edinburgh: Edinburgh University Press, 1978), p. 80.

edged as "classical" from the sixth century B.C. when the Greeks "regarded the creative period of epic poetry as concluded." Following the collapse of the classical Greek polis, Homer was further exalted in the Hellenistic age with its consciousness of "a definitive break between the mighty past and a still uncertain present."[8]

Such a definitive break with a past that came to be viewed as classical occurred more abruptly in China as a result of the political upheavals attending the rise and fall of the Ch'in dynasty in the final decades of the third century B.C. Subject to the proscription and even destruction of their learning by Ch'in authorities, Confucian scholars of the Former Han era were custodians of a tradition that was to some degree lost and fragmented. The extent to which pre-Han Confucian writings and traditions actually did perish under Ch'in rule is a matter of conjecture. Indeed, several modern scholars have questioned the effectiveness of the Ch'in edicts that ordered the destruction of such Confucian texts as the *Documents* and the *Songs*.[9] But the psychological effects of the Ch'in "burning of the books" were nevertheless profound, as Derk Bodde has observed.[10] For many Confucian scholars of the Han era believed that their tradition had survived only in a defective and fragmented condition, and that it was their task to restore its lost unity and coherence. That such a unity and coherence as these scholars conceived never really existed was obscured by the presumed effects of the Ch'in burning of the books, which increasingly took on the proportions of a myth used to justify reconstructions of the canon and its components.

Perhaps the best known of these reconstructions was that of the purportedly lost *Music Classic* (Yüeh-ching), or "Record of Music" (Yüeh-chi), the sixth of the Six Classics canonized in the Former Han era. Han scholars believed that a simulacrum of the "original" might be reconstituted from other classical writings on the subject. Thus, "its compilers made a pastiche of contemporaneous and classical utterances that appeared to support the Confucian positions on music and ritual at court," drawing especially on the *Hsün-tzu*.[11]

The reassembling of a "lost" classic from bits and pieces of surviv-

---

[8] Rudolf Pfeiffer, *History of Classical Scholarship from the Beginnings to the End of the Hellenistic Age* (Oxford: Clarendon Press, 1968), pp. 6, 8, and 87.

[9] See, for example, Derk Bodde, "The State and Empire of Ch'in," in *Cambridge History of China*, vol. 1, pp. 70–71; Kramers, "The Development of the Confucian Schools," p. 751.

[10] Bodde, "The State and Empire of Ch'in," p. 71.

[11] Kenneth J. DeWoskin, *A Song for One or Two: Music and the Concept of Art in Early China*, Michigan Papers in Chinese Studies, no. 42 (Ann Arbor: University of Michigan, Center for Chinese Studies, 1982), p. 91.

ing texts may seem reminiscent of the work of forgers, who indeed had a great future in the history of Chinese culture. But the assumptions on which such reconstructions proceeded were generally not those of conventional forgers. As R. P. Kramers has noted of the compilation of the "lost" *School Sayings of Confucius* (K'ung-tzu chia-yü), traditionally credited to Wang Su (195–256), "there was . . . a great variety of texts, in which, to the mind of the compiler, the old *Chia yü* was embedded. From that situation he started out to collect the fragments which he thought had belonged to this original collection." Although "originally there was no such collection as the *K'ung-tzu chia yü*," the appearance in classical literature of quite a number of quotations from Confucius not found in the extant *Analects* of Confucius seemed to indicate that "such a collection must have existed."[12] Thus, Wang Su's alleged fabrication of the Old Text version of the *Documents Classic*, so thoroughly condemned by such scholars of the Ch'ing era as Yen Jo-chü (1636–1704), may well have been inspired by the belief that he was reassembling a lost text by combining quotations from the primordial *Documents* from various pre-Ch'in texts.

Some Han scholars conceived the more ambitious project of reconstructing the lost unity and coherence of the classics as a whole, not just of one particular text. Among the most notable of these scholars was Liu Hsiang, the imperial librarian in the last years of the Former Han. Liu's *Shuo-yüan* (Garden of Discourses) was a sort of summa of the classics based on the presupposition that "the Five Classics were originally of one body."[13] The lost *Liu-i lun* (Discussions of the Six Arts), by the great Latter Han commentator Cheng Hsüan, may have been a work of a similar nature, as it has been characterized as "a discourse on the history and significance of the entire corpus of early canonical literature."[14] Even Ssu-ma Ch'ien's great work, the *Records of the Historian* (Shih-chi), was "written to comprehend the complete body of the Six Classics and continue the *Spring and Autumn Annals*."[15]

---

[12] R. P. Kramers, *K'ung Tzu Chia Yü: The School Sayings of Confucius; Introduction, Translation of Sections 1–10 with Critical Notes* (Leiden: E. J. Brill, 1950), pp. 136 and 118. Honda Shigeyuki notes that of the twenty-nine quotations from Confucius in the *Mencius*, only eight appear in the extant *Analects*; of the quotations from Confucius in the *Tso-chuan* and *Li-chi*, hardly any appear in the *Analects*. See Honda Shigeyuki, *Chung-kuo ching-hsüeh shih* (History of Chinese Classical Studies) (Taipei: Ku-t'ing shu-wu, 1975 reprint), p. 131.

[13] Ikeda Shuzo, "Ryūkō no gaku to shisō" (The Scholarship and Thought of Liu Hsiang), *Tōhōgakuhō* (Journal of Oriental Studies), no. 50 (February 1978): 143–144 and 146.

[14] Riegel, "The Four 'Tzu Ssu' Chapters," p. 31.

[15] Ikeda, "Ryūkō no gaku to shisō," p. 146.

Few Han scholars, however, attempted to draw out such grand designs, actually to reconstruct the lost unity of the Confucian classics by composing a synthetic work. More often, they contented themselves with the more modest project of explaining how these classics were related to one another, of demonstrating that they were not an arbitrarily assembled congeries of texts. The particular books in this canon may have been fixed by political actions in the reign of Emperor Wu, who appointed erudites to study and expound each of these classics.[16] But this fixing of a canon, the outlines of which had already been set as early as the time of Hsün-tzu, who identified five of the six Confucian classics as such,[17] did not solve the problem of integrating the canon, any more than the mere establishment of a curriculum reveals how its various subjects are related to one another.

The integration of the canon was not, however, so important an issue for Confucians of the Former Han as for those of the Latter Han. In the first place, the classics had more of a practical political function, were often used as manuals of statecraft, under the Former Han. The *Classic of Change*, for example, was purportedly utilized at the Former Han court for political prognostication, the "Tribute of Yü" (Yü-kung) chapter of the *Documents* for the planning of hydraulic works, and the *Spring and Autumn Annals* to judge legal cases.[18] The

[16] The establishment of *po-shih*, or erudites, to teach the classics had precedents in the Ch'in era and even in late-Chou times. See Ch'eng Fa-jen, "Han-tai ching-hsüeh chih fu-hsing" (The Renaissance of Classical Studies in the Han Era), in Wang Ching-chih et al., *Ching-hsüeh yen-chiu lun-chi* (A Collection of Articles on Research in Classical Studies) (Taipei: Li-ming wen-hua shih-yeh, 1981), p. 169; and Bodde, "The State and Empire of Ch'in," p. 73.

[17] On the earliest enumerations of the Five or Six Classics, those which appear in the "Ch'üan-hsüeh" (Encouragement of Learning) chapter of *Hsün-tzu* and the "T'ien-hsia" (World) chapter of *Chuang-tzu*, see Nomura Shigeo, "SenShin ni okeru Shōsho no ryōden ni tsuite no jakkan no kōsatsu" (Some Considerations in the Inheritance of *Shang-shu* in the Period of Pre-Ch'in), *Nippon Chūgoku Gakkai-Hō* (Journal of the Sinological Society of Japan), no. 17 (1965): 12; and Chou Yü-t'ung, "Ch'ün-ching kai-lun" (A General Discussion of All the Classics), in *Chou Yü-t'ung ching-hsüeh shih lun-chu hsüan-chi* (Selected Treatises by Chou Yü-t'ung on the History of Classical Studies), comp. Chu Wei-cheng (Shanghai: Jen-min ch'u-pan she, 1983), p. 208.

[18] Li Huan, "Ch'ün-ching chü-yao chi yen-chiu fang-fa" (On the Important Points and Method of Study of All the Classics), in Wang et al., *Ching-hsüeh yen-chiu lun-chi*, p. 32; Chiang Po-ch'ien, *Shih-san ching kai-lun* (General Discussions of the Thirteen Classics) (Shanghai: Ku-chi ch'u-pan she, 1983), p. 12; P'i Hsi-jui, *Ching-hsüeh li-shih* (History of Classical Studies) (Taipei: I-wen yin-shu-kuan, 1966 reprint), p. 72. On the use of the *Annals* to adjudicate legal cases in the Han era and later, see John D. Langlois, Jr., "Law, Statecraft, and the *Spring and Autumn Annals* in Yüan Political Thought," in *Yüan Thought: Chinese Thought and Religion under the Mongols*, eds. Hok-lam Chan and Wm. Theodore de Bary (New York: Columbia University Press, 1982), pp. 107, 119–120, 122, and 144. On the practical political uses of this same classic in the T'ang era,

use of particular classical texts for such special political and administrative purposes may well have obviated the need to present them as a self-consistent and well-ordered whole, to explain how they were related to one another. Specialists in each of the disciplines or arts represented by one of the classics were probably more concerned with the performance of their political or administrative duties than with the contemplation of the grand unity of the classics as a whole. Too, the relative scarcity of texts in the Former Han era would have made it difficult for any but such well-connected scholars as Liu Hsiang to observe or imagine such a unity, even if they had not been constrained by institutional factors and pedagogical traditions to concentrate on one particular classic.

In the Latter Han, however, several new developments increasingly turned Confucian scholars' attention to the integration and harmonization of the books in the Confucian canon that had been delimited under the Former Han. First, the invention of paper may have made books more widely available, although it probably did not come into general use before the third or fourth century A.D.[19] This might have enabled more scholars and commentators to study the classics as a whole, instead of concentrating on individual texts[20] or depending on the oral transmission of learning from an acknowledged master of one of the classics. Second, the Confucian classics under the Latter Han were used less frequently as manuals of statecraft and became instead primarily objects of study and exegesis.[21] As the study of the classics became less attractive to those interested principally in political preferment, more scholarly types—in fact, the first great conventional exegetes and commentators in Chinese history, men known to history primarily as commentators—came to dominate classical studies in the Latter Han. Some of these figures, notably Ma Jung (79–166) and Cheng Hsüan, established independent private schools that increasingly replaced the Imperial Academy as the main centers of classical studies.[22]

---

see David McMullen, *State and Scholars in T'ang China* (Cambridge: Cambridge University Press, 1988), p. 79.

[19] Michael Loewe, "The Religious and Intellectual Background," in *Cambridge History of China*, vol. 1, p. 650.

[20] Chiang, *Shih-san ching*, pp. 14–15.

[21] Ch'ien Mu, "K'ung-tzu yü Ch'un-ch'iu" (Confucius and the *Spring and Autumn Annals*), in Ch'ien Mu, *Liang-Han ching-hsüeh chin-ku wen p'ing-i* (A Balanced Discussion of the Old and New Text Literature in the Classical Studies of the Han Era) (Taipei: Sanmin shu-chü, 1971), pp. 256–257; Yoshikawa Kōjirō, "Shōsho seigi kaidai" (An Introduction to *Shang-shu cheng-i*), *Tōhōgakuhō* (Journal of Oriental Studies), no. 10, pt. 3 (October 1939): 14 and 20.

[22] Kramers, "The Development of the Confucian Schools," p. 764.

Among Latter Han commentators on the classics, by far the most famous is Cheng Hsüan, whose forte was the study of the three ritual classics: the *Rites of Chou* (Chou-li), the *Deportment and Rites* (I-li), and the *Record of Rites* (Li-chi). Cheng, however, aimed to build a consistent synthesis of all the Confucian classics, even reconciling the divergent readings and interpretations associated with the Old Text and New Text schools.[23] In attempting to reconstruct the agrarian system of high antiquity, for example, Cheng sought to harmonize the conflicting accounts of this system in the classical texts favored by each of these two schools, particularly the *Rites of Chou* and the "Royal Institutes" (Wang-chih) chapter of the *Record of Rites*.[24] Cheng's commentaries, especially those on the ritual classics, took on an almost canonical authority for many later students of the classics, especially in the period of disunion following the fall of the Han.[25]

Cheng was by no means the only grand synthesizer of the classics in the Latter Han era, only the most famous and influential. Others include Ma Jung, Wang Su, Chia K'uei (30–101), Liu Hsüan (d. 25), Hsü Shen (127–200), and Ho Hsiu (129–182). But even Cheng Hsüan's great rival, Ma Jung, followed a similar approach in his classical studies: "In annotating one particular classic, he would necessarily incorporate the other classics. Thus, when in annotating the *Change* he discussed the systems of ritual, he would bring in the *Rites of Chou*; in discussing the *Change*'s obscurities and profundities, he would make use of the *Tso Commentary* and the *Analects*, and also refer back to the *Documents Classic* in order to analyze the principles of the *Change*."[26] This method of reading off one classic in terms of another

[23] For a clear and succinct summary of the main differences between the Old and New Text traditions, see Rodney L. Taylor, "Confucianism: Scripture and Sage," in *The Holy Book in Comparative Perspective*, eds. Frederick Denny and Rodney L. Taylor (Columbia: University of South Carolina Press, 1985), pp. 184–185. As Taylor notes, one of the principal distinctions between the two schools was that "the New Text interpretation tended to see a major role for Confucius himself in the composition of the Classics," while Old Text scholars often "assigned to Confucius the task of transmitting the texts, not creating them" (pp. 184–185). A more extensive discussion of the controversies between the Old Text and New Text schools may be found in Tjan Tjoe Som, "Introduction," *Po Hu T'ung: The Comprehensive Discussions in the White Tiger Hall* [1949], trans. Tjan (Westport, Conn.: Hyperion Press, 1973 reprint), pp. 137–145.

[24] Honda, *Chung-kuo ching-hsüeh shih*, p. 188; Yoshikawa Kōjirō, "Shōsho Kōshi-den kaidai" (An Introduction to the *Shang-shu K'ung-shih chuan*), *Tōhōgakuhō*, no. 11, pt. 2 (July 1940): 32.

[25] Ch'eng Fa-jen, "Han-tai ching-hsüeh chih fu-hsing," p. 188. The high position occupied by Cheng's commentaries, particularly those on the ritual classics, is partly owing to the fact that most other Han commentaries on the Confucian classics either disappeared or survived only in fragments.

[26] Li Wei-hsiung, "Ma Jung yü Tung-Han ching-hsüeh" (Ma Jung and Eastern Han Classical Studies), in Wang et al., *Ching-hsüeh yen-chiu lun-chi*, p. 149.

is one of the strategies that commentators in general commonly employ in order to establish that the canon forms a self-consistent and well-ordered whole, as we shall see in chapter 5.

But this technique was by no means the only one that Han scholars used to re-establish the lost unity (or effect the unification) of the Confucian classics, to reintegrate the fragmented canon. Another such strategy, widely employed particularly during the Han era, was to relate the individual classics to one another and to the cosmos in a systematic way. Adumbrations of this technique may be found in classical Confucian literature—for example, in the statement in the *Mencius*, quoted above in chapter 1, that links two classical texts, the *Songs Classic* and the *Spring and Autumn Annals*, in a chronological order.[27] It appears much more fully developed in the "Encouragement of Learning" (Ch'üan-hsüeh) chapter of *Hsün-tzu* which states that "[with] the respect and refinement of the *Rites*, the centrality and harmony of the *Music*, the breadth of the *Songs* and *Documents*, and the subtlety of the *Spring and Autumn Annals*, cosmic completeness [is achieved]."[28] But even this formulation seems rudimentary when compared with the intricate schemas that Confucian scholars of the Han era devised in order to relate the classics to one another and to various aspects of the universal order.

Formulaic statements of the particular moral and pedagogical functions of each of the classics and of its place in some larger scheme of things are so numerous in Han literature that to quote all of them would be tedious and repetitive. They appear in such diverse sources as the "Author's Preface" (Tzu-hsü) to the *Records of the Historian* of Ssu-ma Ch'ien, the "Treatise on Bibliography" (I-wen chih) of Pan Ku's *Han History*, the "Explanations of the Classics" (Ching-chieh) chapter of the canonical *Record of Rites*, the "Natural Evolutions" (T'ien-yün) chapter of the *Chuang-tzu*, the "Great Gathering" (T'ai-tsu) chapter of the *Huai-nan-tzu*, the "Five Classics" (Wu-ching) chapter of the *Comprehensive Discussions in White Tiger Pavilion* (Po-hu t'ung-i), the *Model Sayings* (Fa-yen) of the Han philosopher Yang Hsiung, and the "Jade Cups" (Yü-pei) chapter in the *Luxuriant Gems of the Spring and Autumn Annals* (Ch'un-ch'iu fan-lu) attributed to Tung Chung-shu. One of the most schematic and succinct of these formulae, which correlates the order of the Confucian classics with the Confucian moral order based on the five constant virtues (*wu-ch'ang*), appears in the "Treatise on Bibliography" of the *Han History*:

[27] *Mencius* 4B, 21:1.

[28] This quotation from the "Encouragement of Learning" chapter of the *Hsün-tzu* may be found in *Hsün-tzu chi-chieh* (*Hsün-tzu* with Collected Explications), annot. Wang Hsien-ch'ien (Taipei: Shih-chieh shu-chü, 1974 reprint), p. 7.

The *Music* is for harmonizing with the divine, the standard of humanity. The *Songs* is for correcting words, the application of rightness. The *Rites* is for clarifying the essence, and since what is clarified is evident, it thus has no [particular] lesson. The *Documents* is for broadening apprehension, the method of [gaining] knowledge. The *Spring and Autumn Annals* is for judging affairs, the sign of trust. These five are thus the Way of the five constant virtues, each incomplete without all the others.[29]

Pan Ku here presents the books of the canon as a comprehensive and integrated whole by relating them to the universal moral order signified by the five constant virtues: humanity, rightness, rites, knowledge, and trust. In so doing, he apparently takes into account the extremely diverse nature of the materials included in the *Rites*, which, he says, has "no [particular] lesson." He also resolves the numerological discrepancy between the Six Classics and the five constant virtues by setting the *Change* apart as the source or origin of all the others.

Another work attributed to Pan Ku, the *Comprehensive Discussions in White Tiger Pavilion*, proposes a slightly different correlation of the classics with the five constant virtues, pairing the *Music* with humanity, the *Documents* with rightness, the *Rites* with ritual, the *Change* with knowledge, and the *Songs* with trust. What is more significant, this source maintains that the sages deliberately patterned the Five Classics after the five virtues, mainly for pedagogical purposes:

> Human feelings have the five natures which harbor the five constant virtues, but which cannot be completed by themselves. Therefore, the sages emblematized heaven's Way of the five constant virtues [in composing the Five Classics], thus clarifying it in order to teach people to complete their virtue.[30]

Other Han scholars correlated each of the Confucian classics with some aspect of the cosmos instead of with the virtues of the Confucian moral order. Yang Hsiung, for example, proposed a schema by which each of the classics illuminated a particular facet of the human or natural world. Taken together, they comprehended the whole:

> In speaking of heaven, nothing is as discerning as the *Change*. In speaking of affairs, nothing is as discerning as the *Documents*. In speaking of es-

---

[29] *Han-shu, I-wen-chih chu-shih hui-pien* (*Han History* "Treatise on Bibliography" with Collected Annotations), comp. Chen Kuo-ch'ing (Beijing: Chung-hua shu-chü, 1983), p. 96.

[30] *Po-hu t'ung shu-cheng* (The Comprehensive [Discussions] in White Tiger Pavilion with Annotations and Verifications), "Wu-ching" (The Five Classics), annot. Ch'en Li (Taipei: Ting-wen shu-chü, 1973 reprint), p. 148 (*chüan* 9).

sences, nothing is as discerning as the *Rites*. In speaking of the will, nothing is as discerning as the *Songs*. In speaking of principles, nothing is as discerning as the *Spring and Autumn Annals*.[31]

Each of the classics, then, had its strong point; and none could be neglected by those who wished to comprehend the full range of phenomena.

Commentators and other scholars of the post-Han era repeated almost endlessly the formulations devised by Han scholars for relating the Confucian classics to one another and to some aspect of the universal order. They also invented a few new such schemas. One of the most popular of these correlated each of the classics with particular eras of ancient history or with the kinds of rulers who held sway during those eras. Thus, the Sung Neo-Confucian cosmologist Shao Yung remarked schematically, if not too accurately, that "the *Change* begins with the three august sovereigns, the *Documents* with the two emperors, the *Songs* with the three kings, and the *Spring and Autumn Annals* with the five hegemons."[32] Chao Shu-sheng similarly arranged the classics in a descending hierarchical order that is also vaguely chronological: "One seeks the Way of heaven and earth in the *Change*, the Way of the emperors and kings in the *Documents*, the Way of the feudal lords in the *Spring and Autumn Annals*, the Way of the great officials in the *Rites*, and the Way of men and things in the *Songs*."[33] Finally, Shao Yung also associated Confucius' manner of editing each of the classics with the era of a particular sage-ruler: "Confucius exalted the *Change* regarding the era beginning with Hsi and Hsüan [= Fu Hsi and the Yellow Emperor]. He set in order the *Documents* regarding the era beginning with [Emperors] Yao and Shun. He expurgated the *Songs* regarding the era from [Kings] Wen and Wu. And he amended the *Spring and Autumn Annals* regarding the era from [Dukes] Huan and Wen."[34]

Later commentators not only keyed the classics comprehensively with the outer world of ancient history and kingship but also did so

[31] Yang Hsiung, *Fa-yen* (Model Sayings), "Kua-chien p'ien" (What Is Rarely Seen), SPPY ed., 7.1b–2a. A similar schema appears in the "Ju-chiao" (Confucian Teaching) chapter of the *Hsün-tzu*. See *Hsün-tzu chi-chieh*, pp. 84–85.

[32] Shao Yung, quoted in *Ching-i k'ao* 296.4a (vol. 8). The Ming philosopher Wang Yang-ming outlined a similar schema in expounding the idea that all the classics are histories. See Wang, *Ch'uan-hsi lu*, (Instructions for Practical Living), annot. Yeh Chün-tien (Taipei: Shang-wu yin-shu-kuan, 1971 reprint), p. 25.

[33] Chao Shu-sheng, quoted in *Ching-i k'ao* 297.15b (vol. 8).

[34] Shao Yung, *Huang-chi ching-shih shu* (Book of the Supreme Polarities Governing the World), "Kuan-wu nei-p'ien" (Inner Chapters on Observing Things), SPPY ed., 5.18a.

with the inner world of human qualities. According to the renowned Sung-era scholar and literatus Ou-yang Hsiu (1007–1072), each of the classics revealed some aspect or attribute of the Sage, Confucius:

> In the *Songs* one can see the Master's mind. From the *Documents* one can know the Master's judgments. From the *Music* one can attain to the Master's virtues. From the *Change* one can investigate the Master's nature. And in the *Spring and Autumn Annals* there is the Master's will.[35]

The Six Classics were thus a macrocosm, or a projection into the outer world, of the Sage, Confucius, who was in himself "a complete concert" (*chi ta-ch'eng*) (*Mencius* 5B, 1:6). Other, later scholars held that the classics comprehended not only every aspect of the Sage, but of the human mind as well. According to the Ming Neo-Confucian philosopher Wang Yang-ming:

> The Six Classics are nothing but the constant Way of our minds. Thus, the *Change* records the waxing and waning of our minds' *yin* and *yang*. The *Documents* records the rules and regulations of our minds' political affairs. The *Songs* records the lyrical expressions of our minds' nature and feelings. The *Rites* records our minds' orderliness and adornments. The *Music* records our minds' pleasure, happiness, harmony, and peace. The *Spring and Autumn Annals* records our minds' integrity, mendacity, depravity, and rectitude.[36]

In sum, the establishment of such systems of correspondence between the books of the Confucian canon on the one hand and a universal moral, cosmological, historical, or mental order on the other supported the idea that the canon was based in the nature of things.[37] It was not, in other words, just a congeries of ill-sorted and fragmented ancient writings that derived its authority more from political

[35] Ou-yang Hsiu, "Chü-shih wai-chi" (Outer Collected Writings of a Retired Scholar), quoted in Ts'ai Shih-ming, *Ou-yang Hsiu ti sheng-p'ing yü hsüeh-shu* (Ou-yang Hsiu's Life and Scholarship) (Taipei: Wen-shih-che ch'u-pan she, 1980), p. 68.

[36] *Wang Yang-ming ch'üan-chi* (Complete Writings of Wang Yang-ming) (Hong Kong: Kuang-chih shu-chü, 1959), 7.65–66; also trans. in Edward T. Ch'ien, *Chiao Hung and the Restructuring of Neo-Confucianism in the Late Ming* (New York: Columbia University Press, 1986), p. 266. A similar quotation, attributed to Chou Tzu-i, appears in *Ching-i k'ao* 297.12a (vol. 8).

[37] Such schemas are not confined to Confucian writings on their canon and even appear in modern literary theory. Northrop Frye, for example, demonstrates what one critic has called a "medieval manner of arbitrary creative schematism" in correlating the "four broad mythoi or narrative categories ('romantic,' 'tragic,' 'comic,' and 'ironic' or satiric)" with the seasons of the year. See Alastair Fowler, *Kinds of Literature: An Introduction to the Theory of Genres and Modes* (Cambridge: Cambridge University Press, 1982), p. 242.

fiat than from its cosmic comprehensiveness. By some accounts, even the fiveness of the Five Classics (or the sixity of the Six Classics) was not arbitrary, but was a matter of metaphysical (or perhaps numerological) necessity. According to Ch'ao Yüeh-chih (1059–1127), "When the five colors are prepared, a painting can be composed. When the five viscera are intact, a person can be completed. Thus, can the scholar dispense with [even] one of the Five Classics?"[38] A modern classicist, Ch'u Po-ssu, however, holds out for sixity, arguing that "five classics would be incomplete and thirteen classics [a common later enumeration] too numerous. The completion of the essence of the Way is in the Six Classics."[39]

Confucian commentators developed systems of correspondence between the individual books in their canon and aspects of universal order more fully and frequently than did their counterparts in any other major tradition. But the Confucian tradition is not unique, not sui generis, even in this regard. Buddhist commentators sometimes formulated such systems in order to relate the various sūtras in their canon to one another and to aspects of the Buddhist cosmos. One renowned Tibetan Buddhist commentator on the *Heart Sūtra*, bsTan-dar-Iha-ram pa, remarked that "the *Heart Sūtra* is the sūtra on view, the *Ātajnāna* is the sūtra on deeds, the *Vajravidāranī* is the sūtra on ablution, the *Bhadracarī* is the sūtra on prayers, and the *Apattideśanā* is the sūtra on the confession of sins."[40] This schema, however, includes only a small fraction of the works in the Mahāyāna canon, in marked contrast to those devised by Han and Sung Confucians respecting their canon.

The Confucian canon was also notable among those of major traditions in the extent to which it remained open, resisting final fixation or complete closure. While subtractions were rare, additions were not infrequent.[41] In the T'ang era, for example, the three primary commentaries on the *Spring and Autumn Annals*—the *Tso Commentary* (Tso-chuan), the *Kung-yang Commentary* (Kung-yang chuan), and the *Ku-liang Commentary* (Ku-liang chuan)—were included in lists of canonical works.[42] By Sung times, thirteen classics were recog-

---

[38] Ch'ao Yüeh-chih, quoted in *Ching-i k'ao* 296.4b (vol. 8).

[39] Ch'u Po-ssu, *Liu-ching tao lun* (A Discussion of the Way of the Six Classics) (Taipei: K'ai-ming shu-tien, 1971), p. 114.

[40] BsTan-dar-Iha-ram pa, *Commentary on the Heart Sūtra, Jewel Light Illuminating the Meaning*, in Donald S. Lopez, Jr., *The Heart Sūtra Explained: Indian and Tibetan Commentaries* (Albany: State University of New York Press, 1988), p. 143.

[41] On various Han and post-Han additions to the number of classics in the Confucian canon, see P'i, *Ching-hsüeh li-shih*, pp. 50 and 64; Honda, *Chung-kuo ching-hsüeh shih*, p. 130; Li, "Ch'ün-ching chü-yao chi yen-chiu fang-fa," p. 29.

[42] P'i, *Ching-hsüeh li-shih*, p. 192.

nized.[43] A prominent scholar of the Ching era, Tuan Yü-ts'ai (1735–1815), enumerated as many as twenty-one classics.[44]

In so doing, however, Tuan was not necessarily stretching the usage of the term "ching" out of all its classical proportions. For in Chou times, the word could refer to almost any book or, rather, to writing on silk or bamboo.[45] Even in the Han era, there was a tendency to designate all pre-Han literature as "ching."[46] Various schools of classical philosophy, including the Taoist, the Mohist, and the Legalist, as well as the scientific, technical, and medical traditions, also developed their own "classics," just as a number of diverse Indian intellectual traditions each had their own sūtras. The elasticity of the term "ching" and the later enumerations of the Confucian classics notwithstanding, few of the other works designated as classics carried nearly as much weight or authority as the established five (or six).

. . . . .

Yet, one major reformation of the Confucian canon did occur in post-Han times which was far more than an enumerative or philological exercise, which saw the emergence of a new canon—that of the Four Books, alongside the Five Classics. These Four Books—the *Analects* of Confucius, the *Mencius*, and two chapters extracted from the canonical *Record of Rites*, the *Doctrine of the Mean* (Chung-yung) and the *Great Learning* (Ta-hsüeh)—were first identified as a unit only by the great Sung Neo-Confucian philosopher Chu Hsi.[47] Prior to the Sung, these four books were not generally recognized as classics or even, in the case of the latter two, as independent texts. Although the *Analects* and *Mencius* were highly regarded by such famous Han and T'ang Confucians as Yang Hsiung and Han Yü (786–824), pre-Sung

[43] Hiraoka Takeo, *Keisho no seiritsu* (The Formation of the Classics) (Osaka: Zenkoku shobō, 1946), p. 3.

[44] Chou, "Ch'ün-ching kai-lun, p. 211.

[45] Chiang, *Shih-san ching*, p. 3; Hua Chung-lin, "Liu-ching t'ao-yüan yü K'ung-tzu shu-tso" (An Examination of the Sources of the Six Classics and of Confucius' Expounding or Composing [These Classics]), in Wang et al., *Ching-hsüeh yen-chiu lun-chi*, p. 14.

[46] Honda, *Chung-kuo ching-hsüeh shih*, p. 6.

[47] Chu Tzu-ch'ing, *Ching-tien ch'ang-t'an* (Common Talks on the Classics) (Hong Kong: T'ai-p'ing shu-chü, 1975), p. 47; Chou Yü-t'ung, " 'Ta-hsüeh' ho 'Li-yün' " (The "Great Learning" and the "Evolution of Rites"), in *Chou Yü-t'ung ching-hsüeh shih lun-chu hsüan-chi*, p. 407. David McMullen, however, argues that the T'ang scholar Ch'üan Te-yü "foreshadowed the Neo-Confucian grouping of the Four Books" in a dissertation written in the year 805. McMullen, *State and Scholars*, pp. 96–97.

scholars often classified the former book as a commentary (*chuan*) and the latter as a work of one of the philosophers (*chu-tzu*).[48] The Sung scholar Ch'en Chen-sun seems to have been the first to identify the two texts jointly as classics.[49] Although the *Doctrine of the Mean* had been the object of independent commentary as early as the Han era, only with the Sung Neo-Confucians was it admitted into any sort of canon.[50] As for the *Great Learning*, Ssu-ma Kuang (1019–1086) was the first to treat it as a separate text and to write a commentary on it.[51] But even he did not attempt to canonize it.

Thus, the movement toward the canonization of the Four Books culminated only with the great Sung Neo-Confucian philosophers, especially Chu Hsi. Chu not only established these books as a new Confucian canon alongside the Five Classics, but he also initiated the practice of writing commentaries on them as a unit.[52] The intellectual and political hegemony of Chu Hsi's brand of Neo-Confucianism in the Yüan, Ming, and Ch'ing eras turned the attention of commentators, scholars, and the educated elite as a whole to the Four Books. Mastery of these texts, with the authorized commentaries by Chu Hsi and his associates, was almost essential for passing the imperial civil service examinations in late-traditional China, for fulfilling the life's ambition of most educated men.

Having identified the Four Books as classics, Chu Hsi and his successors faced an intellectual problem similar to that encountered by Han Confucians, that of integrating or relating the separate books in the canon, of presenting it as a self-consistent and well-ordered whole as opposed to a potpourri of various pre-Han and Han Confucian writings. They confronted the additional task of relating the Four Books to the established canon, that of the Five Classics which they did not reject but rather sought to complement. In dealing with these problems of interrelating the separate books in their canon (or canons), Sung and later Neo-Confucians employed stratagems similar to those used by Han scholars. They also devised a few new ones.

[48] Hiraoka, *Keisho*, pp. 31 and 34; McMullen, *State and Scholars*, p. 81.

[49] Chou, "Ch'ün-ching kai-lun," p. 289.

[50] For an account of the early history of commentaries on the *Mean*, see Tu Wei-ming, *Centrality and Commonality: An Essay on Chung-yung* (Honolulu: University Press of Hawaii, 1976), pp. 13–16. On the apotheosis of the *Mean* during the Sung era, see Riegel, "The Four 'Tzu Ssu' Chapters," p. 48.

[51] Chou, " 'Ta-hsüeh' ho 'Li-yün,' " pp. 406 and 408; Daniel K. Gardner, *Chu Hsi and the Ta-hsüeh: Neo-Confucian Reflection on the Confucian Canon* (Cambridge: Harvard University Press, 1986), p. 23.

[52] Liu Ts'un-yan, "Chu Hsi's Influence in Yüan Times," in *Chu Hsi and Neo-Confucianism*, ed. Wing-tsit Chan (Honolulu: University Press of Hawaii, 1986), pp. 531–532.

An example of the latter is the attempt to link the Four Books with one another by relating their purported authors or subjects through a scholastic genealogy. Thus, the Confucian Way, which began with Confucius (*Analects*), was transmitted first to Tseng-tzu (*Great Learning*), then to Tzu-ssu (*Doctrine of the Mean*), and finally to Mencius (*Mencius*).[53] But the more common way of connecting these four books, one emphasized by Chu Hsi himself, was to arrange them in a pedagogical order that, taken as a whole, constituted a complete Confucian curriculum. As Chu remarked in comments he included in his anthology of Neo-Confucian writings, *Reflections on Things at Hand* (Chin-ssu lu), "I want people first of all to read the *Great Learning* to set a pattern, next to read the *Analects* to establish a foundation, next to read the *Mencius* to observe its development, and next to read the *Doctrine of the Mean* to seek the subtle points of the ancients."[54] Thus, Chu Hsi's Neo-Confucian pedagogy may be regarded as in part a by-product of an attempt to deal with an exegetical issue, that of interrelating various canonical texts.

Neo-Confucian commentators devised pedagogical orders to relate the Four Books not only to one another, but also to the Five Classics. Although some contented themselves with recommending a study of the Four Books in general as a prolegomenon to that of the Five Classics, the Ming scholar Wang Wei (1323–1374) proposed a more intricate schema connecting the two canonical groupings: "In studying the *Change* one must begin with the *Doctrine of the Mean*. In studying the *Documents* one must begin with the *Great Learning*. In studying the *Spring and Autumn Annals* one must begin with the *Mencius*. In studying the *Songs*, *Rites*, and *Music*, one must begin with the *Analects*."[55]

Other Neo-Confucian commentators described the relationships between the Four Books and the Five (or Six) Classics in metaphorical terms. Hu Ping, for example, likened the Six Classics to the heavens and the Four Books to the sun and moon that traverse the heavens.[56] Yang Tsai (1271–1323) remarked that "the Four Books are the mar-

---

[53] Chou, " 'Ta-hsüeh' ho 'Li-yün,' " p. 409; Gardner, *Chu Hsi*, p. 43.

[54] Chu Hsi, in *Chin-ssu-lu* (Reflections on Things at Hand), comps. Chu Hsi and Lü Tsu-ch'ien; annot. Chiang Yung (Taipei: Kuang-wen shu-chü, 1972 reprint), 3.10. Wing-tsit Chan traces the source of this quotation from Chu Hsi to the *Chu-tzu yü-lei* (Classified Conversations of Master Chu), 14.1a. For Chan's translation of this passage, see *Reflections on Things at Hand: The Neo-Confucian Anthology Compiled by Chu Hsi and Lü Ts-ch'ien*, trans. and annot. Wing-tsit Chan (New York: Columbia University Press, 1967), p. 102.

[55] Wang Wei, quoted in *Ching-i k'ao* 297.1b (vol. 8).

[56] Hu Ping, "Tzu-hsü" (Author's Preface) to *Ssu-shu t'ung* (Comprehending the Four Books), in *Ching-i k'ao* 254.2a (vol. 7).

row of the kingly Way and the root of the Five Classics."[57] Finally, a modern Confucian, Ch'en Li-fu, has described the relationships among the Four Books in terms of a building, comparing the *Great Learning* to a "perfect blueprint," the *Doctrine of the Mean* to a "project, complete with all the needed specifications for the foundations of the house," and the *Analects* and *Mencius* to "good materials . . . for the construction of the house."[58]

Such metaphorical statements of the relationships among the books in a canon occasionally appear in other traditions as well. A medieval Hindu devotional text, the *Vaisnaviya Tantrasara*, for example, likens the Upanishads to a cow and the *Bhagavad Gītā* to the milk from the cow.[59] And a medieval rabbinic commentator on the Song of Solomon pairs the vine that has budded (Song of Sol. 7:12) with the masters of Scripture, the vine blossom that has opened with the masters of Mishnah, and the pomegranates in flower with the masters of Gemara (commentary on the Mishnah).[60] But the occasionality and awkwardness of such metaphors in these other traditions highlight the remarkable extent to which Confucian scholars through the ages have been concerned with integrating and relating the separate books in their canon, with presenting it as an ordered whole based on some cosmic or universal principle or prototype. In this respect, the Confucian commentarial tradition is outstanding among the great religious traditions of mankind.

The Confucian tradition, as mentioned above, is also notable in the extent to which the boundaries of its canon remained open, or at least negotiable. For even with the canonization of the Four Books and the attempts to key these new classics harmoniously to the established classics, the Confucian canon (or canons) was not fixed as formally or finally as the canon in most traditions. In the first place, the relationships between the Four Books and Five Classics, and the degree of emphasis that should be given to each, remained a live issue. Many Neo-Confucian commentators, especially in the Southern Sung, Yüan, and Ming eras, practically ignored the Five Classics, with the

[57] Yang Tsai, "Hsü" (Preface) to Ch'eng Fu-hsin, *Ssu-shu chang-t'u* (The Four Books Illustrated by Charts), in *Ching-i k'ao* 255.3b (vol. 7).

[58] Ch'en Li-fu, *The Confucian Way: A New and Systematic Study of "The Four Books,"* trans. Shih Shun Liu (London: KPI, 1986), pp. 9–10.

[59] John G. Arapura, *Gnosis and the Question of Thought in Vedānta: Dialogue with the Foundations* (Dordrecht: Martinus Nijhoff, 1986), p. 103.

[60] Jacob Neusner, *The Wonder-Working Lawyers of Talmudic Babylonia: The Theory and Practice of Judaism in Its Formative Age* (Lanham, Md.: University Press of America, 1987), pp. 151–152.

exception of the *Change*, in their enthusiasm for the metaphysical meat and potatoes of such texts as the *Great Learning* and the *Doctrine of the Mean*. Even Chu Hsi regarded the Five Classics as secondary materials that, unlike the Four Books, were at least once or twice removed from the great Confucian sages, Confucius and Mencius.[61] As Benjamin Elman has written, "the authority of the [old Five] Classics now lay more in their corroboration of doctrines enunciated in the Four Books, rather than in their sacred position as Classics."[62] The seventeenth century, however, saw a "movement away from stress on the Four Books to a re-emphasis on the Five Classics," and there were even attempts to decanonize two of the Four Books, the *Doctrine of the Mean* and the *Great Learning* by reinserting these texts into the *Record of Rites* from which they had been extracted.[63] This proposal, as Elman has noted, implicitly challenged the legitimacy of the Four Books as an independent group of texts and even as part of the Confucian canon.

The canonization of the Four Books was succeeded by attempts both to add and to subtract books from the canon. The precedent of singling out chapters from the *Record of Rites* as canonical having been established with the *Doctrine of the Mean* and the *Great Learning*, a few later commentators proposed to proceed further along this line. Even modern historians of Chinese classical studies have advanced such suggestions, pointing to such chapters as the "Royal Institutes" (Wang-chih) and "Evolution of Rites" (Li-yün) as especially worthy of canonization.[64]

Among most Neo-Confucian commentators of the Sung, Yüan, and Ming eras, however, the most promising new candidates for canonization were some of the writings of the great Neo-Confucian philosophers, especially Chou Tun-i (1017–1073), Chang Tsai (1020–1077), Ch'eng I, and Chu Hsi. Indeed, Ch'ien Mu speculates that the first three of these philosophers set out deliberately to compose new classics.[65] Ch'eng I indicated that Chang Tsai's famous "Western Inscription" (Hsi-ming) might be placed in some canonical category in

[61] Wing-tsit Chan, "Chu Hsi's Completion of Neo-Confucianism," in Chan, *Chu Hsi: Life and Thought* (Hong Kong: Chinese University Press; New York: St. Martin's Press, 1987), p. 136.

[62] Benjamin A. Elman, "Philosophy (*I-li*) versus Philology (*K'ao-cheng*): The *Jen-hsin Tao-hsin* Debate," *T'oung Pao* 69, nos. 4–5 (1983): 185–186.

[63] Ibid., p. 199.

[64] P'i Hsi-jui, *Ching-hsüeh t'ung-lun* (Comprehensive Discussions of Classical Studies) (Taipei: Ho-Lo t'u-shu ch'u-pan she, 1974 reprint), 3.79; Ch'u, *Liu-ching tao lun*, p. 15.

[65] Ch'ien Mu, "Chu-tzu hsüeh t'i-kang" (An Outline of Master Chu's Learning), pp. 15–16, in *Chu-tzu hsin hsüeh-an* (A New Scholarly Record of Master Chu), 5 vols. (Taipei: San-min shu-chü, 1971), vol. 1.

remarking that it equals the *Mencius* in some respects.[66] The Ch'ing
scholar Tou K'o-ch'in ranked Chou Tun-i's "Diagram of the Great
Ultimate" (T'ai-chi t'u) and *Comprehensive Book* (T'ung-shu) with the
Mencius, the *Analects*, and the *Doctrine of the Mean*.[67] But the Neo-Confucian work that most nearly became a classic in its own right, and
the subject of many commentaries and imitations, was the famous anthology of Neo-Confucian writings compiled by Chu Hsi and Lü Tsu-
ch'ien (1137–1181): the *Reflections on Things at Hand*. As William
Theodore de Bary remarks of this and a companion work, the *Elementary Learning* (Hsiao-hsüeh), although "neither of these works
compiled under Chu Hsi's direction would have been thought canonical by Chu himself, . . . among his followers they became virtual 'classics.' "[68]

Even Neo-Confucian commentaries on the classics assumed canonical characteristics for some scholars in late-traditional China. According to Li Ts'an, Chu Hsi's *Collected Commentaries on the Four Books*
(Ssu-shu chi-chu) was so complete and comprehensive that no further
commentaries need be written on these classical texts.[69] The prominent Ming Neo-Confucian scholar Hsüeh Hsüan (1389–1464) remarked of the same work that "it is so broad and great, so refined
and intimate that it completely develops the ideas of the ancient
sages."[70] Chu Hsi himself extolled another commentary, that by Hu
An-kuo (1074–1138) on the *Spring and Autumn Annals*, in terms usually reserved for the classics, remarking that it "clarifies the principles
of heaven and rectifies the minds of people."[71] Another scholar of
the Sung era, Shih Chieh (1005–1045), ranked the commentary by

[66] Ira E. Kasoff, *The Thought of Chang Tsai (1020–1077)* (Cambridge: Cambridge
University Press, 1984), p. 143.

[67] Tou K'o-ch'in, "Li-hsüeh cheng-tsung tzu-hsü" (Author's Preface to the *Orthodox
Transmission of the School of Principle*), in *Ch'ing-ju hsüeh-an* 9.24a (vol. 1).

[68] Wm. Theodore de Bary, "Introduction," *The Rise of Neo-Confucianism in Korea*, eds.
Wm. Theodore de Bary and JaHyun Kim Haboush (New York: Columbia University
Press, 1985), p. 23.

[69] Li Ts'an, "Hsü" (Preface) to Chao Shen, *Ssu-shu chien i tsuan yao* (A Collection of
Important Points on the Meanings of Commentaries on the Four Books), in *Ching-i
k'ao* 253.5a (vol. 7).

[70] Hsüeh Hsüan, *Tu-shu lu* (A Record of My Study of Books), 1.9, quoted in Jung
Chao-tsu, *Ming-tai ssu-hsiang shih* (Intellectual History of the Ming Era) (Taipei: K'ai-
ming shu-tien, 1969), p. 18. An English translation of this passage appears in Mao
Huaixin, "The Establishment of the School of Chu Hsi and Its Propagation in Fukien,"
in Chan, ed., *Chu Hsi and Neo-Confucianism*, p. 510.

[71] Chu Hsi, quoted by Yang Shih-ch'i, in Wang K'o-k'uan, *Ch'un-ch'iu Hu-chuan fu-lu
tsuan-shu* (Hu's Commentary on the *Spring and Autumn Annals* with a Collection of Subcommentaries Attached), in *Ching-i k'ao* 199.3a (vol. 6).

Sun Fu (992–1057) on the *Annals* with the work of Confucius himself.[72]

.   .   .   .   .

The formal raising of the works of later masters and commentators to the level of classics or scriptures is perhaps not so common in most other canonical traditions, especially those of the West. When attempts to do this occur, as with the works of Joachim of Fiore in thirteenth-century Christendom, they are sometimes branded as heretical.[73] Indeed, in the Christian tradition, heretics were often identified by their refusal to recognize the closure of the canon, as was the case with the Gnostics of late antiquity.[74] Even when not regarded as heretical, attempts to add books to the biblical canon, such as the campaign by a group of ministers to include Martin Luther King, Jr.'s "Letter from a Birmingham Jail" in the New Testament, seldom get very far.[75]

But even in traditions in which the canonical text or texts are most well defined, established, and revered, openings may be found for supplements to scripture. In Sunni Islam, for example, the notion that our present Qur'ān text (*mushaf*), as opposed to its heavenly archetype, is incomplete, facilitated the acceptance of sunna (accounts of the actions or practice of Muhammad as transmitted through oral traditions) to fill in the gaps. In some cases, in fact, the sunna could even supersede or abrogate relevant sections in the Qur'ān.[76] In Shia Islam, moreover, the divine revelation was not confined to the Qur'ān, but was communicated to successive Imams after the death of Muhammad.[77]

Rabbinic Judaism, as well as Sunnites in Islam, held that its canon, the original Torah book, was in some sense incomplete or at least in need of elaboration or development, thus paving the way for the later

[72] Shih Chieh, quoted in *Sung-Yüan hsüeh-an* 2.20b (vol. 1).

[73] On Joachim's so-called New Gospel of the Third Age, which supposedly superseded the New Testament, see Beryl Smalley, *The Study of the Bible in the Middle Ages*, 3rd. ed., rev. (Oxford: Basil Blackwell, 1983), pp. 289–290.

[74] Alain Le Boulluec, "La Bible chez les marginaux de l'orthodoxie," in *Le Monde grec ancien et la Bible*, ed. Claude Mondésert (Paris: Editions Beauchesne, 1984).

[75] Bruce M. Metzger, *The Canon of the New Testament: Its Origin, Development, and Significance* (Oxford: Clarendon Press, 1987), p. 271.

[76] Coulson, *Islamic Law*, pp. 57 and 76; John Burton, *The Collection of the Qur'ān* (Cambridge: Cambridge University Press, 1979), pp. 57–58, 117, and 232.

[77] Geo Widengren, "Holy Book and Holy Tradition in Islam," in Bruce and Rupp, eds., *Holy Book and Holy Tradition*, p. 229.

canonization of an "Oral Torah" said to have been originally passed down through Moses on Mount Sinai.[78] Indeed, later rabbis extended the concept of Torah to include the interpretation of Torah by later generations of sages and students. According to the sage R. Yoshua ben Levi, "even what an advanced student will teach before his master has the authority of words spoken by Moses at Sinai."[79] In the words of Jacob Neusner, "Revelation continues in time, so new *torah* becomes part of the Torah, as God speaks to generations without end."[80] However, the recension of the Oral Torah, especially the Mishnah (c. A.D. 200) and the two Talmuds—the *Yerushalmi*, or Palestinian, Talmud (c. A.D. 400) and the *Bavli*, or Babylonian, Talmud (c. A.D. 600)—practically made it more difficult for later recipients of divine revelation to have their works accepted as scripture. Thus, they often found it necessary to devise more ingenious or indirect arguments to avert the premature closure of the canon. Kabbalists, for example, "spoke of a missing twenty-third letter of the Hebrew alphabet, hidden in the white spaces between the letters. From those openings the larger Torah was still to emerge, yet it was there already," and may be seen fully revealed in the works of Harold Bloom.[81]

A rough Hindu counterpart of this missing twenty-third Hebrew letter is the fifth Veda, meant to supplement and in some respects even supplant the original four, which medieval Hindus frequently

[78] Robert Goldenberg, "Talmud," in *Back to the Sources: Reading the Classic Jewish Texts*, ed. Barry Holtz (New York: Summit Books, 1984), p. 130; Susan A. Handelman, *The Slayers of Moses: The Emergence of Rabbinic Interpretation in Modern Literary Theory* (Albany: State University of New York Press, 1982), p. 31. Not all groups or sects within ancient Judaism, however, accepted the authority of the Oral Torah. The Sadducees, for example, accepted only the written law of the Torah book as binding. See Marcel Simon, "The Ancient Church and Rabbinical Tradition," in Bruce and Rupp, eds., *Holy Book and Holy Tradition*, p. 104. Paradoxically, this "Oral Torah," down to the time of its redaction in the Mishnah and the Talmuds, may have been preserved mainly through written records. See Jacob Weingren, "Oral Torah and Written Records," in Bruce and Rupp, eds., *Holy Book and Holy Tradition*, p. 66.

[79] Shmuel Safrai, "Oral Tora," in *The Literature of the Sages, First Part: Oral Tora, Halakha, Mishna, Tosefta, Talmud, External Tractates*, ed. Safrai (Assen/Maastricht: Van Gorcum; Philadelphia: Fortress Press, 1987), p. 66.

[80] Jacob Neusner, *Midrash in Context: Exegesis in Formative Judaism* (Philadelphia: Fortress Press, 1983), p. XIX.

[81] Harold Bloom, *Kabbalah and Criticism* (New York: Continuum, 1983), pp. 53–54. Bloom himself, however, modestly identifies Kafka, Freud, and Scholem as those modern writers whose works are most worthy of Torah status. See Bloom, *The Strong Light of the Canonical: Kafka, Freud, and Scholem as Revisionists of Jewish Culture and Thought*, The City College Papers, no. 20 (New York: The City College, 1987).

regarded as incomplete and even obsolete.[82] Opinions as to the identity of this fifth Veda varied. Such diverse works as the *Purāṇas* ("Ancient Lore"), the epic *Mahābhārata*, Tamil Shaivite literature, Tantric texts, the science of music, and even classical Indian drama were so designated.[83] It seems that just about every major literary, philosophical, religious, and scholastic tradition in medieval India had its own version, most of which were supposed to bridge the gap between ancient Vedic revelation and contemporary Hindu society. The *Purāṇas*, for example, were presented as attempts "to interpret ancient yet eternal truths in ways accessible and comprehensible to later generations."[84]

But the most popular candidates for the fifth Vedic position were the great Indian epics, the *Mahābhārata* and the *Rāmāyaṇa*, which constituted a sort of "second round, so to speak, in revelation."[85] Indeed, the epics, by some accounts, were even weightier and mightier than the original four Vedas.[86] The *Rāmāyaṇa*, in particular, generated as great a mass of exegetical writing as any work in Indian literature, with the possible exception of the *Bhagavad Gītā*.[87] It also inspired countless later imitations and re-creations in just about every major language of India and Southeast Asia. One of these later versions, that by the sixteenth-century Hindi poet Tulsīdās, has even been characterized as the "Bible of Northern India," as noted above. As for the *Mahābhārata*, it was said to be "worshipped by the very gods." Listening to it from beginning to end cleansed one of every sin, even

[82] Arapura, *Gnosis*, pp. 159–160; Lee Siegel, *Laughing Matters: Comic Tradition in India* (Chicago: University of Chicago Press, 1987), p. 116.

[83] Troy Wilson Organ, *Hinduism: Its Historical Development* (Woodbury, N.Y.: Barron's, 1974), pp. 300–301; René Daumal, "To Approach the Hindu Poetic Art," in Daumal, *Rasa; or, Knowledge of the Self: Essays on Indian Aesthetics and Selected Sanskrit Studies*, trans. and intro. by Louise Landes Levi (New York: New Directions, 1982), p. 8.

[84] C. Mackenzie Brown, "The Origin and Transmission of the Two Bhāgavata Purāṇas: A Canonical and Theological Dilemma," *Journal of the American Academy of Religion* 51, no. 4 (December 1983): 556.

[85] J.A.B. van Buitenen, "The Indian Epic," in Edward C. Dimock, Jr., et al., *The Literatures of India: An Introduction* (Chicago: University of Chicago Press, 1978), p. 53.

[86] G. A. Feuerstein, *Introduction to the Bhagavad-Gītā: Its Philosophy and Cultural Setting* (London: Rider and Co., 1974), p. 63. According to the *Mahābhārata*, "Once the divine seers foregathered, and on one scale they hung the four *Vedas* in the balance, and on the other scale *The Bharata*; and both in size and in weight it was the heavier." *The Mahābhārata*, vol. 1: *The Book of the Beginning*, trans. and ed. J.A.B. van Buitenen (Chicago: University of Chicago Press, 1973), p. 31.

[87] Robert P. Goldman, "Introduction," *The Rāmāyaṇa of Vālmīki: An Epic of Ancient India*, intro. and trans. Goldman; annot. Goldman and Sally Sutherland (Princeton: Princeton University Press, 1984), p. 44.

Brahmanicide.[88] The sage Vyāsa, the purported compiler of the epic, was, moreover, celebrated as "a new seer, the son and grandson of illustrious Vedic seers."[89]

In modern times, even the great epics have been in some respects overshadowed by the *Bhagavad Gītā*, which has come to be regarded as "the undisputed statement of all that is most central and important in the Hindu world of ideas."[90] The first great modern Indian intellectual, Ram Mohun Roy (1772–1833), called it "the essence of all Shastrus [scriptures]".[91] Before the nineteenth century, however, this text, originally an interpolation in the massive *Mahābhārata*, "was scarcely known outside the learned world of the pandits." It was traditionally classified as part of the literature of "recollection" (*smriti*), inferior in status to the Vedic revelation (*sruti*).[92]

But even the literature of the *shruti* class was not in the Hindu tradition necessarily closed or fixed for all time. New upanishads, a class of Vedic literature, for example, continued to be composed in medieval and even modern times, although they were not generally accepted as part of the Vedic corpus.[93] Such developments have led at least one modern scholar, Patrick Olivelle, to propose that "a Vedic canon has never existed and we are fooling ourselves if we think that the four classes of Vedic texts provide us with one."[94] Hinduism, according to H. G. Coward, became a "religion of the Book" with a well-defined canon only in modern times when such Hindu revivalists as Dayananda Saraswati (1824–1883), the founder of the Arya Samaj, applied the Protestant principle of *sola scriptura* to the Vedas.[95] Yet, even if Hinduism in general lacked the closed fixed canon that was a major feature of the "Book religions" of the West and Middle East, Vedānta did not. For all schools of Vedānta took three basic texts—

[88] Robert C. Lester, "Hinduism: Veda and Sacred Texts," in Denny and Taylor, eds., *The Holy Book in Comparative Perspective*, p. 141.

[89] James L. Fitzgerald, "The Great Epic of India as Religious Rhetoric: A Fresh Look at the *Mahābhārata*," *Journal of the American Academy of Religion* 51, no. 4 (December 1983): 614.

[90] Eric J. Sharpe, *The Universal Gītā: Western Images of the Bhagavadgītā, A Bicentenary Survey* (London: Duckworth, 1985), p. 69.

[91] Ram Mohun Roy, quoted ibid., p. 12.

[92] Ibid., pp. 69 and 12.

[93] Thomas B. Coburn, " 'Scripture' in India: Towards a Typology of the Word in Hindu Life," *Journal of the American Academy of Religion* 52, no. 3 (September 1984): 445.

[94] Patrick Olivelle, review of *L'Autorité du Veda selon les Nyāya-Vaiśesikas* by George Chemparathy, in *Journal of the American Oriental Society* 107, no. 2 (1987): 364.

[95] Harold G. Coward, "The Response of the Arya Samaj," in *Modern Indian Responses to Religious Pluralism*, ed. Coward (Albany: State University of New York Press, 1987), p. 43.

the Upanishads, the *Bhagavad Gītā*, and the *Brāhma Sūtra*—as the basis of their systems.[96]

In sum, the imperfect closure of the Confucian canon has counterparts in other Eastern traditions. Canons, in any case, are seldom so fixed, sealed, and authoritative as ecclesiastics and ideologues of various persuasions might have it. Even relatively closed canons sometimes face challenges to their authority from within the tradition. Indeed, even the authorities, the guardians of the tradition, at times find it convenient to dim the aura of the canon. In the wake of the Protestant Reformation, for example, "Skillful Jesuits . . . exploited skeptical arguments in order to undermine confidence in the Book and strengthen faith in the Church."[97]

In Neo-Confucianism, the most notable internal challenge to the authority of the canon came from philosophers associated with the "School of Mind" (*hsin-hsüeh*) who taught that the primary locus of the Confucian Way or of universal principle was the innate moral consciousness, not the classics or even the teachings of the ancient sages. Thus, Lu Hsiang-shan (1139–1193), one of the two most famous philosophers of this school, remarked that "the Six Classics annotate me"; the classics, then, were footnotes on the moral mind.[98] Such pronouncements have been widely quoted and analyzed by modern historians of Neo-Confucian thought. But they tend to obscure the fact that even philosophers of this school seldom abandoned classical exegesis. Even Lu advised his students to read the ancient commentaries on the Six Classics.[99] Some pages from the writings of the other most famous philosopher of the School of Mind, Wang Yang-ming, are almost as replete with commentarial concerns and exegetical modes of analysis as are the works of more ordinary commentators.[100]

The persistence of exegetical mentalities, even among those who sought to break free from commentarial concerns, appears in a number of other traditions as well. In medieval Judaism, for example,

[96] P. T. Raju, *Structural Depths of Indian Thought* (Albany: State University of New York Press, 1985), p. 377.

[97] Elizabeth L. Eisenstein, *The Printing Press as an Agent of Change: Communications and Cultural Transformations in Early-Modern Europe*, 2 vols. in 1 (Cambridge: Cambridge University Press, 1980), p. 326.

[98] Lu Hsiang-shan, "Yü-lu" (Recorded Conversations), in *Hsiang-shan ch'üan-chi* (Complete Writings of [Lu] Hsiang-shan), SPPY ed., 34.1b.

[99] Wing-tsit Chan, "The New Fortunes of Chu Hsi," in Chan, ed., *Chu Hsi: Life and Thought*, p. 7.

[100] See, for example, Wang's "Wu-ching i-shuo shih-san t'iao" (Calculated Explanations on the Five Classics, in Thirteen Sections), in *Yang-ming ch'üan-shu* (Complete Works of [Wang] Yang-ming), SPPY ed., 26.7a (vol. 3).

adherents of the Karaist movement, which called for a return to the scriptures and the abandonment of established commentaries, especially the Talmud, remained enmeshed in exegetical enterprises. For "no sooner had the founder of Karaism sounded the Back to Scripture alarm, than exegesis began, Talmudic hermeneutic rules, and extensions of these rules, being used to the full."[101] Likewise, the great medieval Hindu mystic Chaitanya (1485–1523), who once advised an illiterate holy fool that he was a greater authority on the *Bhagavad Gītā* than any pandit,[102] nonetheless commissioned several conventional scholars to establish a proper scholastic basis for the devotional Vaishnava movement that he established. Even Ch'an Buddhism, so renowned for its iconoclasm and for its teaching of a "special transmission outside the scriptures," yet generated a larger literary output than any school of Chinese Buddhism, much of it of a hermeneutical character.[103] Finally, despite the initial determination of the Protestant reformers to remove all glosses from the Bible, there developed by the late sixteenth century a Lutheran scholasticism that "put the Scriptures again under a formalized pattern of interpretation and hermeneutic theory."[104]

In sum, even those medieval writers and thinkers who condemned established commentarial traditions generally continued to operate within an intellectual world dominated by the classics and the modes of thought generated by the demands of classical exegesis. Having examined the antecedents and origins of these classics in the Confucian tradition (chapter 1) as well as the integration, development, and closure (or nonclosure) of canons (chapter 2), let us go on to consider the commentaries.

[101] Judah Goldin, "On the Talmud," in *The Living Talmud: The Wisdom of the Fathers and Its Classical Commentaries*, selected and trans. with an essay by Goldin (New York: New American Library, Mentor Books, 1959), p. 35.

[102] Siegel, *Laughing Matters*, pp. 261–262.

[103] David W. Chappell, "Hermeneutical Phases in Chinese Buddhism," in *Buddhist Hermeneutics*, ed. Donald S. Lopez, Jr. (Honolulu: University Press of Hawaii, 1988), pp. 190 and 198.

[104] Basil Hall, "Biblical Scholarship: Editions and Commentaries," in *The Cambridge History of the Bible*, vol. 3: *The West from the Reformation to the Present Day*, ed. S. L. Greenslade (Cambridge: Cambridge University Press, 1963), p. 87; Gabriel Josipovici, *The Book of God: A Response to the Bible* (New Haven: Yale University Press, 1988), p. 31.

Chapter 3

ORIGINS, DIMENSIONS, AND APOTHEOSIS OF

COMMENTARIES

THE RANGE of works typed as "commentary" may vary widely. By a narrow definition, a commentary may refer only to a running gloss on a text generally recognized as classical or scriptural.[1] A wider conception would identify much of the literature of the postclassical, or "silver," age in several civilizations or traditions as forms of commentary (or, in some cases, hidden commentary) on the classics. Barry Holtz, for example, has remarked that almost all of Jewish literature, from the legal codes of the Middle Ages to the Hasidic homilies of the nineteenth century, "presents itself as nothing more than interpretation, a vast set of glosses on the one true Book, the Torah."[2] Even so unlikely a work as the *Zohar*, a thirteenth-century Jewish mystical speculation, "was given the literary framework of biblical exegesis."[3] Moreover, midrash, "exegesis" or "interpretation" of Scripture, is found in practically every genre of classical and medieval Jewish writing.[4]

A number of the literary genres that flourished in the Greco-Roman world, such as Attic comedy, Greek tragedy, and even Roman satire, may also be typed as modes of commentary on a classical tradition dominated by Homer and the epic tradition. The *Satyricon* of Petronius, for example, has been characterized as a "parody on the *Odyssey*."[5] Even the Pre-Socratic philosophers fell under the "spell of

---

[1] Such a narrow definition of commentary appears in Shaye J. D. Cohen, *From the Maccabees to the Mishnah* (Philadelphia: Westminster Press, 1987), p. 212.

[2] See Barry W. Holtz, "Introduction: On Reading Jewish Texts" and "Midrash," in *Back to the Sources: Reading the Classic Jewish Texts*, ed. Holtz (New York: Summit Books, 1984), p. 13 and pp. 185–186, respectively.

[3] Jacob Neusner, *Midrash in Context: Exegesis in Formative Judaism* (Philadelphia: Fortress Press, 1983), p. xii.

[4] James L. Kugel, "Two Introductions to Midrash," in *Midrash and Literature*, eds. Geoffrey H. Hartman and Sanford Budick (New Haven: Yale University Press, 1986), pp. 91–92. For a brief account of the characteristics of midrash, see John Bowker, *The Targums and Rabbinic Literature: An Introduction to Jewish Interpretations of Scripture* (Cambridge: Cambridge University Press, 1969), pp. 45–46 and 69.

[5] J. P. Sullivan, "Introduction" to *Petronius, The Satyricon; and Seneca, The Apocolocyntosis*, trans. with intros. and notes by Sullivan (Harmondsworth, Eng.: Penguin Books, 1977), p. 17.

epic"—particularly Parmenides, who "sought to represent himself as a new Odysseus, and his philosophical quest as a new *Odyssey*."[6]

Finally, the ideas, themes, and stories contained in the classics of the Hindu tradition, especially the Veda and the two great epics, the *Mahābhārata* and the *Rāmāyana*, informed and even dominated nearly every genre of Indian literature from classical drama and lyric poetry to systematic philosophy. As Edward Dimock has remarked, "this process of commentaries written on commentaries is at the root of a large part of classical Indian literature."[7] If Aeschylus served up slices from the banquet of Homer, the greatest classical Indian dramatist, Kālidāsa, did the same with respect to the epics in his tradition, particularly the *Mahābhārata*.

But the net of commentary may cover an even wider area, enmeshing not only many of the major literary genres in premodern civilizations, but even the classics or scriptures themselves, or at least significant segments of them. It is generally recognized that a number of works composed originally with exegetical intent found their way into texts that were later canonized. Thus, the book of Chronicles in the Old Testament has been characterized as a sort of midrash or commentary on Kings, and the gospel of St. Matthew in the New Testament as a commentary on Mark.[8] According to Jacques Guillet, the New Testament as a whole is primarily a commentary on and a reading of the Jewish scriptures.[9] As Martin Luther reminds us, Jesus and his disciples did not intend to attach an appendix to the Old Testament, but to interpret and apply it.[10] Even the bulk of the Old Tes-

---

[6] Eric Alfred Havelock, *The Literate Revolution in Greece and Its Cultural Consequences* (Princeton: Princeton University Press, 1982), p. 250. Havelock adds: "No less purposeful is the way in which he evokes memories of the *Iliad*, with the implicit claim that he is also another Achilles" (p. 251).

[7] Edward C. Dimock, Jr., "An Overview: the Sutra," in Dimock et al., *The Literatures of India: An Introduction* (Chicago: University of Chicago Press, 1978), p. 2.

[8] David Weiss Halivni, *Midrash, Mishnah, and Gemara: The Jewish Predilection for Justified Law* (Cambridge: Harvard University Press, 1986), p. 17; C.F.D. Moule, *The Birth of the New Testament*, 3rd ed., rev. (San Francisco: Harper and Row, 1982), pp. 94–95. Moule remarks that "a plausible case has been made for the interpretation of Matthew as the result of a 'school' of exegesis" (p. 94). For an account of the various types of intrabiblical exegesis, see James L. Kugel, "Part One. Early Interpretation: The Common Background of Late Forms of Biblical Exegesis," in James L. Kugel and Rowan A. Greer, *Early Biblical Interpretation* (Philadelphia: Westminster Press, 1986), pp. 73–74.

[9] Jacques Guillet, "La Bible à la naissance de l'eglise," in *Le Monde grec ancien et la Bible*, ed. Claude Mondésert (Paris: Editions Beauchesne, 1984), p. 56.

[10] Harold Coward, *Sacred Word and Sacred Text: Scripture in World Religions* (Maryknoll, N.Y.: Orbis Books, 1988), p. 74.

tament, the prophets and the writings, so some rabbinic commentators concluded, was intended "simply [to] explain the Pentateuch."[11]

The incorporation of commentary into canon also appears prominently in classical Chinese literature. In fact, some Chinese canonical texts are formally divided into parts designated as "ching" (classic) and "shuo" (explanation) or "chuan" (commentary). But even whole classics, such as the *Analects* of Confucius and the *Record of Rites* (Li-chi) in the Confucian tradition, have sometimes been typed as "commentaries" in relation to other "classics," such as the *Documents* and the *Songs*. Traditional and modern scholars alike have characterized the *Record of Rites*, one of the Five Classics canonized in the Han era, as a commentary on the *Deportment and Rites* (I-li) or the *Rites of Chou* (Chou-li).[12] According to the great Han commentator Cheng Hsüan, the *Record of Rites* is a "commentary" in relation to the *Rites of Chou*, but a "classic" in relation to the *Tso Commentary* (Tso-chuan).[13]

The broadest conception of commentary might include not only much of premodern literature and parts of the classics, but almost all human acts and artifacts, contexts (and intertexts) as well as texts. As a contemporary deconstructionist would have it, "All facts, figures, and formulas, all runes, readings, and writings, all fashions, fictions, and fantasies, all customs, conventions, and codes, and all laws, loves, and lives, are interpretation."[14]

Whatever its potential for spiritual liberation, such a broad definition of commentary—including almost everything that partakes of interpretation—is inappropriate for this particular examination of commentarial approaches to the classics in the Confucian tradition. Using it would make this study too diffuse by constraining us to treat nearly every cultural form, from popular proverbs to court etiquette, that reflected on material contained in the Confucian classics. It

[11] Ibid., pp. 5–6.

[12] Hsü Fu-ch'üan, "Yüeh-chi wen-hsüeh li-lun ch'u-t'an" (A Preliminary Investigation of the Literary Theory of the "Record of Music"), in Li Yüeh-kang et al., *San-Li yen-chiu lun-chi* (A Collection of Articles on the Study of the Three Ritual Classics) (Taipei: Li-ming wen-hua shih-yeh, 1981), p. 209; Lin Yin, "Hsün-ku yü chih-ching" (Exegesis and the Study of the Classics), in Wang Ching-chih et al., *Ching-hsüeh yen-chiu lun-chi* (A Collection of Articles on Research in Classical Studies) (Taipei: Li-ming wen-hua shih-yeh, 1981), p. 260; Chiang Po-ch'ien, *Shih-san ching kai-lun* (General Discussions of the Thirteen Classics) (Shanghai: Ku-chi ch'u-pan she, 1983), p. 328; Ku Yen-wu, "Chiu-ching" (The Nine Classics), in Ku, *Yüan-ch'ao-pen Jih-chih lu* (The Original Manuscript Version of the Record of Daily Knowledge) (Taipei: Ming-lun ch'u-pan she, 1970), 10.222.

[13] P'i Hsi-jui, *Ching-hsüeh t'ung-lun* (Comprehensive Discussions of Classical Studies) (Taipei: Ho-Lo t'u-shu ch'u-pan she, 1974 reprint), 3.56.

[14] Vincent B. Leitch, *Deconstructive Criticism: An Advanced Introduction* (New York: Columbia University Press, 1983), p. 250.

would also distract attention from the issue of commentarial assumptions regarding the character of the classics and the strategies devised to support those assumptions, the intended focus of this study. On the other hand, neither could this topic be satisfactorily covered by limiting our sources to the works designated as "commentaries" by the narrowest definition: those which take the form of a direct running gloss on a classical text. For many valuable discussions of commentarial presuppositions and procedures appear in other types of works, such as the treatises on bibliography in the standard dynastic histories, the philosophical dialogues of the Neo-Confucian masters, and prefaces to works of classical scholarship. In any case, the present study is more concerned with the development and implications of commentarial and exegetical modes of thought than it is with the historical vicissitudes of a particular literary form or genre. These modes are as likely to be developed and expressed in works we may identify as "hidden commentaries" as in the standard type of running commentary on a classical text.

．　．　．　．　．

Commentary, again taking a broader view of the subject, preceded even the compilation of the classics or scriptures in most civilizations. Its origins, technical as well as intellectual, may be plausibly traced back to the interpretation of omens, oracles, and dreams in various ancient and even preliterate cultures. The divinatory reading of such signs has more in common with classical exegesis than the point that both these forms of hermeneutics interpret obscurities whose meaning is not apparent to the untutored. In some cases, even the methods used by later exegetes were derived, or at least were believed to have been derived, from those used by early diviners in the interpretation of dreams and oracles. In rabbinic Judaism, for example, "the techniques of midrashic interpretation were adapted from ancient procedures of dream interpretation," even with respect to such details as style, spelling, and vocabulary.[15] *Pesher*, a type of exegesis used in the Qumran community, also shows affinities to the interpretation of dreams, especially in its use of symbolism, atomization, and paronomasia.[16] In Christian biblical commentaries, "the terms employed for

[15] Edward L. Greenstein, "Medieval Bible Commentaries," in Holtz, ed., *Back to the Sources*, p. 216. On this subject, James Kugel remarks that "such rabbinic exegetical tools as gematria and notarikon have their parallels in Greek dream-interpretation techniques." Kugel, "Two Introductions to Midrash," pp. 100–101.

[16] D. Domant, "Qumran Sectarian Literature," in *Jewish Writings of the Second Temple*

typological exegesis," a major commentarial strategy used especially in interpreting the historical events recorded in the Old Testament, "originally designated the interpretation of dreams."[17] With respect to Qur'ānic exegesis, the great Islamic philosopher al-Ghazālī (d. 1111) remarked: "Know that interpretation of the Qur'ān (*ta'wīl*) occupies the place of interpretation of dreams (*ta'wīr*)."[18] Even some modern theories of dream interpretation share with classical exegesis not only specific techniques, but also such general assumptions as that the text (or, in Freudian analysis, the latent content of the dream) is an intelligible and unified whole and that no element in it is trivial or superfluous.[19] The main task of the analyst, like that of the classical commentator, is to restore or reveal the original coherence and significance of the text (or dream text) that may not be apparent.

Dreams and their interpretation were not as well connected with classical or scriptural exegesis in ancient China as in the Mediterranean West, although traditional Chinese dream literature is among the most extensive in the world.[20] Confucius himself, the first great commentator in Chinese history, once admitted his failure to dream of the Duke of Chou (*Analects* 7:5), the source of his dream of the good society. But in China the reading of omens and oracles, the practice of various forms of divination, apparently contributed as much to the development of the styles and strategies used by later textual commentators as did dream interpretation in some Western cultures.

The association between divination and commentary is most obvious with the *Classic of Change*. The earliest strata of this collection are primarily concerned with pointing out the degree of fortune or misfortune attached to the sixty-four hexagrams, combinations of six divided or undivided horizontal lines, that are constituted through the

Period: Apocrypha, Pseudepigrapha, Qumran Sectarian Writings, Philo, Josephus, ed. Michael E. Stone (Assen/Maastricht: Van Gorcum; Philadelphia: Fortress Press, 1984), p. 506.

[17] John Wansbrough, *Quranic Studies: Sources and Methods of Scriptural Interpretation* (Oxford: Oxford University Press, 1977), p. 246.

[18] Al-Ghazālī, *The Jewels of the Qur'ān*, a translation, with an introduction and annotation, of al-Ghazālī's *Kitāb Jawāhir al-Qur'ān* by Muhammad Abul Quasem (Kuala Lumpur: University of Malaysia Press, 1977), p. 52.

[19] Sigmund Freud, *On Dreams*, trans. James Strachey (New York: W. W. Norton, 1980), pp. 24–25 and 55–56. Freud remarks: "If what makes their way into the content of dreams are impressions and material which are indifferent and trivial rather than justifiably stirring and interesting, that is only the effect of the process of displacement" (p. 56).

[20] Roberto K. Ong, "Image and Meaning: The Hermeneutics of Traditional Chinese Dream Interpretation," in *Psycho-Sinology: The Universe of Dreams in Chinese Culture*, ed. Carolyn T. Brown (Lanham, Md.: University Press of America, 1988), p. 48.

practice of divination. Only such later strata as the "Great Commentary" (Ta-chuan), one of the "Ten Wings" attributed to Confucius, interpret the meaning of the text as a whole, as opposed to the particular oracular signs, the hexagrams. Some of what may be called the "intermediate strata" of the collection, such as the "Hsiang-chuan" (Commentary on the Images), discuss the characteristics or significance of particular trigrams and hexagrams. They thus constitute a sort of transitional stage between the divinatory reading of signs in terms of good or ill fortune and later modes of moral or cosmological commentary on the words of a classical text.

The links between divination and commentary may not be so strong with the other Confucian classics as with the *Change*. But one historian, David Keightley, has traced the style or procedure of the *Kung-yang* and *Ku-liang* commentaries on the *Spring and Autumn Annals*—that of "nonexploratory interrogation," in which "questions are only asked when the answer is known in advance"—to the oracle-bone divination practiced under the Shang dynasty.[21] Thus, Shang diviners' approaches to interpreting the oracle-bone cracks produced through pyromancy anticipated in at least one respect those used by later exegetes in explaining the historical events recorded in classical texts. The association between these two early forms of hermeneutics is made even closer by the fact that many such events recorded in the *Annals*, such as eclipses, fires, and floods, are construed as omens or portents. In so interpreting these events, or signs, obstensibly for the edification of the ruling powers, the commentator is thus playing the political or social role of the ancient diviners as well as adopting their style and using their techniques. Some of the earliest recognized commentators on such classical texts as the *Annals* may well have been linked occupationally and socially as well as intellectually with diviners.

That exegesis of a classical text comes easily for diviners may be illustrated by a contemporary example from Mayan culture. In translating and interpreting the great epic of that culture, the *Popol Vuh*, Dennis Tedlock relied heavily on the help of Mayan diviners, or "daykeepers," remarking that "diviners are, by profession, interpreters of difficult texts. . . . It should therefore come as no surprise that a diviner might be willing to take on the task of reading the Popol Vuh, whose text presents its own intriguing difficulties of interpretation."[22]

[21] David N. Keightley, "Late Shang Divination: The Magico-Religious Legacy," in *Explorations in Early Chinese Cosmology*, ed. Henry Rosemont, Jr. (Chico, Calif.: Scholars Press, 1984), p. 23.
[22] Dennis Tedlock, "Preface" to *Popol Vuh: The Definitive Edition of the Mayan Book of*

The origins of commentaries on some of the Confucian classics may be traced to oral modes of discourse and transmission as well as to the practice of various forms of divination in early Chinese culture. A venerable tradition traces the sources of the three primary commentaries (*san-chuan*) on the *Spring and Autumn Annals*, particularly the *Tso Commentary*, to the secret teachings of Confucius himself, who conveyed the meaning of the classic orally to a few select disciples. Confucius did this, according to various accounts, in order to avoid the wrath of wicked rulers whose deeds were exposed in the commentaries or, alternatively, to ensure that his teachings concerning the *Annals* would survive the Ch'in burning of the books which he was able to foresee.[23] Although the matter of Confucius' prescience may be open to debate, some of these commentaries, particularly the catechismal form of the *Kung-yang Commentary*, do bear marks of oral composition and transmission.

Traditional and modern scholars alike have developed the theory of the oral origins and transmission of Confucian commentary most fully with respect to the primary commentaries on the *Spring and Autumn Annals*. But several of these scholars also maintain that explanations of the Confucian classics in general were transmitted orally through much of the Former Han era, owing in part to the scarcity and high cost of books in that time as well as to the domination of classical studies by acknowledged masters who transmitted their teachings primarily by word of mouth.[24] Only in the Latter Han did most commentary on classical texts take on written form.

Nevertheless, forms of exegetical writing may be traced even in the literature of the classical age, particularly in works later designated as canonical. Until canonical books are formally fixed or closed, it is a common practice to incorporate commentary into the text that it explains. As noted above, chapters in some classical philosophical works, such as the *Han Fei-tzu*, the *Mo-tzu*, and the *Kuan-tzu*, are even formally divided into separate sections designated as "classic" and

---

the Dawn of Life and the Glories of Gods and Kings, trans. Tedlock (New York: Simon and Schuster, 1985), p. 15.

[23] The former interpretation of Confucius' motives for transmitting orally his teachings concerning the *Annals* may be traced to the *Han History* "Treatise on Bibliography." See *Han-shu, I-wen-chih chu-shih hui-pien* (*Han History* "Treatise on Bibliography" with Collected Annotations), comp. Chen Kuo-ch'ing (Beijing: Chung-hua shu-chü, 1983), p. 74. The latter theory, which maintains that Confucius foresaw the burning of the books, may be found in *Ch'un-ch'iu Kung-yang chuan chu-shu* (The *Kung-yang Commentary* on the *Spring and Autumn Annals* with Subcommentaries), comp. Juan Yüan, SPPY ed., p. 1b of "Hsü" (Preface).

[24] P'i Hsi-jui, *Ching-hsüeh li-shih* (History of Classical Studies) (Taipei: I-wen yin-shu-kuan, 1966 reprint), p. 113; Honda Shigeyuki, *Chung-kuo ching-hsüeh shih* (History of Chinese Classical Studies) (Taipei: Ku-t'ing shu-wu, 1975 reprint), p. 166.

"explanation" or "commentary." The Taoist classics, too, the *Lao-tzu* and *Chuang-tzu*, contain numerous passages and even whole chapters that are primarily exegetical in character. The famous sinologist Naitō Torajirō has proposed, in the words of Burton Watson, that "our present *Lao-tzu* is . . . a somewhat confused combination of a set of ancient philosophical admonitions and a later exegesis by someone called Lao Tzu."[25] As for the *Chuang-tzu*, there are indications that commentary by Kuo Hsiang (d. 312) and subcommentary by Ch'eng Hsüan-ying (fl. 663) crept into the text even in post-T'ang times.[26] With respect to one of the Confucian classics, the *Change*, debate and confusion over which of the so-called Ten Wings are part of the classic and which should be appended as "commentary" continued through much of Chinese history.[27] Even though the text of the *Change* was more effectively fixed or closed than that of the *Chuang-tzu*, thus forestalling new interpolation, there was still some room for maneuver on the question of which portions of the received text were commentary.

Once the books in a canon *are* closed, after they have acquired a sort of supernal aura by virtue of formal canonization and a sense of historical distance separating classical source from exegetical excursion, then commentarial interpolations and exegetical appendices begin to appear as violations of the text. The "text" is no longer conceived of as an ongoing enterprise, as an open anthology of the teachings of a school or tradition, but as a complete embodiment of the wisdom of the ages (or of the sages). Nevertheless, the lines between classic and commentary, or between scripture and gloss, within a canonical text have been blurred or shifted in some traditions even after formal canonization. Chu Hsi himself rearranged the text of one of the canonical Four Books, the *Great Learning*, into one chapter of "classic" and ten chapters of "commentary," and he even made an interpolation to fill what he regarded as a lacuna in the text.[28] Later scholars, however, condemned Chu Hsi for taking such liberties with this classical text.[29]

[25] Burton Watson, *Ssu-ma Ch'ien: Grand Historian of China* (New York: Columbia University Press, 1958), p. 121.

[26] Christopher C. Rand, "Chuang Tzu: Text and Substance," *Journal of Chinese Religions*, no. 11 (Fall 1983): 14.

[27] P'i, *Ching-hsüeh t'ung-lun* 1.27; Ch'ien Hsüan-t'ung, "Ch'ung-lun ching chin-ku-wen hsüeh wen-t'i" (Another Discussion of the Question of New and Old Text Studies of the Classics), in *Ku-shih pien* 5:64–65.

[28] For Chu Hsi's own justification for this interpolation, see pp. 5–6 of his commentary on the *Ta-hsüeh* (Great Learning) in Chu Hsi, *Ssu-shu chi-chu* (The Four Books with Collected Commentaries) (Taipei: Hsüeh-hai ch'u-pan she, 1974 reprint).

[29] See, for example, Ch'ien Te-hung's account of Wang Yang-ming's criticism of Chu Hsi on this subject in Wang's *Ta-hsüeh ku-pen p'ang-shih* (Explanatory Notes on the Old

Even in medieval biblical studies, the line between scripture and gloss sometimes wavered. A noted exegete, Stephen Langton (d. 1228), for example, once remarked that since a certain gloss was exceptionally difficult, he would therefore treat it as part of the text: "Each clause of this gloss is then copied out, underlined, and expounded as though it were a text of Scripture."[30] In some cases, whole packets of extraneous material, such as lives of Alexander, not just exegetical writings, found their way into medieval manuscript Bibles. According to Elizabeth Eisenstein, such corruption or confusion of the Scripture was in part a consequence of the limitations of scribal culture which were overcome after the invention of printing made standardization possible.[31]

In Han China, though, the intermingling of canon and commentary in a single text was less common, for early written commentaries on the newly canonized Confucian classics ordinarily circulated separately from the classics they explained. Although opinions differ on when commentaries began to be commonly interspersed with classical Confucian texts in the form of a running gloss, most trace the origins of this form to the Latter Han at the earliest.[32] Even after this became a common practice, however, the use of special commentarial terminologies, typographical distinctions (after the invention of printing), and the emphasis on lexical problems in much pre-Sung commentary tended to keep commentary distinct from the classical texts.

This distinction was supported by commentators' insistence that there were certain generic differences between classics and commentaries. According to one relatively early definition, commentaries were simply less lengthy or weighty than classics.[33] By this criterion, the relatively brief *Analects* of Confucius, for example, was sometimes characterized as a commentary.[34] Another way of distinguishing the

Version of the *Great Learning*), in *Ching-i k'ao* 159.2b (vol. 5). See also Ch'ai Shao-ping, quoted in *Ching-i k'ao* 297.16a (vol. 8).

[30] Beryl Smalley, *The Study of the Bible in the Middle Ages*, 3rd ed., rev. (Oxford: Basil Blackwell, 1983), p. 218.

[31] Elizabeth L. Eisenstein, *The Printing Press as an Agent of Change: Communications and Cultural Transformations in Early-Modern Europe*, 2 vols. in 1 (Cambridge: Cambridge University Press, 1980), p. 339.

[32] Yü Ta-ch'eng, "Ching-shu ti pan-pen" (Editions of the Classics), in Wang et al., *Ching-hsüeh yen-chiu lun-chi*, p. 294; Chiang Po-ch'ien, *Shih-san ching*, pp. 46–47; Shen Kai, *I hsiao-chuan* (A Small Commentary on the *Change*), in *T'u-shu chi-ch'eng* 55:904.

[33] Chou Yü-t'ung, "Ch'ün-ching kai-lun" (A General Discussion of All the Classics), in *Chou Yü-t'ung ching-hsüeh shih lun-chu hsüan-chi* (Selected Treatises by Chou Yü-t'ung on the History of Classical Studies), comp. Chu Wei-cheng (Shanghai: Jen-min ch'u-pan she, 1983), pp. 273–274.

[34] Ibid.

two, first proposed by the Han-era philosopher Wang Ch'ung (27–97?), was that whereas the classics were composed by the "sages" (*sheng-jen*), commentaries were written by mere "worthies" (*hsien-che*).[35] This hierarchical distinction between classic and commentary according to their respective sources is reminiscent of the division in the Hindu tradition between "revelation" and "recollection," or "Sruti (scriptural teaching actually revealed by God to man)" and "Smriti (teaching of divine incarnations, saints or prophets, who further explain and elaborate the God-given truths of the scriptures.)"[36]

. . . . .

If commentaries thus emanate from relatively inferior beings, worthies as opposed to sages, or saints as opposed to God, then why study them at all? Why not go straight to the supernal source? Why waste time poring over subordinate forms of discourse? A number of later worthies in the Chinese Confucian tradition did advocate a direct approach to the classics without the mediation of commentaries. Ouyang Hsiu, for example, remarked that the classics were, for the most part, simple and clear enough to be read and understood without the aid of a gloss. In many cases, in fact, the gloss actually obscured the meaning of the classical text.[37] Another scholar of the Sung era, Chao P'eng-fei, argued a similar point in regard to the *Spring and Autumn Annals*, querying how Confucius could have been deliberately obscure in writing about such a vital matter as the kingly Way: "The Sage abides in the kingly Way in order to manifest it to ten thousand generations. So how could he have deliberately made his meaning incomprehensible, thus deceiving later generations?" Could he have foreseen that commentaries would later be composed to elucidate his meaning?[38] The Ch'ing scholar K'ung Kuang-sen (1752–1786) advanced a similar argument with respect to two other Confucian classics, the *Change* and the *Songs*: "How could King Wen, in systematizing the *Change* have known that there would later be one who would

[35] Wang Ch'ung, quoted in *Ching-i k'ao* 295.4a (vol. 8).

[36] Swami Prabhavananda and Christopher Isherwood, "Gita and Mahabharata," in *The Song of God: Bhagavad Gita*, trans. Prabhavananda and Isherwood (New York: New American Library, Mentor Religious Classics, 1951), pp. 27–28.

[37] Ts'ai Shih-ming, *Ou-yang Hsiu ti sheng-p'ing yü hsüeh-shu* (Ou-yang Hsiu's Life and Scholarship) (Taipei: Wen-shih-che ch'u-pan she, 1980), pp. 69 and 71.

[38] Chao P'eng-fei, "Tzu-hsü" (Author's Preface) to *Ch'un-ch'iu ching ch'üan* (The *Spring and Autumn Classic* Entrapped), in *Ching-i k'ao* 191.2b (vol. 6). Also quoted in Sung Ting-tsung, *Ch'un-ch'iu Sung-hsüeh fa-wei* (A Disclosure of the Subtleties of Sung Studies on the *Spring and Autumn Annals*) (Taipei: Wen-shih-che ch'u-pan she, 1986), p. 14.

compose for it the 'Ten Wings'? And how could the Duke of Chou in arranging the *Songs* have known that there would later be one who would compose for it the minor prefaces? Must one await a commentary for [the meaning of the classic] to become clear?"[39]

The more common position among commentators in most premodern traditions, however, was that there were obscurities in the classics which were in need of elucidation. Hence, commentaries were necessary, and not necessarily a necessary evil. Indeed, they were often conceived of as means of bringing a scriptural text to life, as has been said of Shankara's commentary on the *Brāhma Sūtra*.[40] A famous *hadīth* attributed to Sa'id ben Jubayr remarks that "someone who recites the Qur'ān and does not then comment on it is like a blind person or a bedouin."[41] A modern Catholic scholar, Roger Ledéaut, chimes in with an aural metaphor, comparing the Bible to a musical score that must be sounded by every new reading.[42] We may complete the round with an agricultural metaphor by Shmuel Safrai, who remarks: "The words of the Tora do not bear fruit by themselves; they must be tended and cultivated in order to bring out their hidden treasures." They are like a *kav* of wheat that the wise servant of the king who gave it to him worked into a loaf of bread.[43]

Indeed, the raw or skeletal state of classical or scriptural texts in some traditions made commentary a virtual necessity. This is especially true of Indian sūtra literature. The text of the *Brāhma Sūtra*, one of the three main canonical works recognized by Vedānta, "would make no sense at all to those who attempt to read it independently" without a commentary.[44] Some books, as Jorge Luis Borges has remarked of a second-century Judaic work, the *Sefer Yesira* (The Book of Creation), were simply "not written for the purpose of being understood; they were made to be interpreted."[45] This may be true

[39] K'ung Kuang-sen, "Ch'un-ch'iu Kung-yang ching chuan t'ung-i hsü" (Introduction to the *Comprehensive Meaning of the Spring and Autumn Classic with the Kung-yang Commentary*), in *Huang-Ch'ing ching-chieh* 691.8191 (vol. 11).

[40] John G. Arapura, *Gnosis and the Question of Thought in Vedānta: Dialogue with the Foundations* (Dordrecht: Martinus Nijhoff, 1986), p. 136.

[41] Quoted in al-Tabarī, *The Commentary on the Qur'ān* by Abū Ja'far Muhammad B. Jarīr al-Tabarī, being an abridged translation of *Jāmi' al-bayān 'an ta'wīl ay al-Qur'ān*, with an introduction and notes by J. Cooper (Oxford: Oxford University Press, 1987), vol. 1, p. 36.

[42] Roger Ledéaut, "The Greek Bible," in *Renewing the Judeo-Christian Wellsprings*, ed. Val Ambrose McInnes, O.P. (New York: Crossroad, 1987), p. 63.

[43] Shmuel Safrai, "Oral Tora," in *The Literature of the Sages, First Part: Oral Tora, Halakha, Mishna, Tosefta, Talmud, External Tractates*, ed. Safrai (Assen/Maastricht: Van Gorcum; Philadelphia: Fortress Press, 1987), p. 104.

[44] Arapura, *Gnosis*, p. 135.

[45] Borges, quoted in José Faur, *Golden Doves with Silver Dots: Semiotics and Textuality in Rabbinic Tradition* (Bloomington: Indiana University Press, 1986), p. xxvii.

even of the Mishnah, which "was written in anticipation that it would have to be supplemented by a commentary."[46]

In the Chinese Confucian tradition, a number of scholars effectively made such a point with respect to the laconic, enigmatic *Spring and Autumn Annals*. Many of them regarded the *Tso Commentary*, one of the three primary commentaries on the *Annals*, as particularly necessary for an understanding of the classic. For the *Tso* filled-in the historical background for the events to which the classic itself only enigmatically alludes. The two, classic and commentary, must thus be read together, as Chia Hsüan-weng (b. 1213) remarked: "The classic sets forth the broad outline, and the commentary records the details. The classic is the beginning, and the commentary expounds the end."[47] Thus, Huan T'an (43 B.C–A.D. 28) maintained that "even a sage who pondered for ten years behind locked doors could not understand the Classic without the [*Tso*] Commentary."[48] A later scholar, Ch'en Hung-hsü (1597–1665), asserted that Confucius in fact composed the *Annals* with the idea that it would have to be supplemented by a more historically oriented work in order to be fully understood: "Thus Confucius' composition of the *Spring and Autumn Annals* [included only] the broad outline. He did not mean to compose a history. He awaited a history for fulfillment [of this project]."[49] The Ming-era philosopher Chan Jo-shui (1466–1560) even constructed a sort of metaphysical chain to establish the necessity of commentaries, particularly the *Tso*, for explaining the *Annals*:

> The *Spring and Autumn Annals* is the mind of the Sage. The mind of the Sage is preserved in meaning. The meaning of the Sage's mind is preserved in affairs. The affairs of the *Spring and Autumn Annals* are preserved in the commentaries. [Through] the classic we know the general, and through the commentaries the particular.[50]

[46] Coward, *Sacred Word*, p. 17.

[47] Chia Hsüan-weng, quoted in *Ching-i k'ao* 169.5b (vol. 5).

[48] Huan T'an, trans. in Timoteus Pokora, *Hsin-lun (New Treatise) and Other Writings by Huan T'an (43 B.C.-28 A.D.)* (Ann Arbor: University of Michigan, Center for Chinese Studies, 1975), p. 94 (translation slightly modified).

[49] Ch'en Hung-hsü, "Pa" (Postscript) to Su Ch'e, *Ch'un-ch'iu chi-chieh* (Collected Explications of the *Spring and Autumn Annals*), in *Ching-i k'ao* 182.7a (vol. 5). Su Ch'e himself expressed a similar idea in his *Ch'un-ch'iu chi-chieh* 1.4b, in *Ching-yüan* (Garden of the Classics), comp. Ch'ien I-chi (Taipei: Ta-t'ung shu-chü, 1970 reprint), 6:2550. According to rabbinic exegetes in the Jewish tradition, God adopted a similar approach in revealing the Law to Moses: "The lawgiver foresaw the interpretation of his statutes [and] deliberately confined himself to a minimum, relying on the rest being inferable by a proper exegesis." David Daube, "Rabbinic Methods of Interpretation and Hellenistic Rhetoric," in *Hebrew Union College Annual* 22 (1949), p. 248.

[50] Chan Jo-shui, "Tzu-hsü" (Author's Preface) to *Ch'un-ch'iu cheng-chuan* (A Correct Commentary on the *Spring and Autumn Annals*), in *Ching-i k'ao* 200.8a (vol. 6).

Although later commentators most frequently cited the *Tso* as the necessary complement to the classic, many argued that all three of the primary commentaries, or *san-chuan*, had their strong points. In fact, they complemented one another just as they complemented the classic. Cheng Hsüan was perhaps the first to distinguish the Three Commentaries in this way. "The Three Commentaries," he remarked, "all have their strong and weak points with respect to the classic. The *Tso Commentary* excels in ritual, the *Kung-yang* excels in omens, and the *Ku-liang* excels in [explaining] the classic."[51] Commenting on this and similar statements, the Sung-era encyclopedist Cheng Ch'iao (1104–1162) remarked that each of the primary commentaries revealed some vital aspect of the classic that might not otherwise be detected: "Having the *Kung-yang* and *Ku-liang* commentaries, we know the strictness of [the Sage's] editing. Having [the commentary of] Mr. Tso, we know the details of the whole story. The scholar cannot but combine [the two]."[52] Later commentarial statements on the merits of each of the *san-chuan* and their relations to the classic tended toward more symmetrical, stylized, and even paradoxical modes of expression. Thus, Ch'en Chen-sun (fl. 1211–1249) commented that "Mr. Tso preserves what the classic does not write about in order to give substance to what it does write about. Kung-yang and Ku-liang take what the classic does write about to infer what it does not write about."[53] And Yeh Meng-te (1077–1148) remarked: "Mr. Tso comments on affairs but does not comment on meaning. . . . Kung-yang and Ku-liang comment on meaning but do not comment on affairs."[54]

In view of the complementarity widely believed to exist, both between the *Annals* and its three primary commentaries and among the Three Commentaries themselves, it is not surprising that a number of T'ang and Sung commentators attempted to combine them all in a single text. Only then could the full import of the Sage's meaning, which could be seen only fragmentarily in each of the individual texts, be fully revealed. Thus, just as some Latter Han commentators set out to restore or reconstruct the lost unity and coherence of the

---

[51] Cheng Hsüan, *Liu-i lun* (Discussions of the Six Arts), quoted in Wang Ying-lin, *Weng-chu K'un-hsüeh chi-wen* (A Record of What I Have Learned in Difficult Studies, with Weng's Commentary), SPPY ed., 6.26a (vol. 3).

[52] Cheng Ch'iao, "San-chuan ko yu te shih" (The Three Commentaries Each Have Their Strong and Weak Points), from *Ch'un-ch'iu chuan* (Commentary on the *Spring and Autumn Annals*), in *T'u-shu chi-ch'eng* 56:1847.

[53] Ch'en Chen-sun, quoted in *Ching-i k'ao* 187.4a (vol. 6).

[54] Yeh Meng-te, "Shih-lin Ch'un-ch'iu chuan hsü" (Preface to Shih-lin's Commentary on the *Spring and Autumn Annals*), quoted in Sung, *Ch'un-ch'iu Sung-hsüeh*, p. 29.

Six Classics, so some T'ang and Sung commentators (or subcommentators) such as Chien Yüeh and Lu Ch'un (d. 805) did the same with the *san-chuan*.[55] As Tan Chu (725–770) remarked, although the Three Commentaries flow separately, their source is the same.[56]

The three primary commentaries on the *Annals* were, however, almost as diverse in their origins as the Six Classics. The *Tso Commentary*, in particular, was apparently not even composed originally as a commentary but, rather, as a sort of historical chronicle. Opinions may differ on whether or not the Han bibliographer Liu Hsin (d. 23) fabricated this work by selecting and rearranging material drawn from the *Kuo-yü* (Conversations of the States), a late-Chou historical chronicle. But it is clear that the themes of the *Tso*, especially the focus on "violent conflict—political, military, and personal,"[57] are unsuited to the style of a moralizing commentary. Too, the considerable discrepancies between the text of the *Annals* and the *Tso* were a source of perplexity to those who tried to coordinate the two.[58] However, the very effort to present such an odd work as the *Tso* as a commentary is an indication of the wide range as well as great prestige of the genre. In almost any canonical tradition, it seems, a work, no matter how already distinguished, acquires further note through its being designated as a commentary on the sacred classics.

. . . . .

Most early commentaries in the Confucian tradition, however, were unlike the *san-chuan*, particularly the *Tso*, in form and style. Some of them, in fact, seem to be limited principally to lexical problems, especially to glossing obscure words and phrases in the classics. The primary justification for the composition of such works was to resolve difficult or doubtful points in the classics, to make fully manifest the meanings of the ancient sages. The clarification of such obscurities was necessary not so much because the sages themselves were unclear or incomplete in their teachings, but because of such historical developments as lexical change, the loss or fragmentation of texts, alterations in the forms of the written characters, and changes in culture and institutions.

The recognition of such developments is probably the most univer-

[55] Chiang, *Shih-san ching*, p. 19; Honda, *Chung-kuo ching-hsüeh shih*, p. 235.

[56] Tan Chu, "Tzu-shu" (Author's Account), in *Ch'un-ch'iu li-t'ung* (The *Spring and Autumn Annals* Systematically United), in *Ching-i k'ao* 176.4a (vol. 5).

[57] David Johnson, "Epic and History in Early China: The Matter of Wu Tzu-hsü," *Journal of Asian Studies* 40, no. 2 (February 1981): 269.

[58] Tu Yü's classic statement on this subject appears in *Ching-i k'ao* 169.2a (vol. 5).

sal motive for the composition of conventional commentaries; at least it is the one most widely recognized. Such commentaries appear in the early stages of nearly all major canonical traditions, particularly in the wake of historical, cultural, and linguistic change that increases the distance from the classical past. But even the simplest and most straightforward type of commentary is seldom concerned solely with elucidating the plain meaning of the text.[59] Although no larger programmatic intent may be evident in such works, even the most unimaginative glossator holds assumptions about the character of the text he is glossing—assumptions that are frequently in accord with those of later, more philosophical commentators. The glossator may even devise strategies designed to support some of these assumptions, although they may seem rudimentary when compared with those used by more sophisticated exegetes.

Even the genre of the gloss is not as simple and unproblematic as is often supposed. There exist various types and subgenres that in some canonical traditions were carefully distinguished from one another.[60] In the Confucian tradition, as well as in others, subcommentaries, intended initially to elucidate the meanings of primary commentaries, made their appearance under Buddhist influence as early as the Six Dynasties era.[61] As the number of commentaries on the classics multiplied, the subgenre of "collected commentaries" (*chi-chu*) came into vogue, some of which assumed almost encyclopedic proportions.[62] Some of the most famous of these later commentaries, such as the seventh-century *Wu-ching cheng-i* (The Correct Meanings

[59] Some scholars have argued otherwise. See, for example, Jacob Neusner, *Judaism, The Classical Statement: The Evidence of the Bavli* (Chicago: University of Chicago Press, 1986), pp. 21–22 and 207.

[60] See, for example, Nikolaus M. Häring, "Commentary and Hermeneutics," in *Renaissance and Renewal in the Twelfth Century*, eds. Robert L. Benson and Giles Constable (Cambridge: Harvard University Press, 1982), pp. 178–179; Tai Chün-jen, "Ching-shu ti yen-ch'eng" (The Elaboration of Commentaries on the Classics), in Wang et al., *Ching-hsüeh yen-chiu lun-chi*, pp. 108–109; Ch'eng Fa-jen, "Han-tai ching-hsüeh chih fu-hsing" (The Renaissance of Classical Studies in the Han Era), in Wang et al., *Ching-hsüeh yen-chiu lun-chi*, p. 170; and Karl H. Potter, *Encyclopedia of Indian Philosophies: Advaita Vedanta up to Śamkara and His Pupils* (Princeton: Princeton University Press, 1981), pp. 4–5.

[61] Yü, "Ching-shu ti pan-pen," p. 293. P'i Hsi-jui, however, contends that Confucius himself wrote the first subcommentaries, really commentaries on his own commentaries on the *Change*. See P'i, *Ching-hsüeh t'ung-lun* 1.13.

[62] Perhaps the most famous example of this genre is Chu Hsi's *Ssu-shu chi-chu* (The Four Books with Collected Commentaries), a work that contains a total of 731 quotations from 32 different scholars. See Dennis A. Levanthal, "Treading the Path from Yang Shih to Chu Hsi: A Question of Transmission in Sung Neo-Confucianism," in *The Bulletin of Sung and Yuan Studies*, no. 14 (1978), p. 52.

of the Five Classics), were composed not by individual scholars but by imperially appointed commissions. Such commissions, as was the case with the *Wu-ching cheng-i*, sometimes received a charge to unify the world of Confucian classical scholarship, and even the intellectual world in general.[63]

Thus, later commentaries in the Confucian tradition came to serve as repositories of learning—as encyclopedias, not simply as glosses on classical texts. The words and phrases of a classical text, for many later commentators, functioned as pegs on which all their knowledge could be displayed. For if the classics were really comprehensive and inexhaustible, as many of these commentators claimed, then what better place could be found to collect all learning than in commentaries on these same classics? A Han-era commentator, Ch'in Chin-chün, is reported to have used more than a hundred thousand words to explain the title of the "Canon of Yao" (Yao-tien) chapter of the *Documents Classic* and thirty thousand words to gloss the meaning of the first phrase in that chapter.[64] The work of a Ming-era commentator, Ch'iu Chün (1420–1495), on the *Great Learning*, the briefest of the Confucian classics, has, according to William Theodore de Bary, "been aptly characterized as 'a comprehensive handbook of public administration, dealing with every aspect of governmental function, including military defense, public finance, personnel management, transportation, water control, etc.' "[65] Ch'iu, moreover, presented his work as a supplement to the encyclopedic *Extended Meaning of the Great Learning* (Ta-hsüeh yen-i) by Chen Te-hsiu (1178–1235), who in writing this commentary "drew on all the resources of his learning and personal experience."[66] Finally, a Ming commentator on the *Analects*, Ch'en Shih-yüan, arranged his voluminous commentary, the *Classified Investigations on the Analects* (Lun-yü lei-k'ao), according to the format of the encyclopedias of the time, beginning with the celestial realm ("astronomical phenomena," "calendrical units"), then pro-

[63] Brief accounts of the background and composition of the *Wu-ching cheng-i* appear in Howard J. Wechsler, *Offerings of Jade and Silk: Ritual and Symbol in the Legitimation of the T'ang Dynasty* (New Haven: Yale University Press, 1985), p. 47; Honda, *Chung-kuo ching-hsüeh shih*, pp. 229–230; and David McMullen, *State and Scholars in T'ang China* (Cambridge: Cambridge University Press, 1988), p. 73. Wechsler notes that "the *Wu-ching cheng-i* provided the basis for classical education throughout the T'ang" (p. 47).

[64] Huan, *Hsin-lun*, p. 89.

[65] Wm. Theodore de Bary, *Neo-Confucian Orthodoxy and the Learning of the Mind-and-Heart* (New York: Columbia University Press, 1981), pp. 180–181. The source of the internal quotation is Chi-hua Wu and Ray Huang, "Ch'iu Chün," in *Dictionary of Ming Biography*, eds. L. Carrington Goodrich and Chaoying Fang (New York: Columbia University Press, 1976), vol. 1, p. 250.

[66] Ibid., p. 91.

ceeding to the terrestrial plane ("territorial states," "mensural rules and schemas") and so forth. Ch'en keyed all of these subjects, though sometimes only tenuously, with terms and short phrases from the *Analects*, to which he appended extensive comments by earlier authorities on these topics as well as his own essays.[67]

The tendency for commentaries to develop into encyclopedic works and for commentators to pose as polyhistors is not peculiar to the Chinese Confucian tradition. In fact, it was probably less pronounced there than in the classical and medieval West. Among Alexandrian scholars, in particular, commentaries on Homer provided a format for displays of immense learning. One such scholar, Demetrius, wrote thirty books of "commentary" on a mere sixty lines in the *Iliad*, mostly on topography and antiquities.[68] The Byzantine erudite Eustathius, bishop of Thessalonica, also surrounded the Homeric poems with "oceans of information," including "grammatical instruction, etymological discourses, cross-references to Greek and Roman literature, [and] historical evidence."[69] The thirteenth-century commentary by Bernard Silvester on the *Aeneid* likewise "covered a good deal of ground, Physics, Ethics, Education, etc." and was in fact modeled on the encyclopedias of late antiquity.[70] One of the most famous of these encyclopedias was that by Cassiodorus, who incorporated into his commentary on the Psalms "among other things, refutations of all the heresies which have ever existed and rudiments of all the sciences the world has ever seen. It is a marvel of erudition."[71] A later Christian scholar, Alexander Nequam, appended his encyclopedia of the natural sciences, the *De naturis rerum*, to his commentary on Ecclesiastes. His work, according to Beryl Smalley, "provides just another example of the early medieval tendency to attach all instruction to *sacra pagina*."[72] But even as knowledge grew in later-medieval times,

---

[67] Ch'en Shih-yüan's *Lun-yü lei-k'ao* may be found reprinted in *Ying-yin ssu-k'u ch'üan-shu chen-pen, chiu-chi* (Reprints of Rare Editions from the *Complete Library in Four Treasuries*, series 9) (Taipei: Shang-wu yin-shu-kuan, 1979), vol. 61.

[68] Rudolf Pfeiffer, *History of Classical Scholarship from the Beginnings to the End of the Hellenistic Age* (Oxford: Clarendon Press, 1968), p. 250.

[69] Don Cameron Allen, *Mysteriously Meant: The Rediscovery of Pagan Symbolism and Allegorical Interpretation in the Renaissance* (Baltimore: Johns Hopkins University Press, 1970), p. 88.

[70] J. Reginald O'Donnell, "The Sources and Meaning of Bernard Silvester's Commentary on the *Aeneid*," *Mediaeval Studies* 24 (1962): 248.

[71] Leslie Webber Jones, "Introduction" to Cassiodorus Senator, *An Introduction to Divine and Human Readings*, trans. and annot. Jones (New York: W. W. Norton, 1969), p. 20.

[72] Beryl Smalley, "Essay I," in *Medieval Exegesis of Wisdom Literature: Essays by Beryl Smalley*, ed. Roland E. Murphy (Atlanta: Scholars Press, 1986), p. 9.

"the natural inclination was to force it into the mold of the Gloss [on biblical texts], so that the Gloss, and glosses on the Gloss, swelled to unwieldy proportions."[73]

Encyclopedic commentaries also appeared prominently in the Islamic tradition. In fact, the first great commentator on the Qur'ān, al-Tabarī (838–923), has been characterized as "primarily an encyclopedist, concerned to preserve as much as he could."[74] A later commentary on the Qur'ān, that by Imam Razi, was intended by its author as a compendium of the rational sciences of the day.[75] Such works have spurred complaints by modern Muslims that "Koran commentaries have become encyclopedias in which law, philology, etc. are discussed, but not 'the Koran itself.' "[76]

On a more popular level, oral commentary on the classical Indian epic the *Rāmāyana* frequently incorporates such diverse material as "parables, folk tales, cosmology, archeology, medicine, and so on." Much of this material, moreover, is quite independent of the classical written text.[77]

Commentaries in postclassical cultures served not only as repositories of learning, as encyclopedias, directed both to elite and to popu-

---

[73] Richard H. Rouse and Mary A. Rouse, "*Statim Invenire*: Schools, Preachers, and New Attitudes to the Page," in Benson and Constable, eds., *Renaissance and Renewal*, p. 210.

[74] Ezzeddin Ibrahim, "Foreword" to al-Tabarī, *Commentary on the Qur'ān*, vol. 1, p. xiv. Al-Tabarī's great work comprises 30 volumes and about 5,400 pages. Geo Windengren, "Holy Book and Holy Tradition in Islam," in *Holy Book and Holy Tradition*, eds. F. F. Bruce and E. G. Rupp (Grand Rapids, Mich.: William B. Eerdmans, 1968), p. 224.

[75] I. H. Azad Faruqi, *The Tarjuman al-Qur'ān: A Critical Analysis of Maulana Abu'l-Kalam Azad's Approach to the Understanding of the Qur'ān* (New Delhi: Vikas Publishing, 1982), pp. 51–52.

[76] J.J.G. Jansen, *The Interpretation of the Koran in Modern Egypt* (Leiden: E. J. Brill, 1974), p. 86. The great value attributed to such encyclopedic commentaries in premodern, preprinting cultures is indicated by the fact that they were frequently copied out, despite "the enormous outlay of time and writing material necessary for the production of each fresh copy." N. G. Wilson, *Scholars of Byzantium* (London: Duckworth, 1983), p. 200. Such commentaries were useful not only for the light they threw on classical texts, but because they could also serve as introductions to classical literature, history, and culture. Hence, the commentator "was expected to fill a large amount of space. His audience expected him to turn any suitable word or phrase into the occasion for an extended digression." Anthony Grafton, *Joseph Scaliger: A Study in the History of Classical Scholarship. 1: Textual Criticism and Exegesis* (Oxford: Clarendon Press, 1983), p. 16.

[77] Stuart H. Blackburn, "Epic Transmission and Adaptation: A Folk Rāmāyana in South India," in *The Heroic Process: Form, Function, and Fantasy in Folk Epic*, Proceedings of the International Folk Epic Conference, University College Dublin, September 2–6, 1985, eds. Bo Almqvist et al. (Dublin: Glandale Press, 1987), p. 584.

lar audiences, but also as fields for the cultivation of the sciences or for specialized branches of scholarship. For inasmuch as the classics or scriptures were comprehensive, comprising all significant knowledge and truth, the study of such diverse subjects as astronomy, geography, and phonetics was required in order to elucidate them properly. Without a knowledge of astrology, logic, and even medicine, declared Roland of Cremona, one could not properly comprehend certain passages in the Holy Scriptures.[78] In fact, no branch of learning, asserted the famed twelfth-century exegete Hugh of St. Victor, is superfluous in biblical studies.[79]

Several of the philological and even natural sciences in a number of civilizations even appear to have originated in classical or scriptural exegesis.[80] In the Hindu tradition, six separate disciplines—phonetics, metrics, grammar, etymology, ritual or religious practice, and astronomy—were formally annexed to the study of the Veda and were designated as "members of the Vedas."[81] In the medieval West, such branches of learning as logic, grammar, and even optics, which historians of science frequently treat as autonomous sciences linked to their modern counterparts, were often exegetical in their orientation. The origins of several medieval literary genres as well as some of the sciences may also be traced to classical and scriptural exegesis. Allegorical literature, for example, has been characterized as "the outgrowth of a tradition of interpretation impinging on a tradition of creative literature."[82] As Beryl Smalley has remarked, we can only speculate on the proportion of material, transmitted to us in other forms, which originated in biblical glosses and ought to be counted as exegesis.[83]

In sum, as commentaries developed from simple glosses to incorporate (or at least accommodate) almost all learning, science, and even literature, they increasingly dominated the intellectual world of postclassical, premodern man (at least of the educated elite). Even

[78] Jacques Verger, "L'Éxègese de l'université," in *Le Moyen Age et la Bible*, eds. Pierre Riché and Guy Lobrichon (Paris: Editions Beauchesne, 1984), p. 214.

[79] Jean Châtillon, "La Bible dans les Écoles du xiiᵉ siècle," ibid., p. 179.

[80] See, for example, Chou Yü-t'ung, "Ching-hsüeh shih yü ching-hsüeh chih p'ai-pieh" (The History of Classical Studies and Schools of Classical Studies), in *Chou Yü-t'ung ching-hsüeh shih lun-chu hsüan-chi*, pp. 95 and 97; H.A.R. Gibb, *Mohammedanism: An Historical Survey*, 2nd ed. (New York: Oxford University Press, Galaxy Books, 1962), p. 93; and Eisenstein, *Printing Press*, p. 336.

[81] Jan Gonda, *Vedic Literature (Saṁhitās and Brāhmaṇas)*, vol. 1 of *A History of Indian Literature*, ed. Gonda (Wiesbaden: Otto Harrassowitz, 1975), p. 34.

[82] Robert Lamberton, *Homer the Theologian: Neoplatonist Allegorical Reading and the Growth of the Epic Tradition* (Berkeley: University of California Press, 1986), p. 147.

[83] Smalley, *Study of the Bible*, p. 76.

many famous figures identified by modern historians as philosophers, scientists, or literati often found their chief forms (or formats) of expression in commentaries on classical or scriptural texts. As Hsü Fu-kuan has pointed out, the only book that the renowned Sung Neo-Confucian philosopher Ch'eng I ever wrote was a commentary on a classical text, his *I-chuan* (Commentary on the Change).[84] The most important and memorable works of the greatest Chinese philosopher of postclassical times, Chu Hsi, were also mainly commentaries on classical and earlier Neo-Confucian texts.[85] In fact, the most noted works of the majority of eminent thinkers in Chinese history, from the second century B.C. (the *Ch'un-ch'iu fan-lu* attributed to Tung Chung-shu) to the eighteenth century A.D. (the *Meng-tzu tzu-i shu-cheng* by Tai Chen), are presented as commentaries on canonical texts.

Commentaries, moreover, were the chief medieval forms of expression in more specialized scientific and technical studies, such as medicine and mathematics, as well as in the major classical and scriptural traditions. As Paul Kristeller has remarked with respect to the late-medieval West, "From the time of the specialization of learning in the twelfth century, the commentary form was ... used in all branches of knowledge and it was cultivated without interruption until the sixteenth century and beyond."[86] In fact, more Latin Aristotelian commentaries were composed between 1500 and 1650 than in the preceding one thousand years.[87]

Commentary dominated much of the intellectual life of postclassical, premodern man not only by virtue of its importance as a genre or form, but also through the habits of mind and modes of thought it fostered. For many medievals, glossing became second nature—to the extent that "they glossed whatever literature came within their reach."[88] Thus, a long-suffering correspondent of one of St. Anselm's pupils complained that one of his own letters was returned "so thickly glossed as to be unintelligible."[89]

[84] Hsü Fu-kuan, "A Comparative Study of Chu Hsi and the Ch'eng Brothers," in *Chu Hsi and Neo-Confucianism*, ed. Wing-tsit Chan (Honolulu: University Press of Hawaii, 1986), p. 52. Hsü adds that "he spent his whole life preparing this work" (p. 52).

[85] Ch'ien Mu, "A Historical Perspective on Chu Hsi's Learning," ibid., p. 35.

[86] Paul Oskar Kristeller, "The Scholar and His Public in the Late Middle Ages and the Renaissance," in *Medieval Aspects of Renaissance Learning: Three Essays by Paul Oskar Kristeller*, ed. and trans. Edward P. Mahoney (Durham, N.C.: Duke University Press, 1974), p. 6.

[87] Charles B. Schmitt, *Aristotle and the Renaissance* (Cambridge: Harvard University Press, 1983), pp. 50–52.

[88] Smalley, *Study of the Bible*, p. 74.

[89] Ibid.

Commentarial habits of mind are also reflected in the importance that medievals attached to the disposition and presentation of classical and scriptural material, often in the form of anthologies, abridgments, epitomes, or summae. As Jaroslav Pelikan has observed of Byzantine exegetes, "The selection and the arrangement of patristic testimonies in their theological treatises may be a more reliable index to their thought than are their own ex professo statements."[90] For "it is in the arrangement of the clippings, whatever their sources, that the meaning of the document lies."[91] Jacob Neusner has likewise remarked of Jewish exegetes that "it is through the work of compilation and redaction, not merely episodic exegesis, that formative minds of diverse kinds of Judaism made their points. Exegesis of Scripture registered at the level of redaction, not merely through discrete remarks on this or that."[92] In the Neo-Confucian tradition, a similar location of meaning at the level of redaction appears in the writings of the renowned Korean scholar Yi T'oegye (1501–1570). Yi, noting that the "Western Inscription" by the famous Sung philosopher Chang Tsai was "entirely composed from the sayings of the ancients," argued that the meaning of the work is best apprehended by considering each phrase in its new, as opposed to its original, context.[93]

In view of the significance that medieval commentators attached to the arrangement of authoritative writings, it is not surprising that some of the greatest writers and thinkers in various medieval cultures devoted their energies to composing anthologies or condensations of canonical or semicanonical works. One of Chu Hsi's most famous works is his concise anthology of the writings of earlier Neo-Confucian masters, his *Reflections on Things at Hand* (Chin-ssu lu). Among Chu's twelfth-century contemporaries in Europe, several noted poets also composed concise anthologies of ancient authorities; these poets "considered that they deserved well by producing abbreviated ver-

[90] Jaroslav Pelikan, *The Christian Tradition: A History of the Development of Doctrine*, vol. 2: *The Spirit of Eastern Christendom (600–1700)* (Chicago: University of Chicago Press, 1977), p. 9.

[91] Jaroslav Pelikan, *The Vindication of Tradition: The 1983 Jefferson Lectures in the Humanities* (New Haven: Yale University Press, 1984), p. 74.

[92] Jacob Neusner, *Judaism in the Matrix of Christianity* (Philadelphia: Fortress Press, 1986), pp. 89–90.

[93] Michael C. Kalton, *To Become a Sage: The Ten Diagrams on Sage Learning by Yi T'oegye*, trans., ed., and with commentaries by Kalton (New York: Columbia University Press, 1988), p. 62. Medieval commentators' idea that the meaning or significance of a work may be profoundly altered by the way in which its various parts are juxtaposed has been affirmed by a contemporary scholar, Gabriel Josipovici, in *The Book of God: A Response to the Bible* (New Haven: Yale University Press, 1988), p. 305.

sions of antique authors and they boast[ed] of it."[94] Even the Bible was the object of such condensational proposals—notably by Erasmus, who remarked that it ought to be accomplished by "men of both piety and learning."[95] Such a work would be as authoritative as the biblical canon itself, while surpassing it in literary value.

. . . . .

Commentaries, epitomes, and related forms thus came to exude a canonical aura in several medieval cultures, as noted in the previous chapter with respect to Chu Hsi's collected commentaries on the Four Books and his anthology of Neo-Confucian writings, the *Reflections on Things at Hand*. Some Sung Neo-Confucian commentators apparently saw their own works in such a light. Thus, Hao Ching (1223–1275) complained that Sung commentators on the *Annals* regarded themselves as reincarnations of Mencius.[96] Several Sung and Ming scholars argued that Neo-Confucians, especially Ch'eng I, had even improved on the ideas of Mencius, particularly on the subject of human nature (*hsing*). Both Chu Hsi and Ch'en Ch'un (1159–1223) contended that Mencius' conception of human nature was one-sided or incomplete and was rectified only by Ch'eng I.[97] According to the Ming Neo-Confucian philosopher Lo Ch'in-shun (1465–1547), while Confucius' characterization of "humanity" (*jen*) was limited and that by Mencius unclear, Master Ch'eng "seems to have understood it fully."[98] Small wonder, then, that Ch'eng I's major works, together with those of the other principal Neo-Confucians of the orthodox line of transmission (*Tao-t'ung*)—namely, Chou Tun-i, Chang Tsai, Ch'eng Hao (1032–1085), and Chu Hsi—came to be regarded as a sort of new subcanon within the Confucian tradition. Chu Hsi, the great synthesizer of the

[94] Ernst Robert Curtius, *European Literature and the Latin Middle Ages*, trans. Willard R. Trask (Princeton: Princeton University Press, 1973), p. 493.

[95] Erasmus, "To Paul Volz, 14 Aug. 1518," quoted in E. Harris Harbison, *The Christian Scholar in the Age of Reformation* (Grand Rapids, Mich.: William B. Eerdmans, 1983), p. 101.

[96] Hao Ching, "Tzu-hsü" (Author's Preface) to *Ch'un-ch'iu wai-chuan* (Outer Commentary on the *Spring and Autumn Annals*), in *Ching-i k'ao* 193.7b (vol. 6).

[97] Chu Hsi, *Chu-tzu yü-lei chi-lüeh* (An Abridgment of the Classified Conversations of Master Chu), comp. Chang Po-hsing (Taipei: Shang-wu yin-shu-kuan, 1973 reprint), 1.26 and 1.28–29; Ch'en Ch'un, *Pei-ch'i tzu-i* (The Meanings of [Confucian Philosophical] Terms [According to Ch'en] Pei-ch'i) (Beijing: Chung-hua shu-chü, 1983 reprint), pp. 7–8.

[98] Lo Ch'in-shun, *K'un-chih chi*, pt. 1, in *Knowledge Painfully Acquired: The K'un-chih chi by Lo Ch'in-shun*, trans., ed., and intro. Irene Bloom (New York: Columbia University Press, 1987), pp. 76–77.

four earlier Neo-Confucian masters, was exalted in the same terms reserved by Mencius to describe Confucius himself, as a "complete concert" (*chi ta-ch'eng*) who harmonized the works of his illustrious predecessors.[99] As Confucius, the first great commentator, was supposed to have set in order the original five Confucian classics, so Chu Hsi, the great commentator once removed, was believed to have done the same with the new Neo-Confucian classics, as well as with the Four Books.

The virtual canonization, or at least considerable apotheosis, of commentaries and commentators is not a peculiarly Chinese phenomenon. In Islam, "the (orthodox) commentaries spring from the oral tradition which accompanied the revelation itself, or else they spring through inspiration from the same supernatural source."[100] In medieval Hinduism a similar development occurred. *Smrti*, reflection by later sages on Vedic revelation, or *shruti*, began to assume Vedic infallibility by virtue of the theory that it was based on lost parts of the Veda.[101] Thus, later commentators established a parity between *shruti* and *smrti*, revelation and recollection.[102] Vedantists, for example, raised the *Brāhma Sūtra*, originally a commentary on some of the metaphysical doctrines in the Upanishads, to the point where it was "almost equal in authority to the *Upanisads*."[103] Even Shankara's commentary on this sūtra has been characterized as "the single most influential philosophical text in India today. . . . Countless Indian adepts commit portions of this text to heart."[104] Shankara himself, moreover, is one of the great cultural heroes of India, revered "to a remarkably great degree by Indians of all walks of life."[105]

Commentators and their works were also apotheosized in medieval Christendom. The writings of such late-ancient and early-medieval biblical exegetes as Origen, St. Gregory the Great, and St. Bernard of Clairvaux were frequently depicted as being just as inspired as those

[99] Ch'en Ch'un, "Lectures at Yen-ling," trans. in Wing-tsit Chan, *Neo-Confucian Terms Explained (The "Pei-hsi tzu-i") by Ch'en Ch'un, 1159–1223* (New York: Columbia University Press, 1986), p. 181.

[100] Frithjof Schuon, *Understanding Islam*, trans. D. M. Matheson (London: George Allen and Unwin, 1963), p. 46.

[101] J. Duncan M. Derrett, *Dharmaśāstra and Juridical Literature*, vol. 4, pt. 2, of *A History of Indian Literature*, ed. Gonda (Wiesbaden: Otto Harrassowitz, 1973), p. 18.

[102] Arvind Sharma, *The Hindu Gītā: Ancient and Classical Interpretations of the Bhagavadgītā* (London: Duckworth, 1986), p. 36. Robert N. Minor, in fact, maintains that "the works which are designated *smrti* have functioned as scripture more often in the lives of Indians than have *śruti*." Minor, "Introduction," *Modern Indian Interpreters of the Bhagavadgītā*, ed. Minor (Albany: State University of New York Press, 1986), p. 1.

[103] Hajime Nakamura, *A History of Early Vedānta Philosophy*, trans. Trevor Leggett et al. (Delhi: Motilal Banarsidass, 1983), pt. 1, p. 438.

[104] Potter, *Advaita Vedānta*, p. 119.

[105] Ibid., p. 16.

of the prophets and evangelists whose compositions were included in the biblical canon. Thus, "St Gregory, composing his commentaries, listens to a dove which perches on his shoulder with its bill to his ear,"[106] just as the evangelists wrote from the dictation of angels. Even as late as the twelfth century, the writings of the fathers of the church were regarded as scriptural.[107] In 1295, in fact, Pope Boniface VIII commanded that the four fathers, Sts. Ambrose, Jerome, Augustine, and Gregory the Great, be venerated with the same solemnity as the four apostles.[108] Moreover, just as some of the works of the great Sung Neo-Confucian masters became primary objects of exegesis in late-traditional China, so in European schools of the High Middle Ages such scholastic works as the *Sentences* of Peter Lombard supplanted even Scripture as the principal objects of study and commentary.[109]

Protestant reformers, however, generally drew sharper and clearer distinctions between canon and commentary, scripture and gloss. John Calvin, for example, maintained that while "the apostles were the certain and authentic amanuenses of the Holy Spirit . . . others have no other office than to teach what is revealed and deposited in the holy Scriptures."[110] The legacy of such statements in the modern West has perhaps helped to obscure the extent to which many medievals regarded canon and commentary as all of a piece. Far from being a dry scholastic exercise, commentary was often the indispensable means of giving life to a canonical text.

Indeed, in late-ancient and medieval Europe, the commentarial tradition on Homer assumed a life of its own in the absence of the Homeric texts it supposedly interpreted. So powerful and pervasive was this tradition that it "survived the text it interpreted," most notably in the works of St. Augustine, Macrobius, and Dante.[111] Thus, while commentary, according to Frank Kermode, is necessary for the survival of a classical text, or at least for the perpetuation of its canonicity, the converse does not seem to be true.[112]

In no major tradition was the place of commentary and the com-

---

[106] Smalley, *Study of the Bible*, p. 12.

[107] Châtillon, "La Bible dans les Écoles," p. 180.

[108] Eugene F. Rice, Jr., "The Renaissance Idea of Christian Antiquity: Humanistic Patristic Scholarship," in *Renaissance Humanism: Foundations, Forms, and Legacy*, vol. 1: *Humanism in Italy*, ed. Albert Rabil, Jr. (Philadelphia: University of Pennsylvania Press, 1988), p. 17.

[109] Verger, "L'Éxegèse de l'université," pp. 219 and 226.

[110] John Calvin, *Institutes* IV, viii 9, quoted in John Murray, *Calvin on Scripture and Divine Sovereignty* (Welwyn, Eng.: Evangelical Press, 1979), p. 17.

[111] Lamberton, *Homer the Theologian*, pp. 193, 261, 272, 282, and 283.

[112] Frank Kermode, *Forms of Attention* (Chicago: University of Chicago Press, 1985), p. 36.

mentator so dignified, exalted, and even divinized as in rabbinic Judaism. Ezra, who was widely regarded as the father of Jewish exegesis, was supposedly "inspired by God in the way that Moses himself had been inspired to make known the Torah on Mount Sinai."[113] Moreover, the Talmud, which presents itself as a commentary, has been characterized as "the central pillar of Jewish culture."[114] Its study was "almost the chief mental occupation of the entire European Jewry" and was "not done only for a few days in school or in the House of Study, but as a way of life and in length of days."[115] Torah study and interpretation so permeated the fabric of medieval Judaism that most of the great figures of postbiblical Jewish cultural history are most celebrated for their exegetical works. For example, the great commentator on the Pentateuch, Rashi (b. 1039/1040), was so influential and revered that his commentaries were for centuries "considered the criterion of Jewish culture and learning."[116] Kabbalists even metamorphosed Rashi, the master of Jewish "plain exegesis," into a mystic who received visions of angels and who learned everything from supernal sources.[117] Such lionized exegetes were an inspiration to Jewish youth even as late as the nineteenth century, as illustrated in the autobiography of Samuel David Luzzatto: "Young as he was, he felt the need of newer and better Bible commentaries than the ones which were ordinarily used by the Jews; and to his companions he confided the hope that some day he would write even a better commentary than Rashi had written."[118]

The works of the great commentators in the medieval rabbinic tradition were an inspiration to God as well as to aspiring Jewish youth.

[113] D. S. Russell, *From Early Judaism to Early Church* (London: SCM Press, 1986), p. 37.

[114] Adin Steinsaltz, *The Essential Talmud*, trans. Chaya Galai (New York: Basic Books, 1976), pp. 266 and 83.

[115] Meyer Waxman, *A History of Jewish Literature*, vol. 2: *From the Twelfth Century to the Middle of the Eighteenth Century* (New York: Thomas Yoseloff, 1960), p. 99; Safrai, "Oral Tora," p. 106.

[116] Esra Shereshevsky, *Rashi: The Man and His World* (New York: Sepher-Hermon Press, 1982), p. 4.

[117] Moshe Idel, *Kabbalah: New Perspectives* (New Haven: Yale University Press, 1988), p. 238.

[118] Samuel David Luzzatto, *Autobiography*, quoted in Nathan Stern, *The Jewish Historico-Critical School of the Nineteenth Century* (New York: Arno Press, 1973), p. 29. A burning desire to be a great commentator also seems to have animated the young Calvin. According to T.H.L. Parker, "Just as Westcott, while still an undergraduate, wrote to his future wife that he intended to edit the New Testament, so Calvin at a hardly later age determined to be a commentator, with the Pauline Epistles as his first subject." Parker, *Calvin's New Testament Commentaries* (Grand Rapids, Mich.: William B. Eerdmans, 1971), p. 4.

According to a well-known Talmudic tale, God himself is an exegete who studies and interprets his own Torah.[119] Moreover, the God of the rabbis was not above learning from rabbinic interpretations of Torah[120] and, in one famous encounter with a rabbinic commentator, even admitted that "my children have bested me."[121]

Such apotheoses of commentaries and commentators help to explain the conception that there is no closed canon in Judaism, that rabbinic exegesis is part of an ongoing revelation, part of Torah.[122] The Jewish people, "the people of the Book," might just as well be described as "the people of biblical exegesis."[123] So little is later exegesis subordinated to earlier canonical writings that some of these writings, such as the Book of Chronicles, were said to have been "written in the first place only to be interpreted midrashically," to provide occasion for commentary.[124]

The elevation of editors and exegetes to the level of poets, prophets, and even God, and of commentary to the level of canon, may seem quaint and peculiar to moderns influenced by Romantic notions of genius and originality and Protestant conceptions of *sola scriptura*. But even canons are as much the products of editing and exegesis as they are of poetry and prophecy, as Han Confucian scholars argued with respect to Confucius. Thus, the "last decisive question" posed by F. A. Wolf nearly two centuries ago regarding the Homeric epics remains open: "Is Homer (the first and best singer of Trojan legends), or are the rhapsodes . . . or the collectors, organizers, revisers, or the later correctors and critics the principal creators of the great artistic compositions that lie before us? Whom do we have to thank for the greater part of this artistry?"[125] With respect to the Bible, where in-

---

[119] Michael Fishbane, "Inner Biblical Exegesis: Types and Strategies of Interpretation in Ancient Israel," in Hartman and Budick, eds., *Midrash and Literature*, p. 19.

[120] Susan A. Handelman, *The Slayers of Moses: The Emergence of Rabbinic Interpretation in Modern Literary Theory* (Albany: State University of New York Press, 1982), p. 42. In some cases, leading exegetes were taken up to heaven to solicit their advice. See Jacob Neusner, *The Wonder-Working Lawyers of Talmudic Babylonia: The Theory and Practice of Judaism in Its Formative Age* (Lanham, Md.: University Press of America, 1987), p. 142.

[121] Jonathan Rosenbaum, "Judaism: Torah and Tradition," in *The Holy Book in Comparative Perspective*, eds. Frederick Denny and Rodney L. Taylor (Columbia: University of South Carolina Press, 1985), p. 19.

[122] Neusner, *Midrash in Context*, pp. 128–129 and 135–136.

[123] Russell, *From Early Judaism*, p. 34.

[124] David Stern, "Midrash and the Language of Exegesis: A Study of Vayikra Rabbah, Chapter 1," in Hartman and Budick, eds. *Midrash and Literature*, p. 115.

[125] F. A. Wolf, "Letter 1. Wolf to Heyne, 18 November 1795," in Wolf, *Prolegomena to Homer, 1795*, trans. with intro. and notes by Anthony Grafton et al. (Princeton: Princeton University Press, 1985), p. 235. That final redactors may exhibit artistry has been affirmed most recently in Josipovici, *The Book of God*, p. 17.

spiration rather than artistry is the main issue, the contemporary critic Northrop Frye asserts more positively that "if the Bible is to be regarded as 'inspired' in any sense, sacred or secular, the editing and conflating and redacting and splicing and glossing and expurgating processes all have to be taken as inspired too. There is no way of distinguishing the voice of God from the voice of the Deuteronomic redactor."[126] Indeed, the redactor may be even more certainly inspired than the supernal source, as a contemporary Catholic scholar implies in posing the question, "Are the sources inspired, or only the final redaction?"[127] But redactors and commentators, unconscious as they are of their own genius or inspiration, often stand in awe of a prior source of authority, particularly of a canon. From this stance, they entertain certain assumptions about the character of this canon which influence their approach to it.

[126] Northrop Frye, *The Great Code: The Bible and Literature* (New York: Harcourt Brace Jovanovich, Harvest/HBJ Books, 1982), pp. 203–204.

[127] Raymond F. Collins, *Introduction to the New Testament* (Garden City, N.Y.: Image Books, 1987), p. 318.

Chapter 4

COMMENTARIAL ASSUMPTIONS

THE MOST UNIVERSAL and widely expressed commentarial assumption regarding the character of almost any canon is that it is comprehensive and all-encompassing, that it contains all significant learning and truth. As Jonathan Z. Smith has written, "Where there is a canon we can predict the necessary occurrence of a hermeneute, of an interpreter whose task it is to continually extend the domain of the closed canon over everything that is known or everything that is."[1] This is true not only of classical or scriptural canons, such as Homer, the Christian Bible, the Torah, the Qur'ān, the Veda, and the Confucian classics, but of some modern literary and ideological ones as well. Modern critics and ideologues have extolled the cosmic comprehensiveness of Shakespeare and Marx in terms similar to those used by traditional commentators with respect to the classics of their respective traditions. Perhaps the persistence and power of this presupposition regarding the character of canons, of this "obsession with exegetical totalization,"[2] reflects a profound desire to see a wholeness or totality somewhere in the world. This is evidently true of some individuals, such as the Marxist philosopher George Lukács, who moved, in his early writings, from an intense admiration for the Homeric epic, which "gives form to the extensive totality of life,"[3] to a commitment to Marx, whose works "form a coherent unity that must be preserved."[4]

The vision of cosmic comprehensiveness, or of totality and wholeness, in a diverse array of canons ranging from Homer to Marx is not, however, simply an illusion that strikes only the eye of the committed or faithful beholder or the confirmed exegete. For, as a general rule, the works that are selected for canonization in various

---

[1] Jonathan Z. Smith, "Sacred Persistence: Towards a Redescription of Canon," in *Approaches to Ancient Judaism: Theory and Practice*, ed. William Scott Green (Missoula, Mont.: Scholars Press, 1978), p. 23.

[2] Ibid.

[3] George Lukács, *The Theory of the Novel: A Historico-Philosophical Essay on the Forms of Great Epic Literature*, trans. Anna Bostok (Cambridge: MIT Press, 1971), p. 46.

[4] George Lukács, 1967 preface to *History and Class Consciousness*, quoted in Martin Jay, *Marxism and Totality: The Adventures of a Concept from Lukács to Habermas* (Berkeley: University of California Press, 1984), p. 61.

traditions do have a wide scope and, in some cases, an almost encyclopedic character. As noted above in chapter 1, most of them originated not as single works by individual authors, but as collections of
diverse materials assembled by "schools" or traditions over long periods of time. Such canons thus grew to incorporate the wisdom or
learning of a whole tradition—and sometimes even a whole culture,
as is arguably the case with the gargantuan Indian epic the *Mahābhārata*; as well as with the Babylonian Talmud, the *Bavli*, which Jacob
Neusner has called "the great vacuum cleaner of ancient Judaism";[5]
and even with Aristotle, whose works have been called "an encyclopedia of ancient knowledge" and the "fruits of an entire civilization."[6]
Even after such works attained a sort of canonical status, some of
them continued to grow more encyclopedic in scope as later editors
and redactors inserted new materials that they hoped would gain
more prestige by being incorporated into a classical corpus.

Further, those bodies or collections of writings which are relatively
comprehensive, which do seem to incorporate heaven, earth, and the
myriad things, generally form more attractive canons than do works
of more limited scope. Confucianism, for example, apparently had
this competitive edge over such rival schools as the Mohist and the
Taoist—that its proposed canon was wider and more comprehensive.[7] The Babylonian Talmud attained a definitive status in Judaism,
eclipsing its less encyclopedic rival, the Palestinian Talmud (*Yerushalmi*) for much the same reason.[8] Conversely, the limited success
and influence of the Samaritans in ancient Palestine has been attributed to the small size of their canon, which included only the Pentateuch, or the five books of Moses.[9]

It might even be argued that the pre-eminence which Plato and
Aristotle gained over other ancient philosophers, particularly in the
later Middle Ages and the Renaissance, derives in part from the comprehensive scope of the works attributed to them. Even in antiquity,
the Platonic dialogues were interpreted as a kind of cosmos as well as

[5] Jacob Neusner, *Judaism, The Classical Statement: The Evidence of the Bavli* (Chicago:
University of Chicago Press, 1986), p. 202.

[6] Fernand Van Steenberghen, *Aristotle in the West: The Origins of Latin Aristotelianism*,
trans. Leonard Johnston (Louvain: E. Nauwelaerts, 1955), p. 15.

[7] A similar point is made in David McMullen, *State and Scholars in T'ang China* (Cambridge: Cambridge University Press, 1988), p. 67.

[8] Neusner, *Judaism*, p. 233. Similarly, the Mishnah of Rabbi Judah the Prince (135–
219) eventually won the day over the less comprehensive, though similarly organized,
Mishnah of Rabbi Akiba. See Hyam Maccoby, *Early Rabbinic Writings* (Cambridge:
Cambridge University Press, 1988), p. 6.

[9] W. D. Davies, "Reflections on the Mormon 'Canon,'" *Harvard Theological Review* 79,
nos. 1–3 (1986): 61.

a complete educational curriculum.[10] And the wide range of Aristotle's works earned him the reputation of a universal intelligence. He was "the master of those who know," "the supreme authority in every branch of secular learning."[11] His reputation for comprehensive knowledge was further enhanced in the Middle Ages by the inclusion of many non-Aristotelian writings, especially Neo-Platonic works, in the Aristotelian corpus.[12]

Among the writings of nineteenth-century political and social philosophers that might be compared with Aristotle in terms of their comprehensiveness, "Marx's canon includes works of sociological theory, economic theory, and history," as Raymond Aron has pointed out.[13] Engels, moreover, proceeded to present Marxism as a "unified objective system encompassing Nature and History."[14] He thus made it more appealing to those in quest of a total or comprehensive vision of man and his world than were the writings of more focused intelligences who were no less perspicacious than Marx.

The actual comprehensiveness of particular canons may vary widely. Few dispassionate observers would, for example, argue that the Qur'ān is as inclusive and ecumenical in scope as the *Mahābhārata* or even the Christian Bible. But the terms in which commentators in various traditions acclaim the comprehensiveness of their respective canons, generally as a self-evident truth not open to discussion or debate, are remarkably similar. Moving from West to East, from Homer's wine-dark sea to Confucius' Yellow River chart, with a sojourn by the waters of Babylon where the Talmudists remembered Zion, let us briefly survey commentators' accounts of the cosmic comprehensiveness of their canons, while recognizing that "comprehensiveness" may have different meanings in different traditions and even within a single tradition.

The omniscience of Homer, the universal scope of his knowledge, is perhaps the most persistent theme in Homeric criticism from ancient to modern times. This notion, which is expressed in Plato, became a commonplace that was seldom questioned or debated in Hel-

[10] Robert Drummond Lamberton, "Homer the Theologian: The *Iliad* and *Odyssey* as Read by the Neoplatonists of Late Antiquity" (Ph.D. diss., Yale University, 1979), pp. 171–172.

[11] John Leofric Stocks, *Aristotelianism* (Boston: Marshall Jones Co., 1925), p. 128.

[12] Robert Lamberton, *Homer the Theologian: Neoplatonist Allegorical Reading and the Growth of the Epic Tradition* (Berkeley: University of California Press, 1986), p. 240.

[13] Raymond Aron, *Main Currents in Sociological Thought*, vol. 1: *Montesquieu, Comte, Marx, Toqueville, and the Sociologists and the Revolution of 1848*, trans. Richard Howard and Helen Weaver (Garden City, N.Y.: Doubleday, Anchor Books, 1968), p. 146.

[14] Russell Jacoby, *Dialectics of Defeat: Contours of Western Marxism* (Cambridge: Cambridge University Press, 1981), p. 52.

lenistic, Roman, and Byzantine writings on the Homeric epics.[15] Of
particular note is Pseudo-Plutarch's treatise *De vita et poesi Homeri*
(first century A.D.), which sought to establish that Homer was a master of all the arts and sciences, of everything from medicine to mete-
orology, and that all the principal literary forms, including tragedy,
comedy, and epigram, were founded by him.[16] According to another
Hellenistic critic, Heraclitus, the later Greek philosophers, such as
Plato and Epicurus, all derived their main ideas from Homer.[17] The
fifteenth-century Italian poet and Hellenist Angelo Poliziano recapit-
ulated these ancient critics' characterizations of Homer, whom he
identified as "the seer, the author and source of all learning and wisdom."[18] Erasmus also expressed the common conviction of his age in
characterizing Homer as the "father of all philosophy" and "an ocean
of all human wisdom."[19] An eighteenth-century English critic,
Thomas Blackwell, traced Homer's universal knowledge to the fact
that he "took his Plan from Nature."[20] Since nature includes all the
sciences, so Homer must comprehend them all as well.

Finally, even modern scholars have affirmed the cosmic inclusiveness of the Homeric epics. Howard Clarke, developing an epic dichotomy broached in Aristotle (*Poetics* 24), posits that the two epics,
the *Iliad* and the *Odyssey*, divide the heroic world, and the world, between them: "the *Iliad* [is] a poem of war, the *Odyssey*, of peace; the
Iliad dominated by men, the *Odyssey*, by women; the *Iliad* with a hero
who is aloof and difficult, the *Odyssey* with one who is worldly and
accommodating; the *Iliad* local and intense, the *Odyssey* broad and lei-
surely."[21] Another contemporary Homeric scholar, Jasper Griffin, attributes the comprehensiveness of Homer in part to his extensive use
of similes which allows him to present information on such diverse
aspects of the world as "wild nature, peaceful agriculture, the various

[15] Kirsti Simonsuuri, *Homer's Original Genius: Eighteenth-Century Notions of the Early Greek Epic (1688–1798)* (Cambridge: Cambridge University Press, 1979), p. 147.

[16] Ibid., p. 6; Lamberton, "Homer the Theologian," pp. 132 and 148–149. Similar arguments occasionally appear even in the works of modern Homeric scholars. See, for example, John A. Scott, *Homer and His Influence* (Boston: Marshall Jones Co., 1925), pp. 159–162.

[17] Michael Murrin, *The Allegorical Epic: Essays in Its Rise and Decline* (Chicago: University of Chicago Press, 1980), p. 9.

[18] Angelo Poliziano, "In Explanation of Homer," quoted in Howard Clarke, *Homer's Readers: A Historical Introduction to the Iliad and the Odyssey* (Newark: University of Delaware Press, 1981), p. 63.

[19] Desiderius Erasmus, "De conscribendis epistolis" and "Epistola de virtute amplectanda," quoted ibid., p. 60.

[20] Thomas Blackwell, *An Enquiry into the Life and Writings of Homer*, quoted ibid., p. 105.

[21] Clarke, *Homer's Readers*, pp. 281 and 292.

trades and skills." Thus, "the whole world can be handled by the epic, not only battle and sudden death. This inclusiveness helps to create the conviction in the reader that justice is being done to reality, not just to specially selected areas of it."[22]

One of the main reasons why the classics, especially the Homeric epics, continue to be widely read and appreciated in modern times, despite their defects when measured by modern literary standards, is that they do seem to comprehend much more of the world than most modern works of literature. Thus, Alexander Pope remarked of Homer that "if he has failed in some of his Flights, it was because he attempted every thing. . . . What he has done admitted no Encrease, it only left room for Contraction or Regulation."[23] Nevertheless, the Homeric epic has inspired many imitations from antiquity to the present century. Poets great and minor, most of whose temperaments, talents, or times were unsuited to composing an epic, could not resist trying their hands at the genre, often with disastrous results.[24] For it seemed that a total vision of the world, a comprehensive view of reality, could be fully presented only in epic form. Only epic, among the major literary genres, "seeks to embrace the totality of a society—as Hegel put it, both its 'world outlook' and its 'concrete existence.' "[25]

The claims that ancient and medieval critics made for the comprehensiveness of the Vergilian epic, the *Aeneid*, are just as extravagant

[22] Jasper Griffin, *Homer* (New York: Hill and Wang, 1980), p. 12. David Marshall speaks similarly of Homer's similes, pointing out that they "add to the encyclopedic fund of knowledge transmitted in the Homeric epic." Marshall, "Similes and Delay," in *Modern Critical Views: Homer*, ed. Harold Bloom (New York: Chelsea House, 1986), p. 233.

[23] Alexander Pope, "Preface [to the *Iliad* (1715)]," in *Eighteenth-Century English Literature*, eds. Geoffrey Tillotson et al. (San Diego: Harcourt Brace Jovanovich, 1969), p. 596.

[24] A notable example of such a failed epic is Ronsard's *La Franciade*. As Gilbert Highet remarks, "The poem was a total failure: Ronsard could not even finish it." Highet, *The Classical Tradition: Greek and Roman Influences on Western Tradition* (Oxford: Oxford University Press, 1976), p. 144. Another illustration of the genre is Goethe's *Achilleis*, "a fragmentary attempt to create pastiche Homer in German." T. J. Reed, *Goethe* (Oxford: Oxford University Press, 1984), p. 83. Perhaps such epic failures stemmed in part from a lack of concentration and commitment. As Northrop Frye has pointed out, "A narrative poet, a Southey or a Lydgate, may write any number of narratives, but an epic poet normally completes only one epic structure, the moment when he decides on his theme being the crisis of his life." Frye, *Anatomy of Criticism: Four Essays* (Princeton: Princeton University Press, 1973) p. 318.

[25] Sheldon I. Pollock, "Introduction" to *The Rāmāyana of Vālmīki: An Epic of Ancient India*, vol. 2: *Ayodhyākānda*, intro., trans., and annot. Pollock; ed. Robert P. Goldman (Princeton: Princeton University Press, 1986), p. 14.

and elaborate as those regarding the *Iliad* and the *Odyssey*.[26] As early as late antiquity, the Latin writer Macrobius (c. 400) characterized Vergil as an authority in every branch of learning, a master of all the arts and sciences.[27] Thus, the discussion on Vergil in Macrobius' *Saturnalia* must call on authorities in such disparate fields as oratory, augury, and philosophy in order to present a comprehensive picture of the universal Vergil.[28] Macrobius' friend, the grammarian Servius, reserved special praise for the sixth book of the *Aeneid*, much of which, he said, was taken from "the deep science of the philosophers, theologians and Egyptians, so that many have written whole treatises on the individual facets of this book."[29] The twelfth-century divine and "best classicist of his age," John of Salisbury, remarked that Vergil had "under the guise of legend expressed the truths of all philosophy."[30] His contemporary Bernard of Chartres wrote a commentary on the *Aeneid* in which he maintained that Vergil "described as a philosopher the nature of human life . . . and all that the human soul does or suffers during its temporary abode in the body."[31] Sir Thomas Elyot, in *The Boke Named the Governor* (1531), also attested to the encyclopedic scope of the *Aeneid*, at least with respect to such practical arts and sciences as botany, husbandry, hunting, music, wrestling, and politics.[32]

Although Vergil's comprehension of the arts and sciences may fall short of modern standards, the *Aeneid* may yet be regarded as micro-

[26] This may in part be a reflection of the Homeric legacy. Philip R. Hardie remarks: "As Virgil imitates Homer, so the commentators on Virgil imitate the commentators on Homer; the universality of Homer naturally led to a claim for the universality of Virgil." Hardie, *Virgil's Aeneid: Cosmos and Imperium* (Oxford: Clarendon Press, 1986), p. 23.

[27] Domenico Comparetti, *Vergil in the Middle Ages*, trans. E.F.M. Benecke (New York: Alfred Hafner, 1929 reprint), pp. 64–65; Leslie George Whitbread, "Introduction" to Fulgentius, "The Exposition of the Content of Virgil According to Moral Philosophy," in Whitbread, ed., *Fulgentius the Mythographer* (Columbus: Ohio State University Press, 1971), p. 106.

[28] Lamberton, *Homer*, p. 268.

[29] Servius, *Ad Aeneid*, quoted in J. W. Jones, Jr., "The Allegorical Traditions of the Aeneid," in *Vergil at 2000: Commemorative Essays on the Poet and His Influence*, ed. John D. Bernard (New York: AMS Press, 1986), p. 111; also trans. in Comparetti, *Vergil*, p. 60.

[30] John of Salisbury, *Polycrat* VI c.22, quoted in Comparetti, *Vergil*, p. 117; John Webster Spargo, *Virgil the Necromancer: Studies in Virgilian Legends* (Cambridge: Harvard University Press, 1934), p. 8.

[31] Bernard of Chartres, quoted in Comparetti, *Vergil*, p. 116.

[32] David G. Hale, "Virgil and Homer in the Early Tudor Period," in *The Early Renaissance: Virgil and the Classical Tradition*, ed. Anthony L. Pellegrini (Binghamton: State University of New York, Center for Medieval and Early Renaissance Studies, 1984), p. 125.

cosmic in a literary sense. Vergil may not have created a new cosmos, "a more judiciously fashioned universe than the one created by the First God."[33] But the *Aeneid* is at least a sort of literary microcosm that incorporates a wide array of different genres, including tragedy, historiography, ethnography, scientific and philosophical poetry, "Hellenistic whimsy," and pastoral and religious hymns.[34] Insofar as literature absorbs life, and text context, there is thus something to be said for Vergil's universality and comprehensiveness.

There is even more to be said for the comprehensiveness of Jewish canonical writings, especially the Babylonian Talmud, or *Bavli*. For the composers of this huge "summa of Judaism," which "covers everything found in all the other writings," intended to "create encyclopedic summaries of all the data at their disposal."[35] Conversely, what earned for the *Bavli* the priority it enjoyed within the Jewish tradition as "Israel's fullest Torah" was its comprehensive character.[36] It includes not only religious law, but also a diverse array of such more mundane topics as occupational hints, medical advice, examinations of human nature, linguistic questions, and ethical problems.[37]

But the claim of comprehensiveness is made even for those forms of the Jewish canon which to the naked eye of the outside observer are much more sketchy and incomplete, particularly the original Torah book, or Pentateuch, which was commonly called "The Book with Everything in It."[38] The scroll of Torah, according to the eleventh-century Kabbalist Gikatilla, includes all the sciences, both exoteric and esoteric.[39] The famous rabbinic commentator Ramban, or Nachmanides (b. 1195), asserted in his commentary on the Pentateuch that "everything can be learned from the Torah," and even Solomon found everything in it:

[33] Clarke, *Homer's Readers*, p. 118. Clarke is here presenting the view of Julius Caesar Scaliger (1484–1558), "the most notorious of the Vergilioators" and the "Aristotle of the Renaissance" (p. 117).

[34] James E. G. Zetzel, "Re-creating the Canon: Augustan Poetry and the Alexandrian Past," in *Canons*, ed. Robert von Halberg (Chicago: University of Chicago Press, 1984), p. 125; Hardie, *Vergil's Aeneid*, p. 24. Hardie argues that "There is a strong suggestion of a striving for comprehensiveness in many aspects of the poem, particularly in the variety of discernible literary models" (p. 24).

[35] Neusner, *Judaism*, pp. 233, 202, and 16.

[36] Ibid., pp. 233 and 240.

[37] Adin Steinsaltz, *The Essential Talmud*, trans. Chaya Galai (New York: Basic Books, 1976), pp. 95–96.

[38] James A. Sanders, *Canon as Paradigm: From Sacred Story to Sacred Text* (Philadelphia: Fortress Press, 1987), p. 182.

[39] Moshe Idel, "Infinities of Torah in Kabbalah," in *Midrash and Literature*, eds. Geoffrey H. Hartman and Sanford Budick (New Haven: Yale University Press, 1986), p. 150.

For every precious thing and every wonder,
Every profound mystery and all glorious wisdom
Are stored up with her.[40]

For many Christian commentators of late antiquity and the Middle
Ages as well, the Bible comprehended all wisdom and learning, secular as well as sacred, practical arts as well as divine mysteries. Its
individual books, according to St. Jerome (340?–420), were repositories of particular arts and sciences. The Book of Numbers, for example, contains "the mysteries of all arithmetic," Job "all the laws of
dialectics," and the Psalms every form of poetry.[41] The sixth-century
Christian encyclopedist Cassiodorus maintained that Psalms, in fact,
includes much more than poetry. It "is filled full with grammar and
etymologies, with schemata, with the art of rhetoric, with topica, with
the art of dialectics, with music, with geometry, with astronomy, and
with the expressions peculiar to the divine law."[42] Cassiodorus went
on to argue that pagan authors had originally learned all of these arts
from Scripture.[43] The Bible was thus the ultimate source as well as
the complete repository of all the major branches of learning and
science.

The development of philosophy, the growth of knowledge, did
not, moreover, render it superfluous in this respect. For as Roger Bacon (1214?–1294) pointed out, "the Scripture deals with creature far
more surely and far better and more truly than philosophical labor is
able to work out." Only the Book of Genesis, for example, reveals the
(Aristotelian) final cause of the rainbow which was not known to any
of the philosophers.[44]

Since the Qur'ān is much shorter and more homogeneous than
most major classical or scriptural texts, it may have been harder to
make a case for its comprehensiveness.[45] In fact, later commentators

[40] Ramban [Nachmanides], *Commentary on the Torah: Genesis*, trans. Charles B. Chavel
(New York: Shilo Publishing, 1971), pp. 4 and 12–13.

[41] St. Jerome, quoted in Ernst Robert Curtius, *European Literature and the Latin Middle
Ages*, trans. Willard R. Trask (Princeton: Princeton University Press, 1973), p. 73.

[42] Cassiodorus, *Com. in. Ps.*, quoted in Beryl Smalley, *The Study of the Bible in the Middle Ages*, 3rd ed., rev. (Oxford: Basil Blackwell, 1983), p. 31.

[43] Cassiodorus Senator, *An Introduction to Divine and Human Readings*, trans. with intro. and notes by Leslie Webber Jones (New York: W. W. Norton, 1969), p. 70.

[44] Roger Bacon, "The *Opus Majus*, Pt. 2, Chap. 8," in *Selections from Medieval Philosophers*, vol. 2: *Roger Bacon to William of Ockham*, ed. and trans. Richard McKeon (New
York: Charles Scribner's Sons, 1958), pp. 37–38.

[45] On this point, Elizabeth L. Eisenstein comments that "the Koran comes closer to
resembling a single prophetic book of the Old Testament, but even then it seems more
homogeneous." This is not surprising inasmuch as "all of the Koran's varied ingredi-
ents were filtered through one mind, articulated in one tongue, and shaped in terms

frequently argued that the received Qur'ān document (*mushaf*) was incomplete in order to legitimate certain elements in Islamic law that could not be found in this source.[46] Nevertheless, the renowned philosopher al-Ghazālī maintained that "the Qur'ān is [like] a sea which has no shore," and that "it is from the Qur'ān that the sciences of the ancients and the moderns branch off."[47] Among the arts and sciences contained in the Qur'ān, observed Ibn Abi al-Fadl al-Mursî (d. 1257), were astronomy, medicine, weaving, spinning, seafaring, agriculture, and even pearl diving.[48] Modern exegetes, moreover, have argued that the Qur'ān alludes to scientific facts and laws that were discovered only in modern times, such as Darwin's idea of evolution.[49] In defense of this view of the Qur'ān as a comprehensive repository of all knowledge, they often cite two of its verses: "We have revealed the Book which manifests the truth about all things," and "we have left nothing out in Our Book."[50] According to a widely accepted tradition (*hadīth*), the Prophet Muhammad also proclaimed the illimitability of the Book: "The Learned shall never be sated of it. It shall not wear out from constant use, nor will its marvels ever be exhausted."[51]

While the notion that the Qur'ān contains all knowledge may be harder to maintain in modern times, modern scholars such as Afzalur Rahman have argued that the Book is comprehensive or all-encompassing in another sense: it "satisfies people of all shades of opinion and degrees of intellect." It speaks to the ordinary man in the street,

---

of a single life span." Eisenstein, *The Printing Press as an Agent of Change: Communications and Cultural Transformations in Early-Modern Europe*, 2 vols. in 1 (Cambridge: Cambridge University Press, 1980), p. 335.

[46] John Burton, *The Collection of the Qur'ān* (Cambridge: Cambridge University Press, 1979), p. 232.

[47] Al-Ghazālī, *The Jewels of the Qur'ān*, a translation, with an introduction and annotation, of al-Ghazālī's *Kitāb Jawāhir al-Qur'ān* by Muhammad Abul Quasem (Kuala Lumpur: University of Malaysia Press, 1977), pp. 46 and 19–20.

[48] J.J.G. Jansen, *The Interpretation of the Koran in Modern Egypt* (Leiden: E. J. Brill, 1974), p. 37.

[49] Ibid., pp. 51–52 and 45; Mohammad Khalifa, *The Sublime Qur'ān and Orientalism* (London: Longman, 1983), pp. 219–220; Jacques Jomier, "Aspects of the Qur'ān Today," in *Arabic Literature to the End of the Umayyad Period*, eds. A.F.L. Beeston et al. (Cambridge: Cambridge University Press, 1983), p. 266.

[50] Qur'ān 16:89 and 6:38, trans. by N. J. Dawood in *The Koran* (Harmondsworth, Eng.: Penguin Books, 1980), pp. 310 and 429.

[51] Quoted in Mahmoud Ayoub, *The Qur'ān and Its Interpreters* (Albany: State University of New York Press, 1984), vol. 1, p. 10. A *hadīth* is a report that "preserved Muhammad's words and his contemporaries' descriptions of his actions. . . . It came to mean a 'tradition' in the form of a brief report." Frederick Denny, "Islam: Qur'ān and Hadīth," in *The Holy Book in Comparative Perspective*, eds. Frederick Denny and Rodney L. Taylor (Columbia: University of South Carolina Press, 1985), p. 14.

98 CHAPTER 4

stimulates philosophers, meets the aspirations of mystics, and encourages scientists.[52]

The Veda was probably the object of more extravagant eulogies than any of the classical or scriptural texts we have surveyed thus far.[53] Many of these focused on its alleged comprehensiveness and inexhaustibility. Shankara held that "like a lamp, it throws light on all things. . . . It is like an omniscient person, because there is nothing with which it does not deal."[54] Modern Vedantists have proclaimed that the Veda contains knowledge of all the latest scientific discoveries and technological advances, and even all knowledge that future research might uncover.[55] Indeed, partisans of the Arya Samaj, a modern Hindu revivalist movement founded by Dayananda Saraswati, have proclaimed that Vedic science is superior to modern science, especially in the field of chemistry.[56] If anything is missing in the Veda, that is because some portions of the original text have been lost; for the extent of the original was infinite.[57]

If infinity may be said to have degrees, then a good case could be made for the great Indian epic, the *Mahābhārata*, being even more infinite. As the *Mahābhārata* says of itself, "That which is found in this work may be found elsewhere, but whatever is not found here, does not occur outside of it."[58] Later commentators argued that the epic

[52] Afzalur Rahman, *Quranic Sciences* (London: Muslim Schools Trust, 1981), p. 14.

[53] For a few examples of such eulogies, see Jan Gonda, *Vedic Literature (Saṃhitās and Brāhmaṇas)*, vol. 1 of *A History of Indian Literature*, ed. Gonda (Wiesbaden: Otto Harrassowitz, 1975), p. 53.

[54] K. Satchidananda Murty, *Revelation and Reason in Advaita Vedānta* (Waltair: Andhra University; New York: Columbia University Press, 1959), pp. 44–45. Shankara's perspective on the Veda is reminiscent of the view of the Brihadāranyaka Upanishad: "As smoke and sparks arise from a lighted fire kindled with damp fuel, even so Maitreyi, have been breathed forth from the Eternal all knowledge and all wisdom—what we know as the Rig Veda, the Yajur Veda, and the rest. They are the breath of the Eternal." *The Upanishads: Breath of the Eternal*, trans. Swami Prabhavananda and Frederick Manchester (New York: New American Library, Mentor Religious Classics, 1957), p. 88.

[55] Troy Wilson Organ, *Hinduism: Its Historical Development* (Woodbury, N.Y.: Barron's, 1974), p. 18; Anslie T. Embree, *The Hindu Tradition* (New York: Vintage Books, 1972), p. 300.

[56] Kenneth W. Jones, *Arya Dharm: Hindu Consciousness in 19th-Century Punjab* (Berkeley: University of California Press, 1976), p. 162.

[57] Murty, *Revelation and Reason*, p. 234.

[58] *Mahābhārata* 1.56.33, quoted in Barend A. Van Nooten, *The Mahābhārata* (New York: Twayne, 1971), p. 3. Compare St. Augustine's comments on Christian scriptures: "And although anyone may find everything which he has usefully learned elsewhere there, he will also find very abundantly things which are found nowhere else at all." Augustine, *On Christian Doctrine* 3.42, trans. D. W. Robertson, Jr. (Indianapolis: Bobbs-Merrill, Library of Liberal Arts, 1979), p. 78. Jacob Neusner makes a similar

presents in story form the fundamentals of all the six systems of Hindu philosophy, which in themselves are all-inclusive, as well as of the Veda. The *Mahābhārata* is "nothing short of an encyclopedia of all ancient knowledge."[59]

But Indian commentators have extolled even the relatively brief *Bhagavad Gītā*, included in the great epic, for its encyclopediacy. The great thirteenth-century commentator on the *Gītā*, Jnāneshvari, characterized it as "the primal abode of learning and the everlasting seat of all the sciences."[60] According to the modern philosopher-statesman S. Radhakrishnan, the *Gītā* "brought together and integrated into a comprehensive synthesis" all the major strands of Indian thought and religious practice, including "the Vedic cult of sacrifice, the Upanisadic teaching of the transcendent Brahman, the Bhagavata theism, and piety, the Samkya dualism and the Yoga meditation."[61] More social-scientifically inclined modern Indians have found in the *Gītā* "an understanding of the principles of Economics, Sociology, Psychology and Management."[62] Thus have commentators pushed the movement toward "exegetical totalization" even with canonical texts that, to outside observers, may seem to fall far short of totality.

A totalistic vision has also dazzled latter-day interpreters of the great Mayan epic, the *Popul Vuh*. As a modern translator of this epic, Dennis Tedlock, remarked of his Mayan diviner informant, "Andrés Xiloj felt certain that if one only knew how to read it perfectly, borrowing the knowledge of the day lords, the moist breezes, and the distant lightning, it should reveal everything under the sky and on the earth, all the way out to the four corners." Through a clear-sighted reading of the *Popol Vuh*, one could recover "the vision of the first four humans, who at first 'saw everything under the sky perfectly.' "[63] More mundanely, the epic does indeed contain accounts of

---

point regarding the Babylonian Talmud, or *Bavli*: "Pretty much anything presented in the other documents we find in this one too. But what we find here we do not necessarily locate elsewhere." Neusner, *Judaism*, p. 10.

[59] N. V. Thadani, "Introduction" to *Mīmāmsā: The Secret of the Sacred Books of the Hindus*, trans. N. V. Thadani (Delhi: Bharati Research Institute, 1952), pp. xi and ccxix.

[60] Shri Jnāneshvar, *Jnāneshvari* [Bhāvārthadipikā], trans. V. G. Pradhān; ed. H. M. Lambert (Albany: State University of New York Press, 1987), p. 3.

[61] John G. Arapura, *Gnosis and the Question of Thought in Vedānta: Dialogue with the Foundations* (Dordrecht: Martinus Nijhoff, 1986), p. 101.

[62] A. K. Srivastava, *Bhagavad Gītā: Economic Development and Management* (New Delhi: Abhinav Publications, 1980), p. 9.

[63] Dennis Tedlock, "Preface" and "Introduction" to *Popol Vuh: The Definitive Edition of the Mayan Book of the Dawn of Life and the Glories of Gods and Kings*, trans. Tedlock (New York: Simon and Schuster, 1985), pp. 20 and 32, respectively.

the various arts and sciences cultivated by the Mayans, including astronomy, navigation, prognostication, as well as genealogies.[64] In its inclusiveness, the Mayan epic, like the Homeric encyclopedia, thus assumed one of the principal functions of myth, which in preliterate societies was "the comprehensive 'encyclopedia' of a culture's several volumes—history, religion, physical science, and domestic lore."[65] Inasmuch as the classics or scriptures in a number of cultures were in part codifications or compilations of a body of myth, they more easily took on myth's comprehensive character.

. . . . .

Chinese Confucianism is nearly unique among the traditions surveyed here in its possession of a distinctly multibook canon of very diverse origins. This perhaps made it easier to argue that the Confucian classics were comprehensive, or at least that they covered a wide range. Thus, it might seem surprising that Confucian commentators more frequently asserted the comprehensiveness of particular books in the canon, especially the *Classic of Change* and the *Spring and Autumn Annals*, than they did of the classics as a whole. But perhaps that point was so widely accepted that it was not felt to require so much special defense or elaboration.

Nevertheless, some testimonies to the comprehensiveness and inexhaustibility of the classics as a whole do appear in Confucian literature. The seventeenth-century Japanese scholar Itō Jinsai (1627–1705) maintained that the Five Classics present "a vast panorama of heaven, earth, the ten thousand creatures, human emotions, and the changes of the world."[66] Chu Hsi marveled that this relatively small corpus of writings, consisting of "only several tens of chapters," yet covered all the subtleties of philosophy and the vicissitudes of history.[67] The prodigious scholar Wang Ying-lin asserted that the philosophy and literature of all times issued forth from the classics.[68] Later commentators maintained that the inexhaustibility of the classics derived from their sagely origins. As Chu Sheng (1299–1371) ob-

[64] Ibid., pp. 32–33 and 210.

[65] Jesse M. Gellrich, *The Idea of the Book in the Middle Ages: Language Theory, Mythology, and Fiction* (Ithaca: Cornell University Press, 1985), p. 38.

[66] Yoshikawa Kōjirō, *Jinsai Sorai Norinaga: Three Classical Philologists of Mid-Tokugawa Japan*, trans. Kikuchi Yuji (Tokyo: Tōhō Gakkai–The Institute of Eastern Culture, 1983), p. 70.

[67] Chu Hsi, quoted in *Ching-i k'ao* 296.7b–8a (vol. 8).

[68] Wang Ying-lin, "Liu-ching" (The Six Classics), from *Yü-hai* (Sea of Jade), in *T'u-shu chi-ch'eng* 57:3170.

served, "The Way of the sages is recorded in the classics. Since the minds of the sages are unlimited, the principles in the classics are also unlimited."[69] Another fourteenth-century commentator, Wang Shen, attributed the cosmic comprehensiveness of the classics to the sages' having patterned them on the Way of nature, on the cosmos at large: "Thus, the reason why the writing in the Six Classics plumbs heaven and earth and extends over past and present without change is that it emanated from nature."[70]

Just as critics and exegetes in the late-ancient and medieval West traced all of the arts and sciences to Homer or the Bible, so some modern historians have asserted that the major branches of learning cultivated in China originated in the Confucian classics. According to Ch'ien Mu, Chinese literature developed from the *Songs Classic*, historiography from the *Spring and Autumn Annals*, and philosophy from the *Classic of Change*.[71] Literary critics in traditional China also traced most literary genres to one or another of the classics. For example, various genres of political writing, including imperial edicts (*chao*), orders (*ming*), memorials (*ts'e*), and manifestos or summons (*hsi*), were believed to have developed from the *Documents Classic*.[72] The classics, asserted Liu Hsieh (462–522), China's most famous and influential literary critic, are "the source of all literary forms."[73]

Although the comprehensiveness of the Confucian canon as a whole may have been more widely assumed among scholars in traditional China, commentators generally argued with more vigor and verve for the all-inclusiveness of particular classics, especially the *Change* and the *Annals*. Even the "Great Commentary" to the *Change*, one of the "Ten Wings" attributed to Confucius, extols that classic as a book which is "broad, great, and all-encompassing. There are in it the Way of heaven, the Way of man, and the Way of earth."[74] Further, "the *Change* encompasses all the transformations in heaven and earth without any defect. In multifarious ways it completes all things, leaving out none."[75] These testimonials to the cosmic comprehensive-

---

[69] Chu Sheng, quoted in *Ching-i k'ao* 297.1a (vol. 8).

[70] Wang Shen, quoted in *Ching-i-k'ao* 297.4a (vol. 8).

[71] Ch'ien Mu, "Fei-yü" (Introduction) to Ch'u Po-ssu, *Liu-ching tao lun* (A Discussion of the Way of the Six Classics) (Taipei: K'ai-ming shu-tien, 1971), p. 3.

[72] Yen Chih-t'ui, quoted in *Ching-i k'ao* 295.7b (vol. 8).

[73] Liu Hsieh, *Wen-hsin tiao lung* 3, in *The Literary Mind and the Carving of Dragons: A Study of Thought and Pattern in Chinese Literature*, trans. and annot. Vincent Yu-chung Shih (New York: Columbia University Press, 1959), p. 21.

[74] This passage from chap. 10 of the "Hsia-chuan" (Lower Commentary) of the "Great Commentary" to the *Change* may be found in Chu Hsi, *Chou-I pen-i* (Basic Meaning of the *Chou Change*) (Taipei: Hua-lien ch'u-pan she, 1971 reprint), 3.36b.

[75] Chap. 4 of "Shang-chuan" (Upper Commentary), ibid., 3.5a.

ness of the *Change* are not isolated expressions. As Benjamin Schwartz has pointed out, this commentary is centrally concerned with "claiming for the system the ultimate key to all matters, mystical, metaphysical, and human."[76]

Later commentators, especially Sung and Ming Neo-Confucians, were even more explicit and enthusiastic in their accounts of the cosmic comprehensiveness of the *Change*. According to Ch'eng I, the *Change* "conjoins everything, from the obscure and bright of heaven and earth to the minuteness of insects, grasses, and trees."[77] So all-encompassing is the *Change*, remarked Chu Hsi, that even the sages could not have composed it by themselves. Rather, they were obliged to take their cues from "the pneumas and regularities of nature that assumed concrete form in patterns and emblems."[78] Even after the *Change* was fully composed, asserted Sun Ch'i-feng (1585–1675), no latter-day sage could fully comprehend it. Moreover, "if after hundreds of thousands of years several more great sages were to arise, and innovate and elaborate, the profundities of the *Change* would still not be exhausted. If the *Change* were once exhausted, then the Great Ultimate would come to an end and the cosmos would come to a standstill."[79] Huang Tsung-hsi (1610–1695) contended that not only were heaven and earth and the myriad things included within the scope of the *Change*, but also the teachings of all the schools of philosophy: "The *Change* is a book that encompasses the cosmos. It is broad, great, and all-inclusive. Therefore, the learning of the nine schools of philosophy and hundred schools of thought can all be incorporated within it."[80]

Finally, even Western students of the *Change* have been entranced by the spell of its alleged cosmic comprehensiveness, although they have been more inclined to emphasize a comprehensiveness of inclusion rather than of accommodation. One of the earliest European expositors of that classic, Joachim Bouvet (1656–1730), maintained that

[76] Benjamin I. Schwartz, *The World of Thought in Ancient China* (Cambridge: Harvard University Press, Belknap Press, 1985), p. 395.

[77] Ch'eng I, in *Chin-ssu lu* (Reflections on Things at Hand), comps. Chu Hsi and Lü Tsu-ch'ien; annot. Chiang Yung (Taipei: Kuang-wen shu-chü, 1972 reprint), 3.17.

[78] Chu Hsi, *I-hsüeh ch'i-meng* (A Primer on the Study of the *Change*) (Taipei: Kuang-hsüeh she yin-shu-kuan, 1975 reprint), p. 1.

[79] Sun Ch'i-feng, "Tu-I ta-chih" (Studying the Great Purport of the *Change*), in Yang Hsiang-k'uei, *Ch'ing-ju hsüeh-an hsin-pien* (A New Compilation of the Scholarly Records of Ch'ing Confucians), vol. 1 (Chinan: Ch'i-Lu shu-she, 1985), p. 25. Frank Kermode makes a similar point regarding canons in general: "Perhaps a perfect interpretation would, as Valéry said of pure reality, stop the heart." Kermode, *Forms of Attention* (Chicago: University of Chicago Press, 1985), p. 91.

[80] Huang Tsung-hsi, quoted in *Ching-i k'ao* 4.15a (vol. 1).

its diagrams "represent in a very simple and natural manner the principles of all the sciences."[81] The great Russian sinologist Iulian Shchutskii found in the "Great Commentary" to the *Change* an ontology, cosmology, gnosiology, ethics, and history of culture.[82] Finally, a renowned contemporary historian of Chinese thought, Hellmut Wilhelm, asserted that the system of the *Change* is so comprehensive that there is "nothing human alien to it," and that "it embraces both the patterns on earth and the images in the heavens."[83]

How can the existence of such extravagant testimonials to the cosmic comprehensiveness of the *Change* by so many scholars over the centuries be explained? They may stem in part from the classic's roots in a system of divination. For divinatory systems are as a rule "held to be complete and capable of illuminating every situation," no matter how small the number of divinatory objects.[84] Hence, as a system of divination, the *Change* must comprehend all of reality, or at least those aspects which are of concern to the diviner and the divinee. But just as canons that originate in systems of divination may be regarded as comprehensive for just that reason, so canons that are thought to be comprehensive are sometimes transformed into systems of divination, even though they did not originate as such. This was true, for example, of Vergil's *Aeneid*, which in the Middle Ages was frequently used as a divinatory manual because it was thought to cover all of life's situations.

The *Spring and Autumn Annals*, a bare historical chronicle of the state of Lu during the period 722–481 B.C., differs markedly in almost every way from the *Change*, a book of divination and a collection of omens and anecdotes with moral commentary and cosmological appendices. Yet, the terms used by Confucian commentators to express the two classics' cosmic comprehensiveness are in some cases remarkably similar. According to the Han cosmologist Tung Chungshu, the *Annals'* comprehensiveness stems from the wide range of its author's investigations: "Confucius, in composing the *Spring and Autumn Annals*, with respect to what is above surveyed the ways of heaven, and with respect to what is below inquired of the feelings of

---

[81] Joachim Bouvet, in *Leibniz-Briefwechsel* 105, quoted in David E. Mungello, *Curious Land: Jesuit Accommodation and the Origins of Sinology* (Stuttgart: Franz Steiner, 1985), p. 314.

[82] Iulian K. Shchutskii, *Researches on the I Ching*, trans. William L. MacDonald and Tsuyoshi Hasegawa with Hellmut Wilhelm (Princeton: Princeton University Press, 1979), pp. 10–11 and 164.

[83] Hellmut Wilhelm, *Change: Eight Lectures on the I Ching*, trans. Cary F. Baynes (Princeton: Princeton University Press, 1973), p. 92.

[84] Smith, "Sacred Persistence," p. 25.

men. He collated it with the past and checked it with the present."⁸⁵
Thus, "by comprehending the *Annals*," wrote the premier Sung commentator on that classic, Hu An-kuo, "we can assess all the affairs of
the world."⁸⁶ The Ch'ing classical scholar K'ung Kuang-sen also
maintained that the *Annals* covers every major realm of the cosmos,
remarking: "In regard to what is above, [this classic] is based in the
ways of heaven; in regard to what is in the middle, [it] applies the
methods of [true] kingship; and in regard to what is below, [it] patterns human feelings."⁸⁷ Wang K'e-k'uan (1304–1372) offered a
more detailed account of those aspects of the cosmos comprehended
by the *Annals*:

> In recording affairs, the *Spring and Autumn Annals* [includes], with respect
> to what is great, heaven and earth and the sun and stars, human ethics and
> political states; with respect to what is small, [it includes accounts of] man-
> sions, utensils and money, plants, birds, and insects. In sum, the principles
> of all the myriad things in the world are complete in it. If one is able to
> comprehend this classic, then there will be no pattern that he does not
> exhaustively [understand].⁸⁸

Ch'en Tsung-chih declared that the *Annals* covers several of the major branches of learning, the arts and sciences, as well as the various
realms of the cosmos: "The *Spring and Autumn Annals* is a history
[composed] by a sage. Thus astronomy, five-phases [cosmology], geography, rites, music, and men and things are all complete in it."⁸⁹
According to Yeh Meng-te (1077–1148), the comprehensiveness of
the *Annals* arose from its incorporating the teachings of all the great
sages of antiquity—including Yao, Shun, Yü, T'ang, King Wen, and
the Duke of Chou—not just those of the Sage, Confucius. Thus, even
if latter-day sages of equal stature were to arise, they would not be
able to add anything to the *Annals*, so complete and perfect it is.⁹⁰
   Modern readers of the *Annals* might well look askance at such vi-

⁸⁵ Tung Chung-shu, "Hsien-liang tui-ts'e" in Pan Ku, *Han-shu* (Han History), 12 vols.
(Beijing: Chung-hua shu-chü, 1962), 8:2515 (*chüan* 56).
⁸⁶ Hu An-kuo, quoted in *Ssu-shu wu-ching*, vol. 3: *Ch'un-ch'iu san-chuan* (The *Spring
and Autumn Annals* with the Three Commentaries), p. 4 of "Kang-ling" (Outline).
⁸⁷ K'ung Kuang-sen, "Tzu-shu" (Author's Account), in *Kung-yang t'ung-i* (The Comprehensive Meaning of the *Kung-yang Commentary*), quoted in Ch'en Li, *Kung-yang i shu*
(Subcommentary on the Meanings of the *Kung-yang Commentary*), SPPY ed., 1.3b.
⁸⁸ Wang K'e-k'uan, quoted in *Ssu-shu wu-ching*, vol. 3, p. 5 of "Kang-ling"; this same
quotation appears in *T'u-shu ch'i-ch'eng* 56:1908.
⁸⁹ Ch'en Tsung-chih, "Tzu-hsü" (Author's Preface) to *Ch'un-ch'iu pei-k'ao* (A Reference Work on the *Spring and Autumn Annals*), in *Ching-i k'ao* 206.6a (vol. 6).
⁹⁰ Yeh Meng-te, "Tzu-hsü" (Author's Preface) to *Ch'un-ch'iu chuan* (Commentary on
the *Spring and Autumn Annals*), in *Ching-i k'ao* 183.7a (vol. 5).

sions of completeness and perfection regarding that classical text. For few if any books in the Confucian canon would seem less likely to be singled out as comprehensive and all-inclusive, as complete reposito- ries of the patterns and principles of heaven, earth, and man. Yet, the *Annals* was (with the possible exception of the *Change*) the Con- fucian classic most frequently and extensively extolled for its cosmic comprehensiveness. This again indicates that commentarial assump- tions regarding the character of the canon and its individual parts sometimes operated rather independently of textual bases. If any one of the Confucian classics merits the imputation of comprehensive- ness, at least with respect to the range of topics included, it is proba- bly the compendious and extremely heterogeneous *Record of Rites*. As one modern scholar has observed, particular chapters in this collec- tion cover such a diverse array of subjects as government, education, music, scholarship, moral philosophy, and political philosophy.[91] In traditional China, however, few scholars celebrated the *Rites* for its comprehensiveness or illimitability. Perhaps the *Rites*, unlike the *Change* and the *Annals*, was not sufficiently oracular and lapidary in its mode of expression to allow later exegetes to read into it their conceptions of cosmic order and plenitude. A prose work compiled during the Han era, its language was not archaic or difficult enough to inspire in most commentators visions of a secret world hidden be- tween the lines.

That difficult and lapidary language may help to inspire such vi- sions may be illustrated by the fact that, of all the Confucian classics besides the *Change* and the *Annals*, the *Songs Classic* was probably the one that later commentators most commended for its encyclopedic range and comprehensive character. According to the late-Ch'ing classicist Ch'en Li (1810–1882), the *Songs* covered all of the four de- partments of learning, including literature, moral conduct, political affairs, and language.[92] Confucius himself, as noted above in chapter 1, remarked on the wide range and diverse applications of the *Songs*, leading Chu Hsi to comment that "the Way of human ethical rela-

[91] Wang Ching-chih, "Ching-shu ti hsien-tai yen-chiu chia-chih" (The Value of the Contemporary Study of the Classics), in Wang et al., *Ching-hsüeh yen-chiu lun-chi* (A Collection of Articles on Research in Classical Studies) (Taipei: Li-ming wen-hua shih- yeh, 1981), p. 7. James Legge also attests to the comprehensiveness of the *Record of Rites*, quoting a statement by P. Callery that it is "the most exact and complete mon- ography which the Chinese nation has been able to give of itself to the rest of the human race." Callery, quoted in Legge, "Introduction" to *The Sacred Books of China: The Texts of Confucianism. Part III: The Li Ki* (Delhi: Motilal Banarsidass, 1966 reprint), p. 12.

[92] Ch'en Li, *Tung-shu tu-shu chi* (Reading Notes of [Ch'en] Tung-shu) (Taipei: Shang- wu yin-shu-kuan, 1970 reprint), 2.12.

tions is complete in the *Songs*."[93] But the world of ethics is small compared with the larger cosmos supposedly comprehended by the *Change* and the *Annals*.

The Confucian commentarial tradition was not the only one in which oracular and lapidary language in canonical works apparently inspired visions of cosmic plenitude and universal order. Indian sūtra literature presents another illustration of this phenomenon. In fact, it often seems that the less comprehensible the sūtra without the aid of commentary, the more comprehensive it was thought to be. The very lacunae and obscurities in some sūtras made it possible for later commentators to fill in the blank spaces imaginatively with their own visions of cosmic order and plenitude, to build a full-fledged system. This is just what the great Vedantist Shankara did with the *Brāhma Sūtra*, one of the three canonical pillars of Vedānta, which even by the standards of the genre is extremely terse and lapidary—to the point of being incomprehensible without a commentary.[94]

.   .   .   .   .

The second most common commentarial assumption regarding the character of canons in most traditions is that they are well ordered and coherent, arranged according to some logical, cosmological, or pedagogical principles. Even modern critics who reject or abandon other traditional commentarial presuppositions show sympathy for the idea that a canon or classical text is organized by some pattern.[95] Indeed, it probably requires a more strenuous effort to believe that a text lacks coherence than to believe that it does not, as Frank Kermode has pointed out.[96] "Where design does not exist," remarks another contemporary critic, K. K. Ruthven, "we feel obliged to invent it, and set about the task as diligently as those early Christians who imposed a symbolic order on that heterogeneous collection of writings known to us as the Holy Bible."[97]

The difficulty of coping with incoherence and confusion (in contexts and intertexts as well as texts) is suggested by the phenomenon

[93] Chu Hsi, *Ssu-shu chi-chu* (The Four Books with Collected Commentaries) (Taipei: Hsüeh-hai ch'u-pan she, 1974 reprint), *Lun-yü* (Analects), p. 121.

[94] Arapura, *Gnosis*, p. 135.

[95] Jacob Neusner, for example, defines a canon as "a mode of classification that takes a library and turns it into a cogent, if composite statement." Neusner, *What Is Midrash?* (Philadelphia: Fortress Press, 1987), p. 79.

[96] Frank Kermode, *The Genesis of Secrecy: On the Interpretation of Narrative* (Cambridge: Harvard University Press, 1982), p. 53.

[97] K. K. Ruthven, *Critical Assumptions* (Cambridge: Cambridge University Press, 1979), pp. 4–5.

of secondary elaboration in memories and dreams. We may "remember" all kinds of things that never really occurred or that we never actually dreamed, because such interpolations are necessary to give coherence and order to the experience. Further scientific validation for this "rage for order," for this tendency to "create order even when evidence of disorder appears to be overwhelming," may also be found in Gestalt psychology, which maintains that humans have "an innate preference for perceiving wholes as distinct from separate parts."[98] Thus, this second general commentarial assumption—that the canon is well ordered and coherent—may be based on a psychological or cultural universal, a "horror of the possibility of randomness,"[99] just as the first—that the classics are comprehensive—may be related to a universal quest for wholeness and totality.

In some traditions, the demonstration of such an order or connection among apparently unrelated parts of the canon was a kind of public performance as well as a considerable tour de force. A common practice among midrashists in the rabbinic tradition, for example, was to begin with a scriptural quotation far from the Torah reading for the day, and then to tie this "verse from afar" with the Torah reading through strings of verbal connections. "The good preacher," weaving this midrashic pattern, would often gather large crowds by his presence.[100] In public view, then, he would perform the primary exegetical task of harmonizing the contradictory and bringing the seemingly discordant into patterns of new and surprising concordance,[101] thus demonstrating the order and coherence of the canon as a whole.

Rabbinic exegetes were, however, also concerned with establishing the order and progression of larger parts of the canon, not just with linking widely separated verses through an intricate web of connecting commentary. Thus Maimonides (1135–1204) tried to find logical

---

[98] Ibid.

[99] This phrase appears in Lamberton, *Homer*, passim.

[100] Barry Holtz, "Midrash," in *Back to the Sources: Reading the Classic Jewish Texts*, ed. Holtz (New York: Summit Books, 1984), p. 198. The guiding principle behind this procedure was that "every verse, no matter how remote, can be seen as a possible source for illuminating the meaning of any other verse." David Stern, "Midrash and the Language of Exegesis: A Study of Vayikra Rabbah, Chapter 1," in Hartman and Budick, eds., *Midrash and Literature*, p. 108. This type of exegesis, especially the use of hook words to interpret one part of scripture by another, also appears prominently in medieval Christian biblical exegesis. See Jean Leclercq, *The Love of Learning and the Desire for God: A Study of Monastic Culture*, trans. Catharine Misrahi (New York: Fordham University Press, 1985), pp. 73–77.

[101] Harold Coward, *Sacred Word and Sacred Text: Scripture in World Religions* (Maryknoll, N.Y.: Orbis Books, 1988), p. 23.

reasons why the various tractates in the Mishnah follow one another in the adopted succession, sometimes even deducing points of law from Mishnaic sequences.[102] The Babylonian Talmud attempts to explain (as do later rabbinic documents) why Jeremiah precedes Isaiah in the canonical order of books, even though he is chronologically later.[103] And Rashi, among many others, attempted to explain why the Torah begins not with the first commandment given to Israel in Exodus 12:1, as it should if its main purpose is to teach law, but with an account of the Creation: "Why, then, did the Torah begin with the account of the Creation? In order to illustrate that God the Creator owns the whole world."[104] An appropriate beginning, so Rashi seems to have realized, was essential to the good order and coherence of the Pentateuch as a whole. Finally, medieval Kabbalists posited that the structure of the Torah had cosmic correspondents, its 248 commandments matching the number of limbs of the human body and its 365 prohibitions resembling the days of the solar year, and even that the structure of the Torah as a whole corresponded to that of the divine body.[105]

More recent scholars of the Hebrew Bible have sought to establish the thematic unity and coherence of that canonical text. Richard Elliott Friedman, for example, has written that "the major unifying component of the biblical plot is the phenomenon of the continually diminishing apparent presence of Yahweh among humans from the beginning of the book to the end."[106] A second, more surprising unifying theme in the Hebrew Bible is "the book's focus on itself," its self-consciousness, especially reflected in the books of Ezra and Nehemiah where the subject is the Torah, the Word of God.[107] Although Friedman calls this phenomenon "an unusual literary datum,"[108]

[102] Meyer Waxman, *A History of Jewish Literature*, vol. 1: *From the Close of the Canon to the End of the Twelfth Century* (New York: Thomas Yoseloff, 1960), p. 259; Salo W. Baron, "Moses Maimonides [1135–1204]," in *Creators of the Jewish Experience in Ancient and Medieval Times*, ed. and annot. Simon Noveck (Washington, D.C.: B'nai B'rith Books, 1985), p. 215.

[103] Gabriel Josipovici, *The Book of God: A Response to the Bible* (New Haven: Yale University Press, 1988), p. 44.

[104] Rashi, *Commentaries on the Pentateuch*, selected and trans. by Chaim Pearl (New York: Viking Press, 1973), p. 31. On this problem, see also David Weiss Halivni, *Midrash, Mishnah, and Gemara: The Jewish Predilection for Justified Law* (Cambridge: Harvard University Press, 1986), p. 8.

[105] Baron, "Moses Maimonides," pp. 213–214; Moshe Idel, *Kabbalah: New Perspectives* (New Haven: Yale University Press, 1988), p. 244.

[106] Richard Elliott Friedman, "The Hiding of the Face," in *Judaic Perspectives on Ancient Israel*, eds. Jacob Neusner et al. (Philadelphia: Fortress Press, 1987), p. 215.

[107] Ibid., p. 221.

[108] Ibid.

quite a number of classical and canonical texts have risen to self-consciousness in the course of their development or maturation, particularly the *Classic of Change*, the Veda, the *Rāmāyana*, the *Mahābhārata*, the Qur'ān, and even *Don Quixote*. The Qur'ān, in particular, seems to be endowed with aspects of a human personality, especially in those episodes where it challenges its opponents. According to the Shi'ites, the Qur'ān will even appear full-bodied on the Day of Judgment, when it will "contend before God with the people, interceding for some and condemning others."[109] The human attributes and self-consciousness of many of the classics or scriptures, especially their emergence as characters or themes in their own stories, no doubt enhance their dramatic appeal, and also contribute to their apparent unity and coherence.[110]

Like many of their Jewish counterparts, medieval as well as modern Christian biblical exegetes have been concerned with explaining the order of books in the Bible. Two of the most famous and influential Christian commentators of late antiquity, Origen (d. 254) and Eusebius (260?–340?), tried both to demonstrate that the four Gospels follow one another in an ordered sequence and to establish their mutual complementarity.[111] Hugh of St. Victor, developing the ideas of earlier biblical commentators, did the same with the wisdom books in the Old Testament—Proverbs, Ecclesiastes, and the Song of Solomon—correlating this progression with the stages of life (youth, maturity, and old age) and with an order of teaching (ethics, physics, and theology).[112] Even modern historians have been loath to abandon the idea the books of the Bible are arranged in some methodical order. Thus, E. J. Goodspeed queried rather plaintively: "Does the literature of the New Testament reveal no clear pattern, no sweep of

[109] Mahmoud Ayoub, "The Speaking Qur'ān and the Silent Qur'ān: A Study of the Principles and Development of Imāmī Shī'ī *Tafsīr*," in *Approaches to the History of the Interpretation of the Qur'ān*, ed. Andrew Rippin (Oxford: Clarendon Press, 1988), p. 181; Issa J. Boullata, "The Rhetorical Interpretation of the Qur'ān: *I'jāz* and Related Topics," ibid., p. 140.

[110] Earl Edgar Elder remarks that "in early Islam there developed a remarkable reverence for the Qur'ān, largely because of its own witness to itself." Elder, "Introduction" to *A Commentary on the Creed of Islam: Sa'd al-Din al-Taftāzāni on the Creed of Najm al-Din al-Nasafi*, trans. and annot. Elder (New York: Columbia University Press, 1950), p. xii.

[111] M. F. Wiles, "Origen as Biblical Scholar," in *The Cambridge History of the Bible*, vol. 1: *From the Beginnings to Jerome*, eds. P. R. Ackroyd and C. F. Evans (Cambridge: Cambridge University Press, 1970), p. 476; Eusebius, *The History of the Church from Christ to Constantine*, trans. G. A. Williamson (Harmondsworth, Eng: Penguin Books, 1984), p. 133.

[112] *The Disascalicon of Hugh of St. Victor: A Medieval Guide to the Arts*, trans. Jerome Taylor (New York: Columbia University Press, 1961), p. 110.

movement in its rise? . . . Is there no broad literary principle that may reduce these reluctant units to a new and significant order?"[113] Northrop Frye has more boldly attempted to establish such an order with respect to the Old Testament. Admitting that "the order of Old Testament books . . . seems very arbitrary at first," Frye avers that "it makes its own kind of sense. The books from Genesis to Esther are concerned with history, law, and ritual; and those from Job to Malachi with poetry, prophecy, and wisdom. In this sequence Job occupies the place of a poetic and prophetic Genesis."[114] The Bible, Frye argues, is "probably the most systematically constructed sacred book in the world."[115]

Qur'ānic exegetes seeking to establish the orderly arrangement of their canon had their work cut out for them more clearly than did their counterparts in most other major scriptural traditions. For the *sūrahs*, or chapters, in the Qur'ān are generally arbitrary and haphazard in their internal arrangement.[116] In most of the *sūrahs*, "not only do abrupt and often bewildering changes of construction, content and situation abound, but there are also numerous repetitions, modifications and even contradictions of arguments."[117] Moreover, the overall order of the *sūrahs* within the Qur'ān is determined principally by the mechanical criterion of diminishing length.

Nevertheless, traditional and modern Muslim commentators have ascribed an almost divine order to the Qur'ān, attributing it to the Prophet who composed the Qur'ān under divine inspiration.[118] According to the great commentator al-Tabarī, "Among the most noble of the meanings by which our Book is distinguished over previous scriptures are its marvellous order, its extraordinary formal coher-

[113] E. J. Goodspeed, *New Chapters in New Testament Study* (New York: Macmillan, 1937), p. 61.

[114] Northrop Frye, *The Great Code: The Bible and Literature* (San Diego: Harcourt Brace Jovanovich, Harvest/HBJ Books, 1982), p. 193; for other arguments by Frye for the unity and coherence of the Bible, see pp. 199–201 and 225.

[115] Northrop Frye, *Anatomy of Criticism: Four Essays* (Princeton: Princeton University Press, 1973), p. 315. Frye's argument regarding the unity and coherence of the Bible has more recently been affirmed by Gabriel Josipovici, who has focused an entire book on "the issue of whether the bible is a unity or a series of fragments" (*Book of God*, p. 28). Pointing to such evidence as the "perfect correspondence between Old and New Testaments," particularly the first of the four New Testament sections (the four Gospels), echoing the five books of Moses, and the second section (the Acts of the Apostles) matching the historical books of the Old Testament (pp. 40–42), Josipovici argues that "the Bible is a unity and not a random collection of books or traditions" (p. 23).

[116] R. Paret, "The Qur'ān - I," in Beeston et al., eds., *Arabic Literature*, p. 186.

[117] A. Jones, "The Qur'ān - II," ibid., p. 233.

[118] Charles J. Adams, "Abū'l-A'lā Mawdūdī's *Tafhīm al-Qur'ān*," in Rippin, ed., *Approaches*, p. 311.

ence, and the unique nature of its compositional structure."[119] Modern scholars as well have proclaimed that "the Qur'ān possesses coherence and order of the highest degree," that "the textual order of the Qur'ān is divine and not random," and that "the whole, once complete, is perfectly closely knit, the themes flowing gracefully throughout."[120] One of these modern commentators even discerns "a mathematical pattern of the alphabet" in the arrangement of the Book, although he does not spell out this pattern.[121] Another contemporary scholar posits an order within the individual *sūrahs*, which he characterizes as "well-knit unit[s] constructed around a main theme with an introduction, a logical enlargement of the subject, and an ending."[122]

Recently, even a speech-act theorist has entered the act, pointing out that the traditional arrangement of the Qur'ān as a whole "preserves a fairly uniform distribution of juridical, theological, and paraenetic materials throughout the text so that liturgical reading (reciting) from beginning to end, or simply continuously, presents auditors with uniform ranges of semantic notions and frames of reference that are generally characteristic of Quranic symbolism." Thus, the reciting of the Qur'ān by the traditional arrangement is "an intelligible speech act within Muslim culture."[123] The speech-act interpretation of the arrangement of the Qur'ān may even find some support in a Qur'ānic verse (*sūrah* 17:107): "We have divided the Koran into sections so that you may recite it to the people with deliberation."[124]

Perhaps speech-act theory could also make some sense of the order and arrangement of the Veda. Modern Hindu philosophers and scholars, such as Aurobindo Ghose, have indeed insisted that such an order exists, that the Vedic *mantras* are coherent and consistent.[125] An

---

[119] Al-Tabarī, *The Commentary on the Qur'ān*, by Abū Ja'far Muhammad B. Jarīr al-Tabarī, being an abridged translation of *Jāmi' al-bayān 'an ta'wīl āy al-Qur'ān*, with an introduction and notes by J. Cooper (Oxford: Oxford University Press, 1987), vol. 1, p. 80.

[120] Khurrmm Murad, *Way to the Qur'ān* (London: Islamic Foundation, 1985), p. 92; Khalifa, *The Sublime Qur'ān*, pp. 62 and 40; Fazlur Rahman, *Islam and Modernity: Transformation of an Intellectual Tradition* (Chicago: University of Chicago Press, 1982), p. 144.

[121] Khalifa, *The Sublime Qur'ān*, p. 107.

[122] Boullata, "Rhetorical Interpretation," p. 149.

[123] Richard C. Martin, "Understanding the Qur'ān in Text and Context," *History of Religions* 21, no. 4 (May 1982): 371–372. According to Kimura Eiichi, the order of the sayings in some chapters of the *Analects* of Confucius may be explained on a similar principle—that they were joined together in their present form for purposes of recital and memorization. Kimura, "Rongo no Gaku-ji-hen ni tsuite" (On *Hsüeh-erh-p'ien* [the *Book of Learning*] of the *Analects of Confucius*), in *Nippon Chūgoku Gakkai-Hō* (Bulletin of the Sinological Society of Japan), no. 19 (1967), p. 57.

[124] Qur'ān 17:107, trans. in Dawood, *The Koran*, p. 241.

[125] A. K. Pateria, *Modern Commentators of Veda* (Delhi: B. R. Publishing, 1985), p. 84.

ascription of a cosmological order to the Veda even appears in the
Prashna Upanishad, which correlates the Rig Veda with the world of
man, the Yajur Veda with the middle heavenly regions, and the Sāma
Veda with the Supreme Spirit.[126] But Vedantic commentators generally limited their systematizing efforts to the more modest confines of
the Upanishads. The *Vedāntasāra*, a popular fifteenth-century introduction to Vedānta, for example, contains an elaborate exposition of
the order of one of the longer upanishads, the Chāndogya, which is
supposedly organized by a number of "character signs."[127] At least
one modern Vedantist has invented a sort of order for the Upanishads as a whole by linking specific schools of Vedānta with particular
upanishads.[128]

The quest for order and coherence in the Upanishads, far from
being a dry scholastic exercise, may have profound spiritual consequences. To those who see only the variety of the Upanishads and
not their underlying unity, as Juan Mascaro has pointed out, the
words of the Brihadāranyaka Upanishad might serve as a warning:
"Who sees variety and not the unity wanders on from death to
death."[129]

The existential or spiritual consequences of a failure to recognize
order and unity in the Homeric poems may not be quite so serious as
with the Upanishads. Nevertheless, critics, especially in modern
times, have devised such extravagant and imaginative testimonials to
the order and coherence of Homer that they are worthy of literary
recognition in their own right. The eighteenth-century critic Henry
Felton, for example, wrote: "Homer's Harp was as powerful to com-
mand his scattered incoherent Pieces into the beautiful Structure of
a Poem, as Amphion's was to summon the Stones into a Wall."[130] A
more geometric imagination, that of Cedric H. Whitman, sees in the
Iliad "a scheme purely and even abstractly architectonic. Not only are
certain whole books of the poem arranged in self-reversing, or bal-
ancing, designs, but the poem as a whole is, in a way, an enormous
hysteron proteron, in which books balance books and scenes balance

[126] *The Upanishads*, trans. Juan Mascaro (Harmondsworth, Eng.: Penguin Books, 1985), p. 73.
[127] Swami Nikhilananda, *Vedāntasāra; or, The Essence of Vedānta of Sadānanda Yogīndra* (Calcutta: Advaita Ashrama, 1978), p. 105.
[128] T. G. Manikar, *The Making of the Vedānta* (Delhi: Ajanta Publications, 1980), p. 159.
[129] Brihadāranyaka Upanishad, quoted in Mascaro, "Introduction" to *The Upani-shads*, p. 11.
[130] Henry Felton, *Dissertation on Reading the Classics, 1713*, quoted in Donald M. Foers-ter, *Homer in English Criticism: The Historical Approach in the Eighteenth Century* (New Ha-ven: Yale University Press, 1947), pp. 18–19.

scenes by similarity or antithesis, with the most amazing virtuosity."[131] The quest for geometric order in the *Aeneid* as well has inspired at least one modern critic to identify more than a thousand Golden Section ratios in that poem.[132]

Confucian commentators were probably even more concerned than their counterparts in most major traditions with establishing the order and coherence of the books in their canon. As discussed above in chapter 2, the integration of the canon, the demonstration of how the Confucian classics were related to one another and to various aspects of the cosmos, was one of the major issues in the intellectual history of the Han era. Han Confucians' particular concern with this issue may be ascribed in part to the prominent role they attributed to the Sage in arranging and editing the classics. If this, after all, was the primary achievement of the Great Sage and Teacher of Ten Thousand Generations, then the classics must be well ordered indeed. God, the Holy Spirit, the Archangel Gabriel, the Breath of the Eternal, or whoever was responsible for the arrangement of the Bible, the Qur'ān, or the Veda, presumably had other personae more significant than that of an organizer or redactor of scriptural or classical texts. But this was not necessarily so with Confucius. Further, the great diversity of the books in the Confucian canon (or canons), and the fact that they were more clearly marked off from one another than were those in most other major traditions, made the issue of their overall order and arrangement an obvious and pressing one.

Once the Confucian canon was integrated and systematized, principally by correlating each book in it with some aspect of the cosmos or of the political or moral universe, later commentators, especially Neo-Confucians, turned their attention to the pedagogical order of the classics. This was an especially important concern with the Four Books canonized in the Sung. For one of the main rationales for identifying these books as a canonical unit was that they supposedly presented a complete Confucian curriculum. According to the early-Ming scholar-official Fang Hsiao-ju (1357–1402), one should "begin with the *Great Learning* to rectify the foundations, follow it with the

---

[131] Cedric H. Whitman, "Geometric Structure of the *Iliad*," in Bloom, ed., *Modern Critical Views: Homer*, p. 120.

[132] Ruthven, *Critical Assumptions*, pp. 17–18. Homer and Vergil were not the only classical authors for whose works ancient and medieval commentators attempted to establish an order. Medieval commentators gave considerable attention to the structure and composition of the Aristotelian corpus, much more so than have modern interpreters of Aristotle. Niels Jorgen Green-Pedersen, *The Tradition of the Topics in the Middle Ages: The Commentaries on Aristotle's and Boethius' 'Topics'* (Munich: Philosophia, 1984), p. 99.

book by Mencius to activate the spirit, proceed to the *Analects* to observe equilibrium, and bind it with the *Doctrine of the Mean* to meet the sources. Afterward one may proceed to the Six Classics."¹³³ The unity of the Four Books, in contrast to that of the Six Classics, was thus more pedagogical than cosmological. As for the order in which the original classics should be approached, the general consensus was that the *Change* and the *Spring and Autumn Annals*, the most profound and subtle books in the canon, should come last in the order of study.¹³⁴

Confucians were not alone in setting out a pedagogical as well as logical or cosmological order for the books in their canon. Christian biblical exegetes beginning with Origen arrayed the wisdom books in the Old Testament (Proverbs, Ecclesiastes, and the Song of Solomon) in such a sequence. According to Beryl Smalley, "the traditional view [was] that Proverbs was written for beginners, Ecclesiastes for the advanced, the Canticle for the perfect."¹³⁵ Origen, moreover, correlated these three books of Solomon with the traditional divisions of Greek philosophy—moral, natural, and contemplative—which, he said, should be studied in just that order, as well as with the three stages of the Christian life—purgative, contemplative, and unitive.¹³⁶ In so prescribing a *cursus* for the wisdom books in the Old Testament, Origen was perhaps influenced by Neo-Platonic commentators who established reading orders for the Platonic dialogues. By following such an order, the student was "to ascend gradually through the different levels of virtues—'political' (the *Gorgias*), 'cathartic' (the *Phaedo*), and 'contemplative' (the *Cratylus*, *Theaetetus*, *Sophist*, *Statesman*, *Phaedrus*, and *Symposium*)—ending at the *Philebus*, 'because in it he [Plato] discusses the Good.' "¹³⁷

¹³³ Fang Hsiao-ju, "Hsüeh-pien" (Critiques on Studies), in *Hsün-chih-chai chi* (Collected Writings from the Hall of the Humble Will), SPPY ed., 6.8a. During the Ming era, however, students of the classics frequently read the Four Books in another order, proceeding from the *Great Learning* to the *Doctrine of the Mean* to the *Analects* to the *Mencius*. See Sano Koji, "Mindai ni okeru kishō—Chūgokujin to keisho" (On the Chinese Method of Learning the Ssu-shu and the Wu-ching, Especially during the Ming Dynasty—The Confucian Classics and the Chinese Mind), in *Nippon Chūgoku Gakkai-Hō* (Bulletin of the Sinological Society of Japan), no. 33 (1981), p. 123.

¹³⁴ See, for example, *Ching-i k'ao* 296.5a (vol. 8), quoting Lu T'ien (1042–1102); and *Ching-i k'ao* 296.13a (vol. 8), quoting Liu Yin.

¹³⁵ Smalley, *Study of the Bible*, p. 137.

¹³⁶ Rowan A. Greer, "Introduction" to Origen, *Origen* [Selections], trans. Greer (New York: Paulist Press, 1979), p. 23; Origen, "The Prologue to the Commentary on the Song of Songs," ibid., p. 232.

¹³⁷ Michael Dunn, "Iamblichus, Thrasyllus, and the Reading Order of the Platonic Dialogues," in *The Significance of Neoplatonism*, ed. R. Baine Harris (Norfolk, Va.: International Society for Neoplatonic Studies, 1976), p. 59.

Confucian commentators, again like their counterparts in other traditions, also attempted to establish the internal order of individual books in their canon. In fact, one of the canonical appendices to the *Classic of Change*, the "Hsü-kua" (Order of the Hexagrams), is devoted to explaining the sequence of hexagrams in that classic, principally by connecting the names of the successive hexagrams with one another. Later exegetes also argued that the chapters in the "Great Commentary" to the *Change* follow one another in good order, with one chapter, for example, discussing the Way of heaven and the next the Way of man.[138] Chu Hsi's commentaries on the Four Books, especially on the *Great Learning* and *Doctrine of the Mean*, placed special emphasis on setting out the order of those newly canonized texts. As Daniel Gardner has observed of Chu's commentary on the *Great Learning*, "Every effort is made by Chu to explain how one statement of the text relates to another, or one chapter to another."[139] Chu even revised the arrangement of the received text of this classic in order to restore what he believed to be the "natural order" of the work intended by the Sage.[140]

· · · · ·

For many of our contemporaries, a third general commentarial assumption common to most major traditions—that the canon is self-consistent, that internal contradictions in it are only apparent—is more of a live issue than the first two. Modern-day adherents of a tradition, believers, might admit that their canon is not comprehensive, that it does not include all knowledge or all truth. They might find some place in the world for secular learning, philosophy, or science. They might also acknowledge that their classical or scriptural text lacks something in the way of orderliness or coherence. Divine revelations and sagely utterances, after all, sometimes proceed by fits and starts, and do not always meet the formal standards of the classical rhetor. But to admit the existence of significant internal contradictions in the canon is a more momentous matter, inasmuch as it seriously undermines the canon's claim to truth. For truth, even if it is not really one and indivisible, must, by most estimations, at least be non-self-contradictory, internally consistent. Moreover, even if a

[138] Wang Fu-chih, *Chou-I nei-chuan* (Inner Commentary on the *Chou Change*), 5.16b, in *Ch'uan-shan I-hsüeh* ([Wang] Ch'uan-shan's Studies on the *Change*) (Taipei: Kuang-wen shu-chü, 1971 reprint), 1:486.

[139] Daniel K. Gardner, *Chu Hsi and the Ta-hsüeh: Neo-Confucian Reflection on the Confucian Canon* (Cambridge: Harvard University Press, 1986), p. 44.

[140] Ibid., pp. 24, 35, and 36.

canon is not believed to harbor "the Truth" in some profound religious sense, the exposure of significant internal contradictions in it would certainly threaten its intellectual respectability. As Maimonides remarked, "If . . . two original propositions are evidently contradictory, but the author has simply forgotten the first when writing down the second in another part of his compilation, this is a very great weakness, and that man should not be reckoned among those whose speeches deserve consideration."[141] Faced with the existence of such contradictory propositions in the *Physics* of Aristotle, the master of those who know, Roger Bacon averred that since "so great an author does not contradict himself," then one of the two statements must be "falsely translated or is in need of exposition."[142] The great eleventh-century Vedantic commentator Rāmānuja similarly argued that "when contradictory statements occur in the Vedas and in the works that follow in the footsteps of the Vedas, one of them must be interpreted differently from what it may seem to convey, so as to reconcile it with the statement (or statements) of which the meaning is otherwise determined."[143]

Nevertheless, the establishment of a canon's internal consistency is much more important in some traditions than in others. Whereas Vedānta, for example, finds its principal raison d'être in harmonizing the key doctrines in the main scriptures of its tradition, chiefly the Upanishads, the *Bhagavad Gītā*, and the *Brāhma Sūtra*,[144] the issue of intellectual harmony is by comparison minor in most Homeric criticism. When great Homer nodded, the result was generally only a literary flaw, not a challenge to the integrity of an entire tradition.

But while Western critics and commentators in late antiquity were not centrally concerned with resolving apparent intellectual contradictions in the Homeric poems, some, such as the Middle Platonist

---

[141] Moses Maimonides, *"Guide of the Perplexed*, Part One, Introduction, in *A Maimonides Reader*, ed. and annot. Isadore Twersky (New York: Behrman House, 1972), p. 245.

[142] Bacon, "The *Opus Majus*, Pt. 2, Chap. 5," in *Selections*, vol. 2, p. 32.

[143] *The Vedānta Sūtras with the Commentary of Rāmānuga* II.i.18., trans. George Thibaut, in *A Source Book in Indian Philosophy*, eds. Sarvepalli Radhakrishnan and Charles A. Moore (Princeton: Princeton University Press, 1957), p. 563.

[144] According to V. S. Ghate, "these five [Vedantic] systems may be supposed to have come into existence in the course of the attempts to reconcile and deduce a system from the apparently contradictory passages of the Upanishads." Ghate, *The Vedānta: A Study of the Brahma-Sūtras with the Bhāsyas of S'amkara, Rāmānuja, Nimbārka, Madhva, and Vallabha*, Government Oriental Series, class c, no. 1 (Poona: Bhandarkar Oriental Research Institute, 1960), p. 47. Hajime Nakamura likewise affirms that "the Vedānta school from its original inception appeared with the explicit purpose of harmonizing the contradictory views in the Upanisads." Nakamura, *A History of Early Vedānta Philosophy*, trans. Trevor Leggett et al. (Delhi: Motilal Banarsidass, 1983), pt. 1, pp. 480–481.

Numenius, were absorbed in trying to reconcile Homer with other great ancient authorities, particularly Plato, on such questions as the fate of souls after death.[145] A later figure in the Neo-Platonic tradition, Macrobius, attempted a still wider synthesis, incorporating Vergil and Cicero as well as Homer and Plato. Macrobius held that since these four authorities were infallible, their teachings must not contradict one another.[146] Establishing a general accord among such a diverse array of sages was a far more formidable task than simply harmonizing Homer and Plato on a particular point. As the circle of ancient authorities to be reconciled widened in late-medieval and Renaissance times, the prospect of their ultimate convergence receded farther into the distance, although it also inspired great interpretive ingenuity.

Exegetes in the rabbinic tradition often had more practical reasons for attempting to resolve discrepancies in their canon, chiefly the legal implications of such resolutions. The Torah was, after all, widely regarded as a book of law, as the record of God's commandments for Israel. But for many later commentators, it seems that the reconciliation of apparent contradictions in various parts of the canon became an end in itself, even an obsession. A prominent scholar of the rabbinic school of Shammai, Hananiah ben Hezakiah, for example, is reported to have burned three hundred jars of "midnight oil" in the course of trying to make the Book of Ezekiel agree with the Pentateuch.[147] Some midrashic commentators developed such a heightened sensitivity to discrepancies that a modern scholar remarks of one such instance that "had the midrash not told us that the verses needed to be reconciled, we probably would not have realized it."[148]

With the possible exception of the Vedantists, Christian biblical exegetes were more concerned with the reconciliation of apparent contradictions in their canon than were their counterparts in any other major tradition here surveyed. For most of them, "The first and foremost of all exegetical imperatives was harmonisation and reconciliation."[149] This was especially true of the great Christian commentators of late antiquity. St. Augustine, for example, focused his exegetical

---

[145] Lamberton, "Homer the Theologian," pp. 169–170.

[146] Curtius, *European Literature*, p. 443.

[147] D. S. Russell, *From Early Judaism to Early Church* (London: SCM Press, 1986), p. 41.

[148] Gary C. Porton, *Understanding Rabbinic Midrash: Texts and Commentary* (Hoboken, N.J.: KTAV Publishing, 1985), p. 72.

[149] G. Vermes, "Bible and Midrash: Early Old Testament Exegesis," in *Cambridge History of the Bible*, vol. 1, p. 209. Vermes adds that "a religion which recognised the totality of its scriptures as word of God and rule of life could not accept that some legal and historical biblical passages disagree, and even flatly contradict one another" (p. 209).

attention on devising explicit rules of interpretation to "prove that these apparently contrary and contradictory statements [in the Bible] are neither contrary nor contradictory."[150] St. Justin Martyr (d. 164) remarked: "I would rather acknowledge that I do not understand what is said" than admit the existence of two contradictory passages in Scripture.[151] In the view of the most influential of all early Christian exegetes, Origen, "failure to maintain a consistent harmony of interpretation from the beginning to end of the Bible" smacked of heresy—indeed, was one of its distinctive marks.[152] Origen devoted his chief exegetical efforts to reconciling apparent discrepancies in Scripture. Later exegetes in the Christian tradition developed what is known as the "scholastic method," principally as a way of reconciling differences in the interpretation of canonical texts. The contemporary literary critic Tzvetan Todorov has characterized the form of interpretation that generally dominated exegesis before the seventeenth century as "the study of the text's internal consistency." Only with Spinoza does the more modern concern with "establishing relationships between the various segments of the text" come to the fore.[153]

Although the Qur'ān itself asserts that it is free from inconsistencies,[154] Qur'ānic exegetes often implicitly recognized the existence of significant internal contradictions and discrepancies in their canon. Perhaps the legalistic orientation of much of the Qur'ān and the fact that it was supposed to govern the life of the Muslim community helped to inspire this recognition, or at least gave it more immediacy. For two rules that evidently contradict one another cannot easily be applied simultaneously. In any case, interpreters of the Qur'ān and of the associated oral traditions emanating from the Prophet developed various means of dealing with discrepancies between two canonical pronouncements—for example, representing one as a particular exception to a general rule propounded in the other.[155] But the most widely used method of resolving apparent contradictions was

[150] St. Augustine, "Letter 147: Augustine to the Noble Lady, Pauline, Greeting," chap. 14, in *Augustine of Hippo: Selected Writings*, trans. and intro. Mary T. Clark (New York: Paulist Press, 1984), p. 373.

[151] St. Justin Martyr, *Dial.* LXV.2, quoted in Willis A. Shotwell, *The Biblical Exegesis of Justin Martyr* (London: SPCK, 1965), p. 5.

[152] Origen, *Comm. in Ioan* x.42 and x.18, quoted in M. F. Wiles, "Origen as Biblical Scholar," in *Cambridge History of the Bible*, vol. 1, p. 480.

[153] Tzvetan Todorov, *Symbolism and Interpretation*, trans. Catherine Porter (Ithaca: Cornell University Press, 1986), p. 154.

[154] Rahman, *Islam and Modernity*, p. 143.

[155] N. J. Coulson, *A History of Islamic Law* (Edinburgh: Edinburgh University Press, 1964), pp. 57–58.

through the doctrine of abrogation (*naskh*), "according to which later pronouncements of the Prophet abrogate, i.e., declare null and void, his earlier pronouncements."[156]

If the legalistic orientation of Islam and the Qur'ān helped open the way for the use of the doctrine of abrogation to deal with apparent contradictions, why was rabbinic exegesis of the Torah not driven along similar paths? Perhaps one reason is the strong conviction, already apparent with the compilers of the Palestinian Talmud (*Yerushalmi*), that there were "no gradations in revelation."[157] For nearly every sect or school of Judaism, "each part of the canon of Judaism speaks equally authoritatively," as Jacob Neusner has pointed out; " 'There is neither earlier nor later.' "[158] Hence there was little room in the Jewish tradition for the idea of abrogation, by which later pronouncements revoked earlier ones, to gain a foothold. Thus deprived of such a convenient device in their attempts to resolve apparent contradictions in their canon, rabbinic exegetes were driven to greater feats of exegetical ingenuity than their counterparts in Islam.

Most Vedantists shared with Jewish midrashists the conviction that every part of their canon was equally authoritative, even if in practice they tended to focus their attention on specific parts or even verses of scripture, particularly in the Upanishads. With Vedantists, too, the doctrine of the abrogation of earlier by later pronouncements was unlikely to arise, since the Veda was, after all, supposed to be eternal and therefore simultaneous. Vedānta as well as the allied school of Mīmāmsā ("the discussion and consideration of doubtful points of the actual performance of the rituals"[159]) were particularly concerned with demonstrating the internal harmony of this Vedic revelation— that "there is no inconsistency or contradiction in the sacred books," that the scriptures "are coherent and consistent in every respect and do not contradict one another."[160] Inasmuch as the scriptures to

---

[156] Arthur Jeffery, *Islam: Muhammad and His Religion* (Indianapolis: Bobbs-Merrill, Library of Liberal Arts, 1958), p. 66. For an account of the Qur'ānic sources of the doctrine of abrogation, see Alfred Guillaume, *Islam* (Harmondsworth, Eng.: Penguin Books, 1986), p. 187. On the great importance of abrogation in Qur'ānic exegesis, see David S. Powers, "The Exegetical Genre *nāsikh al-Qur'ān wa mansūkhuhu*," in Rippin, ed., *Approaches*, p. 123.

[157] Neusner, *Judaism*, p. 44. Another reason why most Jews rejected the doctrine of abrogation is that it implies that the divine will is mutable. Powers, "The Exegetical Genre," pp. 126–127.

[158] Neusner, *Judaism*, p. 1.

[159] This characterization of Mīmāmsā appears in Nakamura, *Early Vedānta*, p. 410.

[160] Thadani, *Mīmāmsā*, p. 8; Sengaku Mayeda, *A Thousand Teachings: The Upadesasahasri of Sankara*, trans. and annot. Mayeda (Tokyo: University of Tokyo Press, 1979), p. 49. On the relationships between Vedānta and Mīmāmsā, "the two great systems of

which the Vedantists referred evidently do contradict one another on such crucial issues as the nature of Brahman,[161] accomplishing this was no easy task. It taxed the ingenuity of the greatest philosophers in the Hindu tradition, including Shankara and Rāmānuja, both of whom took as their point of departure "the task of showing that the Upanishads, the *Bhagavadgītā*, and the *Brāhma Sūtra* represent a single consistent system."[162] Some of the great ideas and profound insights attributed to these Vedantists may be intimately related to their exegetical enterprises, may even be products of them. For example, Shankara evidently formulated his concept of *māyā* ("illusion" or "fabrication") in order to reconcile inconsistencies in the Upanishads.[163]

The obverse of the Vedantists' special concern with the elimination or explanation of apparent contradictions in canonical works was their high regard for harmony and reconciliation. Hindus, both in medieval and in modern times, have been particularly drawn to those canonical texts and philosophical schools, such as the *Bhagavad Gītā* and Vedānta, which seem to synthesize or reconcile most successfully diverse philosophical teachings and sectarian points of view. Thus, this widely recognized attribute of Indian culture may be traced to the exegetical orientation of medieval Hindu commentarial traditions, especially Vedānta.

Confucian commentators were less concerned with reconciling apparent contradictions in their canon than were Vedantists or biblical exegetes. One possible explanation for this is that the Confucian canon, especially the Five or Six Classics, is so diverse that points of conflict were not so conspicuous. It would require even more imagination than that of a midrashist to see a contradiction between a royal court ode included in the *Songs Classic* and a divinatory prognostication from the *Classic of Change*.

---

the orthodox Brahmanical tradition," see Nakamura, *Early Vedānta*, pp. 336 and 409–410.

[161] According to Arvind Sharma, the *Bhagavad Gītā*, one of the principal scriptures that the Vedantists sought to incorporate within their system, is "itself conscious of some apparent contradictions." Sharma, *The Hindu Gītā: Ancient and Classical Interpretations of the Bhagavadgītā* (London: Duckworth, 1986), p. xii.

[162] Eliot Deutsch and J.A.B. van Buitenen, eds., *A Source Book of Advaita Vedānta* (Honolulu: University Press of Hawaii, 1971), p. 72.

[163] Ghate, *The Vedānta*, p. 21. Attempts to resolve exegetical problems stimulated theological developments in other traditions, as Joseph M. Kitagawa has noted: "Jewish, Christian and Islamic theologies have been decisively influenced by the hermeneutical developments of their canons." Kitagawa, "Some Remarks on the Study of Sacred Texts," in *The Critical Study of Sacred Texts*, ed. Wendy Doniger O'Flaherty (Berkeley, Calif.: Graduate Theological Union, 1979), p. 232.

Nevertheless, significant discrepancies did appear in the ideas expressed in some parts of the canon, especially in the relatively homogeneous Four Books canonized by the Sung Neo-Confucians. An example of such a disjunction is on the question of the nature of human nature, an issue on which Mencius disagreed with Hsün-tzu and even, it seemed, with Confucius. When such questions arose, most Confucian commentators sought reconciliation, attempting to establish that the ideas of the ancient sages were really in harmony with one another.[164] In fact, much Neo-Confucian discourse centered on such issues. In Yi dynasty Korea, for example, the so-called four-seven debate, which focused on the question of how to mediate the disjunction between the "four beginnings," or sprouts of virtue, in *Mencius* and the "seven emotions" referred to in the *Doctrine of the Mean* and the "Record of Music" went on for centuries. Absorbing the energies of some of Korea's greatest Neo-Confucian scholars, it was one of the two most important affairs in the history of Confucian thought in Korea. Indeed, "The intellectual fervor aroused by these debates eventually resulted in the formation of four schools of Korean Neo-Confucianism," as Youn Sa-soon has noted.[165]

. . . . .

The three commentarial assumptions discussed above are probably the most universal, or at least the most widely articulated, in the major traditions surveyed. But at least three others are more frequently argued with reference to particular books or parts of canons rather than with reference to canons as a whole: namely, that the classics are moral, that they are profound, and that they contain nothing superfluous or insignificant. A final, more problematic presupposition focuses on the issue of the relative clarity or obscurity of the classics.

That the classics are moral, or that they accorded with contemporary standards of morality, was not generally affirmed in every tradition. Although modern Islamic scholars have insisted that the Qur'ān's ethics are "its essence" and that Islam is "moralistic to the core"—even today, the Qur'ān is used as a primary school text to teach moral and religious duties[166]—no less an authority than Vol-

---

[164] See, for example, Ts'ai Shih-ming, *Ou-yang Hsiu ti sheng-p'ing yü hsüeh-shu* (Ou-yang Hsiu's Life and Scholarship) (Taipei: Wen-shih-che ch'u-pan she, 1980), p. 73.

[165] Youn Sa-soon, "The Korean Controversy over Chu Hsi's View on the Nature of Man and Things," in *Chu Hsi and Neo-Confucianism,* ed. Wing-tsit Chan (Honolulu: University Press of Hawaii, 1986), p. 570.

[166] Rahman, *Islam and Modernity,* p. 154; Adams, "Abū'l-A'lā Mawdūdī's *Tafhīm al-Qur'ān,*" p. 316; Geo Widengren, "Holy Book and Holy Tradition in Islam," in *Holy*

taire wrote that according to the Sunnites, the Qur'ān "has the face of an angel and the face of a beast; do not be shocked by the snout of the beast, and reverence the face of the angel!"[167] A number of Christian exegetes in late antiquity were, however, shocked by the snout of the beast exhibited in parts of the Old Testament, by its crudities and vulgarities, and even sought to decanonize all or parts of that document principally for that reason.[168] But biblical commentators, loath to abandon a large part of their canon, more frequently resorted to such strategies and devices as allegorical and typological exegesis in order to deal with cases in which God or one of the great patriarchs apparently flouted good morality. A medieval exegete, for example, interpreted God's demand that Abraham sacrifice Issac as a sign pointing toward God's own sacrifice of his only begotten Son.[169] The necessity of allegorical exegesis in interpreting the Old Testament was underlined by Origen, who queried: "Who will be so contentious an upholder of the historical sense, who so brutal, that he will not in horror take refuge of necessity in the sweetness of allegory?"[170]

In pedagogically oriented traditions, such as the Homeric and the Confucian, in which the classics were often used as school texts, the issue of apparent immorality in the classics was an especially pressing one. For inasmuch as education in these traditions was much concerned with ethical training, moral lapses in the very texts that were supposed to teach good behavior to the young could hardly be overlooked. In the Confucian tradition, the issue of apparent immorality in the classics arose especially with respect to the *Songs Classic*, which, although it was not a primary school text, did occupy a significant place in Neo-Confucian pedagogy.

It is unlikely that many of the verses in the *Songs* were composed primarily as media for moral instruction. In fact, some of them seem to countenance or depict what later Confucian commentators regarded as lascivious behavior. Nevertheless, by the age of Confucius, the *Songs* had apparently been transposed from the musical to the

Book and Holy Tradition, eds. F. F. Bruce and E. G. Rupp (Grand Rapids, Mich.: William B. Eerdmans, 1968), p. 232.

[167] Voltaire, "Secte: Sect," in *Philosophical Dictionary* (Harmondsworth, Eng.: Penguin Books, 1983), p. 376.

[168] Robert M. Grant, *A Short History of the Interpretation of the Bible*, rev. ed. (New York: Macmillan, 1972), pp. 62 and 69. Grant comments that "among the Christian intelligentsia of the second century, revulsion from the Old Testament must have been widespread. It was, to an educated Greek, an unpleasant book. Its legislation seemed trivial, and some of its morality was clearly immoral" (p. 69).

[169] Gellrich, *Idea of the Book*, pp. 130–131.

[170] Origen, *Homilia in Numeros* XVI.9, quoted in Smalley, *Study of the Bible*, p. 9.

ethical realm.[171] Confucius himself, according to the *Analects*, summed up the purport of the *Songs*: "In thinking do not be depraved."[172] The "Great Preface" (Ta-hsü) to the *Songs*, composed during the Han era, elaborated this ethical emphasis, remarking that the sage-rulers of old composed the *Songs* in order to "regulate [relations between] husband and wife, achieve filiality and integrity, liberalize human ethical relations, praise educational enlightenment, and transform customs and manners."[173] Later commentators, especially Neo-Confucians, took the *Songs* as a repository of models of moral conduct.[174]

The *Songs* was not the only one of the Confucian classics that came to be regarded primarily as a source of moral teaching and ethical exemplars. In fact, some of the classics, especially the Four Books, were so obviously concerned with ethical instruction that the point hardly had to be made at all. But the incorporation of even the *Songs Classic* into the realms of moral pedagogy demonstrates the pervasiveness of the presupposition in the Confucian tradition that the classics are moral, are indeed the touchstones of morality. The same might be said of the *Spring and Autumn Annals*, which, to the naked eye of the outside observer, is not much concerned with ethical instruction, or indeed with much of anything apart from recording scattered historical events as succinctly and dispassionately as possible. Yet, later commentators insisted strongly that the main purport and purpose of the *Annals* is moral pedagogy. "The *Spring and Autumn Annals*," remarked the Sung commentator Lü Ta-kuei (1227–1275), "is a book that upholds heavenly principles and curbs human desires."[175] His contemporary, Wang Hsi, insisted that the essentials of the *Annals* are solely in its "concentrating on the three bonds [in human relationships] and the five constant virtues and in clarifying moral principles to the utmost."[176] But Sung Neo-Confucians were not the first to moralize the *Annals*. Even the three primary commentaries (*san-chuan*) to that classic show a strongly ethical bent. A partic-

---

[171] C. H. Wang, *The Bell and the Drum: Shih Ching as Formulaic Poetry in an Oral Tradition* (Berkeley: University of California Press, 1974), p. 5.

[172] *Analects* 2:2.

[173] *Mao-Shih Cheng chien* (The *Songs* [According to the] Mao [Recension] with the Commentary by Cheng [Hsüan]), SPPY ed., 1.1b.

[174] See, for example, Chu Hsi, *Ssu-shu chi-chu, Ta-hsüeh* (Great Learning), p. 11.

[175] Lü Ta-kuei, "Lun fu-tzu tso Ch'un-ch'iu" (Discussion of the Master's Composition of the *Spring and Autumn Annals*), from *Ch'un-ch'iu lun* (Discussions on the *Spring and Autumn Annals*), in *T'u-shu chi-ch'eng* 56:1890.

[176] Wang Hsi, quoted in Sung Ting-tsung, *Ch'un-ch'iu Sung-hsüeh fa-wei* (A Disclosure of the Subtleties of Sung Studies on the *Spring and Autumn Annals*) (Taipei: Wen-shih-che ch'u-pan she, 1986), p. 42.

ularly famous and widely quoted moralistic characterization of the *Annals*, attributed to the Han cosmologist Tung Chung-shu, appears in the "Author's Preface" (Tzu-hsü) to Ssu-ma Ch'ien's *Historical Records*:

> Now the *Spring and Autumn Annals* with respect to what is above clarifies the Way of the three kings, and with respect to what is below discerns the rules of human affairs. It dispels doubts, clarifies right and wrong, settles hesitations, makes the good [appear] good and the evil evil, praises the worthy and slights the unworthy.[177]

Convinced that the primary purport of the *Annals* was in the exposition of such moral principles and standards, Chu Hsi condemned the *Tso Commentary* on the grounds that it "discusses right and wrong in terms of success and failure and is not based on the correctness of moral principles. It recognizes only that there is profit and harm, and does not recognize that there are moral principles."[178] Thus, the moralizing historiography of the *Tso Commentary*, noted by such observers as P. van der Loon and David Johnson,[179] was apparently not thorough or rigorous enough for Chu Hsi.

The early divinatory strata of the *Change*, as with the *Annals*, are not much concerned with moral pedagogy. But some of the canonical appendices or commentaries to the classic, especially the "Ta-hsiang chuan" (Commentary on the Great Images), the third of the "Ten Wings," contain what might be characterized as moral treatises. In the words of Iulian Shchutskii, this commentary "is systematically occupied with parallels between the images of the text and ethical norms, as if they were reflected in the texts."[180]

The transformation of rather intractable premoralizing classical materials into handbooks of moral instruction occurred in the Homeric tradition as well as in the Confucian. This is surprising inasmuch as the earliest extant Homeric criticism, particularly that by the Pre-Socratic philosophers Heraclitus and Xenophanes, condemned Homer for his apparent immorality, especially for depicting the gods as engaging in scandalous and riotous behavior. Nevertheless, Helle-

---

[177] Ssu-ma Ch'ien, "T'ai-shih-kung tzu-hsü" (Author's Preface by the Grand Historian), to *Shih-chi* (Records of the Historian), 10 vols. (Beijing: Chung-hua shu-chü, 1975), 10:3297 (*chüan* 70).

[178] Chu Hsi, *Chu-tzu yü-lei* (Classified Conversations of Master Chu) 83.6b-7b, quoted in part in Sung, *Ch'un-ch'iu*, p. 78.

[179] P. van der Loon, "The Ancient Chinese Chronicles and the Growth of Historical Ideals," in *Historians of China and Japan*, eds. W. G. Beasley and E. G. Pulleyblank (Taipei: Rainbow Bridge Book Co., 1971 reprint), p. 27; David Johnson, "Epic and History in Early China: The Matter of Wu Tzu-hsü," *Journal of Asian Studies* 40, no. 2 (February 1981): 265.

[180] Shchutskii, *Researches*, p. 169.

nistic educators and commentators managed to "extract from this fundamentally profane epic a veritable catechism . . . a summarization of man's duties to the gods—more, a handbook of practical morality."[181] Thus, Ulysses' escape from the Sirens "teaches us to flee from temptation, both physical and spiritual."[182] Even Aristotle drew moral lessons from the language and events of the *Odyssey*, interpreting Calypso's advice to "keep your ship outside the spray and the waves" as an expression of the difficulty of "hitting the mean just right."[183] And Horace wrote in his "Epistle to Lollius" that Homer "tells us what is fair and what is foul, what is useful and what is not."[184] The Byzantine scholar Eustathius (b. 1115) maintained that the main concern of the *Odyssey* is virtue, that it is "filled with instruction for men"; and even Arabic commentators created "a Homer who was primarily a purveyor of instructions on how to live."[185] Thus Greek, Roman, Byzantine, and Arabic critics seem to have assumed not only that the Homeric canon was moral, but even, in the words of Eric Havelock, that "the warp and woof of Homer is didactic."[186] Yet it is the Renaissance that probably marked the high point in Western history of the moralization of Homer, and of the *Aeneid*.[187] For example, Coluccio Salutati (1331–1406), a humanist annotator of Vergil, "overlooks nothing from the *Aeneid* that could possibly offer edifying instruction." Thus, "Troy under Priam presents a model of luxurious living and the fate that overtakes men who choose this lifestyle."[188] Finally, a prominent modern critic, Simone Weil, has asserted that Homer "presented a moral system simple and true enough to save contemporary humanity."[189]

[181] H. I. Marrou, *A History of Education in Antiquity*, trans. George Lamb (Madison: University of Wisconsin Press, 1982), p. 10.

[182] Ibid., p. 169.

[183] Aristotle, *Ethics*, bk. 2, in *The Philosophy of Aristotle*, trans. A. E. Wardman and J. L. Creed; annot. Renford Bambrough (New York: New American Library, Mentor Books, 1963), p. 314.

[184] Horace, "Epistle to Lollius" 1.2, quoted in Clarke, *Homer's Readers*, p. 110.

[185] N. G. Wilson, *Scholars of Byzantium* (London: Duckworth, 1983), p. 199.

[186] Eric Alfred Havelock, *Preface to Plato* (Cambridge: Harvard University Press, 1982), p. 61.

[187] For examples of the moralization of Homer by English critics of the Renaissance, see Hale, "Virgil and Homer," p. 126; and George deF. Lord, *Homeric Renaissance: The Odyssey of George Chapman* (London: Chatto and Windus, 1956), pp. 24, 34, and 60–61.

[188] Virginia Brown and Craig Kallendorf, "Two Humanist Annotators of Virgil: Coluccio Salutati and Giovanni Tortelli," in *Supplementum Festivum: Studies in Honor of Paul Oskar Kristeller*, eds. James Hankins et al., Medieval and Renaissance Texts and Studies, vol. 49 (Binghamton, N.Y.: Center for Medieval and Early Renaissance Studies, 1987), pp. 82 and 86.

[189] W. F. Jackson Knight, *Many-Minded Homer: An Introduction*, ed. John D. Christie (New York: Barnes and Noble, 1968), p. 205.

The didacticization of morally refractory classical texts appears in many other major literary traditions besides the Homeric and the Confucian. Medieval Japanese interpretations of the classic *Tale of Genji*, for example, were invariably moral interpretations, usually Confucian or Buddhist.[190] Later performers and redactors of the medieval Japanese epic the *Tale of the Heike* inserted sermons based on the teachings of Pure Land Buddhism into what was originally a rather secular narrative of military conflict between two great houses.[191] The compiler of the classic Chinese novel the *Shui-hu chuan* likewise added Confucian principles and moral commentary to that rather profane cycle of stories which had originated in an oral tradition.[192] Finally, Arabic as well as European Renaissance commentators and critics commonly presented Greek tragedy as "a representation of moral order" that "promotes ethical ideals and stabilizes the values of a culture," despite considerable evidence to the contrary.[193] According to Averroës (1126–1198), tragic poetry is primarily concerned with "honest customs, praiseworthy actions and beautifying beliefs."[194] Even some of the great figures in European literary history could not resist the temptation to moralize Greek tragedy. Goethe's *Iphigenie*, for example, was "designed to improve on the ethical crudity of Euripides' version."[195]

The great Indian epic the *Rāmāyana*, was even more thoroughly, consistently, and even obsessively transformed into an exposition of proper morals, particularly of Hindu *dharma*, in such renditions as that by the famous poet Vālmīki: "In his hand, the narrative ceased to be merely an account of an unprecedented war, or that of a palace intrigue. . . . The pattern that Vālmīki has held up before coming generations is that of human relationships, especially family relationships."[196] In thus moralizing the epic, Vālmīki created four great moral figures: Rāma, "champion of righteousness"; Bharata, "a man

[190] Donald Keene, *World within Walls: Japanese Literature of the Pre-Modern Era, 1600–1867* (New York: Holt, Rinehart, and Winston, 1976), p. 327.

[191] Kenneth D. Butler, "The Textual Evolution of the *Heike Monogatari*," *Harvard Journal of Asiatic Studies* 26 (1966): 6 and 35–36.

[192] Ellen Widmer, *The Margins of Utopia: Shui-hu hou-chuan and the Literature of Ming Loyalism* (Cambridge: Harvard University Press, 1987), p. 82.

[193] Michelle Gellrich, *Tragedy and Theory: The Problem of Conflict since Aristotle* (Princeton: Princeton University Press, 1988), pp. 21 and 172.

[194] Averroës, *Averrois Cordubensis Commentarium Medium in Aristolis Poetriam*, quoted ibid., p. 179.

[195] Reed, *Goethe*, p. 57.

[196] Umashankar Joshi, "Welcome Address," in *Asian Variations in Ramayana: Papers Presented at the International Seminar on 'Variations in Ramayana in Asia; Their Cultural, Social, and Anthropological Significance': New Delhi, January 1981*, ed. K. R. Srinivasa Iyengar (New Delhi: Sahitya Akademi, 1983), p. 23.

of brotherly love"; Laksmana, "marked with goodness"; and Sītā, "the daughter of the gods."[197] Even Vālmīki's *sloka* meter has been characterized as "an emotional response to violence and unrighteousness."[198]

But this moralistic metamorphosis of the *Rāmāyana* left its later redactors and re-creators with the problem of explaining apparent moral lapses on the part of the hero Rāma, who was considered to be an avatar of the Supreme Being. Thus, in Kamban's twelfth-century Tamil version of the epic, the narrative is broken, even disfigured, by a long ethical commentary designed to rationalize Rāma's cowardly killing of the monkey-king Vāli.[199] Such episodes, in fact, form the core of most *Rāmāyana* exegesis and are seriously and vigorously debated by many Indians even today. This is apparent in the most popular English-language rendition, that by Chakravarti Rajagopalachari, which is even more replete with moralistic commentary and ethical asides than such earlier versions as those by Vālmīki, Kamban, and Tulsīdās.

Perhaps the immense popularity of the *Rāmāyana*, which next to the Bible is the world's best-known and most beloved literary work, stems in part from the relative ease with which it may be moralized or didacticized. In this respect it had a great advantage over its more comprehensive counterpart in the Indian epic tradition, the *Mahābhārata*, which one modern commentator has characterized as a "treatise on the science of society" as opposed to an "ethical poem."[200] The *Rāmāyana* tradition, moreover, is flexible enough to accommodate ethical interpretations apart from those which focus on the upholding of Hindu *dharma*. In a Jain rendition of *Rāmāyana*, for example, great emphasis is placed on the Jain doctrine of *ahimsā* (nonharming), and the narrative is interspersed with sermons of Jain monks.[201] In Buddhist versions of the story, Rāma appears as a bodhisattva.[202]

---

[197] Pollock, "Introduction" to *Rāmāyana*, vol. 2, p. 50.

[198] Ibid., p. 16.

[199] This appears in chap. 6 of R. K. Narayan's modern adaptation of Kamban's *Rāmāyana*. See Narayan, *The Ramayana: A Shortened Modern Prose Version of the Indian Epic* (Harmondsworth, Eng.: Penguin Books, 1985), pp. 108–113. For an extensive discussion of the moral ramifications of this episode in Kamban's *Rāmāyana*, see David Shulman, "Divine Order and Divine Evil in the Tamil Tale of Rāma," *Journal of Asian Studies* 38, no. 4 (August 1979): 651–669.

[200] Vinoba Bhave, quoted in Boyd H. Wilson, "Vinoba Bhave's Talks on the Gītā," in *Modern Indian Interpreters of the Bhagavadgītā*, ed. Robert N. Minor (Albany: State University of New York Press, 1986), p. 115. Rāma, moreover, is much more easily presented as a paragon of morality than is Yudhisthira in the *Mahābhārata*, who is "a victim of his own moral vacillation, lack of judgment, and ambition." Pollock, "Introduction" to *Rāmāyana*, vol. 2, p. 40.

[201] K. R. Srinivasa Iyengar, "Introduction," to Iyengar, ed., *Asian Variations*, p. 7.

[202] H. Daniel Smith, *Reading the Rāmāyana: A Bibliographic Guide for Students and Col-*

While the potential and flexibility for moralizing is perhaps not so great with the *Mahābhārata* as with the *Rāmāyana*, numerous didactic treatises interrupt the narrative flow of this other great Indian epic as well. Perhaps the most glaring example is the famous deathbed sermon of Bhimsa which lasts for a record fifty-eight days.[203] Moreover, philosophers in medieval India as well as pedagogues in modern India have emphasized didactic themes in the epic, such as the duties of the warrior caste, honesty, and brotherly love.[204] A modern Western student of the *Mahābhārata* characterizes it as "the tutor of the people for higher religious and moral ideas."[205]

In sum, it seems peculiar that as the gap between the mores portrayed in such classics as the *Songs*, the Homeric poems, and the *Rāmāyana*, on the one hand, and contemporary morality, on the other, widened with the passage of time and with changes in culture and customs, these classics came to be regarded increasingly not only as intrinsically moral, but as standard guides to moral conduct and handbooks of ethical instruction. As K. K. Ruthven observes, "Whenever an admired book is not explicitly moral, moralistic critics often take it upon themselves to show that it is much more moral than we suspect."[206] Thus, Sainte-Beuve affirmed that one of the marks of a "true classic" is that it be written by an author "who has discovered some unequivocal moral truth."[207] Perhaps it is the natural fate of the classics to fall into the hands of didactic critics and exegetes who regard questions of value primarily as questions of morality and who overlook the irony and ambiguity in the classics and in *Existenz* in general. As Jesse Gellrich has remarked of the tale of David and Bathsheba in the Bible, "The biblical narrative makes no attempt to explain away the ironic aspect of events, but exegesis, like myth, refuses to tolerate irony."[208] The ironic and ambiguous aspects of the Book of Job are also frequently overlooked by exegetes as well as by more

---

lege Teachers; Indian Variants on the Rāma-Theme in English Translations, Foreign and Comparative Studies, South Asian Special Publications, no. 4 (Syracuse: Maxwell School of Citizenship and Public Affairs, Syracuse University, 1983), p. 110.

[203] Robert N. Minor, *Bhagavad-Gītā: An Exegetical Commentary* (Columbia, Mo.: South Asia Books, 1982), p. xxii.

[204] Van Nooten, *The Mahābhārata*, pp. 87 and 116.

[205] Joseph Dahlmann, *Genesis des Mahābhārata* (Berlin: F. L. Dames, 1899), p. 142, quoted in James L. Fitzgerald, "India's Fifth Veda: The *Mahābhārata*'s Presentation of Itself," *Journal of South Asian Literature* 20, no. 1 (Winter/Spring 1985): 126.

[206] Ruthven, *Critical Assumptions*, p. 187.

[207] Charles-Augustin Sainte-Beuve, *Qu'est-ce qu'un classique?* quoted in Jan Gorak, *Critic of Crisis: A Study of Frank Kermode* (Columbia: University of Missouri Press, 1987), p. 53.

[208] Gellrich, *Idea of the Book*, pp. 128–129. Robert Lamberton similarly remarks of Proclus' exegesis of Plato's *Cratylus* that it is "indifferent to the irony that most modern readers have detected throughout the dialogue." Lamberton, *Homer*, p. 207.

ordinary readers who see in the rather unlikely figure of Job a moral model of patience.[209] Insofar as morality has more popular appeal than irony and ambiguity, ethical exegesis attracts a larger and more enthusiastic audience than does the bare classic stripped of its moralizing adornments. Small wonder, then, that the moralization of the classics or scriptures is an almost universal theme in world cultural history. Confucian classical scholars, their image as inveterate moralizers notwithstanding, were not unique or even unusual in having advanced such a trend in their own tradition.

However, the Confucian classics, particularly the Neo-Confucian Four Books, are unusual, perhaps even sui generis, in the degree to which they are primarily concerned with moral issues and in the extent to which ethical systems can be convincingly extracted from them without obvious commentarial contortions. The Confucius of the *Analects* probably merits the mantle of moralist more than his counterparts in any other major classical or scriptural tradition. On the other hand, it was after all the Neo-Confucians who canonized the Four Books, including the *Analects*, and who de-emphasized the study of those established books of the Confucian canon which could not be so easily accommodated to their moral philosophy.[210] In this respect, they resembled medieval Christian exegetes who commented most extensively on those books of the Bible that lent themselves most readily to moralization, including the Psalms, the Song of Solomon, and the Gospels.[211]

. . . . .

Of all the major commentarial presuppositions, that the classics or scriptures are profound is probably the least commonly articulated in most traditions. Modern scholars do occasionally offer testimonials to

---

[209] Cyprian was a particularly influential moralizer of Job in the Christian tradition. Victor Saxer, "La Bible chez les pères latins du IIIe siècle," in *Le Monde latin antique et la Bible*, eds. Jacques Fontaine and Charles Pietri (Paris: Editions Beauchesne, 1985), p. 359.

[210] Joseph Adler remarks that the Sung Neo-Confucians "turned to the Four Books in part because these contained more reflections than the Five Classics on such topics as human nature, the source of morality, and humanity's relation to the cosmos." Adler, review of *Chu Hsi and the Ta-hsüeh: Neo-Confucian Reflection on the Confucian Canon* by Daniel K. Gardner, in *The Bulletin of Sung Yuan Studies*, no. 19 (1987), p. 36.

[211] Jacques Verger, "L'Exégèse de l'université," in *Le Moyen Age et la Bible*, eds. Pierre Riché and Guy Lobrichon (Paris: Editions Beauchesne, 1984). Beryl Smalley remarks that "of the Aristotelian corpus both the *De animalibus* and the *Ethics* were favourites with biblical commentators." Smalley, "Essay IV," in *Medieval Exegesis of Wisdom Literature: Essays by Beryl Smalley*, ed. Roland E. Murphy (Atlanta: Scholars Press, 1986), p. 128.

the "unfathomable profundity of the divine speech" recorded in the Torah or the "profundity and depth of idea" of the Upanishads.[212] Among earlier commentators, though, evidence that this was a common assumption often appears more in the form of a negative confirmation than of a positive assertion. For example, as Bernhard Karlgren has pointed out, Confucian commentators frequently argued that a work identified as part of the canon was really a later forgery on the grounds that its contents are "shallow and vulgar."[213] Although Karlgren, the modern philologist, calls this criterion of canonicity "curious and naive," it is evidently based on the assumption that the classics must be profound and refined, the opposite of shallow and vulgar. Another instance of this commentarial assumption being revealed negatively, in places where the rule of profundity or significance apparently lapses, may be found in Origen's commentary on the Book of Numbers. Regarding the meaning of the name of "Oboth" in Numbers 33:43, Origen declares: "Although we have not found an interpretation of this name, nonetheless we do not doubt that in this name as in all the others the logic of the progresses is preserved."[214] Origen thus assumes that every name and number in this canonical book is fraught with significance, that each can be fit in with his own profoundly allegorical interpretation of the text.

Although commentators in most of the traditions surveyed seldom asserted directly and specifically the profundity of their canon, they did extend to great lengths the related idea that the canon is comprehensive, that it includes all significant knowledge or truth or that it covers every realm of the cosmos. A canon of such wide dimensions could hardly fail to measure up to almost any standard of profundity. The "Treatise on Bibliography" of the *Han History*, in fact, indicates that the profundity of the *Classic of Change* arises from its comprehensiveness: "The Way of the *Change* is profound [inasmuch as], with respect to men, it has passed through the [hands of the] three sages [identified by the commentator Wei Chao as Fu Hsi, King Wen, and

[212] Gershom Scholem, *Kabbalah* (New York: New American Library, Meridian Books, 1978), p. 172; Ghate, *The Vedānta*, p. 7.

[213] Bernhard Karlgren, "The Authenticity of Ancient Chinese Texts," in *Bulletin of the Museum of Far Eastern Antiquities*, no. 1 (1929), p. 166. Commentators on the Taoist classics also made such assertions. Kuo Hsiang (d. 312), discussing questionable passages in the received text of the *Chuang-tzu*, argued that "the style of these admixtures is vulgar and unseemly, and has neither profundity nor subtlety." Hence, they must be later interpolations or forgeries, inasmuch as they do not manifest "Master Chuang's vast talent." Quoted in Christopher C. Rand, "Chuang Tzu: Text and Substance," *Journal of Chinese Religions*, no. 11 (Fall 1983): 12–13. Rand discusses the possible sources of this quotation in n. 25, p. 13, of his article.

[214] Origen, "Homily XXVII on Numbers," trans. in Greer, *Origen*, p. 266.

Confucius] and, with respect to eras, lasted through the three ancient [periods of history]."[215]

The idea that the canon is profound may be associated with the last of our traditional commentarial assumptions—that it contains nothing superfluous or trivial, and that there are no unnecessary repetitions. The classics, in other words, are profound throughout, not just in certain key passages. Again, establishing this presupposition was particularly important in the Confucian tradition, for Confucius himself was supposed to have edited or expurgated the precanonical collections that fell into his hands with a view toward eliminating what was superfluous or trivial. To admit that such elements yet remained in the classics was to question Confucius' most celebrated achievement.

On the other hand, Confucian commentators' frequent assertions that the essence of a particular classical text could be summed up in a short compass, even in a phrase or two, might be construed as relegating the preponderance of the text to a less weighty role, perhaps even a weightless one. That such conclusions were drawn by traditional commentators is indicated by Hsü Yu-wang's criticism of Chu Hsi's statement that "the main intent of the *Spring and Autumn Annals* is to punish rebellious ministers and chastise unruly sons . . . to exalt kings and debase hegemons." Hsü objects that this idea does not accord with earlier scholars' assertions that every written character in the *Annals* has some significance.[216]

Aside from Confucian commentators, medieval rabbinic and Christian exegetes also frequently asserted that superfluities and trivialities did not exist in their canons, that significance was to be found everywhere in them.[217] In Jewish exegetical tradition, this belief in "the nonsuperfluous nature of each detail"[218] helped justify the use of such special interpretive techniques as *gematria*, by which each letter of the Hebrew alphabet was read as a numerical value. The numerical values of the letters in the sacred text could then be rearranged or recombined to reveal new levels of meaning. Such interpretations were based on the presupposition that God "in His infinite wisdom

[215] *Han-shu, I-wen-chih chu-shih hui-pien* (Han History "Treatise on Bibliography" with Collected Annotations), comp. Chen Kuo-ch'ing (Beijing: Chung-hua shu-chü, 1983), p. 18.

[216] Hsü Yu-wang, "Hsü" (Preface) to Chang Chün-li, *Ch'un-ch'iu chi-i* (The *Spring and Autumn Annals* with Collected Discussions), in *Ching-i k'ao* 194.11a (vol. 6).

[217] For examples of such statements regarding the Confucian canon, see the quotation from Chao Meng-fu in *Ching-i k'ao* 296.13a (vol. 8) and that from Feng Shih-k'o in *Ching-i k'ao* 297.12b (vol. 8).

[218] Joel Rosenberg, "Bible A: Biblical Narrative," in Holtz, ed., *Back to the Sources*, pp. 36–37.

counted carefully each word" in the entire biblical corpus; nothing in the canon was a product of mere chance.[219] Even syntactical particles and calligraphic ornamentations were fraught with significance.[220] Moreover, apparently superfluous words in the Torah often became objects of special study, inasmuch as "superfluity is taken to imply emphasis."[221] For example, the appearance of three synonymous references to Abraham's homeland in Genesis 12:1 attracted special attention by rabbinic commentators as a highly significant point requiring extensive exegesis.[222]

In sum, the explication of apparent superfluities or repetitions was as important a concern in rabbinic exegesis as the elimination or reconciliation of apparent contradictions was in Vedānta or the explanation of moral lapses was in Rāmāyana commentary. It profoundly influenced the character and development of rabbinic Judaism and distinguished it from other commentarial traditions, which generally focused more of their attention on other issues or assumptions. According to one modern scholar, "The rapt attention given by the rabbis to every nuance of the biblical text is only rivalled by the approach of some modern literary critics to the analysis of poetry."[223]

Prominent Christian commentators of late antiquity and the early Middle Ages also stressed that every detail in the sacred canon had some significance, though not quite as single-mindedly as their rabbinic counterparts. "There is not one jot or tittle," asserted Origen, "written in the Bible which does not accomplish its special work for those capable of using it." St. Jerome (340?–420) likewise affirmed that "in the divine Scriptures every word, syllable, accent and point is packed with meaning."[224] According to the early-medieval encyclopedist Cassiodorus, "there is nothing empty and nothing idle in divine literature, but what is said is always said for some useful purpose."[225] Even the chronological figures and catalogs of names in the

[219] Arthur Green, "Teachings of the Hasidic Masters," ibid., p. 371. A Hindu analogue to gematria, associated with the Mīmāmsā school, is outlined in The Mīmāmsā Sutras of Jaimini, chaps. 1–13, trans. Pandit Mohan Lal Sandal, vol. 27 of The Sacred Books of the Hindus (New York: AMS Press, 1974 reprint), esp. p. x.

[220] José Faur, Golden Doves with Silver Dots: Semiotics and Textuality in Rabbinic Tradition (Bloomington: Indiana University Press, 1986), p. xxviii.

[221] Steinsaltz, The Essential Talmud, p. 225.

[222] James L. Kugel, "Part One. Early Interpretation: The Common Background of Late Forms of Biblical Exegesis," in James L. Kugel and Rowan A. Greer, Early Biblical Interpretation (Philadelphia: Westminster Press, 1986), p. 85.

[223] Maccoby, Early Rabbinic Writings, p. 29.

[224] Origen, Hom. in Ierem. 39, 1, and Jerome, In Eph. 2 (3, 6), quoted in J.N.D. Kelly, Early Christian Doctrines, rev. ed. (San Francisco: Harper and Row, 1978), pp. 61–62.

[225] Cassiodorus, Introduction to Divine and Human Readings, pp. 124–125.

Bible, St. John Chrysostom (345?–407) maintained, have their profound value.[226]

Prominent exegetes in the other traditions here surveyed also contended that there are no superfluities in their sacred texts. The first great Qur'ānic commentator, al-Tabarī, insisted that "there is nothing in the Qur'ān of which people have no need."[227] A prominent contemporary interpreter of the Qur'ān, Ā'isha'Abd al-Rahmān, has asserted that "not even one particle in the Qur'ān is otiose or elliptic."[228] And expounders of the *Rāmāyana* hold that "profound meanings, reflecting the underlying order of the cosmos, inhere in every line of scripture."[229]

Some commentarial traditions do admit that parts of their canon are superfluous. Mīmāmsā, one of the six orthodox schools of Hindu philosophy, for example, maintains that since the purpose of the Veda is to lay down injunctions, to regulate ritual conduct, "those portions of it which do not do so are meaningless."[230] But even Mīmāmsā attempts to save these apparently meaningless passages by relating them in some way to the meaningful ones, or those with injunctions. For example, what appear to be purely factual statements in the Veda, such as that "Vāyu is the swiftest of all deities," are really means of preparing auditors to perform certain actions, to follow certain injunctions, such as that which enjoins the offering of sacrifices to Vāyu. For "Vāyu is a god who will surely be swift in awarding the desired results."[231] Thus, the commentarial assumption that the classics contain no superfluities exerts a powerful attraction even on those who begin their exegetical efforts by denying it.

· · · · ·

There is such a wide range of commentarial opinion on our final proposition—that the classics or scriptures are clear and accessible to

---

[226] Kelly, *Early Christian Doctrines*, p. 62.

[227] Jane Dammen McAuliffe, "Quranic Hermeneutics: The Views of al-Tabarī and Ibn Kathīr," in Rippin, ed., *Approaches*, p. 53.

[228] Boullata, "Rhetorical Interpretation," p. 153.

[229] Philip Lutgendorf, "The View from the Ghats: Traditional Exegesis of a Hindu Epic," *Journal of Asian Studies* 48, no. 2 (May 1989): 281.

[230] Murty, *Revelation and Reason*, p. 214.

[231] Francis X. Clooney, "Why the Veda Has No Author: Language as Ritual in Early Mīmāmsā and Post-Modern Theology," *Journal of the American Academy of Religion* 55, no. 4 (Winter 1987): 672. Mīmāmsā scholars also use allegory to establish the injunctive character of scriptural statements. Shlomo Biderman, "Orthodoxy and Philosophy in India: Philosophical Implications of the Mīmāmsā School," in *Orthodoxy, Heterodoxy and Dissent in India*, eds. S. N. Eisenstadt et al. (Berlin: Mouton, 1984), p. 76.

all—that it had better be called a question, rather than an assumption, in most traditions. While some commentators maintain that the classics are plain and simple enough to be readily understood even without the aid of commentary, others assert that the canon is clear only on certain essential matters, or that extensive exegesis is necessary for understanding the classics. Still others not only declare that the meanings of the classics are obscure, even impenetrable in places, but even say that they were meant to be so. To cite opinions representing all these points of view would require too long a digression.

However, there is one especially notable perspective on the question of the relative clarity or obscurity of the classics that is sharply reflected in the Confucian tradition: the apparent paradox that the classics are easy yet difficult, plain yet obscure. Confucian commentators were especially inclined to so characterize the *Spring and Autumn Annals*, which the Han cosmologist Tung Chung-shu described as "exceedingly obscure yet clear."[232] According to Ch'eng I, although the "*Annals'* larger meaning is easy to see, its subtle words and hidden meanings are hard to know."[233] The Ch'ing commentator Chung Wen-cheng (1818–1877) elaborated on just what was easy and what was difficult about this classic: "Although its statements are easy, getting a thorough understanding is difficult. The words of the Sage are plain, but within them are places of profundity."[234]

The idea that the classics are plain yet mysterious, accessible yet remote, is not confined to Confucian commentary on the *Annals*. A prominent modern Hindu interpreter of the *Bhagavad Gītā*, Vinoba Bhave, characterized that text as both a *shāstra*, which is "meant to be read and understood by everyone," and a *sūtra*, which is "arcane and mystical, requiring an adept interpreter."[235] A modern Homeric scholar, John A. Scott, says of Homer that "a child can comprehend him, and that the wisest man knows that the greatness of Homer, with its simplicity, lies just beyond his grasp," just as the Ch'ing commentator Tiao Pao (1603–1669) wrote of the *Change* that although a child can practice it, a white-haired man cannot fathom it.[236] According to a contemporary Muslim scholar, Fazlur Rahman, the Qur'ān is "simple and uncomplicated," yet "highly complicated—as complicated as

[232] Tung Chung-shu, *Ch'un-ch'iu fan-lu* (Luxuriant Gems of the *Spring and Autumn Annals*) (Taipei: Shang-wu yin-shu-kuan, 1968 reprint), 2.25 ("Chu-lin" chap.).

[233] Ch'eng I, quoted in *Ku-liang pu-chu* (The *Ku-liang Commentary* with Supplementary Commentaries), comp. Chung Wen-cheng, SPPY ed., p. 4a of "Lun-ching" (A Discussion of the Classic). A slightly different rendition of Ch'eng I's words on this point may be found in Sung, *Ch'un-ch'iu*, p. 242.

[234] Chung Wen-cheng, in *Ku-liang pu-chu*, p. 4a of "Lun-ching."

[235] Wilson, "Vinoba Bhave's Talks," p. 115.

[236] Scott, *Homer*, p. 162; Tiao Pao, *I-cho hsü* (Preface to Deliberations on the *Change*), in *Ch'ing-ju hsüeh-an* 15.2b–3a (vol. 1).

life itself."[237] And Maimonides held that the Torah "is both a code of laws for the unlearned and an introduction to philosophy for the elite."[238]

Frank Kermode has suggested that "the belief that a text might be both an open proclamation, available to all" and "a repository of secrets" is widely entertained in regard not only to sacred books but also to secular canons. "Shakespeare is an inexhaustible source of occult readings . . . yet at the same time he is believed to speak plainly, about most of human life, to any literate layman."[239] Similarly, "the themes of Marx's thought are simple and deceptively clear but lend themselves to interpretations among which it is impossible to choose with certainty," as Raymond Aron has pointed out. Marx lends himself to "simplification for the simple and to subtlety for the subtle,"[240] just as "the wise get to the depths [of the *Spring and Autumn Annals*] and their inferiors get to the shallows" (although both obtain some benefit).[241] The classics are thus comprehensive, inexhaustible with respect to their pedagogical as well as cosmological range. This marvelous quality of the classics justifies their use both as primary school texts and as bases for the most arcane philosophical and literary works. That the classics have been widely and successfully used in a number of civilizations for both these purposes indicates that this commentarial proposition regarding the clarity and obscurity, or simplicity and profundity, of the classics may have some basis.[242]

. . . . .

In conclusion, one more question regarding the six or seven commentarial assumptions outlined in this chapter might be raised. That

[237] Rahman, *Islam and Modernity*, p. 137.

[238] Martin D. Yaffe, review of *Joseph Ibn Kaspi's Gevia' Kesif: A Study in Jewish Philosophic Biblical Commentary* by Basil Herring, *Journal of the American Academy of Religion* 52, no. 1 (March 1984): 182.

[239] Kermode, *Genesis of Secrecy*, p. 144.

[240] Aron, *Main Currents*, p. 149.

[241] Tan Chu, *Ch'un-ch'iu tsuan-li* (The *Spring and Autumn Annals* with a Compilation of Examples), quoted in Sung, *Ch'un-ch'iu*, p. 22.

[242] Su Hsün recognized that a canon, if it is to be accepted must contain both clarity and simplicity, on the one hand, and obscurity or profundity on the other, albeit not necessarily in the same canonical book: "The doctrine of the sage was not rejected because the *Rites* gave it clarity and the *Changes* gave it profundity." Su, "I-lun" (Discussion of the *Change*), in *Su Hsün chi* (Collected Writings of Su Hsün) (Taipei: Ho-Lo t'u-shu ch'u-pan she, 1975 reprint), 6.52. I have followed the translation of this passage given in Shchutskii, *Researches*, p. 230. Su credits the *Change* with being obscure as well as profound: "What is clear is easily understandable; what is easily understandable is profaned; and what is profaned is easily rejected. The Sage feared that the Way would be rejected and that the world would return to chaos. Thus, he created the *Change*" (*Su Hsün chi* 6.51).

is, to the extent that this set of assumptions is based on my own rather idiosyncratic reading and understanding, is it not arbitrary? Have I covered all the major possibilities? Could some of the assumptions that evidently overlap with one another be combined to present a more streamlined set of commentarial presuppositions? In short, are not other schemas possible, perhaps even preferable?

I have no ready answer to the above questions except to say that I am not the first to have engaged in such an enterprise and that I have compared my set of commentarial assumptions with a few earlier ones.[243] One of the most useful and illuminating of these is Tzvetan Todorov's set of five "triggers" for exegesis, his "indices" calling for interpretation in the explication of a scriptural text. Todorov's list, which he illustrates by quotations from Philo of Alexandria (d. A.D. 40), consists of "contradiction," "discontinuity," "superfluity," "implausibility," and "inappropriateness."[244] These five, as explained by Todorov (and Philo), may be correlated with my set of commentarial assumptions in the following way: (1) contradiction: the canon is self-consistent; (2) discontinuity: the canon is well ordered or coherent; (3) superfluity: the canon contains no superfluous or trivial elements; (4) implausibility: the canon is everywhere profound and meaningful; and (5) inappropriateness: the canon is moral. The only one of mine missing from Todorov's list is the one having to do with the canon's comprehensiveness; and this point would not normally arise in day-to-day exegesis of a particular scriptural or classical text, but is more frequently discussed by meta-commentators whose Olympian vision spans the canon as a whole.

Other lists of exegetical imperatives or assumptions also contain points in common with my set. These include the account proposed by Geza Vermes, in volume 1 of the *Cambridge History of the Bible*, of

[243] Perhaps the most obvious place to look for concise statements of such assumptions is in the rabbinic rules of exegesis, of which the best known are the seven rules of Hillel, the thirteen rules of Rabbi Elisher ben Ishmael, and the thirty-two rules of Rabbi Eliezer ben Jose the Galilean. See Shotwell, *The Biblical Exegesis of Justin Martyr*, p. 90. But most of these rules have to do with specific techniques and are not statements of general commentarial assumptions or presuppositions regarding the character of the canon. They were, however, held in such high esteem in medieval Judaism that they were actually incorporated into daily morning prayers, and were even regarded as part of the revelation handed down from Sinai. See Susan A. Handelman, *The Slayers of Moses: The Emergence of Rabbinic Interpretation in Modern Literary Theory* (Albany: State University of New York Press, 1982), p. 52.

[244] Todorov, *Symbolism and Interpretation*, pp. 37–38. Another account of what Todorov calls "triggers" for interpretation in Philo, which accords almost as well with my set, may be found in Frederic W. Farrar, *History of Interpretation* [1886] (Grand Rapids, Mich.: Baker Book House, 1961 reprint), p. 22.

"four principal causes" of "pure exegesis": "(I) a scriptural passage contains a word whose exact meaning escaped the interpreter [which may be related to the question of whether the classics are clear or obscure]; (II) it lacks sufficient detail [which may be associated with the assumption that the classics are well ordered or that they are comprehensive]; (III) it seems to contradict other biblical texts [which ties in with the assumption that the classics are self-consistent]; (IV) its apparent meaning is unacceptable [which usually means that the commentator assumes the classics must be moral, and perhaps profound as well]."[245] Again, all but one or two of the assumptions in my set may, with a little imagination, be correlated with points in this list of "triggers" for exegesis. The same may be true of a similar list offered by Shaye J. D. Cohen in his book *From the Maccabees to the Mishnah*: "Usually exegesis is prompted by some sort of difficulty: two laws or narratives seem to contradict each other; the heroes of scripture act in a manner unbecoming their piety and grandeur; the scriptural account seems dull, trivial, obscure, pointless, or absurd, and so on."[246]

The reasons why medieval scribes suppressed or rejected certain passages in a canonical or scriptural text may provide a sort of negative confirmation of my schema, since their reasons for suppression usually reflect their assumptions regarding the character of the canon. According to Marie-Émile Boismard, "a scribe was inclined to suppress words that seemed to him to be obscure, difficult, superfluous, bizarre, scandalous, erroneous, or in contradiction with other scriptural passages."[247] This list, too, may be correlated with all but one or two of the points in my set of universal commentarial assumptions regarding the character of canons.

Finally, even Jonathan Swift's satiric account of the attributes of his *Tale of a Tub* which entitled it to the status of a classic may be related to my schema. First, Swift remarks of this "comprehensive discourse" that "the reader . . . will here find sufficient matter to employ his speculations for the rest of his life," indicating that the *Tale* is at least comprehensive enough to provide for one lifetime's cogitations. Second, Swift argues that if seven of the deepest scholars in Christendom were employed separately to write ample commentaries on the *Tale*, all of what they would write would be "manifestly deducible

[245] Vermes, "Bible and Midrash," p. 203.

[246] Shaye J. D. Cohen, *From the Maccabees to the Mishnah* (Philadelphia: Westminster Press, 1987), p. 206.

[247] Marie-Émile Boismard, "L'Hypothese synoptique de Griesbach," in *Le Siècle des Lumières et la Bible*, eds. Yvon Belaval and Dominique Bourel (Paris: Editions Beauchesne, 1986), p. 133.

from the text," implying that it is clear (at least to profound scholars) and perhaps self-consistent as well. Lastly, Swift reveals that he has in the *Tale* "couched a very profound mystery in the number of O's multiplied by seven, and divided by nine." He also promises that "whoever will be at the pains to calculate the whole number of each letter in this treatise, and sum up the difference exactly between the several numbers, assigning the true natural cause for every such difference, the discoveries in the product will plentifully reward his labour."[248] Thus, nothing is superfluous or trivial in Swift's new classic; every detail is heavy with significance. Some profound meaning may be extracted even from the arrangement of the letters in the text.

Apart from revealing several common commentarial assumptions regarding the character of the classics or scriptures, Swift's satire also adumbrates a few of the strategies devised by exegetes to establish or support those presuppositions. For example, he insists that his new classic, the *Tale*, is keyed simultaneously to at least three different pedagogical scales or classes of readers, "the superficial, the ignorant, and the learned,"[249] an idea that commentators in some canonical traditions used to explain apparent inconsistencies or vulgarities in the classics. But the bounds of Swift's satire are not ample enough to encompass a fair description of many of these strategies. Hence, we are constrained to fill in the gaps in Swift's canonical account by appending our own commentary (really a hidden commentary) in the following chapter.

---

[248] Jonathan Swift, *A Tale of a Tub*, in Swift, *Gulliver's Travels and Other Writings*, ed. and annot. Louis A. Landa (Boston: Houghton Mifflin, 1960), pp. 339–340.

[249] Ibid., p. 339.

Chapter 5

COMMENTARIAL STRATEGIES

L IKE THE SIX OR SEVEN basic commentarial assumptions outlined in the preceding chapter, the strategies and arguments used by exegetes to support those assumptions are common to several classical and scriptural traditions. It is, after all, reasonable that similar sets of presuppositions regarding the character of the classics or scriptures should have called forth similar arguments for establishing the truth of those conceptions. But although such common commentarial strategies as allegory, the idea of accommodation, and scholastic or modal distinctions appear *somewhere* in most major traditions, these traditions differ significantly among themselves in the extent to which they employ particular strategies and toward what ends. Some methods may be used to establish more than one commentarial assumption. Commentators have employed allegory, for example, to support such diverse ideas as that the classics are well ordered, self-consistent, moral, and profound, that they contain no superfluities, and even that they are clear (or obscure). The intellectual differences among major scholastic or commentarial traditions arose, to some extent, from the degree to which those traditions stressed or developed particular strategies for supporting their assumptions regarding the character of the classics. Traditions in which the modal distinction, for example, was widely employed tended to cultivate a specialized, highly technical scholastic language.

On the other hand, such distinctions among various traditions were perhaps even more the products of how much emphasis they gave to establishing one or another of the various commentarial assumptions. Thus, rabbinic Judaism is distinguished by its special concern to demonstrate the nonsuperfluous nature of each detail in its scriptures, and Vedānta by its stress on resolving apparent contradictions in its canon. In some commentarial traditions, however, significant historical changes occurred in the focus of commentarial concern—that is to say, which issues or assumptions were thought to be the most important or pressing. For example, the work of F. A. Wolf, according to Howard Clarke, served to "shift the basis of Homer study" from "morality and meaning" to "logic and consistency,"[1] to matters having

---

[1] Howard Clarke, *Homer's Readers: A Historical Introduction to the Iliad and the Odyssey*

to do with the third in our set of commentarial assumptions as outlined in the previous chapter.

. . . . .

The most nearly universal of commentarial assumptions—that the classics are comprehensive and all-encompassing—did not call forth the most numerous or ingenious arguments in its defense. Perhaps this idea seemed so obvious and was so widely accepted in most traditions that it was not felt to require any elaborate demonstration. Nevertheless, some traditional commentators, including Confucians, did recognize that the classics (or the teachings of the sages which they presented) did in some respects seem to fall short of cosmic comprehensiveness. Several of these commentators developed explanations for such apparent deficiencies and lacunae.

With respect to the Confucian classics as a whole, one of the commonest of these arguments was that although the original vision of the sages as expressed in the archetypal classics was indeed all-inclusive, later disciples and commentators were able to retain only one aspect or another of the complete view. According to the great T'ang Confucian scholar and literatus Han Yü (768–824), "the Way of Confucius was great and could be broadened. But his disciples could not observe everything or completely know [it]. Thus when they studied it, they each obtained only what was [in] close [accord] with their natural inclinations."[2] A later Neo-Confucian commentator on the Four Books, Chou Ju-teng, thus maintained that while one of Confucius' disciples, Yen-tzu, excelled in literature and ritual, another, Tseng-tzu, emphasized the moral virtues of fidelity and altruism.[3] According to Chu Hsi, even Tseng-tzu, the purported composer of the *Great Learning*, did not fully express the ineffable unitary principle of Confucius.[4] While Tseng-tzu's characterization of the Confucian Way in terms of "fidelity" (*chung*) and "altruism" (*shu*) approached the mark, wrote the Sung Neo-Confucian scholar Ch'en Hsiang-tao, it yet fell

---

(Newark: University of Delaware Press, 1981), p. 161. On the general intellectual influence of Wolf's *Prolegomena ad Homerum*, Cedric H. Whitman remarks that "few books in modern times, least of all books written in Latin, can claim to have roused such intellectual turmoil or to have created such a widespread climate of opinion as this one." Whitman, *Homer and the Heroic Tradition* (Cambridge: Harvard University Press, 1958), p. 3.

[2] Han Yü, quoted in *Ching-i k'ao* 231.1b (vol. 7).

[3] Chou Ju-teng, *Ssu-shu tsung-chih*, *Shang-Lun* (The Purport of the Four Books, First Part of *Analects*), p. 50a, in *Chung-kuo tzu-hsüeh ming-chu chi-ch'eng* 20:377.

[4] Chu Hsi, *Ssu-shu chi-chu* (The Four Books with Collected Commentaries), *Shang-Lun* (First Part of *Analects*) (Taipei: Hsüeh-hai ch'u-pan she, 1974 reprint), p. 23.

short of a complete and comprehensive understanding. But this was to be expected. For "the Way of Confucius is all-encompassing and universal. Those who are humane regard it as 'humanity.' Those who are wise regard it as 'wisdom.' Tseng-tzu's regarding the Master's Way as 'fidelity' and 'altruism' may be seen in this perspective."[5]

Modern historians as well have argued that the Sage's comprehensive vision was narrowed by his less perspicacious followers. Chou Yü-t'ung, for example, has declared that each of the major schools of classical interpretation developed only one aspect of Confucius' learning: the Old Text school his historiography, the New Text school his political science, and the Sung Neo-Confucians his philosophy.[6] And Benjamin Schwartz speaks of "the Master's apprehension that his disciples have only a limited or one-sided grasp of his total vision."[7]

Later commentators and historians in the Confucian tradition also expressed such an idea with respect to particular classical texts, arguing that the major schools of interpretation each had only a one-sided grasp of the whole. According to P'i Hsi-jui (1850–1908), "Cheng [Hsüan] explains the *Songs* in terms of rites and Chu [Hsi] explains the *Songs* in terms of principle. But neither is completely satisfactory."[8] The fourteenth-century scholar Wang Shen-tzu maintained that each of the major Sung commentaries on the *Change* developed only one aspect of that classic's manifoldness:

> The *Change* has the Way of the sages in fourfold. But Ch'eng I's *Commentary on the Change* esteems only its words. Shao Yung's numerological stud-

[5] Ch'en Hsiang-tao, *Lun-yü ch'üan-chieh* (Complete Explications of the *Analects*), 3.29b–30a, in *Chung-kuo tzu-hsüeh ming-chu chi-ch'eng* 4:116–117.

[6] Chou Yü-t'ung, "Ch'ün-ching kai-lun" (A General Discussion of All the Classics), in *Chou Yü-t'ung ching-hsüeh shih lun-chu hsüan-chi* (Selected Treatises by Chou Yü-t'ung on the History of Classical Studies), comp. Chu Wei-cheng (Shanghai: Jen-min ch'u-pan she, 1983), p. 221.

[7] Benjamin I. Schwartz, *The World of Thought in Ancient China* (Cambridge: Harvard University Press, Belknap Press, 1985), pp. 130–131. Modern historians and critics have also argued that Homer's comprehensive vision, as expressed in his presentation of Odysseus in the *Odyssey*, was slighted by later interpreters. According to George deF. Lord, "Odysseus' unequalled power to arouse strong personal feelings throughout the history of Western civilization proves the comprehensiveness of Homer's characterization," although few, most notably George Chapman, "avoided the ever-present danger of splitting Homer's many-sided hero and leaving us with a fragment." Lord, *Homeric Renaissance: The Odyssey of George Chapman* (London: Chatto and Windus, 1956), p. 53.

[8] Hsiung Kung-che, "K'ung-tzu Shih-chiao yü hou-shih Shih chuan" (Confucius' Teachings on the *Songs* and Later Generations' Commentaries on the *Songs*), in Hsiung Kung-che et al., *Shih-ching yen-chiu lun-chi* (A Collection of Articles on the Study of the *Songs Classic*) (Taipei: Li-ming wen-hua shih-yeh, 1981), p. 11.

ies esteem only its images. Chu Chen's (1072–1138) explanations of the *Change* esteem only its changes, and Chu Hsi's *Basic Meaning* [*of the Chou Change*] esteems only its divinations.[9]

Hellmut Wilhelm, likewise affirming the "universality and completeness of this *I Ching* system," lamented that "the clear vision which enabled Confucius and his early followers to comprehend the totality of this system has not been given to all periods."[10] In sum, if the classics appeared to be less than comprehensive, the fault was with the later expositors, not in the classics.

In several cases, however, exegetes acknowledged that even the ideas in the classics or the teachings of the sages which they presented were one-sided or incomplete. But such apparent distortions or blind spots in the comprehensive vision of the sages were deliberate, calculated to make up for the particular deficiencies of the age in which they lived. According to the late-Ch'ing classicist Liao P'ing (1852–1930), the "Royal Institutes" (Wang-chih) chapter of the *Record of Rites* was designed to remedy the Chou era's inclination toward refinement (*wen*) at the expense of simplicity (*chih*). Hence that classical text's apparent bias toward the latter.[11] Ch'eng I followed a similar line of argument in explaining Mencius' blanket condemnation of profit (*li*). Asserting that "never does the gentleman not desire profit," Ch'eng claimed that in the time of Mencius, "the people of the world sought profit alone and knew nothing of humanity and rightness. Therefore, Mencius spoke of humanity and rightness and did not speak of profit."[12] Although this statement might well be read as a denial of the universal applicability of the ideas expressed in the classics, as indicative of a movement toward historical relativism,[13] Ch'eng I probably intended it more as an explanation of why Mencius apparently failed to admit an important human value or activity into his total system. Ch'eng is not debunking or even relativizing the ideas expressed in a classical text—merely seeking to account for an apparent limitation, a flaw in its supposedly comprehensive vision.

Later commentators identified other such limitations in classical

[9] Wang Shen-tzu, quoted in *Ching i k'ao* 4.10b (vol. 1).

[10] Hellmut Wilhelm, *Change: Eight Lectures on the I Ching*, trans. Cary F. Baynes (Princeton: Princeton University Press, 1973), p. 80.

[11] Liao P'ing, *Chin-ku hsüeh k'ao* (Investigations of New and Old Text Studies) (Ch'ang-an ch'u-pan she, 1974 reprint), 2.5b, 33a.

[12] Ch'eng I, quoted in Chu, *Ssu-shu chi-chu, Shang-Meng* (First Part of *Mencius*), p. 2.

[13] Maruyama Masao so interprets similar statements by the Japanese Confucian philosopher Ogyū Sorai (1666–1728). Maruyama, *Studies in the Intellectual History of Tokugawa Japan*, trans. Mikiso Hane (Princeton: Princeton University Press; Tokyo: University of Tokyo Press, 1974), pp. 78 and 86–87.

texts. Among the most important of these, concerning the assumption that the classics are comprehensive, are the lacunae and lack of detail especially obvious in such canonical texts as the extremely terse *Spring and Autumn Annals*. If the *Annals*, like the rest of the canon, is really comprehensive in scope, then why does it apparently neglect to present a detailed or even adequate account of the events of the era it covers? Why does it, in some respects, even fail to measure up to the standards of a conventional history?

One explanation for this apparent anomaly is that the Sage did not intend the *Annals* to be a conventional history. Unlike its historiographic counterpart, the *Documents Classic*, the *Annals* speaks of principles (*li*), not of affairs (*shih*) or historical events. Thus, the late-Ch'ing commentator Chung Wen-cheng (1818–1877), declared that "those who read the *Spring and Autumn Annals* should not seek [its meanings] through historians' studies."[14] The Sung scholar-official Su Ch'e (d. 1112), however, argued that historical studies, especially of the *Tso Commentary*, were a necessary supplement to the laconic *Annals*, that they were needed to make the text of the classic fully comprehensible (and comprehensive). Confucius, in fact, composed the *Annals* with the idea that it would be supplemented by such histories.[15] Thus, the ultimate intent of the Sage was to present a complete and comprehensive account of the subjects covered by the *Annals*, even if the text of the classic itself does not reveal such a full picture.

Confucian commentators seeking to establish the comprehensiveness of their canon were also concerned with explaining apparent lacunae at the micro level—in particular passages in classical texts. Ch'eng I and Chu Hsi, for example, noted that the Mencian account of the "four beginnings" (*ssu-tuan*), or sprouts of virtue, does not include anything corresponding to *hsin* (trust or good faith), indicating that the *Mencius* apparently fails to comprehend the entire moral universe represented by the five Confucian norms which does include *hsin*. They explain this omission by postulating as follows: since it is understood that *hsin* is at the basis of all other virtues or norms, or is their necessary foundation, it is unnecessary to mention it separately.[16] Thus, Ch'eng I and Chu Hsi ingeniously turn an apparent liability, a lacuna in a classical text, to good account while implicitly

[14] Chung Wen-cheng, "Lun-ching" (A Discussion of the Classic), pp. 7b–8a, in *Ku-liang pu-chu* (The *Ku-liang Commentary* with Supplementary Commentaries), comp. Chung Wen-cheng, SPPY ed.

[15] Su Ch'e, *Ch'un-ch'iu chi-chieh* (The *Spring and Autumn Annals* with Collected Explications), 1.4b, in *Ching-yüan* (Garden of the Classics), comp. Ch'ien I-chi (Taipei: Ta-t'ung shu-chü, 1970), 6:2550.

[16] Ch'eng I and Chu Hsi in Chu, *Ssu-shu chi-chu, Shang-Meng*, p. 47.

affirming the classic's claim to comprehensiveness. In so doing, they make a philosophical point, indicating that metaphysical ideas, such as that a single virtue or quality may serve as a basis for all the rest, may develop from exegetical requirements or concerns.

Commentators in other traditions besides the Confucian also identified omissions or oversights in their canonical texts. But not all of the explanations they devised to account for these lacunae impinged on the realm of high philosophy. A Muslim tradition, for example, explains the loss of certain verses in the Qur'ān by saying that the sheet on which they were written was eaten by a domestic animal.[17] A Qur'ānic commentator rationalized the apparent omission of a certain verse by arguing that "the Qur'ān, the Word of God, is inimitable in, among other respects, its brevity."[18] On the other hand, a later Vedantic commentator formulated a more profound cosmological explanation for the omission of ether and air from a list of the elements given in a fifteenth-century semicanonical text, the *Vedānta-sāra*, similar to that proposed by Ch'eng I to explain the absence of *hsin* from the Mencian account of the moral virtues. Remarking that "as ether is all-pervading and without it nothing can exist, and as force, symbolized by air, is also at the root of all movement, and nothing can exist apart from it, therefore ether and air are to be taken for granted along with fire, water, and earth."[19] In other words, the canonical passage in question really is cosmologically comprehensive. Indeed, its apparent omissions make it a more accurate and profound account of the elements of the cosmos than it would be if it had simply included the two omitted elements in the list, undistinguished from the rest.

A midrashic commentator on the Hebrew Bible, Rabbi Yohanah, devised an equally ingenious explanation for an apparent omission in Psalm 145. Although each verse in this "alphabetical psalm" should begin with a new letter of the Hebrew alphabet, the psalm lacks a verse that should start with the Hebrew letter "N" (*nun*). This "N" verse, Yohanah argues, is missing because of David's foreknowledge that one of the direst prophecies in the entire Bible, Amos' prediction that Israel would fall to rise no more, begins with the same letter. David, moreover, not only avoided invoking this dread prophecy by omitting the "N" verse from Psalm 145, but he also mitigated or defused it in the very next verse by proclaiming that "the Lord lifts up

---

[17] John Burton, *The Collection of the Qur'ān* (Cambridge: Cambridge University Press, 1979), pp. 94–95.

[18] Ibid., p. 104.

[19] Vidvattamācārya, paraphrased in Swami Nikhilananda, *Vedāntasāra; or, The Essence of Vedānta of Sadānanda Yogīndra* (Calcutta: Advaita Ashrama, 1978), pp. 59–60.

all who are fallen, and straightens up all who are bent" (Psalms 145:14).[20]

If the arguments that Confucian commentators used to explain or repair apparent omissions in their canon, to establish its comprehensiveness, seem to be relatively limited or unimaginative, it should be recalled that this was not a pressing issue for many exegetes after the Han era. Moreover, the correlative schemas (described above in chapter 2) that Han commentators devised to integrate the canon, to relate the classics to one another and to aspects of the cosmos, were also a means of establishing its cosmic comprehensiveness. For example, the Han historian Pan Ku's (32–92) correlation of the books of the canon with the complete set of Confucian moral virtues was supposed to demonstrate that the classics comprehended the moral universe. Likewise, Sung Neo-Confucians' presentation of the Four Books as a complete Confucian curriculum was intended to establish that this new canon encompassed the entire pedagogical range. In sum, one of the basic strategies that Confucian commentators used to confirm the comprehensiveness of their canon was to correlate its individual books or parts with a larger whole, with some realm of the greater universe, whether moral, pedagogical, or cosmological. Once this was established, the appearance of rather isolated omissions and oversights did not seem to pose such a serious challenge to the conception that the classics are comprehensive. The presence of such omissions, moreover, could be rationalized by invoking Confucius' remark, recorded in the *Analects*, that if after raising one point (or corner) of an argument my auditors do not come up with the other three points, I do not go over the one point again (*Analects* 7:8). The comprehensiveness of Confucius' teaching thus lay not so much in its explicit coverage of every detail as in its wide appreciation of the principles and patterns of human life.

. . . . .

The second basic commentarial assumption—that the classics or scriptures are well ordered and coherent—was neither so early or efficiently established nor so widely accepted in most traditions. Practical exegetes could generally leave the proposition that the classics are comprehensive to the care of meta-commentators and cosmologists. But they could not so easily overlook the numerous parts and pas-

---

[20] James L. Kugel, "Two Introductions to Midrash," in *Midrash and Literature*, eds. Geoffrey H. Hartman and Sanford Budick (New Haven: Yale University Press, 1986), pp. 77–78.

sages in the classics that seemed to lack proper order or sense. To deal with such problems, to verify that the words of the sages or divines were well ordered and systematic despite appearances, required the formulation of more intricate strategies and diverse arguments. Moreover, various exegetes felt constrained to demonstrate that such a good order and sense existed at every level, from the integration of the canon as a whole to the sequence of terms or words in particular classical phrases.

Commentators in some major classical or scriptural traditions might well regard the importance that Confucians attached to establishing the good order of their canon as unwarranted (although many notable early Christian and Muslim exegetes held that the form of Scripture as well as its content was divinely inspired). Why, they might ask, devote so much attention to matters of form at the expense of more crucial points, such as that the canon is self-consistent or that it is moral? For many Confucians, however, there could be no more important proposition regarding the classics than that they are well ordered—if for no other reason than that Confucius himself was supposedly responsible for such order.

Apart from the cosmological schemas devised for integrating the canon, outlined above in chapter 2, the most common strategy used by Confucian commentators for demonstrating that the classics were related systematically to one another was by reading off the terms and concepts of one classic by those in others. This strategy was not unknown in other traditions, and was in fact widely used by Platonic commentators on Aristotle who sought to establish the unity of the two great ancient Greek authorities. In the High Middle Ages, commentators on Vergil read the *Aeneid* in terms borrowed from such antique philosophical texts as Boethius' *Consolation of Philosophy*. These two texts, in fact, interpenetrated in late-medieval exegesis to the extent that they coalesced into a monotext.[21] Even in modern times, Christian biblical scholars and theologians have often read the terms and concepts of various books of the Bible, such as the ancient covenant idea in the book of Exodus, in light of their simulacra in the other books, on the theory that "every book added to the Bible modifies the meaning of all the former books."[22] In Chinese Confucianism, with its diverse multibook canon, the demonstration of conceptual and terminological accord among the separate classics, the

---

[21] Christopher C. Baswell, "Boethian Readings of the *Aeneid*," a paper presented at the 22nd International Congress on Medieval Studies, Kalamazoo, Mich., May 7, 1987.

[22] James Tunstead Burtchaell, "Catholic Theories of Biblical Inspiration since 1810," in *The Catholic Tradition, Sacred Scripture*, vol. 2, eds. Rev. Charles J. Dollen et al. (McGrath Publishing Co., Consortium, 1979), p. 392.

establishment of proto-intertextuality, was more difficult than in most Western traditions. But it was also more essential for confirming the integrity of the canon as a whole.

The strategy of reading off one classic in terms of another was probably most highly developed and systematically pursued by Ch'ing commentators on the *Spring and Autumn Annals* who were of the New Text school and who favored the *Kung-yang Commentary* to that classic. Because many adherents of this school regarded Confucius as the composer of the Five Classics, not just the editor or expurgator, it was all the more important to demonstrate their conceptual unity—perhaps even necessary in order to confirm Confucius' authorship. But it also had to do with the New Text scholars' view of the *Annals* as the master key to all the classics. As Liu Feng-lu (1776–1829) remarked, "if one does not understand the *Spring and Autumn Annals*, one cannot talk about the Five Classics. The *Annals* is the key to the Five Classics."[23] Thus, a number of noted New Text scholars of the Ch'ing era read the ideas and schemas associated with the *Kung-yang Commentary* on the *Annals* into some of the other classics, including the *Change*, the *Documents*, the *Songs*, and the *Analects*.[24]

Some of these readings simply correlated numerological sets in the *Kung-yang Commentary* with their supposed correspondents in other classics. The philosophical essayist Kung Tzu-chen (1792–1841), for example, paired the three ages (*san-shih*) associated with the *Annals* with the eight rules of government (*pa-cheng*) that appear in the "Great Norm" (Hung-fan) chapter of the *Documents Classic*.[25] And Liao P'ing matched the six lines in the hexagrams of the *Change* with the three ancient calendrical systems that were associated with the *Kung-yang Commentary* to the *Annals*.[26] An earlier commentator, Hung Tz'u-k'uei (d. 1236), paired the six lines of the *po* hexagram with the 242 years covered by the *Annals*, assigning approximately 40 years to each line. He explained this correlation as follows: "As the *yin* increasingly advances [as one proceeds from the top line to the bottom

---

[23] Liu Feng-lu, *Kung-yang Ho-shih shih-li* (The *Kung-yang* with Mr. Ho's Explanatory Examples), quoted in Sun Ch'un-tsai, *Ch'ing-mo ti Kung-yang ssu-hsiang* (The *Kung-yang* Thought of the Late-Ch'ing Era) (Taipei: Shang-wu yin-shu-kuan, 1985), p. 37.

[24] Brief accounts of these scholars and some of their works on this subject appear in Lu Pao-ch'ien, *Ch'ing-tai ssu-hsiang shih* (Intellectual History of the Ch'ing Era) (Taipei: Kuang-wen shu-chü, 1978), p. 269; Chou, "Ch'ün-ching kai-lun," p. 268; and Sun, *Ch'ing-mo ti Kung-yang ssu-hsiang*, p. 48.

[25] Kung Tzu-chen, "Wu-ching ta-i chung-shih ta-wen i" (Answers to Questions on the Entire Scope of the Great Meanings of the Five Classics, Part 1), in *Kung Tzu-chen ch'üan-chi* (Complete Writings of Kung Tzu-chen) (Taipei: Ho-Lo t'u-shu ch'u-pan she, 1975 reprint), 1.46.

[26] Sun, *Ch'ing-mo ti Kung-yang ssu-hsiang*, p. 110.

line in the *po* hexagram], then the chaos [recorded in the *Annals*, which proceeds in chronological order] increasingly waxes."[27]

Other commentators correlated ideas and phrases associated with the *Kung-yang*, rather than its numerological sets or units, with their purported correspondents in other classics. The reason behind some of these associations is not obvious. Liu Feng-lu, for example, paired the "learning" of the Confucian *Analects* with the "expurgation and establishment of the Six Classics" of the *Kung-yang*, and correlated the *Analects'* "human nature and the Way of heaven" with the *Kung-yang's* "subtle words."[28] Kan Wen-ch'uan more plausibly compared terms by which the *Annals* and the *Change* establish hierarchical arrangements:

> The *Spring and Autumn Annals* clarifies the honorable and the humble, and thus the way of the subject is established. The *Change* says, "Heaven is exalted and earth is lowly, and thus the *ch'ien* [hexagram corresponding to heaven] and *k'un* [hexagram corresponding to earth] are fixed." The high and low [associated with the *Change*] thereby display the positions of the honorable and humble [related in the *Annals*].[29]

The commentarial strategy of demonstrating the order and interrelatedness of the canon as a whole by reading off one classic in terms of another was most refined by nineteenth-century New Text commentators on the *Annals*. Some of these scholars' classical studies centered on interpreting the entire Confucian canon in terms of the ideas and categories associated with the *Kung-yang* school. But the use of this strategy was not confined to this school, to Ch'ing scholars, or to studies that involved the *Annals*. A diverse array of commentators, many of whom did not assume that the *Annals* was the master key to the canon as a whole, used it to relate a number of the other classics to one another.

Several such commentarial readings focused on the *Change*, the other of the Confucian classics besides the *Annals* that was most often identified as the key to all the rest. Sometimes, these readings simply correlated numerological sets or formulae. Thus, Hao Ching (1223–1275) paired the "four qualities" (*yüan, heng, li, chen*), divinatory terms that appear in the *Change*, with the "four beginnings," or

---

[27] Hung Tz'u-k'uei, "Tzu-hsü" (Author's Preface) to *Ch'un-ch'iu shuo* (Explanations on the *Spring and Autumn Annals*), in *Ching-i k'ao* 190.6a (vol. 6).

[28] Sun, *Ch'ing-mo ti Kung-yang ssu-hsiang*, p. 41.

[29] Kan Wen-ch'uan, "Hsü" (Preface) to Wang Yüan-chieh, *Ch'un-ch'iu yen-i* (Judgments on the Meanings of the *Spring and Autumn Annals*), in *Ching-i k'ao* 196.6b (vol. 6).

sprouts of virtue, in the *Mencius*.[30] Sung Hsiang-feng (1776–1860) matched these same four qualities with the "five beginnings" (*wu-shih*) associated with the *Annals*.[31] A Ch'ing commentator on the Four Books, Chang Tai (1597–1684?), devised a more intricate system of correspondence between the phrases in the opening line of book 1 of the *Analects* and those explaining the inner trigram of the first hexagram of the *Change*, the *ch'ien*. Some of his correspondences seem rather forced, such as the pairing of the *Analects*' "Friends come from afar" with the *Change*'s "seeing the dragon in the field."[32]

Neo-Confucian commentators frequently related the *Great Learning*'s eight-step pedagogical order for self-cultivation and the achievement of good government—which runs the gamut from the investigation of affairs (*ko-wu*) to the pacification of the realm (*p'ing t'ien-hsia*)—to key passages in other classics. Ts'ai Shen (1167–1230), the premier Sung Neo-Confucian commentator on the *Documents*, interpreted the phrases at the beginning of the "Kao-yao mo" (Plans of Kao-yao) chapter of the *Documents* in terms of this order.[33] The late-Ch'ing classicist Ch'en Li did the same with the first section of the *Analects*—for example, pairing the *Analects*' admonition to frequently review one's studies with the "investigation of affairs and the advancement of knowledge" of the *Great Learning*.[34] A Sung commentator cited in Chu Hsi's commentary on the Four Books paired this same phrase from the *Great Learning* with a characterization of Confucius' pedagogical technique drawn from the *Analects*, a disciple's remark that Confucius "broadens me with culture."[35] In sum, it seems that just about every passage or phrase in the canon that had any pedagogical purport was fair game for correlation with the eight-step order of the *Great Learning*, the touchstone of Neo-Confucian pedagogical discourse.

Apart from demonstrating the order and interrelatedness of the canon as a whole through such strategies as reading off one classic in terms of another, Confucian commentators also sought to establish that individual books in the canon were systematically arrayed or or-

[30] Hao Ching, quoted in *Ching-i k'ao* 231.4b (vol. 7). A more cosmologically oriented explanation of the meanings of these terms from the *Change* appears in Wilhelm, *Eight Lectures*, p. 51.

[31] Sung Hsiang-feng, *Kuo-t'ing lu* (Taipei: Kuang-wen shu-chü, 1971 reprint), 4.2a.

[32] Chang Tai, *Ssu-shu yü* (Close Encounters with the Four Books) (Hangchou: Che-kiang ku-chi ch'u-pan she, 1985 reprint), p. 69.

[33] Ts'ai Shen, *Shu-ching chi-chuan* (*Documents Classic* with Collected Commentaries), p. 15, in *Ssu-shu wu-ching*, vol. 1.

[34] Ch'en Li, *Tung-shu tu-shu chi* (Reading Notes of [Ch'en] Tung-shu) (Taipei: Shang-wu yin-shu-kuan, 1970 reprint), p. 8.

[35] Quoted in Chu, *Ssu-shu chi-chu*, *Shang-Lun*, p. 57; the reference is to *Analects* 9:10.

ganized. One way of doing this was through the formulation of numerological correspondences between the order or organization of the text and the order of some aspect of the cosmos. Chao T'ai-ch'ing, for example, correlated the number of sections in the *Mencius*, seven, with the "seven governors" in the heavens, including the sun, moon, and five planets; he also related the 261 chapters of the *Mencius* to the approximate number of days in three seasons of the year.[36] Sun Shih (962–1033) matched these same seven sections with the seven major kings and kingdoms of the Warring States era in which Mencius lived.[37] According to the Han-era skeptical philosopher Wang Ch'ung (27–100?), one argument used by Han exegetes to establish that the received version of the *Documents Classic* was complete was that the number of its chapters, twenty-nine, corresponded to the twenty-eight lunar lodges plus the northern dipper asterism in the heavens.[38]

Attempts to establish numerological correspondences between the arrangement of canonical texts and that of the cosmos appeared in the Christian exegetical tradition as well. An early Christian commentator, Irenaeus (c. 130–200), found cosmic correspondents for the fourness of the four Gospels, correlating them with the four regions of the world, the four universal winds, and the four principal covenants.[39] St. Jerome correlated the twenty-two books of the Old Testament with the twenty-two letters of the Hebrew alphabet, remarking: "As, then, there are twenty-two elementary characters by means of which we write in Hebrew all we say, and the compass of the human voice is contained within their limits, so we reckon twenty-two books, by which, as by the alphabet of the doctrine of God, a righteous man is instructed."[40] Finally, the idea that the apostle Paul wrote to precisely seven churches was used as a way of overcoming the particularity and occasionality of Paul's correspondence, since "the number seven was a symbol of wholeness," and the seven churches thus symbolized the universal church.[41]

---

[36] Chao T'ai-ch'ing, quoted in Lin Chih-ch'i, "Tzu-hsü" (Author's Preface) to *Meng-tzu chiang-i* (Explanations of Meanings in *Mencius*), in *Ching-i k'ao* 234.4a (vol. 7).

[37] Sun Shih, *Meng-tzu chu-shu* (*Mencius* with Explanatory Commentaries), 1.2a, in *Chung-kuo tzu-hsüeh ming-chu chi-ch'eng* 9:7.

[38] Wang Ch'ung, *Lun-heng* (Discussions Weighed in the Balance) (Shanghai: Jen-min ch'u-pan she, 1974), 28.426 ("Cheng-shuo" chap.).

[39] "Irenaeus on Why There Are Only Four Gospels" (from Irenaeus, *Against Heresies* 3.11.8), in *The Church Fathers on the Bible*, ed. Frank Sadowski (New York: Alba House, 1987), pp. 31–33.

[40] "Jerome's Preface to the Books of Samuel and Kings," ibid., p. 201.

[41] Harry Y. Gamble, "Christianity: Scripture and Canon," in *The Holy Book in Comparative Perspective*, eds. Frederick Denny and Rodney L. Taylor (Columbia: University of South Carolina Press, 1985), p. 40; Brevard S. Childs, *The New Testament as Canon: An Introduction* (Philadelphia: Fortress Press, 1985), p. 424.

Confucian commentators also attempted to demonstrate that the arrangement or sequence of chapters within the books of their canon followed some logical or cosmological pattern. This was a particular problem with the *Documents Classic*, supposedly a "history," but one that did not follow any clear chronological or logical arrangement. Ts'ai Shen, however, found another sort of pattern in the chapters of that classic: namely, the division between the earlier *tien* (canon) chapters, which "recorded events," and the later *mo* (plan) chapters, which "recorded words."[42] Ts'ai also maintained that particular chapters in the *Documents* followed one another in good order, commenting in one instance that "the preceding chapter speaks of according with the times and this one of according with affairs."[43]

Other Neo-Confucian commentators, especially Ch'eng I and Chu Hsi, focused their attention on establishing the orderliness of the newly canonized *Doctrine of the Mean* and *Great Learning*. As Jeffrey Riegel has pointed out, "there is no 'internal' unity to the *Chung Yung* but only one that appears ephemeral and contrived."[44] But Ch'eng I maintained that the work as a whole followed a sort of metaphysical progression: "The book begins by discussing the one principle, which in the middle [it treats as something that] disperses to become the myriad affairs, which in the end again unite to become the one principle."[45] Chu Hsi perceived a similar general order in the *Great Learning*, remarking that the first four chapters of what he denoted as the "commentary" portion of the text "discuss in summary the broad outline and point the direction," while the final six chapters "discuss in detail the particulars and the required effort"[46] In sum, Ch'eng I and Chu Hsi interpret the arrangements of the *Doctrine of the Mean* and the *Great Learning* as gravitating between the poles of generalities or cosmic wholes, on the one hand, and particulars or the myriad affairs, on the other. The texts of these classics are thus cosmologically comprehensive as well as systematically organized.

Establishing the orderliness and coherence of the relatively short and concentrated *Doctrine of the Mean* and *Great Learning* was a rather simple matter when compared to accomplishing the same with respect to the *Change*, with its multiple strata and complex appendices.[47] Indeed, some traditional commentators admitted, even cele-

---

[42] Ts'ai, *Shu-ching chi-chuan*, pp. 15–16.

[43] Ibid., p. 3.

[44] Jeffrey Kenneth Riegel, "The Four 'Tzu Ssu' Chapters of the *Li Chi*: An Analysis of the *Fang Chi, Chung Yung, Piao Chi*, and *Tzu I*" (Ph.D. diss., Stanford University, 1978), p. 99.

[45] Ch'eng I, in Chu, *Ssu-shu chi-chu, Chung-yung* (Doctrine of the Mean), p. 1.

[46] Chu, *Ssu-shu chi-chu, Ta-hsüeh* (Great Learning), pp. 14–15.

[47] The difficulty of accomplishing this enterprise may be illustrated by Hellmut Wilhelm's characterization of the "Ten Wings," the canonical appendices to the classic:

brated, that classic's diverse origins, multiple authorship, and numerous strata. Such an admission would hardly seem a propitious beginning for a demonstration that the text was well ordered or coherent. But commentators turned these apparent liabilities to good account by arguing that the ancient sages who supposedly composed the successive strata of the *Change* proceeded in an ordered sequence, each one complementing his predecessor's work.[48]

Following the "Treatise on Bibliography" of the *Han History*, most commentators maintained that the ancient sage Fu Hsi drew the lines of the original eight trigrams of the *Change*, and that King Wen later combined these to make the sixty-four hexagrams.[49] Confucius, in turn, explicated these figures in his "Appended Words" (Hsi-tz'u). The noted Sung scholar Su Hsün (1009–1066) explained how each of these three steps or strata illuminated some aspect of cosmic reality: "[Fu Hsi] observed the images of heaven and earth to make the lines [of the trigrams]. [King Wen] comprehended the alternations of the *yin* and *yang* to make the hexagrams. [And Confucius] investigated the situations of ghosts and spirits to make the words [which form the canonical appendices to the *Change*]."[50] Kuo Yung, another commentator of the Sung era, proposed a simpler but similar schema, remarking that Fu Hsi's trigrams which "illuminated heaven" were complemented by King Wen's hexagrams which "illuminated man."[51] The philosophical historian Chang Hsüeh-ch'eng (1738–1801) gave an historicist twist to this theory of the cosmological

"Important and unimportant matters are mingled indiscriminately; there are repetitions, and also many regrettable gaps; the titles often no longer fit the contents. In short, they form a conglomerate, apparently put together not very skillfully toward the end of the Chou era from remnants still extant, and then added to the *I Ching* as appendices." Wilhelm, *Eight Lectures*, p. 66.

[48] The idea that a classic had been properly ordered through its having passed through several sagely hands appears with respect to other Confucian canonical texts as well. See, for example, the description by the Ch'ing scholar Feng Ching (1652–1715) of the composition of the *Erh-ya*, in his "Ta-hsüeh wen-ta" (Questions and Answers on the *Great Learning*), from *Chieh-ch'ung chi* (Writings of [Feng] Chieh-ch'ung), in *Huang-Ch'ing ching-chieh* 206.2047 (vol. 3). Ou-yang Hsiu took a similar view of the composition of the *Songs Classic*. See Michael A. Fuller, review of *The Literary Works of Ou-yang Hsiu (1007–72)* by Ronald C. Egan, in *The Bulletin of Sung Yuan Studies*, no. 19 (1987), p. 53.

[49] See, for example, Wang Ying-lin, "I" ([On the] *Change*), in *Yü-hai* (Sea of Jade), 35.1a (Taipei: Ta-hua shu-chü, 1977 reprint), 2:695. As Wang points out, however, there were at least four different theories on who doubled the trigrams to make the hexagrams.

[50] Su Hsün, "I-lun" (Discussion of the *Change*), in *Su Hsün chi* (Collected Writings of Su Hsün) (Taipei: Ho-Lo t'u-shu ch'u-pan she, 1975 reprint), 6.51–52.

[51] Kuo Yung, "Ch'uan-chia I-shuo tsung-lun" (A General Discussion to be Transmitted to My Heirs Explaining the *Change*), in *Sung-Yüan hsüeh-an* 28.4b (vol. 2).

complementarity of the different strata of the *Change*, declaring that "in high antiquity [the time of Fu Hsi] they interpreted the ways of heaven. But from middle antiquity on [the era of King Wen], they interpreted the great beginnings of the affairs of men."[52] Chang thus indicates that the order or arrangement of the *Change* reflected the general course of ancient Chinese intellectual history.

Not every Confucian commentator maintained that a good order existed everywhere in the canon. Some, especially Neo-Confucians, even rearranged or "reconstructed" sections of the classics that they considered to be disorganized or otherwise unfit to communicate the teachings of the sages. Perhaps the most famous such rearrangement was Chu Hsi's recension of the text of the *Great Learning*, which he divided into "classic" and "commentary" chapters. He also filled in what he regarded as lacunae in the text and excised some characters that he judged to be superfluous. Although Chu's doctoring of the *Great Learning* is perhaps the most celebrated such affair in the annals of Neo-Confucianism, he performed much more radical surgery on the so-called ritual classics, particularly the *Record of Rites* and the semicanonical *Deportment and Rites* (I-li). Specifically, he compiled a sort of composite work, the *Comprehensive Explications of the Text and Commentaries of the Deportment and Rites* (I-li ching-chuan t'ung-chieh), which not only rearranged the sequence of chapters and altered some passages of the original *I-li*, but also used passages from the *Record of Rites* as annotations.[53] He thus used a canonical work, one of the Five Classics, to annotate one that was only semicanonical.

Chu Hsi was not the last Confucian commentator to have rearranged or altered classical texts to make them conform to the more perfect order supposedly intended by their original sagely authors. Two eighteenth-century Japanese Confucian scholars, Nakai Riken and Matsui Rashu, reorganized the texts of the *Mean* and the "Great Commentary" to the *Change*, respectively, in order to eliminate inconsistencies or repetitions.[54] Even in modern times, scholars have com-

---

[52] Chang Hsüeh-ch'eng, *Wen-shih t'ung-i* (The Comprehensive Meaning of Literature and History) (Taipei: Kuang-wen shu-chü, 1967 reprint), 1.5. Chang's saying on this point is echoed in Mou Tsung-san, *Li-shih che-hsüeh* (Philosophy of History) (Taipei: Le-t'ien ch'u-pan she, 1971), pp. 12–13.

[53] Kao Ming, "Chu Hsi's Discipline of Propriety," in *Chu Hsi and Neo-Confucianism*, ed. Wing-tsit Chan (Honolulu: University Press of Hawaii, 1986), pp. 321–322. Kao notes that this book "was not completed by Chu Hsi himself; parts were revised by Huang Wan and Yang Fu" (p. 322).

[54] Tetsuo Najita, *Visions of Virtue in Tokugawa Japan: The Kaitokudō Merchant Academy of Osaka* (Chicago: University of Chicago Press, 1987), p. 198; Iulian K. Shchutskii, *Researches on the I Ching*, trans. William L. MacDonald and Tsuyoshi Hasegawa with Hellmut Wilhelm (Princeton: Princeton University Press, 1979), p. 162.

posed such revisions. K'ang Yu-wei (1858–1927), for example, reorganized the text of the *Mencius*, complaining that "in the seven sections [of the standard arrangement] of the *Mencius*, the 'great meanings and subtle words' are confused and scattered."[55] More recently, Ch'en Li-fu accomplished the larger project of rearranging the whole of the Four Books "with a scientific spirit and method."[56]

Such radical rearrangements of classical or scriptural texts have precedents in other traditions. In the early Christian centuries, for example, there were several attempts to reorganize the texts of the four Gospels into a single narrative that would eliminate repetitions and inconsistencies.[57] Even in the conservative rabbinic tradition, rearrangements of the traditional order of the books of the Bible as well as of chapters within some of these books, such as that by Don Isaac Abravanel (1437–1508), were not unknown.[58] Moreover, the practice of bridging apparent gaps in received versions of canonical works was common in several traditions—most conspicuously in the Homeric, in which the "epic cycle" was composed primarily to make good the lacunae in Homer's narratives. Apocryphal gospels that covered obscure phases in the life of Jesus often served a similar purpose in early Christian literature. In rabbinic Judaism, one of the purposes of *haggadah*, a type of midrash,was to "fill in the gaps" in the narrative material of the Hebrew Bible.[59] Such additions and alterations were frequently justified on the grounds that they conformed to the original order conceived by the sagely or divine composers of the classics or scriptures, which was obscured in the received versions of canonical texts. In other words, rearrangement or "reconstruction" could actually be used as a strategy to demonstrate that the archetypal text, at least, was well ordered.

In some cases, though, commentators acknowledged that even the

[55] K'ang Yu-wei, *Meng-tzu wei* (The Subtleties of *Mencius*) (Taipei: Shang-wu yin-shu-kuan, 1976 reprint), 1.1.

[56] Ch'u Po-ssu, *Liu-ching tao lun* (A Discussion of the Way of the Six Classics) (Taipei: K'ai-ming shu-tien, 1971), p. 6 of "Hsü-yen" (Preface). The book that resulted from this project has recently been translated into English as *The Confucian Way: A New and Systematic Study of 'The Four Books,'* trans. Shih Shun Liu (London: KPI, 1986).

[57] For brief accounts of such attempts, see C. F. Evans, "The New Testament in the Making," in *The Cambridge History of the Bible*, vol. 1: *From the Beginnings to Jerome*, eds. P. R. Ackroyd and C. F. Evans (Cambridge: Cambridge University Press, 1970), p. 266; and Raymond F. Collins, *Introduction to the New Testament* (Garden City, N.Y.: Doubleday, Image Books, 1987), p. 22.

[58] Jacob S. Minkin, "Don Isaac Abravanel [1437–1508]," in *Creators of the Jewish Experience in Ancient and Medieval Times*, ed. and annot. Simon Noveck (Washington, D.C.: B'nai B'rith Books, 1985), p. 260.

[59] John Bowker, *The Targums and Rabbinic Literature: An Introduction to Jewish Interpretations of Scripture* (Cambridge: Cambridge University Press, 1969), p. 43.

original or archetypal text was not coherent or well ordered, at least not by conventional standards. Yet, this apparent lack of order, some commentators hastened to add, might serve a higher purpose. A contemporary scholar, Adin Steinsaltz, for example, remarks that few works in Jewish canonical literature have clear schematic frameworks because "Torah, as a reflection of life itself, cannot be artificially compartmentalized, but must develop naturally from subject to subject."[60] A more ingenious explanation for the apparent lack of order in the Torah appears in the *Midrash Tehillim* (on Psalm 3): "Had the chapters of the Torah been given in their correct order, anyone who read them would have been enabled to raise the dead and work miracles; therefore the Torah's [true] order has been hidden and is known [only] to God."[61]

Inasmuch as Muslims attribute the present sequence of the *sūrahs*, or chapters, of the Qur'ān to the Prophet himself and, in some instances, even to God, Qur'ānic commentators have been particularly concerned with accounting for the fact that the sūrahs are apparently not arranged in any logical order. Usually a higher purpose or principle is invoked. One modern scholar, for example, comments that "in order to avoid one-sidedness at any stage of its study," the *sūrahs* dealing with similar topics are not grouped together. Thus, "the entire picture of the complete Iman" is always before the reader.[62] An earlier tradition, cited by the great commentator al-Tabarī, however, indicated that such a topical order did exist in correlating the organization of the Qur'ān with that of the Bible. Thus, the "seven long" *sūrahs* corresponded with the Torah, the "hundreds (*as-mi'un*)" with the Psalms, and the "duplicated (*al-mathani*)" with the Gospels.[63]

· · · · ·

Traditional commentators generally maintained that order and coherence existed on both the micro and the macro level; that is, with respect to the arrangement of words and phrases in the classics or scriptures as well as in their overall organization and relationships to

[60] Adin Steinsaltz, *The Essential Talmud*, trans. Chaya Galai (New York: Basic Books, 1976), p. 62.

[61] *Midrash Tehillim*, quoted in Gershom Scholem, *Kabbalah* (New York: New American Library, Meridian Books, 1978), p. 170.

[62] Maulana Abūl Alā Maudūdī, "An Introduction to the Study of the Qurān," in *The Holy Qurān*, ed. Khurshid Ahmed (Karachi: Jamiyat-ul-Falah Publications), p. 35.

[63] Al-Tabarī, *The Commentary on the Qur'ān* by Abū Ja'far Muhammad B. Jarīr al-Tabarī, being an abridged translation of *Jāmi' al-bayān 'an ta'wīl āy al-Qur'ān*, with an introduction and notes by J. Cooper (Oxford: Oxford University Press, 1987), vol. 1, p. 44 of "Introduction."

one another. These scholars attempted to explain the sequence of words in particular sentences as well as the order of chapters in the work as a whole, thus accounting for apparent anomalies, inconsistencies, and randomness.

The issue of order at the micro level of word and phrase was especially important with respect to the one of the classics that Confucius himself was supposed to have composed, the *Spring and Autumn Annals*. As James Legge has pointed out, this terse chronicle appears to convey little of the author's view of the events it records: "The notices . . . are absolutely unimpassioned. . . . No details are given; no judgment is expressed."[64] Yet, Confucius was supposed by Mencius and later commentators to have composed this work primarily to express his moral judgments on the men and events chronicled therein and even to set a pattern for the future. Hence, he must have expressed such judgments and patterns very subtly through the arrangement and variations of particular words and phrases in the *Annals*, leaving nothing to chance. Some significant order must underlie the apparent randomness of many of the entries in this bare chronicle. This order, even the sequence of terms in the *Annals*, must express Confucius' teachings on statecraft, morality, and the cosmos. This view is illustrated in Ho Hsiu's (129–182) subcommentary on the *Kung-yang Commentary* to the *Annals*, especially in a passage explaining the order of the "five beginnings" (*wu-shih*) associated with the *Kung-yang* school.[65]

First, the original entry in the *Spring and Autumn Annals* for the first month of the first year of Duke Yin:

> [It was the] first [or original] year, the spring, the king's first month.

Ho Hsiu's subcommentary on this entry:

> If the feudal lords do not respectfully serve the king's government, then he will not be able to mount the throne. Therefore, [the text of the *Annals*] first says the "first month" [when the feudal lords pay homage] and afterward says [or omits to say] "mount the throne." If the government does not proceed from the king, then it cannot be a [proper] government. Therefore, [the text] first says "the king's" and afterwards says the "first month." If the king does not accede to heaven to regulate his commands, then there will be no law. Therefore, [the text] first says "spring" [one of the seasons

---

[64] James Legge, *The Chinese Classics*, vol. 5: *The Ch'un Ts'ew with the Tso Chuen*, 2nd ed. (Taipei: Wen-shih-che ch'u-pan she, 1971 reprint), p. 3 of "Prolegomena."

[65] For an account of the provenance of these "five beginnings," see Li Tun, *Ch'ün-ching hsiao-chih* (Small Notes on All the Classics), in *Huang-Ch'ing ching-chieh* 723.8439 (vol. 12).

that is given by heaven] and afterward says "the king's." If heaven does not profoundly rectify its origins, then it will not be able to accomplish its transformations. Therefore, [the text] first says "the origin" [or "first"] and afterward says "spring." These five [namely, the first or original year, spring, the king, the first month, and mount the throne] jointly appeared on the same day, complementing one another to become one essence. Thus, the great foundations of heaven and man and the connections of the myriad things must be investigated [by the student of the *Annals*].[66]

A Ch'ing commentator, Sung Hsiang-feng, maintained that the omission or inclusion of any of the "five beginnings" in particular entries in the *Annals* was Confucius' way of expressing moral judgments, of dispensing praise and blame in the classic: "Since the *Spring and Autumn Annals* has the five beginnings, the meaning of [Confucius'] praising the good and censuring the evil over 240 years is made clear."[67]

Such attempts to explain an apparently random or puzzling word order as a sort of code that expresses significant moral or philosophical ideas appear in other traditions as well. One of the most notable of these is the mythographer Fulgentius' (468–533) explanation (which he puts into the mouth of Vergil) of the anomalous order of words in the first line of the *Aeneid*, "Arma virumque cano":

> According to logic one should mention the person first and then the things relating to the person, so that substance precedes accidents—for example, "man" would come first and then "arms," since the virtue is in the person. But I [Vergil] wrote according to the formulas of praise, and therefore I mentioned the merit of the man before the man himself.[68]

Qur'ānic exegetes were likewise concerned with explaining the logic behind apparently random word orders in their canonical text, especially those which recount the names or attributes of God.[69] For example, al-Tabarī in one instance argued that God's name "al-rahmān" comes second to his name "Allah" "because it is permissible to describe someone other than Him by it."[70]

---

[66] Ho Hsiu, *Ch'un-ch'iu Kung-yang chuan* (The *Spring and Autumn Annals* with the *Kung-yang Commentary*) (Taipei: Hsin-hsing shu-chü, 1974 reprint), p. 5.

[67] Sung, *Kuo-t'ing lu* 4.2a

[68] Fulgentius, "The Exposition of the Content of Vergil According to Moral Philosophy," quoted in *Medieval Literary Criticism: Translations and Interpretations*, eds. O. B. Hardison, Jr. et al. (New York: Frederick Ungar, 1974), p. 66.

[69] I. H. Azad Faruqi, *The Tarjuman al-Qur'an: A Critical Analysis of Maulana Abu'l-Kalam Azad's Approach to the Understanding of the Qur'ān* (New Delhi: Vikas Publishing, 1982), p. 39.

[70] Al-Tabarī, *Commentary on the Qur'ān*, vol. 1, p. 58.

Confucian commentators on the *Spring and Autumn Annals* drew moral and cosmological lessons not only from the anomalous or puzzling word-order sequences in the classic, but also from discrepancies in the *Annals'* use of terminology to characterize men and events. In so doing, commentators, especially those associated with the *Kung-yang* and *Ku-liang* schools, again turned an apparent liability into an asset, indicating that what might be regarded as literary disorder was the vehicle for the expression of a higher moral or cosmological order.

The most noticeable terminological inconsistencies in the *Annals* are in its use of the chronological terms with which most of the entries in this chronicle begin. In some cases, the classic omits to record the year, season, month, or day in which a particular event occurred. In other instances, such chronological terms appear where they are superfluous or inappropriate. The *Ku-liang Commentary* to the *Annals* frequently draws moral lessons from such instances, as the following examples illustrate:[71]

> The day of the entering is given in order to condemn those who entered. [Duke Yin 10.7]

> For ten years of (Duke) Yin's reign there is no *cheng-yüeh* ("first month"). (This is due to the fact that) Yin did not consider himself the correct heir. [Duke Yin 11.4]

> (The *Ch'un-ch'iu*) condemns him, and therefore carefully records the month. [Duke Huan 2.7]

> That the Text gives the day (is due to the fact that the *Ch'un-ch'iu* considered that the duke) over-emphasized military matters. Therefore it exercises care and records the day. [Duke Huan 6.3]

Other commentators drew moral and historical lessons from inconsistencies in the *Annals'* renderings of titles and ranks. The premier Sung commentator on the *Annals*, Hu An-kuo, for example, explained the omission of the written character for "Heavenly" in the title "Heavenly King" in four out of twenty-six instances in the text by saying that "the kingly patterns were abandoned, and human ethical relationships were disordered. Therefore, [the *Annals*] does not write 'Heavenly' in order to censure them."[72] Commentators adduced

---

[71] All of these examples are drawn from the translations given by Göran Malmqvist, "Studies on the Gongyang and Guuliang Commentaries, I," in *Bulletin of the Museum of Far Eastern Antiquities*, no. 43 (1971), pp. 86, 87, 97, and 101. I have changed Malmqvist's transliterations into Wade-Giles.

[72] Hu An-kuo, quoted in Shih Kuang-ch'i, *Ch'un-ch'iu shu-fa kuo-yüan* (A Probe into the Origins of the Method of [Historical] Writing in the *Spring and Autumn Annals*) (Taipei: I-wen yin-shu-kuan, 1976 reprint), 1.3. An earlier commentator, Chia K'uei

cosmological as well as moral lessons from such omissions. The Ch'ing New Text scholar Liu Feng-lu, for example, explained the *Annals*' having in one case recounted an event while failing to record the month in which it occurred as an indication that "when the Way of man is rectified, the Way of heaven is settled."[73] Conversely, another Ch'ing commentator on the *Annals* accounted for certain entries' having recorded the year and season while omitting to mention the king and the accession of a duke as the *Annals*' way of asserting the priority of the "ways of heaven" over the "affairs of men."[74]

As modern scholars have noted, the terminological and stylistic inconsistencies in the *Spring and Autumn Annals* do not follow any pattern that would lend much support to the idea that they express moral evaluations or cosmological conceptions.[75] Yet traditional commentators, especially those associated with the *Kung-yang* school, even devised a general theory of history from their reading of such discrepancies. They took their cue from a few scattered entries in the *Kung-yang Commentary* that inquire why the classic does not record the day or circumstances of a particular event. The answer sometimes given in this catechismal commentary is that "[it was a] distant [event]. [Confucius, in describing] what he himself witnessed, [used] distinctive expressions. For what he himself heard [he used other] distinctive expressions; and for what he himself heard by way of transmission [he used still other] distinctive expressions."[76] Later commentators on the *Kung-yang* associated the three periods of Confucius' recollection in this passage with three historical ages—those of disorder (*chü-luan*), approaching peace (*sheng-p'ing*), and great peace (*t'ai-p'ing*)—that were supposed to follow one another in succession. In writing about each of these three ages, Confucius was said to have modulated carefully his language and his coverage of events to the circumstances of the times, thereby producing the apparent disjunc-

(30–101), accounted for this discrepancy in the terms used for "king" by way of geographic reference: "In the capital district he is called 'the king.' Among the other states of China he is called 'the heavenly king.' Among the barbarians he is called the 'son of heaven.' " Quoted in Hung Liang-chi, *Ch'un-ch'iu Tso-chuan ku* (The *Tso Commentary* on the *Spring and Autumn Annals* with Explanatory Notes), SPPY ed., 1.1b–2a. For a more extended account of various Sung commentators' explanations of this discrepancy, see Sung Ting-tsung, *Ch'un-ch'iu Sung-hsüeh fa-wei* (A Disclosure of the Subtleties of Sung Studies on the *Spring and Autumn Annals*) (Taipei: Wen-shih-che ch'u-pan she, 1986), pp. 152–155.

[73] Liu Feng-lu, *Ch'un-ch'iu Kung-yang Ho-shih shih-li* (The *Kung-yang* Version of the *Spring and Autumn Annals* with Mr. Ho's Explanatory Examples), in *Huang-Ch'ing ching-chieh* 1281.1a (vol. 19).

[74] *Ch'un-ch'iu Kung-yang chuan chu-shu* (The *Kung-yang Commentary* on the *Spring and Autumn Annals* with Subcommentaries), comp. Juan Yüan , SPPY ed., 1.4a.

[75] On this point, see, for example, Malmqvist, "Studies," p. 68.

[76] *Ch'un-ch'iu Kung-yang chuan*, p. 8.

tions and unevenness in the text. Thus, an attempt to explain terminological and stylistic inconsistencies in the recording of events
helped inspire the formulation of a general theory of historical development, and also contributed to the image of Confucius as a seer
with preternatural insight into the historical progress of humankind.

The *Spring and Autumn Annals* was not the only one of the Confucian classics for which commentators sought to establish the existence
of a significant order beneath apparent anomalies, inconsistencies,
and randomness at the micro level. Commentators on other classics
may not have developed systematic formulae and procedures for sig-
nifying and explaining such order, as did exegetes of the *Annals*;[77]
but they often tried to demonstrate that apparently random succes-
sions of written characters in various classical texts really manifested
some logical-temporal sequence or order. Ts'ai Shen, for example, a
prominent Sung Neo-Confucian commentator on the *Documents*, proposed the following explanation of the order of the "five affairs" (*wu-
shih*)—"appearing, speaking, looking, listening, and thinking"—given
in the "Great Norm" chapter of the *Documents Classic:*

> When man is first born, his appearance is manifested. After being born,
> his sound is emitted. After a while he is able to see, and then able to hear,
> and then able to think.[78]

Chu Hsi also read a temporal order into the *Analects'* famous characterization of Confucius' lack of negative qualities—its statement that
Confucius had no prejudices, no inflexibilities, no stubbornness, and
no egotism:

> These four in tandem form a temporal cycle. It arises with prejudice, pro-
> ceeds to inflexibilities, rests in stubbornness, and is completed in egotism.
> In general, prejudices and inflexibilities constantly [appear] before an af-
> fair has begun, and stubbornness and egotism after the affair has been
> concluded.[79]

An earlier Sung commentator on the *Analects*, Ch'en Hsiang-tao
(1053–1093), attempted to explain the apparently random order of a
similar set—that which says Confucius "did not speak of prodigies,
force, disorder, and gods" (*Analects* 7:20)—as follows:

> The harm caused by prodigies is not so great as that caused by force. The
> harm caused by force is not so great as that caused by disorder. Prodigies,

---

[77] A list of various formulae widely used in exegesis of the *Spring and Autumn Annals*
appears in Ch'en Li, *Kung-yang i shu* (Subcommentary on the Meanings of the *Kung-
yang Commentary*), SPPY ed., 1.3a.

[78] Ts'ai, *Shu-ching chi-chuan*, p. 75.

[79] Chu, *Ssu-shu chi-chu, Shang-Lun*, p. 56.

force, and disorder are man-made. Therefore, [Confucius] puts them first. Gods are not man-made. Therefore, [Confucius] puts them last.[80]

Like commentators on the *Spring and Autumn Annals*, Confucian exegetes of other classical texts attempted to explain terminological inconsistencies and anomalies as well as apparently random word order. The great Han commentator Cheng Hsüan, for example, queried why the "Appended Judgments" on the third line of the first, or *ch'ien*, hexagram in the *Classic of Change* mentions the "gentleman" while those on the other five lines refer to the "dragon." He explains this apparent anomaly by invoking a cosmological theory relating the Way of man to that of the cosmos at large:

> The positions of the six lines [of the hexagram] emblematize the three powers [of heaven, earth, and man]. The third line is the end of the inner [or lower] trigram and the beginning of the Way of man. Yet, it has the merit of tallying with heaven and earth. Therefore, the [other] five lines all rise with the dragon, but only the third mentions the gentleman.[81]

In sum, just as attempts to explain terminological and stylistic inconsistencies in the *Spring and Autumn Annals* helped to inspire the formulation of grand theories of historical development, so did similar discrepancies in the *Change* apparently stimulate cosmological cogitations on the relationships between heaven, earth, and man.

Ts'ai Shen's endeavor to explain an inconsistency in the use of particles in the account of the five elements or phases given in the "Great Norm" chapter of the *Documents* also gave rise to metaphysical musings. Ts'ai noted that the descriptions of the qualities of four of the five (water, fire, metal, and wood) are preceded by the particle "yüeh" while only earth is preceded by "yüan." He accounts for this by saying that while the text characterizes the first four of the elements in terms of their "natures" (*hsing*), it characterizes the last, earth, in terms of its "virtue" (*te*): namely, "planting and harvesting." According to Ts'ai, this signifies that "the earth element combines the five elements," that it is primary among them. "Therefore, [the text of the 'Great Norm'] does not say 'yüeh' [with respect to the qualities of earth] but says 'yüan.' "[82]

Attempts to explain such grammatical inconsistencies in canonical texts also led commentators in other exegetical traditions to draw cos-

[80] Ch'en, *Lun-yü ch'üan-chieh* 4.13b–14a.

[81] Cheng Hsüan, quoted in *Chou-I chi-chieh tsuan-shu* (The *Chou Change* with Collected Explications and Commentaries), comp. Li Ting-tso (Taipei: Kuang-wen shu-chü, 1971 reprint), 1.6b. This work, compiled during the T'ang era, is the major source for Han commentaries on the *Change*, most of which are lost.

[82] Ts'ai, *Shu-ching chi-chuan*, p. 75.

mological or theological conclusions. Witness, for example, Genesis 1:5 ("And there was evening and there was morning, one day") together with Rashi's commentary:

> According to the style of the rest of this passage, Scripture should have written "first day," since in the case of the other days the ordinal number is given—second, third, fourth, etc. Why, then, is an exception made here? The explanation in the Mishnah is that it is because God was then the only being in existence. (And the term "first" in reference to any existence other than God would be wrong.)[83]

Confucian commentators used cosmological and metaphysical concepts not only to explain terminological and grammatical inconsistencies, as in the examples cited above, but also to account for apparently illogical or puzzling associations of ideas in classical texts. An illustration of such an association, which appears in the "Great Commentary" to the *Change*, is that "the hard and soft are the emblems of day and night." A Han-era commentator on the *Change*, Hsün Shuang (128–190), introduced what might be called "cosmological middle terms"—in this case, "heaven" and "earth"—to help bridge the gap between these two ill-matched dualities, hard and soft and day and night: "Hard is heaven [or the *ch'ien* hexagram], and soft is earth [or the *k'un* hexagram]. Heaven is day and earth is night. Day thus represents the lord, and night the subject."[84]

The use of such cosmological terms as heaven and earth and *yin* and *yang* to explain such perplexing associations was not confined to commentaries on the *Change*. Cheng Hsüan employed a similar strategy to interpret the puzzling passage in the "Royal Institutes" chapter of the *Record of Rites* that "in the spring and autumn one teaches the Rites and Music, and in the winter and summer one teaches the *Songs* and *Documents*." According to Cheng, "the spring and summer are *yang*. The sounds of the *Songs* and Music are also *yang*. The autumn and winter are *yin*. The affairs of the *Documents* and Rites are also *yin*."[85] A later commentator on the "Record of Music" chapter of the *Record of Rites* also used the *yin-yang* duality to account for an earlier commentator's perplexing association of drums with the civil, and bells with the military: "The sound of the drums is *yang*; therefore, one calls it 'civil.' The sound of the bells is *yin*; therefore, one calls it

---

[83] Rashi, *Commentaries on the Pentateuch*, selected and trans. by Chaim Pearl (New York: Viking Press, 1973), p. 32.

[84] Hsün Shuang, quoted in *Chou-I chi-chieh tsuan-shu* 8.711.

[85] Cheng Hsüan, quoted in *Lun-yü chu-shu* (The *Analects* with Commentaries and Subcommentaries), comp. Hsing Ping, SPPY ed., 1.1b.

'military.' "[86] Although such cosmological dualities as *yin-yang* were probably not formulated in the first place to serve exegetical ends, they were developed through being widely used to support such commentarial assumptions as that the classics are well ordered and coherent. Cosmology is, after all, the science of order par excellence. Thus, the strategic use of cosmological ideas to establish the orderliness of classical discourse is not surprising.

But to confirm this proposition that the classics are well ordered and coherent required that the terms of order themselves, the cosmological and metaphysical concepts scattered throughout the Four Books and Five Classics, be properly arrayed and related to one another. Neo-Confucian commentators, for whom such concepts as *li* (principle or pattern), *ch'i* (pneuma), *hsin* (mind or heart), and *hsing* (human nature) were the touchstones of Confucian thought, were particularly concerned with integrating these terms into some kind of larger order or system.[87] Indeed, so important was this project in Neo-Confucianism that various schools of Neo-Confucian thought, such as the "School of Principle" (*li-hsüeh*) and the "School of Mind" (*hsin-hsüeh*), are sometimes distinguished from one another by the particular ways in which they relate such cosmological or metaphysical terms as *li* and *hsin*. Some Neo-Confucian writings even give the impression that a type of enlightenment might proceed from a realization of the proper order and interrelationships of such terms. The great Korean Neo-Confucian scholar Yi T'oegye (1501–1570) constructed elaborate diagrams showing the relationships of various Neo-Confucian terms and concepts to one another. By correctly contemplating some of these diagrams, one could achieve "a level of insight in which discordant notes fall into place and the whole may be grasped as a polyphonic unity."[88] Thus, what began as attempts by exegetes to demonstrate that the scattered and unsystematic occurrences and usages of metaphysical terms in the classics could be resolved into a good order developed into descriptions of ultimate re-

[86] Fang-shih (Mr. Fang), quoted in *Li-chi chi-shuo* (The *Record of Rites* with Collected Explanations), annot. Ch'en Hao, pp. 215–216, in *Ssu-shu wu-ching*, vol. 2.

[87] A similar concern inspired Renaissance aestheticians who inherited from classical antiquity only "a number of scattered notions and suggestions" on aesthetics which "had to be carefully selected, taken out of their context, rearranged, reemphasized and reinterpreted or misinterpreted before they could be utilized as building materials for aesthetic systems." Paul Oskar Kristeller, *Renaissance Thought and the Arts: Collected Essays* (Princeton: Princeton University Press, 1980), p. 174.

[88] Michael C. Kalton, *To Become a Sage: The Ten Diagrams on Sage Learning by Yi T'oegye*, trans., ed., and commentaries by Kalton (New York: Columbia University Press, 1988), pp. 108–109.

ligious experience or intellectual illumination in Neo-Confucian thought.

Neo-Confucian commentators frequently related classical metaphysical terms to one another by defining them as aspects or applications of some master term. Chu Hsi, for example, remarked that "humanity is humanity's basic substance. Rites are humanity's gradations. Rightness is humanity's regulations. And knowledge is humanity's discriminations."[89] Lest this statement be interpreted solely as an expression of Chu's special love of humanity, rather than of his desire to establish the order and interrelatedness of various key terms in Neo-Confucian discourse, witness his account of the functions of the mind, which follows a similar pattern: "The mind is the master of the body. Ideas are what the mind emits. Feelings are what the mind moves. The will is what the mind changes."[90]

The Ming Neo-Confucian philosopher Wang Yang-ming related a slightly higher order of metaphysical entities to the mind: "The mind is one, and that is all. In terms of its completely embodying commiseration it is called 'humanity.' In terms of its attainment of what is proper, it is called 'rightness.' In terms of its orderliness it is called 'principle.' "[91] Like Chu Hsi, Wang Yang-ming in other places related or defined major classical metaphysical concepts by master terms other than "mind"—by "principle" and "human nature," for example.[92] In so doing, Wang gives the impression that the project of arraying these terms in a proper order was more important than the raising of any particular term or concept, such as "mind," to a superior status. Indeed, Wang subsumed more than twice as many such terms to "principle" than to "mind," including "human nature," "mind," "intention," "knowledge," "things," "sincerity," and "rectification."[93]

[89] Chu Hsi, *Chu-tzu yü-lei chi-lüeh* (An Abridgment of the Classified Conversations of Master Chu), comp. Chang Po-hsing (Taipei: Shang-wu yin-shu-kuan, 1973 reprint), 1.36.

[90] Ibid., 1.33. Chu Hsi devised similar systems keyed to other metaphysical master terms, such as heaven (*t'ien*) and principle (*li*). For accounts of these, see *Chin-ssu lu* (Reflections on Things at Hand), annot. Chu Hsi and Lü Tsu-ch'ien; comp. Chiang Yung (Taipei: Kuang-wen shu-chü, 1972 reprint), 1.4–5, 7.

[91] Wang Yang-ming, *Ch'uan-hsi lu* (Instructions for Practical Living), annot. Yeh Chün-tien (Taipei: Shang-wu yin-shu-kuan, 1971 reprint), 2.159.

[92] Ibid., 1.39–40 and 2.168.

[93] Ibid., 2.168. A parallel to Neo-Confucian philosophers' subordination of an array of metaphysical terms to the one they are discussing at a particular time may be found in the kathenotheism, or one-by-one monotheism, of the Veda. Various Vedic hymns give the particular god to whom they are addressed hegemony over all the others, although that god may be ranked in a subordinate position in hymns addressed to other deities.

The systematic relation to one another of such diverse and scattered classical metaphysical terms was something of a tour de force. Revealing the hidden connections among these terms was a means of formulating grand intellectual syntheses and even perhaps of communicating a sort of religious enlightenment. Those Neo-Confucian thinkers who devised or revealed such connections often qualified as sages. But demonstrating the orderliness of classical discourse also required accomplishing the less spectacular task of resolving ambiguities among key classical terms whose meanings appeared to overlap or otherwise to confound one another. For if the canon was really a unified and coherent whole whose texts had been edited by Confucius himself, then the meanings of its key concepts must be distinguished from one another in a clear and consistent fashion.

That the formulation of such distinctions was an important issue in Neo-Confucian thought is illustrated by Chu Hsi's having been asked frequently by his disciples and students to differentiate the meanings of two or more classical metaphysical terms, as the following examples from the *Classified Conversations of Master Chu* (Chu-tzu yü-lei) make clear:

> *Question*: "What is the difference between the Way and principle?"
> *Answer*: "The Way is greatly inclusive. Principles are the numerous patterns and lineaments inside the Way."[94]

> *Question*: "What is the difference between the allotment of human nature and the allotment of destiny?"
> *Answer*: "The allotment of human nature speaks of it in terms of principle. The allotment of destiny speaks of it by connecting pneuma [with principle]."[95]

> *Question*: "What is the difference between sincerity and trust?"
> *Answer*: "Sincerity is a product of nature. Trust is a product of man [or is artificial]. Therefore, it is said that sincerity is the Way of heaven. This is the trust of the sage. In regard to the trust of the common man, it can only be called 'trust,' and cannot be called 'sincerity.' "[96]

In this last illustration, Chu Hsi uses his statement of the essential difference between two related metaphysical terms as a vehicle for expressing a moral hierarchy among men, between sage and commoner.

One of Chu Hsi's disciples, Ch'en Ch'un (1159–1223), devoted a

[94] Chu, *Chu-tzu yü-lei* 1.34.
[95] Ibid., 1.27.
[96] Ibid., 1.35.

special treatise to explaining and distinguishing the meanings of such terms. Regarding the Neo-Confucian formula that "human nature is principle," Ch'en asks why, if the two are really the same, two terms are used instead of one. His answer is that " 'principle' refers generally to the common principle of the cosmos and man. 'Human nature' is the principle within ourselves."[97] Finally, Ch'eng I distinguished between the fidelity (*chung*) and altruism (*shu*) that, according to Tseng-tzu in the *Analects*, constituted the Way of Confucius. "Fidelity," commented Ch'eng, "is the Way of heaven and altruism the Way of man." Further, "fidelity is the essence (*t'i*) and altruism the application (*yung*)."[98]

The preceding examples show that the Sung Neo-Confucians commonly employed certain dualities, especially *li-ch'i* (principle/pneuma), *t'ien-tao–jen-tao* (Way of heaven/Way of man), *t'i-yung* (essence/application), and *yin-yang*, to clarify and distinguish the meanings of key terms in the Neo-Confucian lexicon, and to locate them on a sort of metaphysical map. Indeed, the wide use of these terms in Neo-Confucian writings was at least partly a product of their usefulness for this purpose—that is, for establishing the orderliness and coherence of classical discourse on philosophical topics. Thus, the centrality of the *li-ch'i* and *t'i-yung* dichotomies in Neo-Confucian cosmology may have sprung more from exegetical requirements, broadly conceived, than from pure speculation regarding the structure of the cosmos. They may be treated as a part of the scholastic language that Neo-Confucian commentators devised in order to support the general commentarial assumption that the classics are well-ordered.[99]

Neo-Confucians were not the first commentators in the Confucian tradition to have attempted systematically to distinguish metaphysical terms whose meanings apparently overlap with one another. Li Ting-tso, a T'ang-era commentator on the *Change*, for example, differen-

---

[97] Ch'en Ch'un, *Pei-ch'i tzu-i* (The Meanings of [Confucian Philosophical] Terms [According to Ch'en] Pei-ch'i) (Beijing: Chung-hua shu-chü, 1983 reprint), p. 6; also translated by Wing-tsit Chan in *Neo-Confucian Terms Explained (The "Pei-hsi tzu-i") by Ch'en Ch'un, 1159–1223*, trans., ed., and intro. Chan (New York: Columbia University Press, 1986), pp. 46–47.

[98] Ch'eng I, quoted in Chu *Ssu-shu chi-chu, Shang-Lun*, p. 23. The characterization of fidelity as essence and altruism as application also appears in Chang Shih, *Lun-yü Chang Hsüan-kung chieh* (The *Analects* with Explications by Chang Hsüan-kung), in *Chung-kuo tzu-hsüeh ming-chu chi-ch'eng* 3:175.

[99] Such a special scholastic language, designed to demonstrate the coherence of scriptural texts, was also developed by ancient and medieval Christian biblical exegetes. See, for example, Jean-Nöel Guinot, "Théodoret de Cyr," in *Le Monde grec ancien et la Bible*, ed. Claude Mondésert (Paris: Editions Beauchesne, 1984), p. 345.

tiated the terms *t'ien* (heaven) and *ch'ien* (the "creation" hexagram corresponding to heaven in the *Classic of Change*) by calling the former the "essence of heaven" and the latter the "application of heaven,"[100] again invoking the useful *t'i-yung* dichotomy. One of the apocrypha to the *Change*, the *I-wei ch'ien-tso-tu*, even formulates a cosmogony in the course of differentiating various classical terms used to denote the beginning of the cosmos:

> There is a "grand change," a "grand incipience," a "grand beginning," and a "grand simplicity." [With the] grand change, the pneuma has not yet appeared. The grand incipience is the beginning of the pneuma. The grand beginning is the beginning of forms. The grand simplicity is the beginning of matter.[101]

Thus, cosmogony may take its place among the various commentarial strategies used by exegetes to establish the orderliness of classical discourse. In fact, some cosmogonies may well have been devised for just that purpose.

The highly formalized parallelistic modes of expression used by many Confucian commentators may also have been designed to demonstrate or perhaps simulate the ideal of classical orderliness. Models for such expressions appear in the classics themselves, as in this paradoxical parallelism from the *Doctrine of the Mean*: "When clarification comes from sincerity, it is called 'human nature.' When sincerity comes from clarification, it is called 'teaching.' With sincerity there is clarification; with clarification there is sincerity."[102] Whatever sense may be made of this passage, it at least serves the purpose of relating key Confucian metaphysical terms to one another in an ordered and symmetrical way. To accomplish this end was, as noted above, one of the marks of Neo-Confucian sagehood.

So it is not surprising that parallelistic modes of discourse were highly developed by Neo-Confucian commentators. In some cases, the demands (or attractions) of symmetry and stylization may have affected the structure of thought, not just provided a fitting means for its expression. For example, it appears that Chu Hsi's delight in parallelism inspired him to relate "humanity" and "rightness" to one another in the following way: "The essence of humanity is hard but its application soft. The essence of rightness is soft but its application

---

[100] *Chou-I chi-chieh tsuan-shu* 1.1a.

[101] *I-wei ch'ien-tso-tu*, quoted in Hui Tung, *I-li* (Exempla from the *Change*) (Taipei: Shang-wu yin-shu-kuan, 1965 reprint), p. 3; another English translation of this passage from the *I-wei ch'ien-tso-tu* appears in Wilhelm, *Eight Lectures*, p. 82.

[102] *Chung-yung* (Doctrine of the Mean), chap. 21.

hard."[103] The mid-Ching philosopher Tai Chen (1723–1777), often identified as an iconoclastic critic of Sung Neo-Confucian metaphysics, did not abandon his predecessors' manner of discourse, their highly formalized, symmetrical modes of expression. He thus related orthodoxy and heterodoxy to one another by remarking that "the Way of the [Confucian] sages and worthies has no egotism but is not without desires. Lao-tzu, Chuang-tzu, and the Buddha have no desires but are not without egotism."[104]

Such parallelistic language, which may well serve mnemonic purposes, appears in other commentarial traditions besides the Confucian, and it is in fact one of the marks of scholastic discourse, even that of Jesus: "For with what judgment ye judge, ye shall be judged; and with what measure ye mete, it shall be measured to you again" (Matthew 7:2). "The scholastic machine," as Jacques Le Goff has remarked of Western medieval theological formulations, was "always intent on finding symmetries."[105]

. . . . .

In the West, if not in Confucian China, the scholastic machine was even more intent on resolving apparent contradictions in the classics or scriptures, on demonstrating that the canon is self-consistent. This is true not only of biblical exegesis, but of Western hermeneutics in general. As a recent interpreter of Hellenistic exegesis on Homer remarks, "from its beginnings hermeneutics seems to have been bent to the task of reconciling apparent contradictions whether within the work of a single author or between authors."[106]

In ancient and medieval biblical exegesis, attempts to resolve such discrepancies helped to inspire the development of the best-known of all commentarial strategies—the positing of different levels of meaning or interpretation apart from the literal sense, the most celebrated of which is the allegorical. Commentators in some traditions, especially the Homeric and the biblical, took the appearance of superficial contradictions in the canon as a signal calling for a deeper level of interpretation—notably allegory—that went beyond the lit-

---

[103] Chu, *Chu-tzu yü-lei* 1.36.

[104] Tai Chen, *Meng-tzu tzu-i shu-cheng* (Explications and Verifications on the Meanings of Terms in *Mencius*) (Taipei: Shih-chieh shu-chü, 1966 reprint), 2.80.

[105] Jacques Le Goff, *The Birth of Purgatory*, trans. Arthur Goldhammer (Chicago: University of Chicago Press, 1984), p. 266.

[106] Robert Lamberton, "Introduction" to *Porphyry: On the Cave of the Nymphs*, trans. and intro. Lamberton (Barrytown, N.Y.: Station Hill Press, 1983), p. 5.

eral sense.[107] Indeed, some early Christian commentators, among them Origen, seem to have regarded such contradictions as a divinely inspired means of prompting the search for the more profound spiritual sense of Scripture.[108]

In other traditions, though, the resort to allegory in order to explain apparent discrepancies or contradictions in a classical or scriptural text was not so immediate or automatic. Chinese Confucian commentators, in fact, hardly used allegory at all for this purpose. In their attempts to establish that the canon is self-consistent, however, they did use strategies that had counterparts in other major commentarial traditions. One of the most common of these is the idea of accommodation, the doctrine that the sages or divines whose words are recorded in the classics or scriptures keyed their teachings to different pedagogical levels in order to meet the needs and correct the views of different classes of disciples or auditors. Hence, sagely sayings and divine utterances that apparently contradicted one another were not interpreted as statements of absolute or immutable truths, in which case discrepancies among them would have posed serious problems, but as means of instructing and cultivating particular kinds of students.

Confucian commentators used the idea of accommodation to resolve apparent discrepancies particularly in their interpretations of the *Analects*. In fact, the *Analects* itself provides justification for this procedure in a saying attributed to Confucius: "To those who are above average, one can speak of higher [things]. To those below average, one cannot speak of higher things" (*Analects* 6:19). Elsewhere, Confucius explains his having given conflicting admonitions to two different disciples as follows: "Since Ch'iu was backward, I urged him on. Since Yu outstripped others, I held him back" (*Analects* 11:21). Later Confucian commentators and philosophers, including Han Yü, Chang Tsai (1020–1077), and Wang Yang-ming, used this same principle to explain other instances in the *Analects* where Confucius gave different answers to the same question: his responses were intended to meet the needs or to accord with the intellectual or spiritual attainments of particular disciples.[109]

[107] See, for example, ibid., p. 11; and M. F. Wiles, "Origen as Biblical Scholar," in *Cambridge History of the Bible*, vol. 1, p. 476. The pervasiveness of allegory in Western traditions is underlined by Stephen Prickett who remarks that "allegorical interpretation has roots in pre-biblical Babylonian and Egyptian hermeneutics, and . . . lasts until well on into the nineteenth century." Prickett, *Words and the Word: Language, Poetics, and Biblical Interpretation* (Cambridge: Cambridge University Press, 1986), p. 23.

[108] Childs, *New Testament as Canon*, p. 146.

[109] See, for example, Charles Hartman, *Han Yü and the T'ang Search for Unity* (Prince-

Despite its importance in exegesis of the *Analects*, the idea of accommodation was not so widely used by Confucian commentators on most of the other classics. This strategy was, however, more commonly employed in other major Eastern religious traditions—particularly the Vedantic and Buddhist, whose canons contained more direct and flagrant internal contradictions on crucial issues. For example, the Upanishads seemed to teach both that the divine nature, Brahman, is above form and that it is qualified by form, that it is both nondual and dual. Likewise, various Buddhist sūtras present the Buddha as preaching both the doctrine of nonexistence and the doctrine of neither existence nor nonexistence of the individual soul or being. Such contradictions were more serious than those appearing in the *Analects* which generally only present Confucius as giving different answers to his disciples' practical questions. For they concerned the central metaphysical questions in the Vedantic and Buddhist traditions. The resolution of such contradictions preoccupied some of the most profound commentators in these traditions and inspired the development of important philosophical ideas.

Among these was the Buddhist doctrine of *upāya* (skill in means), according to which the historical Buddha preached divergent doctrines keyed to the different intellectual capacities or spiritual dispositions of various classes of auditors. For example, the Buddha preached the doctrine of nonexistence to those who adhered to existence, and the doctrine of neither existence nor nonexistence to those who adhered to nonexistence, by most accounts a higher stage of mental or spiritual development.[110] According to some commentators, especially those associated with the Mādhyamika school, all of the teachings of the Buddha were merely provisional or pedagogical, designed to cut off false views.[111] Nowhere in the canon did there appear any final or complete statement of absolute truth.

Vedantic commentators, unlike some of their Mādhyamika Buddhist counterparts, did not generally assert that their scriptures contain no statement of final truth. But Shankara, at least, held that even the ultimate truth of the nondual absolute Brahman as stated in the Veda is provisional or pedagogical in the sense that it is intended only to instruct the unenlightened.[112] To those who are especially unen-

---

ton: Princeton University Press, 1986), p. 184; Ira E. Kasoff, *The Thought of Chang Tsai* (Cambridge: Cambridge University Press, 1984), p. x; Wang, *Ch'uan-hsi lu* 1.100–101.

[110] Kogen Mizuno, *Buddhist Sutras: Origin, Development, Transmission*, trans. Moroi Takanashi et al. (Tokyo: Kosei Publishing Co., 1982), p. 140.

[111] Richard H. Robinson, *Early Mādhyamika in India and China* (Madison: University of Wisconsin Press, 1967), p. 40.

[112] K. Satchidananda Murty, *Revelation and Reason in Advaita Vedānta* (Waltair: An-

lightened, it may be necessary to teach the conflicting lower doctrine of the dual or personal Brahman. The Upanishads, in fact, contains clear statements of both doctrines, of both the nondual and the dual. But once the primarily pedagogical purport of both is realized, the seriousness of their mutual contradiction is vitiated.

The general idea that apparent imperfections in the canon arise from God, the Godhead, or the sages having made concessions to limited human capacities and understanding is not confined to Eastern religious traditions. Expressions of this concept may be found in Christian, Muslim, and even Neo-Platonic writings.[113] But commentators in these Western traditions less frequently used the idea of accommodation specifically as a device for resolving apparent contradictions in the canon. When they did so, such ventures were sometimes branded as heretical. For example, the Valentinian idea that discrepancies in Jesus' teachings as recorded in the Gospels arose from his having spoken "sometimes from the Demiurge, sometimes from the middle power, sometimes from the highest" was condemned by the church.[114]

A second commentarial strategy that Confucian exegetes often employed to resolve apparent contradictions in their canon has closer orthodox counterparts in Western traditions. This is the use of the standard scholastic or modal distinction.[115] By this method, apparent disjunctions in the meanings of words and concepts in the classics or scriptures are reconciled by saying that the same term is being used in two or more different senses or is being approached from more than one point of view. A familiar, if somewhat forced, example of a modal distinction may be found in the doctrine of the Trinity. By this doctrine, the apparently divergent characterizations of "God" that

---

dhra University; New York: Columbia University Press, 1959), p. 99. In his *Crest Jewel of Discrimination*, Shankara comments that "when Brahman has been experienced, it is useless to read the scriptures." *Shankara's Crest Jewel of Discrimination (Viveka Chudamani) with A Garland of Questions and Answers (Prasnottara Prabhavananda)*, trans. and intro. Swami Prabhavananda and Christopher Isherwood (New York: New American Library, 1970), p. 43.

[113] See, for example, Wiles, "Origen as Biblical Scholar," pp. 464–465; Burton, *Collection of the Qur'ān*, pp. 152–153; and Michael J. B. Allen, *Marsilio Ficino and the Phaedran Charioteer* (Berkeley: University of California Press, 1981), p. 41.

[114] Irenaeus, *Against the Heresies* III, preface–4.2, trans. E. R. Hardy, in *Documents in Early Christian Thought*, eds. Maurice Wiles and Mark Santer (Cambridge: Cambridge University Press, 1983), p. 129.

[115] For an explanation and application by Origen of the modal distinction, which he bases on Aristotle's definition of equivocal terms (*Categories* 1.1), see Origen, "Homily XX on Jeremiah," trans. in Joseph W. Trigg, *Biblical Interpretation* (Wilmington, Del.: Michael Glazier, 1988), p. 75. I was first apprised of this term and its hermeneutical application by a former colleague, Stephen Farmer.

appear in Scripture may be explained by assigning them to the different persons of the Trinity. God in his capacity as the Son, or Word, may perform acts or have attributes that differ from those of God in his capacity as the Father. Thus, St. Justin Martyr accounted for the puzzling mention of two "Lords" in Genesis 19:24—"the Lord rained upon Sodom and Gomorrah fire and brimstone from the Lord out of heaven"—by saying that the first "Lord" is Christ, or God the Son, and that the second, the one in heaven, is God the Father.[116] It is possible that the idea of the Trinity may itself have been formulated partly to solve the exegetical problem of explaining divergent accounts of God given in Scripture, of characterizing a being that manifested apparently inconsistent divine and human attributes. A central doctrine of the Christian faith may thus be regarded as a product of an exegetical technique, the modal distinction.[117]

A more clearly and precisely formulated modal distinction appears in a fourteenth-century attempt to reconcile the biblical reference to the waters above the firmament with the Aristotelian doctrine that none of the four earthly elements—including water—inheres in the superlunary regions, which are composed of a fifth celestial element, ether. Fourteenth-century scholastics resolved this apparent contradiction between two canonical authorities, the Bible and Aristotle, by positing that while water did not inhere "formally" (*formaliter*) in the superlunary ether, it existed there "virtually" (*virtualiter*).[118] Thus, Aristotle and the Scriptures did not contradict one another on this important cosmological question; they were simply speaking from different points of view in their characterizations of the watery element.

Commentators in other traditions used the modal distinction not only to mediate conflicts between different authorities, such as Aristotle and the Bible, but also to resolve contradictions within single canonical works. The Neo-Platonist Proclus (410–485?), for example, explained Plato's characterization of "Homer" as both "divine" and "third from the truth" by proposing that "insofar as Homer is possessed by the Muses, he is divine; but insofar as he is an imitator, he

[116] Willis A. Shotwell, *The Biblical Exegesis of Justin Martyr* (London: SPCK, 1965), pp. 34–35; Rowan A. Greer, "The Christian Bible and Its Interpretation," in James L. Kugel and Rowan A. Greer, *Early Biblical Interpretation* (Philadelphia: Westminster Press 1986), p. 147.

[117] For an example of how the doctrine of the Trinity was used, particularly in the biblical exegesis of Theodore of Mopsuestia, to explain apparent contradictions in the Gospels' characterizations of Christ's relationship to the Father, see M. F. Wiles, "Theodore of Mopsuestia as Representative of the Antiochene School," in *Cambridge History of the Bible*, vol. 1, p. 505.

[118] Edward Grant, "Cosmology," in *Science in the Middle Ages*, ed. David C. Lindberg (Chicago: University of Chicago Press, 1978), pp. 277–278 and 287.

is third from the truth."[119] Another Neo-Platonic commentator on Homer, Porphyry, accounted for the divergence between two epithets describing the Cave of the Nymphs in book 13 of the *Odyssey*, "lovely" and "murky," as follows: "Thus, as far as its exterior is concerned, and viewed superficially, it is 'lovely,' but as far as its interior is concerned, and viewed in depth, 'murky.' "[120]

Vedantists, primarily concerned as they were with reconciling apparent inconsistencies in the Upanishads and in other parts of their canon, commonly used modal distinctions in their exegetical works. Shankara employed such a distinction to mediate two conflicting statements in the *Bhagavad Gītā*—that the *Ātman*, or Supreme Self, in the form of Krishna dwells in the heart of every being and that the *Ātman* does not dwell in beings. He resolved this apparent discrepancy by stating that the indwelling *Ātman* refers to the physical and material nature of Brahman as opposed to the true *Ātman*.[121] Vyasatirtha, a later Vedantic commentator of the rival Dvaita school, used a similar scholastic distinction in order to reconcile the contradiction between Upanishadic characterizations of Brahman as both dual and nondual. Brahman is one, or nondual, in its own essence (*svarupena*) and dual by virtue of a peculiarity of its nature.[122] The popular fifteenth-century synopsis of Vedānta, the *Vedāntasāra*, also used a kind of modal distinction in order to explain conflicting accounts in the Upanishads of Brahman's relation to the physical world, of the sense in which Brahman brought the universe into being. Thus Brahman, "when considered from its own standpoint is the efficient cause, and when considered from the standpoint of its *Upādhi* or limitation is the material cause [of the universe]."[123]

A noted medieval biblical exegete, Hugh of St. Victor, also employed a kind of modal distinction in order to resolve a conflict in the Scriptures on a cosmogonic question. In seeking to reconcile the contradiction between the six-day account of the Creation in Genesis 1

[119] Proclus, "On the More Difficult Questions in the *Republic*: The Nature of Poetic Art," trans. Thomas Taylor and Kevin Kerrane, in Hardison et al., eds., *Medieval Literary Criticism*, p. 63.

[120] *Porphyry. On the Cave of the Nymphs*, pp. 24–25. A fuller explanation of this distinction, from the point of view of Porphyry's Neo-Platonic model of perception, may be found in Robert Lamberton, *Homer the Theologian: Neoplatonist Allegorical Reading and the Growth of the Epic Tradition* (Berkeley: University of California Press, 1986), pp. 126–127.

[121] Arvind Sharma, *The Hindu Gītā: Ancient and Classical Interpretations of the Bhagavadgītā* (London: Duckworth, 1986), p. 63.

[122] B.N.K. Sharma, *History of the Dvaita School of Vedānta and Its Literature: From the Earliest Beginnings to Our Own Times* (Delhi: Motilal Banarsidass, 1981), p. 329.

[123] *Vedāntasāra*, p. 40 (see n. 19 above).

and the "day" of Genesis 2:4 as well as the statement in Ecclesiasticus 18:1 that "he that liveth forever created all things together," Hugh affirmed that God first created all things at once *in matter* and that later, over the course of six days, differentiated them *in form*.[124] Hugh thus distinguished between two different senses or modes of "creation."

As with Western scholasticism, Neo-Platonism, and Vedānta, the modal distinction was most highly developed and frequently used in Chinese Confucian exegesis in a later, more philosophical tradition— that of Neo-Confucianism. Prominent Neo-Confucians such as Ch'eng I and Chu Hsi used this device particularly to resolve apparent discrepancies in the newly canonized Four Books. One such disjunction was in the differing Confucian and Mencian accounts of "human nature" (*hsing*). Whereas the Confucius of the *Analects* remarked that men's natures are merely close to one another's, Mencius maintained that human nature is basically good.[125] Ch'eng I commented that Confucius was "speaking of the temperamental side of human nature, and not speaking of the basis of human nature. If one speaks of its basis, human nature is the same as principle. And there is no principle that is not good—thus Mencius' saying that human nature is good. How [then could men's basic natures be merely] close to one another's?"[126] The Ming philosopher Feng Ts'ung-wu (1556– 1627) reconciled these same two characterizations of human nature in Confucius and Mencius by using a similar modal distinction. While Confucius, he said, was speaking of the temperamental aspect of human nature, Mencius was referring to the nature mandated by heaven.[127]

Neo-Confucian commentators also used modal distinctions to resolve discrepancies within single books of their canon. Chu Hsi, for example, employed such a device in order to explain why in one chapter the "Great Commentary" to the *Change* associates "knowledge" with heaven and "humanity" with earth, while in the next it links "knowledge" with *yin* (which is associated with earth) and "hu-

[124] Beryl Smalley, *The Study of the Bible in the Middle Ages*, 3rd ed., rev. (Oxford: Basil Blackwell, 1983), pp. 132–133.

[125] *Analects* 17:2; *Mencius* 6A, 2:2.

[126] Ch'eng I, quoted in Chu, *Ssu-shu chi-chu*, *Hsia-Lun* (Second Part of *Analects*), p. 119.

[127] Feng Ts'ung-wu, *I-ssu lu* (Record of Doubtful Thoughts), from *Feng Ts'ung-wu wen-chi* (Literary Works of Feng Ts'ung-wu), in *T'u-shu chi-ch'eng* 57:2884. Neo-Confucians devised a similar kind of modal distinction in order to reconcile the divergent characterizations of human nature in *Mencius* and *Hsün-tzu*, as explained in Donald J. Munro, *Images of Human Nature: A Sung Portrait* (Princeton: Princeton University Press, 1988), pp. 69–70.

manity" with *yang* (which is associated with heaven). The first chapter, Chu declared, "speaks [of heaven] in terms of clarity and turbidity," while the next "speaks in terms of movement and quiescence."[128] Ts'ai Shen used a modal distinction to mediate between divergent characterizations of "felicity" or "happiness" (*fu*) in two adjoining passages in the "Great Norm" chapter of the *Documents Classic*: "Whereas the preceding passage refers to the complete essence of felicity, this one issues from the one origin of felicity."[129]

In some cases, Neo-Confucian commentators arrayed the two parts of a modal distinction hierarchically, as the following example from Ch'en Ch'un's *Pei-ch'i tzu-i* (The Meanings of [Confucian Philosophical] Terms [According to Ch'en] Pei-ch'i) illustrates:

> The *Doctrine of the Mean* says that "fidelity and altruism are not far from the Way," correctly speaking of the fidelity and altruism of scholars. Tseng-tzu [in the *Analects*] says that "the Way of the Master [Confucius] is fidelity and altruism," speaking of the fidelity and altruism of sages. The fidelity and altruism of sages is the Way of heaven. The fidelity and altruism of scholars is the Way of man.[130]

Although they used it most frequently, Neo-Confucians were not the only commentators in the Confucian tradition to employ the modal distinction in order to reconcile discrepancies in canonical texts. A T'ang commentator on the *Classic of Change*, for example, explained two different characterizations of the *ch'ien* hexagram in the canonical appendices to that classic as follows: "The 'Tsa-kua' (Miscellaneous [Remarks on the] Hexagrams) says that *ch'ien* is 'hard,' speaking of its essence (*t'i*). The 'Shuo-kua' (Explanations of the Trigrams) says that *ch'ien* is 'strong,' speaking of its application (*yung*)."[131] Even modern historians of Confucian persuasion occasionally use modal distinctions, particularly to resolve apparent conflicts among Neo-Confucian philosophers. Lu Pao-ch'ien, for example, attempted to reconcile divergent conceptions of "mind" in Wang Yang-ming and Chu Hsi by arguing: "What Wang Yang-ming refers to is the basic metaphysical mind, and what Chu Hsi refers to is the practical nonmetaphysical mind."[132]

The ambiguity and multivalency of such basic terms in the Neo-Confucian lexicon as "mind," "human nature," and "humanity" lent

[128] Chu Hsi, *Chou-I pen-i* (Basic Meaning of the *Chou Change*) (Taipei: Hua-lien ch'u-pan she, 1971 reprint), 3.5b.

[129] Ts'ai, *Shu-ching chi-chuan*, p. 76.

[130] Ch'en, *Pei-ch'i tzu-i*, p. 30.

[131] *Chou-I chi-chieh tsuan-shu* 1.47.

[132] Lu, *Ch'ing-tai ssu-hsiang shih*, pp. 173–174.

itself particularly well to the use of the standard scholastic or modal distinction. Hence, Neo-Confucian philosophers employed this device more than any other as a means of reconciling apparent contradictions in their canon, of establishing that the classics are self-consistent.

Ch'ing commentators having more practical interests in history and statecraft often employed other strategies or arguments to resolve canonical contradictions. One of these is the idea that conflicting concepts and schemas in the classics were not intended as timeless absolutes, but were meant to be applied in different historical ages. This strategy for explaining discrepancies was used particularly by nineteenth-century New Text scholars. K'ang Yu-wei, for example, accounted for the disjunction between Hsün-tzu's theory that human nature is evil and Mencius' that it is good by arguing that the former was meant to provide the basis for government in the age of disorder, the latter in the age of peace.[133] K'ang also held that the reason why Hsün-tzu spoke much of rites but little of humanity, whereas Mencius did the opposite, was that the former was intended to accord with the era of small prosperity (*hsiao-k'ang*) and the latter with that of great harmony (*ta-t'ung*).[134]

Nineteenth-century New Text scholars were also concerned to explain the disjunctions between the account of the ancient political order given in the classical *Rites of Chou* and that which appears in the "Royal Institutes" chapter of the *Record of Rites*. According to P'i Hsi-jui, these discrepancies arose from the fact that while the *Rites of Chou* described the system prevailing under the Chou dynasty, the "Royal Institutes" delineated Confucius' own plan for a future political order. It was, P'i claimed, "the system of the uncrowned king," Confucius.[135] Earlier commentators, however, beginning with Cheng Hsüan in the Han era, accounted more mundanely for the disjunctions between these two classical descriptions of the ancient political order, arguing that while the *Rites of Chou* described the system of the Chou dynasty, the "Royal Institutes" outlined that of the preceding Shang or Yin dynasty.[136] Finally, the Yüan Neo-Confucian commentator Hsü Ch'ien (1269–1337) indicated that such formal or technical disjunctions in classical accounts of the ancient political and social order

[133] K'ang, *Meng-tzu wei*, p. 3

[134] K'ang Yu-wei, *Nan-hai K'ang hsien-sheng k'ou-shuo* (Oral Sayings of Mr. K'ang of Nan-hai) (Chung-shan ta-hsüeh ch'u-pan she, 1985), p. 31.

[135] P'i Hsi-jui, *Ching-hsüeh t'ung-lun* (Comprehensive Discussions of Classical Studies) (Taipei: Ho-Lo t'u-shu ch'u-pan she, 1974 reprint), 3.69.

[136] Honda Shigeyuki, *Chung-kuo ching-hsüeh shih* (History of Chinese Classical Studies) (Taipei: Ku-t'ing shu-wu, 1975 reprint), p. 171.

were of little moment, inasmuch as the purport of such systems in general was to ensure the support and comfort of the aged and the moral education of the young.[137]

.   .   .   .   .

The problem of explaining apparent immorality and improprieties in the classics or scriptures was more important in Western exegesis of Homer and the Bible than in most Eastern commentarial traditions, perhaps because moral outrages were more frequent or conspicuous in these Western canons. As noted above, Homeric and Christian commentators frequently employed allegory in order to account for apparent moral lapses and offenses in the scriptures. As the Hellenistic exegete Heraclides remarked, "If Homer was not speaking in allegorical terms, he was guilty of the greatest impieties."[138] The same might be said of the composers of some of the books of the Old Testament. Indeed, as Origen pointed out, commentators who eschewed allegorical interpretations of such phrases from the Old Testament as that "an evil spirit from God suffocated Saul" (1 Samuel 18:10) were frequently driven to espouse such heretical doctrines as that the God of the Old Testament was an imperfect one, different from the God of the New.[139] The only feasible nonheretical alternative to allegorical readings of the Old Testament, it seemed, was the abandonment of a large part of that canon.

Confucian commentators did not generally confront such stark choices when they turned their attention to instances of apparent immorality and inhumaneness in the classics of their tradition. Moreover, their explanations for the appearance of such improprieties were seldom allegorical. Wang Yang-ming, for example, claimed that the licentious selections contained in the *Songs Classic* were not edited by Confucius but were added by ordinary scholars of the Han dynasty in order to replace missing parts after the Ch'in burning of the books.[140] The Ch'ing philologist and philosopher Li Kung (1659–1733) saw some positive moral value in these selections, remarking that reading of the depravities recorded in the *Songs* taught one to

[137] Hsü Ch'ien, *Tu Meng-tzu ts'ung-shuo* (A Reading of *Mencius* with Collected Explanations), p. 4a, in *Chung-kuo tzu-hsüeh ming-chu chi-ch'eng* 11:303.

[138] Heraclides, quoted in Jean Seznec, *The Survival of the Pagan Gods: The Mythological Tradition and Its Place in Renaissance Humanism and Art*, trans. Barbara F. Sessions (Princeton: Princeton University Press, 1972), p. 84.

[139] Origen, *On First Principles*, bk. 4, in *Biblical Interpretation in the Early Church*, trans. and ed. Karlfried Froehlich (Philadelphia: Fortress Press, 1984), p. 55.

[140] Wang, *Ch'uan-hsi lu* 1.26.

avoid them.[141] Chu Hsi posed a similar explanation for the preponderance of negative examples, as opposed to positive exemplars, contained in the *Spring and Autumn Annals*, interpreting them as warnings to future generations.[142] In his commentary on the *Analects*, Chu even used a sort of modal distinction to account for what might be construed as an inhumane remark by Confucius—that obtaining the people's trust is more important than feeding them (*Analects* 12:7). According to Chu, Confucius was here "speaking in terms of the people's virtue," not "in terms of human feelings."[143] Chu, together with Ch'eng I and other Neo-Confucian scholars of the Sung era, also defended Mencius against an apparent moral lapse—specifically, the charge that he did not honor and respect the House of Chou—by arguing that the circumstances of the time made it impossible for him to do so.[144]

Much of the commentary on the great Indian epic the *Rāmāyana* is also centered on explaining apparent moral lapses, especially those of the hero, Rāma, in such episodes as his killing of the monkey-king Vāli and his subjecting his wife Sītā to a horrible fire ordeal, at the end of the epic, in order to prove her chastity. A modern expositor of the *Rāmāyana*, Chakravarti Rajagopalachari, remarks of the latter episode that "Raama's avataar came to an end with the slaying of Raavana [the demon king]. After that battle, Raama remained only as a king" whose conduct "can be explained simply as the behaviour of a king in accordance with the customs of the time."[145] A related argument—that "when God takes a lower and limited form by His own ordinance, limitations follow"—is the most frequent one employed by *Rāmāyana* exegetes to account for Rāma's apparent moral imperfections in the epic.[146]

A more drastic means that some Confucian commentators used to deal with apparent improprieties in the classics was simply to delete

[141] Li Kung, "Lun-yü chuan-chu wen" (Queries Regarding Commentaries and Annotations on the *Analects*), in *Ch'ing-ju hsüeh-an* 13.28a (vol. 1).

[142] Chu Hsi, "Ch'un-ch'iu kang-ling" (An Outline of the *Spring and Autumn Annals*), in *T'u-shu chi-ch'eng* 56:1874. The Hellenistic commentator Pseudo-Plutarch offered a similar explanation for why Homer depicts vices as well as virtues. See Robert Drummond Lamberton, "Homer the Theologian: The *Iliad* and *Odyssey* as Read by the Neoplatonists of Late Antiquity" (Ph.D. diss., Yale University, 1979), p. 119.

[143] Chu, *Ssu-shu chi-chu, Hsia-Lun*, p. 80.

[144] Chu, *Ssu-shu chi-chu, Shang-Meng*, p. 5. K'ung Ying-ta, in the T'ang era, defended Confucius against a similar accusation. See David McMullen, *State and Scholars in T'ang China* (Cambridge: Cambridge University Press, 1988), p. 80.

[145] Chakravarti Rajagopalachari, *Ramayana* (Bombay: Bharatiya Vidya Bhavan, 1986), p. 311.

[146] Ibid., p. 190.

them, following in the footsteps of Confucius. Some commentators proposed to do this not only with the *Songs*, but even with the *Mencius*. According to Feng Hsiu, parts of the *Mencius* that contravened the other classics had been added to the text by some of his later disciples. Feng thus deleted such parts from his own *Expurgated Mencius* (Shan Meng-tzu).[147] In so doing, he was to some extent following the example of Mencius himself, who refused to accept as authentic a passage in the *Documents Classic* which says that pestles floated in the blood shed by the people when they were fighting for a humane ruler (*Mencius* 7B, 3).

Among commentators in other traditions, Homeric scholars are most renowned for excising or at least signaling lines they consider to be offensive or immoral. The Alexandrian scholar Aristarchus, for example, deleted four lines from the *Iliad* in which Phoenix expresses his desire to kill his father, as well as a line that characterized the goddess Aphrodite by her "voluptuousness."[148] Zenodotus also deleted lines that seemed to show insufficient respect for the gods, as well as those in which such heroes as Agamemnon were said to "tremble."[149] More commonly, though, Alexandrian critics simply marked such passages, rather than eject them altogether.[150]

. . . . .

Establishing a fourth basic commentarial assumption—that the classics are profound—did not generally require such drastic measures as deletion or expurgation. However, one of the main strategies that Confucian commentators, especially Neo-Confucians, used to substantiate this proposition has some resemblance to expurgation. Those parts of the canon which were not especially profound or philosophical were all but ignored, and attention was focused on a few particular books, passages, and ideas in the classics which were. This tendency to narrow the scope of classical studies to a few privileged parts of the canon appeared as early as Han times. But it was exaggerated among Sung and Ming Neo-Confucians, some of whom

[147] Ch'ao Kung-wu (summarizing the views of Feng Hsiu), quoted in *Ching-i k'ao* 233.2b (vol. 7).

[148] F. A. Wolf, *Prolegomena to Homer, 1795*, trans. with intro. and notes by Anthony Grafton et al. (Princeton: Princeton University Press, 1985), p. 6; Marchinus H.A.L.H. van der Valk, *Textual Criticism of the Odyssey* (Leiden: A. W. Sithoff's Uitgeversmaatschappij N.V., 1949), p. 15.

[149] P. M. Fraser, *Ptolemaic Alexandria: I. Text* (Oxford: Clarendon Press, 1972), p. 451; van der Valk, *Textual Criticism*, p. 92.

[150] John L. Myres, *Homer and His Critics* (London: Routledge and Kegan Paul, 1958), p. 13.

took a small number of selected phrases in the *Doctrine of the Mean* and the *Great Learning* as the mainstay of their canonical cogitations. Wang Yang-ming, for example, maintained that the first chapters of each of these two classics "taught the complete task of Confucian learning."[151]

Such a narrowing of classical studies to focus on a few selected ideas, issues, or passages is a common feature in late-scholastic traditions, especially those with large, heterogeneous canons such as Vedānta and Mahāyāna Buddhism. Although prominent Vedantists frequently affirmed the value and authoritativeness of all scripture, of the entire Veda, in practice they concentrated their attention on the Upanishads, by far the most profound and philosophical part of the Vedic canon. According to Eliot Deutsch and J.A.B. van Buitenen, "very little of the Revelation literature preceding the Upanishads was of systematic interest to the Vedantins."[152] Early Vedantic texts such as the *Brāhma Sūtra*, moreover, focused on only one or two of the Upanishads, considering the others only incidentally.[153] Later Vedantic commentators not only concentrated their attention on particular parts of the Upanishads, but also seized upon a few ideas or expressions in those parts which, they said, summed up the purport of the entire Veda. According to Shankara and other Vedantists of his school, the sentence "That Thou art," which expresses the identity of Brahman and *Ātman*, of the oversoul and the soul, exhausts the meaning of all the scriptures. Thus, "To teach this cardinal truth—the identity of the soul and Brahman—is the aim of all the Upanisads."[154]

The very size and diversity of the Buddhist canon, the largest of any major tradition, virtually required that those who undertook its study concentrate on a few particular books. As the noted Japanese

[151] Wing-tsit Chan (citing *Wang Wen-ch'eng kung ch'üan shu* 26.2a), in *Instructions for Practical Living and Other Neo-Confucian Writings by Wang Yang-ming*, trans. and annot. Chan (New York: Columbia University Press, n.d.), p. 271.

[152] Eliot Deutsch and J.A.B. van Buitenen, eds., *A Source Book of Advaita Vedānta* (Honolulu: University Press of Hawaii, 1971), pp. 7–8.

[153] Hajime Nakamura, *A History of Early Vedānta*, trans. Trevor Leggett et al. (Delhi: Motilal Banarsidass, 1983), pt. 1, p. 430.

[154] Murty, *Revelation and Reason*, p. 90. According to Frits Staal, "Sankara was wrong, or at any rate unfair, when he isolated a few so-called 'great statements' from all the others that are equally great—and arbitrary. His attitude is simply anachronistic and has little to do with the Upanisads themselves. What is remarkable is that Sankara's perspective has determined the approach of almost all students of Indian philosophy." Staal, "Is There Philosophy in Asia?" in *Interpreting across Boundaries: New Essays in Comparative Philosophy*, eds. Gerald James Larson and Eliot Deutsch (Princeton: Princeton University Press, 1988), p. 223. But what is perhaps even more remarkable is that Staal apparently expects commentators like Shankara to be true to the spirit of the classics.

Buddhist cleric Dōgen (1200–1253) remarked, "A monk who approaches the vast, sublime subject of Buddhism by studying several aspects at once will fail to understand a single one."[155] This natural inclination toward selectiveness, however, was accentuated by the belief that there were some sūtras whose meaning was truly profound and comprehensive, so much so that the rest of the canon could be practically ignored. In East Asian Buddhism, the most famous example of such a sūtra is the *Lotus* beside which all the other sūtras were merely accommodations and preliminary teachings.[156] The great Japanese prophet and prelate Kūkai (774–835), asserted that the very brief *Heart Sūtra* occupied a similar position: "It is simple yet comprehensive; it is terse yet profound. The expositions on wisdom in the Five Collections are contained in one clause without omission, and the goals of the seven Buddhist schools are entered in one line without deletion."[157]

The tendency to concentrate on the more profound or philosophical parts of the canon, while not so pronounced as in Vedānta and Mahāyāna Buddhism, appears in Western religious traditions as well. The early-medieval Christian encyclopedist Cassiodorus, for example, wrote: "I have spent the greatest and most zealous toil upon the Psalter and the Prophets and the Epistles of the Apostles, since they seemed to me to stir up greater profundity of thought and, as it were, to encompass the height of all Scripture and its most glorious depth."[158] The later-medieval scholastic and composer of the famous *Sentences*, Peter Lombard, maintained that the Book of Psalms contained all theology.[159] In the later Middle Ages, moreover, the area of commentarial concern narrowed even more from whole books of the biblical canon to particular issues and doctrines such as the Eucharist and the Trinity. Qur'ānic exegetes, the relative brevity and homogeneity of their canon notwithstanding, identified certain chapters and verses as "the essence of the Qur'ān," "the heart of the

---

[155] Dōgen, *Shōbō Genzō Zuimonki* 2,344, quoted in Konishi Jin'ichi, "Michi and Medieval Writing," in Sumie Jones et al., *Principles of Classical Japanese Literature*, ed. Earl Miner (Princeton: Princeton University Press, 1985), p. 194.

[156] The great Japanese Buddhist prophet Nichiren maintained this view of the *Lotus*. See Laurel Rasplica Rodd, *Nichiren: A Biograghy*, Occasional Paper no. 11 (Tempe: Arizona State University, 1978), p. 15.

[157] Kūkai, "The Secret Key to the Heart Sutra" (Hannya shingyō hiken), in *Kūkai: Major Works*, trans. Yoshito S. Hakeda (New York: Columbia University Press, 1972), p. 264.

[158] Cassiodorus Senator, *An Introduction to Divine and Human Readings*, trans. with intro. and notes by Leslie Webber Jones (New York: W. W. Norton, 1969), p. 71.

[159] Jean Châtillon, "La Bible dans les Écoles du xiie siècle," in *Le Moyen Age et la Bible*, eds. Pierre Riché and Guy Lobrichon (Paris: Editions Beauchesne, 1984), p. 192.

Qur'ān," "the chief of all Qur'ānic verses," or "the key to all the doors of Paradise."[160] Hellenistic commentators on Homer also tended to concentrate on certain episodes in the *Iliad* and *Odyssey*, principally the "divine scenes" which portrayed the gods.[161] Even the Mishnah, in the rabbinic tradition, focused its discussion on a limited number of topics in the Torah book, particularly the calendar, the family, and the institutions of the community.[162] The Talmuds as well were based mainly on the exegesis of only a few provisions contained in the Hebrew Bible.[163]

Commentators in almost all of these traditions frequently affirmed the equal authoritativeness of canonical writings, and even the homogeneity of their canons.[164] Orthodox rabbinic commentators, in fact, went so far as to brand as heretics those who claimed that the Ten Commandments contained the essence of Torah and that all the rest was marginal.[165] Early fathers of the Christian church likewise affirmed that "only heretics would exalt one portion of the New Testament scriptures against another."[166] But the history of hermeneutics in most major canonical traditions seems to revolve around a concentration on progressively narrower selections from the classics or scriptures, generally those thought to be the most philosophical or profound. The development of thought in such traditions often hinged upon shifts in the focus of commentarial concern, shifts of view on the issue of which particular parts or aspects of the canon were most worthy of attention.[167] Classical revivals, renaissances, and reformations within these traditions have frequently centered on such shifts or changes, although the rhetorical claims of these move-

[160] Muhammad Abul Quasem, "Introduction" to al-Ghazālī, *The Jewels of the Qur'ān*, a translation, with an introduction and annotation, of al-Ghazālī's *Kitāb Jawāhir al-Qur'ān* by Quasem (Kuala Lumpur: University of Malaysia Press, 1977), p. 11.

[161] Michael Murrin, *The Allegorical Epic: Essays in Its Rise and Decline* (Chicago: University of Chicago Press, 1980), p. 3.

[162] Jacob Neusner, *Judaism, The Classical Statement: The Evidence of the Bavli* (Chicago: University of Chicago Press, 1986), p. 3.

[163] David Daube, "Rabbinic Methods of Interpretation and Hellenistic Rhetoric," in *Hebrew Union College Annual* 22 (1949), p. 239.

[164] For illustrations of this viewpoint, see Sharma, *Dvaita School*, p. 162; and Earl Edgar Elder, *A Commentary on the Creed of Islam: Sa'd al-Din al-Taftāzāni on the Creed of Najm al-Din al-Nasafi*, trans. with intro. and notes by Elder (New York: Columbia University Press, 1950), p. 135.

[165] Steinsaltz, *Essential Talmud,* p. 104.

[166] David G. Meade, *Pseudonymity and Canon: An Investigation into the Relationship of Authorship and Authority in Jewish and Earliest Christian Tradition* (Tübingen: J.C.B. Mohr [Paul Siebeck], 1986), p. 202.

[167] A similar idea may be found expressed in Frank Kermode, *Forms of Attention* (Chicago: University of Chicago Press, 1985), p. 92.

ments—that they are restoring the authentic core of classical teaching—sometimes obscures this process. One man's classical core, however, may be another man's exegetical rind. As E. Harris Harbison remarks of a verse from Romans that inspired Martin Luther, "A verse which had been a window into Paul's character for Colet and a problem in grammar for Valla and Erasmus had become a key to the whole meaning of Scripture for Luther."[168]

· · · · ·

Among Confucian commentators, Sung Neo-Confucians were most concerned with identifying those parts of the canon that they believed conveyed the essence of the sages' teachings, and they were adept at ignoring the other, inessential or less profound parts. Several of them singled out the newly canonized *Doctrine of the Mean* as the "source of sagely teaching" or "the summation and pivot of all the classics," or remarked that "the conclusions of the Four Books are assembled in the *Doctrine of the Mean*."[169] A Ming Neo-Confucian, Ch'iu Chün (1421–1495), characterized the *Great Learning* in similar terms, calling it the "epitome of the Six Classics and the great canon for myriad ages."[170] Most major Neo-Confucian thinkers did, however, devote attention to a somewhat wider selection of classical texts, usually including the Four Books and some of the "Ten Wings," the canonical commentaries on the *Classic of Change* attributed to Confucius. These were the major components of the new Neo-Confucian canon.[171]

Neo-Confucian philosophers, though, faced the difficulty that important parts of this canon apparently failed to discuss or explain adequately the most profound philosophical conceptions and metaphysical terms in Neo-Confucian thought. This was especially a problem with the *Analects* of Confucius, the main source of the Sage's teaching.

[168] E. Harris Harbison, *The Christian Scholar in the Age of Reformation* (Grand Rapids, Mich.: William B. Eerdmans, 1983), p. 120.

[169] Lo Ts'ung-yen and Li Li-wu, quoted in *Ching-i k'ao* 151.1b (vol. 5); Yang Shih, "Tzu-hsü" (Author's Preface) to *Chung-yung chieh* (Explications of the *Doctrine of the Mean*), in *Ching-i k'ao* 151.6b (vol. 5); Huang Chen, *Chung-yung chang-chü* ([A Commentary on] the *Doctrine of the Mean* by Paragraphs and Sentences), in *Ching-i k'ao* 152.5b (vol. 5).

[170] Ch'iu Chün, "Tzu-hsü" (Author's Preface) to *Ta-hsüeh yen-i pu* (Supplement to the *Extended Meanings of the Great Learning* [of Chen Te-hsiu]), in *Ching-i k'ao* 158.4a (vol. 5).

[171] On the "canon" of the Neo-Confucians, see Mao Huaixin, "The Establishment of the School of Chu Hsi and Its Propagation in Fukien," in Chan, ed., *Chu Hsi and Neo-Confucianism*, p. 503.

Confucian commentators' consideration of this issue frequently focused on the remark recorded in the *Analects* that Confucius' discourses on human nature (*hsing*) and the Way of heaven (*t'ien-tao*) could not be heard (*Analects* 5:12). They proposed several explanations for Confucius' not having directly communicated his teachings on these most profound topics. One of the earliest of these, by the third-century commentator Ho Yen (d. 249), was simply that these conceptions were too "profound and subtle. Thus, [Confucius' disciples] could not hear of them."[172] Another, posed by Chu Hsi, was that "the Sage [Confucius] taught people the broad outline. He spoke only of filiality, brotherliness, fidelity, and trust, words for daily use and constant practice. . . . Such terms as 'mind' and 'human nature' were not spoken of in detail until Tzu-ssu and Mencius."[173] The most common Neo-Confucian explanation for these apparent omissions in the *Analects*, for that text's superficial lack of profundity, was that Confucius really did communicate his teachings on human nature, the Way of heaven, and other profound conceptions, but only indirectly, not explicitly through words. To support this idea, commentators cited another passage in the *Analects* in which Confucius attempted to justify his remark to a disciple that he would prefer not to have to speak at all. Heaven, said Confucius, does not speak, and yet "the four seasons run their course by it, and all things are produced by it" (*Analects* 17:19). So too Confucius, although seldom speaking of human nature and the Way of heaven, was able to subtly and indirectly convey the meanings of these ideas.[174] A Ming Neo-Confucian philosopher, Lo Ch'in-shun (1465–1547), however, asserted that Confucius did indeed directly explain the meanings of human nature and the Way of heaven, but that he did so in the canonical appendices to the *Change* which he is supposed to have composed, not in the *Analects*.[175] Finally, the redoubtable Ch'ing scholar Ch'ien Ta-hsin (1728–1804) excused Confucius' not having spoken in the *Analects* of the "Way of heaven" by arguing that the phrase really referred to occult and astrological matters beyond the ken of the proper Confucian sage.[176]

[172] Ho Yen, *Lun-yü Ho-shih teng chi-chieh* (The *Analects* with Collected Explications by Mr. Ho and Others), SPPY ed., 5.4b.

[173] Chu, *Chu-tzu yü-lei* 2.40.

[174] This argument appears in Hsieh Liang-tso, "Tzu-hsü" (Author's Preface) to *Lun-yü chieh* (Explications of the *Analects*), in *Ching-i k'ao* 214.3a (vol. 6).

[175] Lo Ch'in-shun, *K'un-chih chi*, pt. 2, in *Knowledge Painfully Acquired: The 'K'un-chih chi' by Lo Ch'in-shun*, trans., ed. and intro. Irene Bloom (New York: Columbia University Press, 1987), p. 113.

[176] Ch'ien Ta-hsin, "Ta-wen, liu" (Questions and Answers, no. 6), in *Ch'ien-yen-t'ang wen chi* (Literary Collections from the Hall of Hidden Study) (Taipei: Shang-wu yin-

Neo-Confucian commentators were also concerned with explaining why Confucius apparently neglected to discuss fully or define adequately such profound Confucian concepts as "humanity" (*jen*). The Sung scholar-official Chen Te-hsiu (1178–1235), noting the saying that Confucius seldom spoke of "humanity," averred: "that of which Confucius seldom spoke was only the essence of humanity. As for the methods of seeking humanity and the essentials for practicing humanity, there are instances in all twenty chapters [of the *Analects*]."[177] Chu Hsi, answering a disciple's complaint that Confucius was unclear in his expositions of "humanity," explained that this manifold concept cannot be reduced to words without doing it violence. Chu also maintained that Confucius intended to lead his pupils to humanity through their experiencing it, not through giving them a definition.[178] A Ch'ing scholar, Wu T'ing-tung (1793–1873), argued that Confucius' reticence on "humanity" arose from his fear that discussing it too much would drive his auditors to aim too high.[179] When the Sage did discuss or characterize it, claimed the Sung commentator Cheng Ju-hsieh, he defined it rather inadequately or incompletely in terms of "filiality" and "brotherliness," simply because this provided an accessible approach to "humanity" for his auditors: "If he had taught them by [attempting to explain] the 'Way' and 'humanity,' they would not have known what was the 'Way' or what was 'humanity.' Only by instructing them regarding 'filiality' and 'brotherliness' could they all know the proper point of entry."[180] Confucius thus accommodated his teachings concerning "humanity" to his audience.

Sung Neo-Confucian philosophers were concerned not only with explaining the apparent absence of a profound metaphysics in the *Analects*, but also with accounting for the presence of apparently superficial material in that classical text. Ch'eng I, noting one such instance in the *Analects*, again invoked the idea of accommodation, re-

shu-kuan, 1968), 9.109. Ch'ing scholars were by no means the last to comment on this issue of why the Sage's discourses on human nature and the Way of heaven could not be heard. For a discussion of this question by two of our more philosophical contemporaries, see David L. Hall and Roger T. Ames, *Thinking through Confucius* (Albany: State University of New York Press, 1987), pp. 197–199.

[177] Chen Te-hsiu, "Hsü" (Preface) to Ch'en Tzu, *Lun-yü fa-wei* (A Disclosure of the Subtleties of the *Analects*), in *Ching-i k'ao* 219.3a–3b (vol. 6).

[178] Sato Hitoshi, "Chu Hsi's 'Treatise on Jen,' " in Chan, ed., *Chu Hsi and Neo-Confucianism*, p. 214.

[179] Wu T'ing-tung, "Yü Fang Ts'un-chih lun tu Lun Meng chi i" (A Record of Doubts Concerning a Discussion with Fang Ts'un-chih on the Reading of the *Analects* and *Mencius*), in *Ch'ing-ju hsüeh-an* 159.4b (vol. 7).

[180] Cheng Ju-hsieh, *Lun-yü i yüan* (The Sources of the Ideas in the *Analects*), in *Ching-yüan* 159.4b (vol. 7).

marking that "the words of the sages change according to the person [addressed]. Although it seems that there are superficial words [among them], what they encompass is inexhaustible."[181] Regarding another admittedly superficial phrase in the *Analects*, Ch'eng argued that "although the sayings of the Sage are very commonplace, if one puts these three sayings in context and extends them to their ultimate degree, then even the regulations of [the sage-kings] Yao and Shun do not surpass them."[182] In sum, Ch'eng I proposed at least two explanations for the seeming superficiality of some of Confucius' utterances as recorded in the *Analects*: first, that they were adapted to the audience that the Sage was addressing; second, that when extended and related to a larger context, they are really profound.

Confucian scholars who were oriented toward concerns of statecraft were more inclined to admit the classics' lack of intellectual profundity and literary polish. But this for them was not a serious shortcoming since, as the prominent Ming scholar-official Fang Hsiao-ju (1357–1402) maintained, "The classics are instruments for governing the world," not works of literature or philosophy.[183] The Ch'ing philosophical historian Chang Hsüeh-ch'eng affirmed that "the Six Classics are all the political statutes of the ancient kings," not, as some later scholars proposed, the private teachings of later sages.[184]

. . . . .

Establishing our sixth commentarial assumption—that superfluities and needless repetitions do not exist in the canon—was an especial concern of rabbinic exegetes, as noted above in chapter 4. A large part of Rashi's great commentary on the Pentateuch is devoted to accounting for such apparent redundancies as the repetition of the phrase "and the child [Moses] grew" in two adjoining verses in Genesis 2. Rashi, quoting a previous authority, accounts for this repetition by invoking a type of modal distinction, arguing that "the first refers to physical growth, and the second to greatness, when Pharoah appointed him [Moses] over his household."[185] A more ambitious and momentous rabbinic explication of an apparent redundancy in Scripture refers to Leviticus 26:46, which states that "these are the statutes and ordinances and laws" given to Moses on Mount Sinai. Rabbinic exegetes keyed these three ill-distinguished or overlapping categories

[181] Ch'eng I, quoted in Chu, *Ssu-shu chi-chu, Hsia-Lun*, p. 85.

[182] Ibid., *Shang-Lun*, p. 2.

[183] Fang Hsiao-ju, quoted in *Ching-i k'ao* 297.4b (vol. 8).

[184] Chang, *Wen-shih t'ung-i* 1.1.

[185] Rashi, *Commentaries*, pp. 86–87.

to three distinct classes of rabbinic literature or teaching, specifically legal exegesis of Scripture, the rulings promulgated by Israel's sages, and the two Torahs, written and oral. As M. S. Jaffee explains, "Scripture's redundancy permits the inference that the revelation to Moses consisted not only of the Torah, but of authoritative interpretations and amplifications of it," and thus allowed the rabbis to sketch out or confirm the contours of their canon.[186]

Among commentators in other major traditions, Qur'ānic exegetes proposed the most varied and ingenious arguments to account for apparent superfluities, especially repetitions, in their scriptural text. In fact, this is as important a concern in Qur'ānic exegesis as the resolution of apparent contradictions is in Vedānta, particularly among modern Muslims sensitive to Western imputations that their holy book is monotonous and repetitive. One modern commentator, Maulana Abūl Alā Maudūdī, explains such Qur'ānic repetitiveness by arguing that during the lifetime of the Prophet, it was necessary that "the same things [be] repeated over and over again as long as the movement remains in the same stage."[187] Another twentieth-century commentator, al-Mashriqi, views repetitions in the Qur'ān from a more timeless perspective, asserting that they serve "as an incentive for man, lazy by nature, to take thought."[188] Qur'ānic repetitions may even have an aesthetic attraction, as they remind one modern scholar of "the monotony of the desert landscape which has for the Beduins a charm of its own."[189] Another Western commentator remarks that without its reiterations, the Qur'ān "would lack its existential quality and its cumulative force."[190] Premodern exegetes were more apt to emphasize the more practical benefits that Qur'ānic repetitions supposedly conferred. The philosopher al-Ghāzalī, for example, maintained that the reiteration of the phrase "Most Gracious, Ever Merciful" in a chapter of the Qur'ān was not superfluous inasmuch as it bestowed an "additional benefit" in "expanding the channels of mercy."[191] But the great early commentator on the Qur'ān, al-Tabarī, simply explained "the use of extended expression and added words, of repetition and varied expressions for the same meaning" in the

[186] Martin S. Jaffee, "Oral Torah in Theory and Practice: Aspects of Mishnah-Exegesis in the Palestinian Talmud," *Religion* 15 (October 1985): 391.

[187] Maulana Abūl Alā Maudūdī, "Introduction to the Study of the Qurān," p. 33.

[188] Al-Mashriqi, *Tadhkira* II, 38, quoted in J.M.S. Baljon, *Modern Muslim Koran Interpretation (1880–1960)* (Leiden: E. J. Brill, 1968), p. 51.

[189] Baljon, *Modern Muslim Koran Interpretation*, p. 46.

[190] Kenneth Cragg, *The Mind of the Qur'ān: Chapters in Reflection* (London: George Allen and Unwin, 1973), pp. 32–33.

[191] Al-Ghāzalī, *Jewels of the Qur'ān*, p. 67.

Qur'ān as adaptations to the rhetorical devices employed by the Arabs of the time.[192]

Among Indian commentators, exegetes and interpreters of the two great epics, especially of the *Mahābhārata*, faced the task of explaining repetitions and apparent superfluities of monumental proportions. To account for such superfluities satisfactorily required a good deal of imagination and inventiveness. Thus, one *Mahābhārata* commentator, arguing that "the unifying purpose of the *Mahābhārata* is to produce a cumulative effect of disillusionment," opens up "the perverse possibility of justifying every tedious accretion in the poem on the ground of its own contribution to the frustration of the reader."[193] In this respect, the bulk of modern scholarship might be regarded as the legitimate heir of India's great epic.

Confucian commentators were generally less expansive and imaginative in their explanations of apparent superfluities and repetitions in the books of their canon. But they were concerned with this issue—especially with respect to the *Spring and Autumn Annals*, in the composition of which Confucius was supposed to have carefully weighed every word. One of the most common explanations for repetitions in that classical text, used particularly in the *Kung-yang Commentary*, is that they were inserted for emphasis, "in order to magnify the event."[194] Ch'eng I followed a similar line of argument in accounting for the repetition in the *Annals* of the names of four states, which he says was the Sage's way of accentuating their crimes.[195] The subtle words of Confucius in apportioning praise and blame in the *Annals* were no less subtle for their being repeated, in fact more so.

Confucian commentators, especially Neo-Confucians, used a number of other standard strategies to account for repetitions in other classical texts, particularly the *Analects*. One of the most common of these is the modal distinction, also widely employed to establish the proposition that the classics are self-consistent. Chu Hsi, for instance, explained the appearance of a repeated phrase in the *Analects* by commenting that "the former instance speaks in terms of action,

---

[192] Al-Ṭabarī, *Commentary on the Qur'ān*, vol. 1, p. 12.

[193] Gary A. Tubb, "*Śāntarasa* in the *Mahābhārata*," *Journal of South Asian Literature* 20, no. 1 (Winter/Spring 1985): 159.

[194] See, for example, *Ch'un-ch'iu Kung-yang chuan*, p. 97.

[195] Ch'eng I, quoted in *Ch'un-ch'iu san-chuan* (The *Spring and Autumn Annals* with the Three Commentaries), p. 48, in *Ssu-shu wu-ching*, vol. 3. Calvin posed a somewhat similar explanation of the repetitions in prophetic works of the Old Testament. As recounted by T.H.L. Parker, Calvin reasoned as follows: "Micah was contemporary with Isaiah. Why the need for two witnesses? Was not Isaiah's word sufficient? Certainly, but the Lord wanted to make the Jews quite inexcusable by publishing his message through more than one Prophet." Parker, *Calvin's Old Testament Commentaries* (Edinburgh: T.& T. Clark, 1986), pp. 39–40.

while this one speaks in terms of knowledge."[196] He accounted for the puzzling repetition of the written character *chih* (knowledge) in a sentence from the "Record of Music" chapter of the *Record of Rites* by remarking that "the first *chih* is the essence and the second *chih* is the application," again invoking the useful *t'i-yung* dichotomy.[197] Li Kung ferreted out a more subtle superfluity from Confucius' remark, recorded in the *Analects*, that "the gentleman is broadly learned in culture and restrains himself with rites" (*Analects* 6:25). That is, to say, since rites is one of the six arts or disciplines covered by the term "culture" (*wen*), is not the second phrase of this sentence from the *Analects* superfluous? Li answered that "the rites [involved] in being broadly learned means to be trained in the rules of the five rites. The rites [involved] in restraining with rites speaks in terms of synthesizing the six arts."[198]

Finally, ancient and modern commentators alike have quite sensibly linked repetitions both in the *Analects* and the *Mencius* to the circumstances of their composition or delivery. Chao Ch'i (d. 201), in the earliest extant commentary on the *Mencius*, pointed out that the importance of the subjects on which Mencius spoke, such as "the foundations of kingly government," required that they be expounded in similar terms before different rulers.[199] The late-Ch'ing historian of classical studies Ch'en Li maintained that similar repetitions in the *Analects* arose from "the disciples each having recorded what he heard."[200] Since the *Analects* was a composite of these disciples' records or reminiscences, small wonder that repetitions appeared in the text. The great T'ang-era literatus and scholar Han Yü remarked of one such repetition that it could well be deleted from the text of the *Analects*,[201] thus indicating that Confucian commentators were perhaps not so insistent as their counterparts in other traditions on the nonsuperfluous nature of each detail in canonical works.

．．．．．

The proposition that the classics are clear was less a commentarial assumption than it was a question. As pointed out in the previous

[196] Chu, *Ssu-shu chi-chu, Hsia-Lun*, p. 105.

[197] Chu Hsi, quoted in *Li-chi chi-shuo*, p. 206.

[198] Li Kung, *Sheng-ching hsüeh kuei-tsuan* (A Compilation of Schemas on the Study of the Sacred Classics) (Taipei: Shang-wu yin-shu-kuan, 1965 reprint), 1.4.

[199] Chao Ch'i, *Meng tzu Chao-chu* (*Mencius* with Chao's Commentary), SPPY ed., 1.18a.

[200] Ch'en, *Tung-shu tu-shu chi* 2.9.

[201] Han Yü, *Lun-yü pi-chieh* (The *Analects* with Explanatory Notes) B.5b, in *Chung-kuo tzu-hsüeh ming-chu chi-ch'eng* 3:52.

chapter, there was no general consensus on this issue among commentators in most traditions. But while aficionados of "dark conceits" who identify obscurity with sublimity have appeared in almost every age, most traditional commentators do seem to have assumed that it is reasonable to expect the classics to be clear.[202] They were, after all, composed primarily to communicate to the world the teachings of the sages or the message of the divine. Thus, the obscurities that most commentators acknowledged in the classics or scriptures had somehow to be accounted for. To do this, commentators devised several strategies and arguments related to those which were used to establish the other assumptions outlined above.

One such strategy, favored especially by commentators in the Christian and Vedantic traditions, was to admit that the scriptural texts were full of obscurities but to maintain that the canon was nonetheless clear on all essential matters. As Harbison characterizes Martin Luther's view on this matter, "Scripture may be obscure in certain places, but not in things that count."[203] John Dryden expressed a similar sentiment in poetical form in his "Religio Laici":

> And that the *Scriptures*, though not every where
> Free from Corruption, or intire, or clear,
> Are uncorrupt, sufficient, clear, intire,
> In *all* things which our needfull *Faith* require.[204]

Yet, while Dryden held that "points not clearly known, / Without much hazard may be left alone,"[205] the early Christian exegetes Origen and St. Augustine maintained that the clear passages in Scripture might be used to illuminate the more obscure. As Augustine remarked, "Hardly anything may be found in these obscure places which is not found very plainly said elsewhere."[206]

The great Vedantic commentator Shankara was perhaps less san-

---

[202] A notable exception to this rule was the great early Christian exegete Origen, who wrote that "the gospel so desires wise men among believers that, in order to exercise the understanding of hearers, it has expressed certain truths in enigmatic forms, and some in the so-called dark sayings, some by parables, and others by problems." *Contra Celsum* 3.45, in *Origen: Contra Celsum*, trans. Henry Chadwick (Cambridge: Cambridge University Press, 1965), pp. 159–160.

[203] Harbison, *Christian Scholar*, p. 108.

[204] John Dryden, "Religio Laici; or, A Layman's Faith. A Poem," in *Eighteenth-Century English Literature*, eds. Geoffrey Tillotson et al. (San Diego: Harcourt Brace Jovanovich, 1969), p. 161.

[205] Ibid., p. 163.

[206] St. Augustine, *On Christian Doctrine* 2.6, trans. D. W. Robertson, Jr. (Indianapolis: Bobbs-Merrill, Library of Liberal Arts, 1979), p. 38; Tzvetan Todorov, *Symbolism and Interpretation*, trans. Catherine Porter (Ithaca: Cornell University Press, 1986), p. 107.

guine that the obscurities in the Veda could be similarly illuminated. But he was equally insistent that the scriptures were clear and consistent on one really essential point, that Brahman is "omniscient, omnipotent, and cause of the birth, existence and dissolution of the universe."[207] According to Shankara, contradictions and confusion in the Veda regarding such ancillary issues as the exact order of creation are unimportant, "since the creation of the world and similar topics are not at all what Scripture wishes to teach. For we neither observe nor are told by Scripture that the welfare of man depends on those matters in any way."[208]

Some commentators in the Confucian tradition also indicated that the classics were clear on essential matters while obscure in other places.[209] In seeking to clarify their canon, however, they more frequently invoked the related argument that the essential message or meaning of a classical text or even of the canon as a whole was encompassed in a single phrase or passage. Although there was certainly no guarantee that the meanings of these phrases and passages were clear, this position did simplify the study of the classics. For it indicated that whatever obscurities and confusion existed in the bulk of the classical texts could be lightly passed over.

Confucian commentators on particular classical texts often argued that the purport of the entire classic could be summed up in one phrase. They did so even though this might well have led others to question the value of their extensive exegetical labors on the text as a whole, and possibly even to suspect that the classics do indeed contain some superfluous elements. Chung Wen-cheng (1818–1877), for example, remarked that the *Spring and Autumn Annals* is from beginning to end concerned only with the "rectification of names" (*cheng-ming*): "To exhaust [the meaning of] these words in order to illuminate the kingly Way—this directly reveals the purport of the entire book."[210] Li Kuang-ti (1642–1718) argued that the 64 hexagrams and 384 lines of the *Change* could also be covered by a single phrase: "Goodness mends deviations."[211] Ch'ien Ta-hsin reduced the purport of that

[207] Shankara, *Brahmasūtra Bhāsya* I:1, in *The Hindu Tradition*, ed. Ainslie T. Embree (New York: Vintage Books, 1972), p. 204.

[208] Shankara, *Brahmasūtra Bhāsya* I:4, in Deutsch and van Buitenen, eds., *Source Book of Advaita Vedānta*, p. 172.

[209] See, for example, Ray Huang, "Ni Yuan-lu: 'Realism' in a Neo-Confucian Scholar-Statesman," in Wm. Theodore de Bary and the Conference on Ming Thought, *Self and Society in Ming Thought* (New York: Columbia University Press, 1970), p. 434; and Lo, *K'un-chih chi*, pt. 2, p. 117.

[210] Chung, "Lun-ching," p. 1a, in *Ku-liang pu- chu*.

[211] Li Kuang-ti, *Tu Lun-yü cha-chi* (Reading Notes on the *Analects*), A.33a, in *Ying-yin*

classic even further, to one word or character: "centrality" (*chung*).[212] According to Ch'en Yüan (d. 1145), "all seven chapters of *Mencius* are exclusively [concerned with] illuminating the goodness of human nature."[213] And Ts'ai Shen found the essence of the *Documents Classic* in a short passage at the beginning of the "Canon of Yao" chapter, rather than in a particular idea or doctrine.[214]

More ambitious Confucian commentators found a central idea or unifying theme in a number of the classics, and even in the canon as a whole. In Chu Hsi's view, each of the original classics was focused on a central duality or dichotomy, *yin* and *yang* in the *Classic of Change*, depravity and correctness in the *Songs Classic*, and order and chaos in the *Documents*.[215] The famous early-Ch'ing scholar Ku Yen-wu (1613–1682) summed up the purport of several of the Five Classics with quotations from Confucius. He remarked, for example, that "although the three hundred songs [in the *Songs Classic*] are very extensive, yet [Confucius] said, 'One saying can cover them: In thinking do not be depraved.' "[216] The early-Ming Neo-Confucian scholar Hsüeh Hsüan (1392–1464) maintained that each of the Four Books as well has an essential or central idea: "To illuminate virtue is the essential idea of the *Great Learning*. Sincerity is the essential idea of the *Doctrine of the Mean*. Humanity is the essential idea of the *Analects*. And the goodness of human nature is the essential idea of the *Mencius*."[217] According to Wu Kuei-fang (1521–1578), even the Five Classics as a whole have such a central theme: namely, the constant ethical

---

Ssu-k'u ch'üan-shu chen-pen, chiu-chi (Reprints of Rare Editions from the *Complete Library in Four Treasuries*, series 9) (Taipei: Shang-wu yin-shu-kuan, 1979), vol. 64.

[212] Ch'ien Ta-hsin, "Chung-yung shuo" (Explanations of the *Doctrine of the Mean*), in *Ch'ien-yen-t'ang wen-chi* 3.37.

[213] Ch'en Yüan, quoted in *Ching-i k'ao* 231.3b (vol. 7).

[214] Ts'ai, *Shu-ching chi-chuan*, p. 1.

[215] Chu Hsi, "Tu chu ching fa" (On the Method of Studying All the Classics), in *T'u-shu chi-ch'eng* 57:3163. The late-Ch'ing scholar-statesman Chang Chih-tung (1837–1909) proposed a slightly more elaborate schema along these lines, remarking, for example, that "the great meaning of the *Change* is [in its depiction of the alternations of] *yin* and *yang* and waxing and waning," and that of the *Spring and Autumn Annals* in its "clarifying the kingly Way and punishing the rebellious traitors." Chang, "Shou-yüeh, ti-pa" (Keeping the Faith, no. 8), in *Ch'ing-ju hsüeh-an* 187.21b (vol. 8).

[216] Ku Yen-wu, "Yü i i kuan chih" (I Bind It with One Thread), in *Yüan-ch'ao pen Jih-chih lu* (The Original Manuscript Version of the *Record of Daily Knowledge*) (Taipei: Ming-lun ch'u-pan she, 1970), 9.202.

[217] Hsüeh Hsüan, quoted in *Ching-i k'ao* 297.5b (vol. 8). The medieval Christian biblical exegete Nicholas of Lyra (1270–1349) proposed a somewhat similar schema for the four Gospels, positing that "Matthew emphasized Jesus' humanity, John his divinity, Luke his ministry, and Mark his kingdom." Jerry H. Bentley, *Humanists and Holy Writ: New Testament Scholarship in the Renaissance* (Princeton: Princeton University Press, 1983), p. 26.

rules for daily use.[218] Yü Shu also found the essence of all the classics in a few easily practiced ethical rules and relationships: "Although the Six Classics number tens of thousands of words, with only ten written characters one can exhaust their meaning. Their essentials are confined to [teaching the proper relationships between] ruler and subject, father and son, husband and wife, elder and younger, and friend and friend."[219]

The reduction of the complexities of the canon to a few relatively clear and simple phrases or ideas was not a practice confined to Chinese Confucian commentators. It is a strategy that is almost universal in commentarial traditions. As Frank Kermode has remarked in his study of the Christian Gospels, "Sometimes it appears that the history of interpretation may be thought of as a history of exclusions which enable us to seize upon this issue rather than on some other as central, and choose from the remaining mass only what seems most compliant."[220] Two students of Vedantic literature, Deutsch and van Buitenen, observe: "Every tradition that bases itself on revealed truth makes its selection, and in the end it is often no more than a few handfuls of assertions that finally constitute the scriptural foundation of a faith."[221]

Such exclusions and selections are not always concerned primarily with clarifying the meanings of the canon, with eliminating or minimizing the significance of its apparent obscurities. Commentators also used them to establish the proposition that the classics are profound and even that they are moral, mainly by focusing attention on the more philosophical or edifying parts of the canon. Thus, the idea that the essence of a classic or scripture can be summed up in a short compass has, like the modal distinction, the idea of accommodation, and allegory, been employed as a strategy to establish a number of commentarial assumptions regarding the character of canons. But in several traditions, including the Christian biblical and Vedantic as well as the Confucian, this strategy was widely used in order to deal with apparent obscurities in the canon or to demonstrate its essential clarity.

Martin Luther's quest for such clarity was partly responsible for his having identified the books of Romans, Galatians, the fourth gospel, and 1 Peter as containing the kernel of Christianity. It was perhaps

[218] Wu Kuei-fang, in *Ching-i k'ao* 297.11b (vol. 8).

[219] Yü Shu, *Yü-ch'üan yü-lu* (Recorded Conversations from Jade Springs), in *Sung-Yuan hsüeh-an* 25.16a (vol. 2).

[220] Frank Kermode, *The Genesis of Secrecy: On the Interpretation of Narrative* (Cambridge: Harvard University Press, 1982), p. 20.

[221] Deutsch and van Buitenen, eds., *Source Book of Advaita Vedānta*, p. 33.

his focus on these books that led him to conclude: "There is not on earth a book more lucidly written than the Holy Scriptures."[222] The search for clarity and simplification in Scripture through the reduction of its meaning to a few essential points or parts had many precedents in the Christian tradition. It appears, for example, in St. Augustine's assertion that "Scripture teaches nothing but charity"— which, according to Jesse Gellrich, "made the entire Bible the signifier of a single concept, the New Law of Charity."[223] A similar reductive simplification appears in a verse, concerning the love of God and neighbor, spoken by Jesus in the gospel according to St. Matthew. "On these two commandments hang all the Law and the Prophets."[224] Like Confucius with the *Songs* and Shankara with the Veda, part of the genius of Jesus was supposedly his ability to extract brevity and clarity from obscure and confused masses of canonical writings.[225]

This quality seems to have been shared by a number of great figures in several traditions. The rabbi Hillel (d. A.D. 8), when accosted by a heathen who said that he wished to learn the whole Torah while standing on one foot, replied: "Do not unto others that which you would not have them do unto you. That is the entire Torah; the rest is commentary."[226] Shankara is likewise renowned for having reduced the complexities of the Veda to the single phrase "That thou art," which expressed the identity of Brahman and *Ātman*.[227] The founders of most major sects in ancient and medieval Japanese Buddhism

[222] Martin Luther, quoted in Robert M. Grant, *A Short History of the Interpretation of the Bible*, rev. ed. (New York: Macmillan, 1972), pp. 132–133.

[223] St. Augustine, *On Christian Doctrine* 3.10, p. 88; Jesse M. Gellrich, *The Idea of the Book in the Middle Ages: Language Theory, Mythology, and Fiction* (Ithaca: Cornell University Press, 1985), p. 136.

[224] Matthew 22:40; see also Mark 12:29–31.

[225] On the other hand, part of the genius, or at least the reputation, of some modern critics apparently stems from their ability to extract obscurity and confusion from brevity and clarity. See, for example, Paul Ricoeur's discourse on Marx's pithy observation that "the philosophers have only interpreted the world; the point, however, is to change it," in Ricoeur, *Hermeneutics and the Human Sciences: Essays on Language, Action, and Interpretation*, ed. and trans. John B. Thompson (Cambridge: Cambridge University Press, 1985), p. 87.

[226] Hillel, quoted in Steinsaltz, *Essential Talmud*, p. 26. According to Hyam Maccoby, this statement of the Golden Rule "has many hellenistic parallels, including the version attributed to Jesus in the Gospels (Matt. 7:12; Luke 6:31)." Maccoby, *Early Rabbinic Writings* (Cambridge: Cambridge University Press, 1988), p. 41.

[227] Murty, *Revelation and Reason*, p. 90. One of the reasons why Vedānta, despite its difficult metaphysics and obscure forms of expression, has been so predominant in Indian thought is its association with this famous and simple formula which is taken to express a great truth. Even though the higher philosophical implications of this statement may not be understood by many, still it resonates throughout Indian culture. I owe this insight to Professor Gail Sutherland, my LSU colleague whose class on Hinduism I audited in the spring of 1988.

also based much of their appeal on "some specific single text, phrase, symbol, vow, ritual, or concept that, raised to central importance, reduced or completely dissolved the most vexing problems."[228]

In some commentarial traditions, such reductive simplifications or clarifications were even institutionalized, or at least were identified by a special term. Perhaps the most famous example of such a term is the Buddhist "mantra," which was in many cases supposed to sum up the meanings of an entire sūtra, and even several sūtras.[229] In rabbinic Judaism, Hillel's version of the Golden Rule, quoted above, is probably the most renowned example of "Kelal," "a kind of total statement which would embrace more detailed particulars."[230] Indian commentators, particularly Vedantists, were more apt to extract such a statement directly from some canonical text, such as the Upanishads or the *Bhagavad Gītā*. This they called the *mahāvākya*, or "great utterance," the key phrase by which they interpreted the remainder of the text and which supposedly embodied its core or essence.[231] Traditional Vedantic commentators sometimes identified four of these *mahāvākyas* in the Veda, including the famous "That thou art" from the Chāndogya Upanishad.[232] Even a folk version of the *Rāmāyana* has its *mahāvākya*, a verse that supposedly tells the essence of the story.[233] In modern times, Mahatma Gandhi found the *mahāvākya* of the *Gītā* in the last verses of chapter 2 of that text.[234] Once the purport of these verses was grasped, the "embellishments, obscurities, dogmatic elaborations, mythical cycles, and ritualistic discourses" in other Hindu texts could be passed over.[235]

[228] William R. LaFleur, *The Karma of Words: Buddhism and the Literary Arts in Medieval Japan* (Berkeley: University of California Press, 1986), p. 58.

[229] For an example of this characterization of *mantra*, see Gung-thang dkon-mchog-bstan-pa'i-sgron-me, *An Explanation of the Heart Sūtra, Illuminating the Hidden Meaning*, in Donald S. Lopez, Jr., *The Heart Sūtra Explained: Indian and Tibetan Commentaries* (Albany: State University of New York Press, 1988), pp. 178, 183, and 185.

[230] Bowker, *The Targums*, p. 51. Geza Vermes notes that "there was a general tendency among Jews in the early postbiblical centuries to discover a small number of all-inclusive precepts." Vermes, "Jesus and Christianity," in *Renewing the Judeo-Christian Wellsprings*, ed. Val Ambrose McInnes, O.P. (New York: Crossroad, 1987), p. 137.

[231] Robert N. Minor, "Introduction," *Modern Indian Interpreters of the Bhagavadgītā*, ed. Minor (Albany: State University of New York Press, 1986), p. 3; Sharma, *The Hindu Gītā*, p. 250.

[232] Karl H. Potter, ed., *Encyclopedia of Indian Philosophies: Advaita Vedānta up to Śaṃkara and His Pupils* (Princeton: Princeton University Press, 1981), p. 59.

[233] Stuart H. Blackburn, "Epic Transmission and Adaptation: A Folk Rāmāyana in South India," in *The Heroic Process: Form, Function, and Fantasy in Folk Epic*, Proceedings of the International Folk Epic Conference, University College, Dublin, September 2–6 1985, eds. Bo Almqvist et al. (Dublin: Glandale Press, 1987), p. 581.

[234] Robert N. Minor, "Conclusion," in Minor, ed., *Modern Indian Interpreters*, p. 225.

[235] J.F.T. Jordens, "Gandhi and the Bhagavadgītā," ibid., p. 93.

In fact, one of the great appeals of the *Gītā* is the ease with which various *mahāvākyas*, often of mutually contradictory purport, can be extracted from it. *Mahāvākyas* from the *Gītā* have, for example, been used to support both the doctrine of nonviolence and that of just wars, as well as such varied ways to spiritual liberation as yogic practice, devotion to a personal god (*bhakti*), and gnosis (*jnāna*). Thus, the appearance of apparently contradictory statements in the *Gītā*, of diverse *mahāvākyas*, may actually have widened that text's appeal and audience.

Classical Chinese lacks an equivalent of the Sanskrit "mahāvākya." But a similar concept did acquire a sort of institutional expression in late-traditional China in the exaltation of those passages or phrases in the classics which were most apt to appear on the imperial civil service exams. Although the mastery of such passages and phrases might not bring about enlightenment, it might well lead to the acquisition of acceptable consolation prizes, such as wealth, power, and glory.

On the other hand, the mastery of a *mahāvākya* might be dangerous as well as rewarding, as illustrated in Jorge Luis Borges' "Parable of the Palace" in which the Yellow Emperor showed the poet through his palace:

> It was at the foot of the penultimate tower that the poet (who seemed remote from the wonders that were a marvel to all) recited the brief composition that today we link indissolubly to his name and that, as the most elegant historians repeat, presented him with immortality and death. The text has been lost; there are those who believe that it consisted of a line of verse; others, of a single word. What is certain, and incredible, is that all the enormous palace was, in its most minute details, there in the poem, with each illustrious porcelain and each design on each porcelain and the penumbrae and light of each dawn and twilight, and each unfortunate and happy instant in the glorious dynasties of the mortals, of gods and dragons that had inhabited it from the unfathomable past. Everyone was silent, but the Emperor exclaimed: *You have robbed me of my palace!* And the executioner's iron sword cut the poet down.[236]

While commentators in several traditions dealt with obscurities and confusion in their canons by practically ignoring them and by concentrating on what they regarded as scripture's clear and essential message, others sought to explain why such obscurities existed. One of

---

[236] Jorge Luis Borges, "Parable of the Palace," in Donald S. Lopez, Jr., "Interpretation of the Mahāyāna Sutras," in Lopez, ed., *Buddhist Hermeneutics* (Honolulu: University Press of Hawaii, 1988), p. 67.

the most common of these explanations, especially favored by Christian biblical exegetes, is that such difficulties promoted interpretive zeal and ingenuity. As St. Augustine remarked, "[The authors of the Holy Books] have spoken with a useful and healthful obscurity for the purpose of exercising and sharpening, as it were, the minds of the readers and of destroying fastidiousness and stimulating the desire to learn."[237] Origen agreed that the obscurities in the Scriptures were put there deliberately, but not so much to exercise the wit of the pious interpreter as because "the sheer attractiveness of the language might otherwise have led us either to abandon their teachings entirely . . . or else through not moving beyond the letter, never to discover anything of a more divine character."[238]

Commentators in other scriptural traditions also celebrated obscurities in their canons as a means of promoting the quest for deeper levels of meaning. According to the great philosophical historian Ibn Khaldhûn (1332–1406), there is a hidden aspect of revelation that is couched in analogies, hints, contradictions, and variants in the Scripture which indicate to the few, the intellectual elite, the need to employ a special method of interpretation.[239] The revered Qur'ānic exegete al-Zamakhsharī (1055–1144) affirmed that ambiguities and obscurities in the Qur'ān encouraged research and meditation on that text.[240] Hindu exegetes associated with the Mīmāmsā school likewise interpret the "strange, extraordinary and inconsistent statements" in the Vedic hymns as spurs to interpretive ingenuity.[241] Pseudo-Plutarch, a Hellenistic commentator on Homer, excused the latter's use of "enigmatic and mythic language" by remarking: "That which is couched in hidden meanings . . . may be attractive where that which is spoken explicitly is useless." Such language quickens exegetical zeal and makes it possible for lovers of learning to "more easily seek and more easily find the truth."[242] Finally, even modern critics such as Thomas Greene and Frank Kermode have expressed a

[237] St. Augustine, *On Christian Doctrine* 4.8, p. 132.

[238] Origen, *On First Principles* IV, 2.9, in Wiles and Santer, eds., *Documents in Early Christian Thought*, p. 144.

[239] Muhsin Mahdi, *Ibn Khaldûn's Philosophy of History: A Study in the Philosophic Foundation of the Science of Culture* (Chicago: University of Chicago Press, 1971), pp. 93–94.

[240] "Zamakhsharī on Sūra 3:7/5," in Helmut Gätje, *The Qur'ān and Its Exegesis: Selected Texts with Classical and Modern Interpretations*, trans. and ed. Alford T. Welch (Berkeley: University of California Press, 1976), p. 56.

[241] N. V. Thadani, "Introduction" to *Mīmāmsā: The Secret of the Sacred Books of the Hindus*, trans. Thadani (Delhi: Bharati Research Institute, 1952), p. xiv.

[242] Pseudo-Plutarch, *De vita et poesi Homeri* 92, in Lamberton, "Homer the Theologian," p. 124.

preference for difficult and obscure classical texts that allow reader participation or promote interpretive action.[243]

Confucian commentators seldom used such arguments to account for obscurities in their canon. But the noted Sung literatus Su Hsün did contend in a famous essay that the abstruseness of the *Classic of Change* promoted respect for that classical text and for the teachings of the sages. For "the reason why people hold something in reverence is that there is in it something that cannot be seen through." Thus, "since the *Change* has something in it which cannot be seen through, the people of the world trusted the Way of the sages and revered it."[244]

Commentators on the *Spring and Autumn Annals* posed other sorts of explanations for that classic's obscurities and subtleties. One of these is that such expressions hid the purport of the *Annals* from evil rulers who might have retaliated against its author. According to the *Kung-yang Commentary* to the *Annals*, "In [the records about Dukes] Ting and Ai there are many obscure expressions. If these rulers had familiarized themselves with this text and asked about its explanation, they would not have known whether they were charged with crime or not."[245] Another interpretation of the obscurities in the *Annals*, proposed by the T'ang-era commentator Chao K'uang (fl. c. 770), is that the subtleties of the Sage's words match those of the men and affairs they describe: "Men's goodness and evil necessarily have [degrees of] depth and shallowness. If one does not regulate one's expressions, then they will not be adequate for differentiating these [degrees]."[246]

As commentators in several traditions have recognized, dwelling too much on the obscurities and subtleties in canons may be theologically suspect as well as hermeneutically futile. Indeed, ambiguities may well have been planted in some scriptural texts in order to entrap those bent on sowing dissension, as the Qur'ān itself suggests:

> It is He who has sent down upon thee the Book, some of whose verses are clear, which are the mother (i.e., the essential matter) of the Book, but

[243] Jerome McGann, *A Critique of Modern Textual Criticism* (Chicago: University of Chicago Press, 1983), p. 98; Frank Kermode, *The Classic: Literary Images of Permanence and Change* (Cambridge: Harvard University Press, 1983), pp. 129–130.

[244] Su, "I-lun," p. 52; an English translation of this essay appears in Shchutskii, *Researches*, pp. 230–233.

[245] *Ch'un-ch'iu Kung-yang chuan*, p. 175.

[246] Chao K'uang, quoted in *Ch'un-ch'iu san-chuan*, p. 3 of "Kang-ling" (Outline). A modern biblical scholar, Stephen Prickett, sets forth a similar rationale for the Bible's apparent obscurities and ambiguities: "How far is it possible . . . 'to use language that is natural, clear, simple, and unambiguous,' when the Bible is not about things that are natural, clear, simple, and unambiguous?" Prickett, *Words and the Word*, p. 10.

others are ambiguous. Now as for those in whose hearts is deviation, they follow what is ambiguous in it, seeking dissension, seeking its interpretation, whereas none knows its interpretation save Allah.[247]

Thus, we may appropriately close this chapter with a prayer that appears in al-Tabarī's monumental commentary on the Qur'ān:

O my God, inspire us with a firm devotion to (this Revelation) so that we may have recourse (only) to its unambiguous parts, while being firm in submission to the obscure parts, (not seeking definitive interpretations for them).[248]

[247] Qur'ān 3:7, trans. in Arthur Jeffery, *Islam: Muhammad and His Religion* (Indianapolis: Bobbs-Merrill, Library of Liberal Arts, 1958), p. 49.
[248] Al-Tabarī, *Commentary on the Qur'ān*, p. 8.

Chapter 6

DEATH AND TRANSFIGURATION OF

COMMENTARIAL WORLD VIEWS

THE TRANSITION from commentarial forms and modes of discourse to modern scholarship and criticism is one of the most important in the intellectual history of mankind. Prior to the twentieth century, though, such a transition occurred in only three of the major traditions surveyed here: the biblical, the Homeric, and the Confucian (and in this last only incompletely). Despite the similarities in the commentarial assumptions and strategies employed in all the major traditions covered here, they parted ways in the speed and direction with which they entered (or made) the modern intellectual world. In at least two of these traditions, particularly the Qur'ānic and the Vedantic, commentarial forms are still vital, even perhaps dominant.[1] At the other end of the spectrum, they have not been abandoned completely even in Homeric scholarship, in which the line between traditional commentary and modern criticism is often difficult to draw. In addition, the virtual canonization of the writings of the founders of certain modern ideologies, such as Marx and Freud, has inspired the revival of commentarial modes in the twentieth century. Even some of the traditional commentarial assumptions and strategies outlined in chapters 4 and 5 of this book appear in the works of modern ideologues. Contemporary literary

---

[1] J.J.G. Jansen points out that "commentaries on the Koran which were written before the twentieth century are also still widely read. The so-called *Tafsîr al-Galâlayn*, written in 1466/7, saw at least seven editions between 1926 and 1940 in Cairo, and the Koran commentary by Az-Zamaksharî, written in 1131/2, was printed at least five times before 1919." Jansen, *The Interpretation of the Koran in Modern Egypt* (Leiden: E. J. Brill, 1974), p. 10. According to Jacques Jomier, "problems of historical criticism have not yet (in 1983) arisen in the Islamic world where the Qur'ān is concerned." See Jomier, "Aspects of the Qur'ān Today," in *Arabic Literature to the End of the Umayyad Period*, eds. A.F.L. Beeston et al. (Cambridge: Cambridge University Press, 1983), p. 265. Geo Widengren adds that "Islamic exegesis in modern times on principle has not moved far from traditional mediaeval exegesis." Widengren, "Holy Book and Holy Tradition in Islam," in *Holy Book and Holy Tradition*, eds. F. F. Bruce and E. G. Rupp (Grand Rapids, Mich.: William B. Eerdmans, 1968), p. 225. For a brief account of the "continuation of traditional exegesis and explication" in modern Indian literature, see Wilhelm Halbfass, *India and Europe: An Essay in Understanding* (Albany: State University of New York Press, 1988), p. 258.

criticism, moreover, has adapted traditional modes of commentarial discourse, such as midrash.[2]

Since fundamental and extensive criticism of traditional commentarial presuppositions and procedures appeared before the present century principally in Europe and China, the present chapter will be concerned primarily with developments in those areas. This is not to deny the existence of significant departures from established commentarial modes of interpreting classical or scriptural texts in pre-twentieth-century rabbinic Judaism,[3] Islam, and Vedānta, but only to remark that they did not develop into general intellectual movements that radically transformed whole traditions. The reasons why such movements did arise in the other three traditions surveyed—the Christian biblical, the Homeric, and the Confucian—probably have less to do with any special intellectual qualities they might have than with such developments as the differential impact of the printing revolution in early-modern Europe and China, as opposed to the Near East and India (where printing was not introduced until the nineteenth century).[4] By making large selections of ancient writings widely available, printing helped foster examinations of the relationships between the classics or scriptures and the general intellectual and social milieus of the eras in which they were composed. The results of these examinations, of this historical recontextualization of the classics, frequently challenged some of the basic commentarial assumptions outlined above in chapter 4. For example, by revealing that ancient customs and mores differed markedly from modern ones, these investigations undermined the belief that the ordinances

[2] Joshua Wilner, "Romanticism and the Internalization of Scripture," in *Midrash and Literature*, eds. Geoffrey H. Hartman and Sanford Budick (New Haven: Yale University Press, 1986), p. 237. Jacob Neusner also identifies similarities between traditional rabbinic hermeneutics and contemporary literary criticism, particularly the "intertextual reading of texts." Neusner, *Canon and Connection: Intertextuality in Judaism* (Lanham, Md.: University Press of America, 1987), p. xii. According to Philip Rieff, psychoanalysis also resembles religious hermeneutics; in fact, "parodies" it. See Rieff, "The Tactics of Interpretation," in *Sigmund Freud's "The Interpretation of Dreams,"* ed. Harold Bloom (New York: Chelsea House, 1987), p. 54.

[3] On the reluctance of nineteenth-century Jewish scholarship to indulge in the higher criticism, see Nathan Stern, *The Jewish Historico-Critical School of the Nineteenth Century* (New York: Arno Press, 1973), p. 56. According to Harold Coward, "Even today it is not unusual to find Orthodox Jews who as an avocation are devoting much of their life to writing a Torah commentary." Coward, *Sacred Word and Sacred Text: Scripture in World Religions* (Maryknoll, N.Y.: Orbis Books, 1988), p. 26.

[4] William A. Graham remarks that printing was "long available to the Turkish and Arab world but not taken up until late, primarily for religious and cultural reasons." Graham, *Beyond the Written Word: Oral Aspects of Scripture in the History of Religion* (Cambridge: Cambridge University Press, 1987), p. 20.

or morality of the classics or scriptures provided a timeless or universal standard.

Printing also cheapened the currency, not only by making the canon available to everyman, often in inflated forms, but also by creating a flood of books in which the classics were only one current. The sight of the classics or scriptures occupying only a small shelf in the stacks of a great library might well have led even the most committed classicist to question the assumption that the classics are comprehensive or encyclopedic. Even the Bible, which many ancient and medieval writers had regarded as a sort of encyclopedia, assumed but a modest place in the greater *Encyclopedia* of the French Enlightenment which, moreover, treated that sacred text with indifference, even with "a certain negligence."[5] "Henceforth," notes François Laplanche, "the Bible was no longer considered as the source and sum of all culture, since it on the contrary had itself entered culture."[6]

Challenges to traditional commentarial assumptions in early-modern Europe and China may be traced to the accelerated development of the philological sciences in those areas as well as to the printing revolution. First of all, by applying the critical methods and standards used in the study of profane texts to the classics or scriptures, philologists at least implicitly questioned the latter's claim to such special qualities or attributes as cosmic comprehensiveness or unfathomable profundity. More specifically, philologists' increasingly expert investigations of the grammatical structures and vocabularies of sacred and canonical texts such as the Bible revealed "lacunae, errors, ambiguities, and even contradictions in the canon."[7]

·   ·   ·   ·   ·

The most nearly universal of all our commentarial presuppositions— that the classics or scriptures are comprehensive and all-encompassing, that they embrace all significant knowledge and truth—was also one of the first to be subjected to significant criticism in both Europe and China. Homer was the first canon in Western history to receive critical scrutiny on this account. In book 10 of the *Republic*, Plato attacked the prevailing belief in an omniscient Homer, who was re-

[5] B.-E. Schwarzbach, "L'Encyclopédie de Diderot et de d'Alembert," in *Le Siècle des Lumières et la Bible*, eds. Yvon Belaval and Dominique Bourel (Paris: Editions Beauchesne, 1986), p. 761.

[6] François Laplanche, "La Bible chez les Réformés," ibid., p. 469.

[7] Anna-Ruth Löwenbrück, "Johann David Michaelis et les débuts de la critique biblique," ibid., p. 114.

puted to be the master of all the arts and sciences.[8] Seneca mocked the tendency to trace the doctrines of all schools of philosophy to Homer.[9] But such isolated criticisms of the notion that Homer comprehended all learning, from moral philosophy to the practical arts, apparently had little impact in antiquity and the Middle Ages.

Early-modern European critics of the notion of Homer's comprehensiveness, however, apparently reflected a general point of view and did not just express an eccentric insight. Among the great French writers of the era, Rabelais, Montaigne, and Fontenelle all challenged the idea that the Homeric poems are the repositories of all knowledge and wisdom.[10] By the eighteenth century, the notion of an omniscient Homer was a subject appropriate for satire, notably in Jonathan Swift's *Tale of a Tub*. Swift wrote that "whereas we are assured he designed his work for a complete body of all knowledge, human, divine, political, and mechanic, it is manifest he hath wholly neglected some, and been very imperfect in the rest." For example, "he seems to have read but very superficially either Sendivogius, Behmen, and *Anthroposophia Theomagica*," three kabbalistic works.[11] Swift's contemporary Alexander Pope represents a more general trend toward the aestheticization of Homer, the celebration of his epics for their poetical beauties rather than for their alleged comprehension of the arts and sciences.[12] He characterized the encyclopedic approach to Homer as "occasion'd by the Ostentation of Men who had more Reading than Taste, and were fonder of showing their Variety of Learning in all kinds, than their single Understanding of Poetry."[13]

Programmatic denials of the Bible's comprehensiveness also appear in early-modern European literature. One of the most famous and influential of these is Spinoza's statement that "Scripture does not aim at imparting scientific knowledge."[14] But even some late-me-

---

[8] *The Republic of Plato*, trans. and annot. Francis MacDonald Cornford (New York: Oxford University Press, 1945), pp. 328ff.

[9] Ernst Robert Curtius, *European Literature and the Latin Middle Ages*, trans. Willard R. Trask (Princeton: Princeton University Press, 1973), pp. 205–206.

[10] Howard Clarke, *Homer's Readers: A Historical Introduction to the Iliad and the Odyssey* (Newark: University of Delaware Press, 1981), p. 98.

[11] Jonathan Swift, *A Tale of a Tub*, in Swift, *Gulliver's Travels and Other Writings*, ed. and annot. Louis A. Landa (Boston: Houghton Mifflin, 1960), p. 308.

[12] Michael Murrin, *The Allegorical Epic: Essays in Its Rise and Decline* (Chicago: University of Chicago Press, 1980), p. 178. Baxter Hathaway traces this "shift in attitudes by which literary works were to be looked on as literary works, not merely as repositories of wisdom and learning," to the sixteenth century. Hathaway, *Marvels and Commonplaces: Renaissance Literary Criticism* (New York: Random House, 1965), p. 9.

[13] Alexander Pope, notes to the *Iliad* 7.82, quoted in Murrin, *Allegorical Epic*, p. 178.

[14] Benedict de Spinoza, *Tractatus Theologico-Politicus* 13, trans. R.H.M. Elwes (London: George Routledge and Sons, 1895), p. 176. A number of twentieth-century

dieval commentators such as William of Auvergne seem to have sensed the limitations of Scripture in this respect.[15] Many of them, in fact, wrote separate tracts and treatises on issues and topics not adequately covered in the Bible; for attempts to present all learning on all subjects, ranging from politics to linguistics, in the form of biblical commentaries frequently miscarried as the new knowledge burst out of the commentarial framework.[16]

The growth of knowledge in early-modern Europe led to the supersession of the commentary and even of the canon in other fields as well. In European cartographic works prior to the sixteenth century, new maps were commonly presented as supplements to those which appeared in Ptolemy's *Geography*, the most authoritative classical work in this field. But from the publication of the *Theatrum* of Abraham Ortelius (c. 1570), ancient maps were set off in a separate section after the contemporary ones, "so that the reader could see 'how maimed and imperfect' were ancient world views which comprised 'scarce one quarter of the whole globe now discovered to us.' "[17] In few fields could the noncomprehensive nature of the classics be so sharply illustrated as in geography and cartography, especially in the wake of the European Age of Discovery.

General challenges to the proposition that the classics are comprehensive seldom appear in premodern Confucian literature. But Confucian commentators did occasionally question the idea that particular classical texts such as the *Classic of Change* and the *Spring and Autumn Annals* were the sources or repositories of the various branches of learning. According to Chang Ju-yü (fl. 1195),

> the sages composed the *Change* basically to illuminate the Way. As for the rest, it can [also] be used for divination and that is all. But afterward, those who spoke of *yin-yang*, astronomy and the calendar, and music and the pitchpipes all sought these [subjects] in the *Change*. Seeking them, they believed that they had obtained [them there]. And tallying [these subjects with the *Change*], they believed that they had reached accord. But this is contrary to the intention of the sages.[18]

Qur'ānic exegetes have rather belatedly reached the same conclusion. See Kenneth Cragg, *The Pen and the Faith: Eight Modern Muslim Writers and the Qur'ān* (London: George Allen and Unwin, 1985), p. 21.

[15] Beryl Smalley, "Essay I," in *Medieval Exegesis of Wisdom Literature: Essays by Beryl Smalley*, ed. Roland E. Murphy (Atlanta: Scholars Press, 1986), p. 18.

[16] For examples, see Beryl Smalley, *The Study of the Bible in the Middle Ages*, 3rd ed., rev. (Oxford: Basil Blackwell, 1983), pp. 327–331.

[17] Elizabeth L. Eisenstein, *The Printing Press as an Agent of Change: Communications and Cultural Transformations in Early Modern Europe*, 2 vols. in 1 (Cambridge: Cambridge University Press, 1980), p. 193; the internal quotations are from Ortelius' "Message to the Reader."

[18] Chang Ju-yü, quoted in *Ching-i k'ao* 4.8b (vol. 1).

An eighth-century commentator on the *Spring and Autumn Annals*, Lu Ch'un (d. 805), also denied that classic's comprehensiveness (although perhaps only implicitly) by maintaining that the good words (*shan-yen*) of later ages should not be read into the *Annals* or included in its commentaries. For "how could they all be interpolated into the *Spring and Autumn Annals*? What ought to be made known to later ages naturally should be recorded only in historical books [apart from the *Annals* and its commentaries]."[19] The idea that the classical commentary is not an appropriate format for the recording of all knowledge and wisdom also appears in Chu Hsi's criticism of Ch'eng I's having included moral lessons in his commentary on the *Classic of Change*. Ch'eng I, said Chu, "intended to give moral instructions [in the Commentary]. But he should have said them elsewhere, not in connection with the *Book of Changes*."[20] The extent to which Sung and Ming Neo-Confucians did in fact discuss such topics elsewhere was a source of perplexity to later scholars such as Ku Yen-wu, who proposed to reintegrate studies of principle or philosophy (*li-hsüeh*) into classical studies (*ching-hsüeh*).[21]

On the other hand, Ku himself was one of the main precursors of new specialized modes of scholarship in such fields as geography, epigraphy, and phonology which flourished in Ch'ing times. Although these studies were frequently justified and presented as adjuncts to classical scholarship, especially as ways of illuminating difficult or obscure points in the classics, in practice they often assumed the status of autonomous disciplines cultivated for their own sake by professional scholars.[22] The vast increase in knowledge in a wide range of fields that issued from these studies made the proposition that the classics embrace all learning even less plausible or defensible. Moreover, many Ch'ing scholars' commitment to or focus on the ad-

[19] Lu Ch'un, "Tan Chao ch'ü-she san-chuan i li" (Examples of What [the Commentators] Tan [Chu] and Chao [K'uang] Choose and Reject Regarding the Meanings of the Three Commentaries [on the *Spring and Autumn Annals*]), in *Ch'un-ch'iu Tan Chao chi-chuan tsuan-li* (A Compilation of Exempla from the Collected Commentaries on the *Spring and Autumn Annals* by Tan [Chu] and Chao [K'uang]), in *Ching-yüan* (Garden of the Classics), comp. Ch'ien I-chi (Taipei: Ta-t'ung shu-chü, 1970 reprint), 5:2364.

[20] Chu Hsi, *Chu-tzu yü-lei* (Classified Conversations of Master Chu), chap. 69, quoted in Ying-shih Yü, "Morality and Knowledge in Chu Hsi's Philosophical System," in *Chu Hsi and Neo-Confucianism*, ed. Wing-tsit Chan (Honolulu: University Press of Hawaii, 1986), p. 236.

[21] Chou Yü-t'ung, "Ching chin-ku-wen hsüeh" (Studies on the Old and New Text [Versions of the] Classics), in *Chou Yü-t'ung ching-hsüeh shih lun-chu hsüan-chi* (Selected Treatises by Chou Yü-t'ung on the History of Classical Studies), comp. Chu Wei-cheng (Shanghai: Jen-min ch'u-pan she, 1983), p. 18.

[22] This process is examined in Benjamin A. Elman, *From Philosophy to Philology: Intellectual and Social Aspects of Change in Late Imperial China* (Cambridge: Harvard University Press, 1984), esp. p. 67ff.

vancement of particular academic disciplines, such as astronomy, geography, and philology, inclined them to treat the classics more as source materials for these specialized studies than as complete repositories of the wisdom of the sages. As such, the classics had no privileged status over other types of ancient historical and literary sources. By the early twentieth century, some scholars drew the logical conclusion from this development, proposing to do away with the category "classical studies" and to reapportion its components into studies of history, literature, and philosophy.[23]

A final indication of the slippage of the notion that the Confucian classics are comprehensive is that it became the object of satire, or perhaps parody, in Tokugawa Japan at a time when a form of Neo-Confucianism was established as the state ideology. In his work "The Larger Meaning of the Bathhouse of the Floating World" (Ukiyo-buro), Shikitei Sanba (1776–1822), a near contemporary of Jonathan Swift, characterized the bathhouse institution as a comprehensive repository of moral learning. "At the bathhouse," he wrote, "one sees demonstrated every one of the Five Virtues." For example: "Hot water warms the body, removes dirt, cures ills, and heals fatigue. This is Benevolence. . . ." In sum, "there is, one realizes on careful reflection, no shortcut to moral learning like the public bath. It is, after all, the way of Nature, and of Heaven and Earth, that all are naked when they bathe."[24]

. . . . .

Challenges to the notion that the classics are well ordered and coherent are particularly prominent in Homeric criticism from early-modern times. As early as the seventeenth century, the noted critic François Hédelin Abbé d'Aubignac attempted to demonstrate that the *Iliad*, contrary to what Aristotle, Horace, and Longinus had said, was an aesthetic confusion.[25] His contemporary Charles Perrault remarked that this epic was composed originally "all in pieces and sections independent of one another."[26] The great Homeric scholar

[23] Kumaichiro Uchino, "Mingoku sho-chū-ki no keigaku kan" (Views on Classical Studies during the Early and Middle Periods of the Chinese Republic), in *Nippon Chūgoku Gakkai-Hō* (Bulletin of the Sinological Society of Japan), no. 9 (1957), p. 4.

[24] Shikitei Sanba, "The Larger Meaning of the Bathhouse of the Floating World," trans. in Robert W. Leutner, *Shikitei Sanba and the Comic Tradition in Edo Fiction* (Cambridge: Harvard University Press, 1985), pp. 137–138.

[25] Murrin, *Allegorical Epic*, pp. 174–175.

[26] Charles Perrault, *Parallele des anciens et des modernes en ce qui regarde les arts et les sciences* 3:98, quoted in "Introduction" to F. A. Wolf, *Prolegomena to Homer, 1795*, trans., intro., and notes Anthony Grafton et al. (Princeton: Princeton University Press, 1985), p. 9.

F. A. Wolf (1759–1824) also interpreted the apparent lack of a general order or design in Homer as evidence that the Homeric epics are really compilations of the works of different poets that were stitched together by later redactors.[27] In attempting to demonstrate how this stitching was done, Wolf may have anticipated deconstruction by concentrating on the awkward passages in the epics, rather than upon those elements which supposedly gave them order and unity.[28]

Several famous Confucian scholars of premodern times also challenged the conception that some of the classics, especially the original five canonized in the Han era, were well ordered and coherent. Chu Hsi, for example, remarked of the *Documents Classic* that it was "put together from fragments. So attempts to connect [the text] sentence by sentence by meaningful patterns must lead to farfetched results."[29] Ch'eng I likewise attributed the apparent disorder of another classic, the *Record of Rites*, to the circumstances of its composition: "The extant books on ritual [or the ritual classics] were all collected from the ashes [after the Ch'in burning of the books] and, for the most part, emerged from the forced interpretations of scholars of the Han era. Thus, how could one presume to trust completely and explain them sentence by sentence?"[30] Such comments were perhaps meant to enhance the status of the relatively orderly Four Books newly canonized by the Neo-Confucians of the Sung era. But at least one Neo-Confucian scholar, Wang Po (1194–1274), identified quite a number of discontinuities and inconsistencies even in one of the Four Books, the *Doctrine of the Mean*, and queried how the sagely Tzu-ssu could have composed so illogical a work.[31]

. . . . .

Challenges by traditional Confucian commentators to the idea that the classics are internally consistent are rather rare and limited in scope. But admissions of internal contradictions in the books of the

[27] See Murrin, *Allegorical Epic*, p. 194.

[28] Ibid. Murrin does not make the point about deconstruction. According to Kugel, midrashists in the rabbinic tradition also searched their scriptures for such "irritations and irregularities" as contradictions, unusual words, and words that do not fit their contexts. See James L. Kugel, "Two Introductions to Midrash," in Hartman and Budick, eds., *Midrash and Literature*, p. 92.

[29] Chu Hsi, "Tu chu ching fa" (On the Method of Studying All the Classics), in *T'u-shu chi-ch'eng* 57:3164.

[30] Ch'eng I, quoted in *Li-chi chi-shuo* (The *Record of Rites* with Collected Explanations), annot. Ch'en Hao, p. 66, in *Ssu-shu wu-ching*, vol. 2.

[31] Jeffrey Kenneth Riegel, "The Four 'Tzu Ssu' Chapters of the *Li Chi*: An Analysis of the *Fang Chi, Chung Yung, Piao Chi,* and *Tzu I*" (Ph.D. diss., Stanford University, 1978), p. 78.

Confucian canon were not unknown even in the works of earlier commentators. Han Yü, for example, identified such a contradiction between the following two sayings recorded in the *Analects* of Confucius:

> The Master said: Men are by nature close to one another, but by practice are far apart from one another. [*Analects* 17:2]

> The Master said: Only [those of] the highest wisdom and lowest stupidity do not change. [*Analects* 17:3]

Han Yü's comment on these sayings:

> The first passage, in saying that men are by nature close to one another, indicates that men can through practice [move] upward or downward. But this [second] passage, in saying that the highest and the lowest do not change, indicates that men cannot change through practice. These two meanings contradict one another.[32]

Nineteenth-century criticisms of the notion that the classics are internally consistent are generally more programmatic and wider in scope than this rather isolated *aperçu* by Han Yü. Such criticisms frequently reprove earlier commentators for having attempted to impose a spurious order and consistency on two or more mutually contradictory parts of the canon. P'i Hsi-jui, for example, remarked that Cheng Hsüan's commentaries on the three ritual classics had attempted to "reconcile the theories of the Old and New Text schools. Even in cases in which he could not harmonize them, he forcibly sought to bring them into accord." P'i offered as an illustration Cheng's effort to synthesize or harmonize the fundamentally incommensurable systems of land mensuration outlined in the *Rites of Chou* and in the "Royal Institutes" chapter of the *Record of Rites*.[33] P'i's contemporary Liao P'ing, also a scholar associated with the New Text school, likewise criticized earlier commentators for their efforts to reconcile inconsistent accounts of ancient political and administrative systems given in the *Rites of Chou*, the "Royal Institutes," and the *Documents Classic*.[34] On a less polemical note, Ch'en Li (1810–1882) remarked that Chu Hsi's definition of "humanity" (*jen*) as "the principle of love and the virtue of the mind" did not fit all the occurrences of

---

[32] Han Yü, *Lun-yü pi-chieh* (The *Analects* with Explanatory Notes), B.17a, in *Chung-kuo tzu-hsüeh ming-chu chi-ch'eng* 3:75.

[33] P'i Hsi-jui, *Ching-hsüeh t'ung-lun* (Comprehensive Discussions of Classical Studies) (Taipei: Ho-Lo t'u-shu ch'u-pan she, 1974 reprint), 3.54.

[34] Liao P'ing, *Chin-ku hsüeh k'ao* (Investigations of New and Old Text Studies) (Ch'ang-an ch'u-pan she, 1974 reprint), B.20b.

the term in the *Analects* of Confucius.[35] Ch'en thus seems to have recognized that disharmonies among various characterizations of *jen*, even within one classical text, precluded the possibility that any unitary definition, such as that proffered by Chu Hsi, could ring true. Unlike some earlier commentators in the Neo-Confucian tradition, Ch'en was apparently unimpressed by the syncretic brilliance of Sung Neo-Confucian sages' formulaic relation of such classical metaphysical terms as *jen* (humanity), *li* (principle), and *te* (virtue) to one another. Instead of praising Chu for his synthetic insight, he faults him for his empirical oversights.

In early-modern Europe, the criticism and demise of attempts to harmonize apparently conflicting classical texts and authorities was more extensive and abrupt. There are at least two reasons for this, both related to the amount and complexity of the material to be synthesized. First, European syncretists sought to reconcile apparent contradictions among a wider range of great ancient authorities—from biblical patriarchs to Hellenistic philosophers, not just within a limited set of classical texts. Second, the explosion of the number of printed texts in the sixteenth and seventeenth centuries greatly complicated the syncretists' task of resolving conflicts among these authorities.[36] According to Elizabeth Eisenstein, one of the reasons why "Montaigne perceived greater 'conflict and diversity' in the works he consulted than had medieval commentators" was that he had access to more ancient texts.[37] Montaigne's century nevertheless saw the development of a number of great syncretic enterprises, such as that by Pico della Mirandola, despite the increasing odds against their successful resolution.

By the following century, however, the perception of such "conflict and diversity" as Montaigne recognized had begun to inspire opposition to and abandonment of syncretic projects, which eventually became objects of ridicule. Spinoza criticized attempts to reconcile one passage of Scripture with another as "a pretty piety . . . which accommodates the clear passages to the obscure, the correct to the faulty, the sound to the corrupt."[38] Descartes took the appearance of so many conflicts and contradictions in the works of earlier philosophers as the occasion for his (temporary) abandonment of philosophy, not

[35] Ch'en Li, *Tung-shu tu-shu chi* (Reading Notes of [Ch'en] Tung-shu) (Taipei: Shang-wu yin-shu-kuan, 1970 reprint), 2.21.

[36] Elizabeth Eisenstein suggests that "the initial increase in output did strike contemporary observers as sufficiently remarkable to suggest supernatural intervention." Eisenstein, *Printing Press*, p. 50.

[37] Ibid., p. 74.

[38] Spinoza, *Tractatus* 10, p. 153.

as a challenge to create a new synthesis of ancient authorities that would resolve all such contradictions.[39] Voltaire lamented the sad fate of the "theologian," the last professional syncretist, who "for thirty years ... tried to reconcile the gospels and bring the fathers into union." But "the difficulty of organizing in his head so many things whose nature is to be confused, and to throw a little light into so many dark clouds, often disheartened him, but as these researches were his professional duties, he devoted himself to them in spite of his disgust."[40] The evident failure of syncretic projects, the apparent impossibility of reconciling so many diverse classical authorities, even inspired a nightmare in the great nineteenth-century German philosopher of history Wilhelm Dilthey. Having seen in a dream a disharmonious version of Raphael's *School of Athens* in which the philosophers were engaged in quarrels instead of reconciliation, Dilthey sadly concluded that "to contemplate all the aspects in their totality is denied us."[41]

Dilthey's resignation and despair in the face of the failure of syncretic endeavors has, however, been transcended in the present century by deconstructive man, who revels in what Jacques Derrida has called a reality of "holes" rather than "wholes" or, as Roland Barthes has remarked, "who endures contradiction without shame."[42] But such "holeness" and endurance is beyond the limited capacity of most of us, the undeconstructed, who still have not managed to transvalue pre-post-structuralist ideologies. Even Nietzsche, the transvaluator par excellence in modern Western intellectual history, was transfixed by the mystique of the unitary classical core, supposedly hidden beneath commentarial accretions. Although this classical core might be rotten, as Nietzsche maintained was the case with the great world religions known to him, it was nevertheless a palpable whole whose es-

[39] René Descartes, *Discourse on the Method of Rightly Conducting One's Reason and Seeking Truth in the Sciences*, in *The Essential Descartes*, ed. Margaret D. Wilson (New York: New American Library, Mentor Books, 1969), p. 111.

[40] Voltaire, "Théologien: Theologian," in *Philosophical Dictionary*, ed. and trans. Theodore Besterman (Harmondsworth, Eng.: Penguin Books, 1983), p. 387.

[41] Wilhelm Dilthey, "The Dream," from *Gesammelte Schriften* VIII, 218–224, trans. in William Kluback, *Wilhelm Dilthey's Philosophy of History* (New York: Columbia University Press, 1956), pp. 106–107.

[42] Martin Jay, *Marxism and Totality: The Adventures of a Concept from Lukács to Habermas* (Berkeley: University of California Press, 1984), p. 516; Roland Barthes, *The Pleasure of the Text*, trans. Richard Miller (New York: Hill and Wang, 1975), p. 3. This concern with avoiding contradictions was also apparently transcended by Martin Luther, who once remarked that "when a contradiction occurs in Holy Scripture, so let it go." Quoted in Frederic W. Farrar, *History of Interpretation* [1886] (Grand Rapids, Mich.: Baker Book House, 1979 reprint), p. 337.

sence could be probed by philology, "one of the two great opponents of all superstitions."[43]

. . . . .

By Nietzsche's time, the commentarial assumption that the classics and scriptures, particularly the Homeric epics and the Old Testament, were moral had been challenged so frequently that Nietzsche's assertion that they were repositories of morality (albeit that of *Untermenschen*) might well have provoked some surprise.[44] Indeed, the great Homeric scholar F. A. Wolf wrote that "the most offensive readings [in Homer] have all the marks of truth"; they were closest to the Homeric originals.[45] A prominent modern Hellenist, Wolfgang Schadewaldt, has even attempted to prove that those portions of the *Odyssey* which are moral, which emphasize man's moral accountability, were introduced into the epic by a later interpolator.[46]

Premodern Confucian scholars, however, especially Neo-Confucian commentators, were hardly in a position to disparage the moral value or meaning of their canon. Unlike a noted modern biblical scholar, they could not easily assert (with respect to their own canon) that "to look for models of morality in the Bible is very nearly a futile task."[47] For the main value of the Confucian classics was in their function as teachers of morality rather than in their literary excellence, intellectual profundity, or divine inspiration. Thus, the prominent Ming Neo-Confucian philosopher Lo Ch'in-shun remarked: "There is no great harm in having slight differences in interpreting the classics, but when it comes to the foundations of moral principle, there must not be even the slightest discrepancy."[48]

Nevertheless, several noted Confucian commentators did challenge moralistic interpretations of the *Spring and Autumn Annals*, denying

[43] Friedrich Nietzsche, *The Anti-Christ* 47, in Nietzsche, *Twilight of the Idols and The Anti-Christ*, trans. and annot. R. J. Hollingdale (Harmondsworth, Eng.: Penguin Books, 1972), p. 163.

[44] For examples of such challenges in eighteenth-century Homeric criticism to the idea that the classics are moral, see Donald M. Foerster, *Homer in English Criticism: The Historical Approach in the Eighteenth Century* (New Haven: Yale University Press, 1947), pp. 7, 12, and 23.

[45] Wolf, *Prolegomena*, p. 59.

[46] See Clarke, *Homer's Readers*, p. 183.

[47] James A. Sanders, *Canon as Paradigm: From Sacred Story to Sacred Text* (Philadelphia: Fortress Press, 1987), p. 71.

[48] Lo Ch'in-shun, *K'un-chih chi*, pt. 2, in *Knowledge Painfully Acquired: The K'un-chih chi by Lo Ch'in-shun*, trans., ed., and intro. Irene Bloom (New York: Columbia University Press, 1987), p. 128.

the prevailing theory that the various anomalies and inconsistencies in that classical text were Confucius' way of subtly expressing his moral judgments on the men and events chronicled therein. According to the great T'ang-era commentator K'ung Ying-ta (574–648), the *Annals'* inconsistencies in its recording of dates arose from omissions in the historical chronicle of the state of Lu on which it was based. Such variations were not, in other words, devised by Confucius in order to express moral judgments, to apportion praise and blame.[49] Chu Hsi, remarking that it was difficult to distinguish the words of the original chronicle of Lu from Confucius' alterations, also rejected moralistic interpretations of inconsistencies in the usages and expressions in the text: "As for the opinion that the addition or subtraction of a written character is [a way of expressing] praise and blame, I do not dare believe it."[50] Another Sung commentator on the *Annals*, Lü Ta-kuei (1227–1275), asserted that "the calamity of forced interpretations of the *Spring and Autumn Annals* has two general sources: first, the saying that [variations in the recording of] dates express praise and blame; second, the saying that [variations in] names and titles express praise and blame."[51] Such statements did not deny that the *Annals* could be used for moral instruction; they simply said that moral judgments should not be sought in the linguistic variations and terminological inconsistencies of the classical text.

Prior to the Ch'ing era, challenges to the idea that the Confucian classics are profound usually focused on specific classical texts rather than on the canon as a whole. Some of these challenges, such as Wang An-shih's (1021–1086) characterization of the *Spring and Autumn Annals* as "disconnected and fragmentary court reports," were used politically as arguments for excluding these texts from the approved canon and curriculum. But most were reactions to earlier commentators' having read excessively recondite and philosophical conceptions into the classics, thus obscuring their plain sense. Yü Ju-yen (1614–1679), for example, remarked that commentators' interpretations of the classics, especially of the *Annals*, suffered not from being

---

[49] K'ung Ying-ta, quoted in *Ch'un-ch'iu san-chuan* (The *Spring and Autumn Annals* with the Three Commentaries), p. 3 of "Kang-ling" (Outline), in *Ssu-shu wu-ching*, vol. 3.

[50] Chu Hsi, quoted ibid., p. 5. Cheng Ch'iao and Ma Tuan-lin, among other famous Sung scholars, also rejected such moralistic interpretations of the language of the *Annals*. See Hok-lam Chan, " 'Comprehensiveness' (T'ung) and 'Change' (Pien) in Ma Tuan-lin's Historical Thought," in *Yüan Thought: Chinese Thought and Religion under the Mongols*, eds. Hok-lam Chan and Wm. Theodore de Bary (New York: Columbia University Press, 1982), pp. 43–44 and 46.

[51] Lü Ta-kuei, quoted in *Ch'un-ch'iu san-chuan*, p. 5 of "Kang-ling."

too shallow, but from being too deep.[52] And Chu Hsi complained that although the pre-Confucian strata of the *Change* are "very plain and simple, modern commentaries mistakenly devise abstruse and subtle theories [to interpret them]."[53] Chu elsewhere criticized commentators in general on similar grounds:

> People of today who discuss the classics frequently have four faults: what was originally lowly they raise up to make lofty; what was originally shallow they bore to make deep; what was originally near they extend to make far; what was originally clear they must make obscure.[54]

Wang Jo-hsü (1174–1243) identified a similar set of faults among commentators on the *Analects*, whom he accused of "three excesses": being "excessively profound, excessively lofty, and excessively opaque." Wang added that "the words of the Sage were only of human feelings. Thus, they are readily understandable and easy to know, commonplace and yet enduring." As for "the Master's words concerning human nature and the Way of heaven," two profound metaphysical topics, Confucius' disciple "Tzu-kung himself said that they could not be heard. And yet the Sung Confucians all suppose that they have really heard them."[55] Although lack of philosophical profundity in the classics might well be perceived as a shortcoming, Wang turns this apparent debit to good account by indicating that the Sage spoke simply and accessibly of matters close to the human heart.[56] In bringing the classics, or at least the *Analects*, down to earth,

[52] Yü Ju-yen, *Ch'un-ch'iu p'ing-i tzu-hsü* (Author's Preface to the *Plain Meanings of the Spring and Autumn Annals*), in *Ch'ing-ju hsüeh-an* 201.4b (vol. 8).

[53] Chu Hsi, "Ta Lü Po-kung shu" (A Letter in Reply to Lü Po-kung), in *Chu-tzu ta-ch'üan* (Complete Works of Master Chu), SPPY ed., 33.32b (vol. 4).

[54] Chu Hsi, *Chu-tzu yü-lei chi-lüeh* (An Abridgment of the Classified Conversations of Master Chu), comp. Chang Po-hsing (Taipei: Shang-wu yin-shu-kuan, 1973 reprint), 2.65. Compare Spinoza's remark: "I am consequently lost in wonder at the ingenuity of those . . . who detect in the Bible mysteries so profound that they cannot be explained in human language, and who have introduced so many philosophical speculations into religion that the Church seems like an academy, and religion like a science, or rather a dispute." *Tractatus* 13, pp. 175–176.

[55] Wang Jo-hsü, "Tzu-shu" (Author's Account), in *Lun-yü pien-huo* (A Straightening Out of Confusing Points on the *Analects*), in *Ching-i k'ao* 220.3b–4a (vol. 6). Peter K. Bol, commenting on similar passages in Wang's writings, remarks that "Wang draws his readers away from a quest for philosophical foundations, deeper meanings, and enduring tensions." Bol, "Seeking Common Ground: Han Literati under Jurchen Rule," *Harvard Journal of Asiatic Studies* 47, no. 2 (December 1987): 517.

[56] Nakai Riken, a Confucian scholar in Tokugawa Japan, also praised the *Analects* for its down-to-earth human morality, remarking that this was the source of that classic's timelessness. See Tetsuo Najita, *Visions of Virtue in Tokugawa Japan: The Kaitokudō Merchant Academy of Osaka* (Chicago: University of Chicago Press, 1987), p. 193. His more famous contemporary, Itō Jinsai, asserted that the *Analects* was the "greatest book in

Wang, moreover, might well have found canonical support for his position in Mencius' famous saying that "though the Way be close at hand, it is sought in distant places; though affairs be easy, they are sought in what is difficult" (*Mencius* 4A, 11). In any case, Wang's doubts regarding the philosophical profundity of the *Analects* did not lead him to any denial of the classics' unique value as sources of sagely wisdom.

Several famous Confucian scholars of the Ch'ing era, however, did challenge such uniqueness—and thus, implicitly, the assumption that the classics are special repositories of the most profound sagely teachings. They generally did so not directly, but by relegating the classics to the same status as other categories of literature, especially histories. According to the great Ch'ing historian Ch'ien Ta-hsien, the division between the classics and histories was an artificial one that had not existed in antiquity.[57] Ch'ien and other scholars of his time approached the classics not so much as expressions of the wisdom of the Confucian sages, but as source materials for the study of the ancient eras in which they were composed. They thus treated the classics as they did noncanonical works dating from the same period, using the same methods of study and verification.[58] For all these works, both canonical and noncanonical, were of value in reconstructing the history, society, culture, and institutions of the classical era.

This shift in hermeneutical focus from the classics to the classical era, "from the *chefs-d'oeuvre* of mankind to the historical interconnection which supports them,"[59] was one of the most momentous in the history of the human sciences. Such a transition occurred in eighteenth- and nineteenth-century European historical studies as well as in Ch'ing scholarship. For nineteenth-century German historicists, in particular, the main loci of profound meaning in the past were not classical texts, but the historical eras that these texts and other source materials illuminated. As Paul Ricoeur has remarked of these historicists' approach, "Before the coherence of the text comes the coherence of history, considered as the great document of mankind, as the

all the universe" because it deals with matters that are "humble and familiar." Quoted in Yoshikawa Kōjirō, *Jinsai Sorai Norinaga: Three Classical Philologists of Mid-Tokugawa Japan*, trans. Kikuchi Yūji (Tokyo: Tōhō Gakkai–Institute of Eastern Culture, 1983), p. 62.

[57] See Elman, *From Philosophy to Philology*, p. 73.

[58] Yamanoi Yū, "Minmatsu Shinsho ni tsuite no kōsatsu" (A Study on the Thoughts in the Late-Ming and Early-Ch'ing Dynasty), *Tokyo Shingaku-Hō* (Bulletin of the Tokyo Sinological Society), no. 11 (June 1965): 46.

[59] Paul Ricoeur, "The Task of Hermeneutics," in *Paul Ricoeur, Hermeneutics, and the Human Sciences: Essays on Language, Action, and Interpretation*, ed. and trans. John B. Thompson (Cambridge: Cambridge University Press, 1985), p. 48.

most fundamental expression of life."[60] While Ch'ing scholars may not have directly articulated the notion of the *Zeitgeist*, some of them did approach ancient texts, both canonical and noncanonical, primarily as sources for an understanding of the spirit and institutions of the age in which they were composed. Thus P'i Hsi-jui remarked that in reconstructing the ritual traditions of the Chou era, one should proceed by piecing together relevant selections from a wide range of works, including the *Deportment and Rites* (I-li), the *Record of Rites*, the *Elder Tai's Record of Rites* (Ta-Tai Li-chi), the *Spring and Autumn Annals* with its three primary commentaries, and the writings of scholars of the Han era.[61]

Not all Ch'ing scholars were entranced by the historicist vision. Some continued the quixotic quest for an authentic classical core which, they believed, could be revealed by removing the layers of heterodox accretions and confusing commentaries that had accumulated over the centuries. Ironically, some of those scholars whom modern historians have most celebrated as iconoclasts, such as Ts'ui Shu (1740–1816), maintained this thoroughly traditional attitude toward the classics. For Ts'ui, the classics, not the spirit and institutions of the age in which they were composed, were the primary repositories of truth and value. "The Way of the sages," he wrote, "is only in the Six Classics."[62]

Ts'ui's Confucian fundamentalism was not unmatched in other classical and scriptural traditions in modern times. But the continued appeal among nineteenth-century Confucian scholars of the idea that there is an irreducible classical core which contains the most concentrated wisdom available to mankind indicates that traditional commentarial assumptions, such as that the classics are profound, remained vital in Chinese Confucianism at least until the present century.

. . . . .

Even in the twentieth century, some of these assumptions and the strategies used for supporting them have survived, both inside and outside the Confucian tradition. On the one hand, traditional commentarial presuppositions and procedures have continued to be favored by a wide range of modern Confucian writers, from philosophers such as T'ang Chün-i and Mou Tsung-san to ideologues in

[60] Ibid.

[61] P'i, *Ching-hsüeh t'ung-lun* 3.86.

[62] Ts'ui Shu, "K'ao-hsin lu t'i-yao" (A Summary of the *Record of Investigations of Evidence*), in *Ch'ing-ju hsüeh-an* 97.2a (vol. 4).

Republican China. On the other hand, even some of the radical iconoclasts associated with the New Culture Movement, who challenged
nearly every one of these traditional assumptions with respect to the
Confucian classics, yet proceeded to establish new canons, especially
in literature. The new advocates of vernacular literature touted five
(or six if one includes *Chin P'ing-mei*) classic Chinese novels in terms
similar to those which traditional commentators had used to characterize the Five (or Six) Confucian classics. They particularly emphasized the idea, inherited from Ch'ing commentators on these novels,
that these works present a comprehensive view of man and the cosmos.[63] Indeed, some Ch'ing novelists themselves announced their encyclopedic intent in prefaces to their works. The author of one eighteenth-century novel, for example, stated that his work would "cover
a multitude of topics, reason (*li*), classics, history, filial piety, loyalty,
military science, medicine, poetry, mathematics, emotions, moral
learning (*daoxue*), sexuality (*chuntai*), and the comic."[64] Even contemporary Western scholars have commented on the encyclopedic character of some of these classic vernacular novels, especially the *Dream
of the Red Chamber* (Hung-lou meng), "a microcosm of traditional Chinese culture."[65] According to Andrew Plaks, the scope and texture of
this great novel is similar to that of the Confucian Four Books, specifically in "the broad range of human emotional response covered by
the canonic 'joy, anger, pain, and pleasure' of the Four Books."[66]

The classic vernacular novel was not the only new literary canon in
which twentieth-century scholars found a comprehensive view of human life or of man and the cosmos. As Chang-tai Hung has remarked
of the Chinese folklore movement of the 1920s, "Folklorists felt that
the gamut of human experience could be comprehended through

[63] For examples of Ch'ing commentators' characterizations of these novels as comprehensive and coherent, see Andrew H. Plaks, "Allegory in *Hsi-yu Chi* and *Hung-lou
Meng*" and "Towards a Critical Theory of Chinese Narrative," in *Chinese Narrative: Critical and Theoretical Essays*, ed. Plaks (Princeton: Princeton University Press, 1977), pp.
199 and 332, respectively; Ellen Widmer, *The Margins of Utopia: Shui-hu hou-chuan and
the Literature of Ming Loyalism* (Cambridge: Harvard University Press, 1987), pp. 89–
90; and John Ching-yu Wang, *Chin Sheng-t'an* (New York: Twayne, 1972), p. 45.

[64] R. Keith McMahon, "A Case for Confucian Sexuality: The Eighteenth-Century
Novel *Yesou Puyan*," *Late Imperial China* 9, no. 2 (December 1988): 45. McMahon adds
that "like other scholar-novelists, he has chosen the novel as a form into which he can
pour his vast erudition: besides the usual core of Confucian learning in history, poetry
and moral thought, he is fluent in mathematics, astronomy, military science and medicine" (p. 33).

[65] Richard J. Smith, *China's Cultural Heritage: The Ch'ing Dynasty, 1644–1912* (Boul-
der, Colo.: Westview Press, 1983), p. 210.

[66] Plaks, "Allegory," p. 200.

what Zhou Zuoren called 'songs of life.' "[67] Ku Chieh-kang, one of the most incisive and effective modern critics of traditional approaches to the Confucian classics, yet found a somewhat new canon in folk literature which, he indicated, encompassed the accumulated wisdom and experience of the common people: "Proverbs are their moral laws; their idioms are their rhetoric; their riddles are their keys to wisdom."[68]

In the modern West, as well as in twentieth-century China, the most common assumption made about the character of new classics or canons, both literary and ideological, is that they are in some sense comprehensive. In the words of Frank Kermode, such canons are regarded as "heterocosms" or "miniature Torahs"; "the text is a world system."[69] In English literary theory, such a view may be traced back to the eighteenth century. John Dryden, for example, remarked of Chaucer that he was "learn'd in all sciences, and therefore speaks properly on all subjects" and, further, that "he must have been a man of most wonderful comprehensive nature because . . . he has taken into the compass of his *Canterbury Tales* the various manners and humours of the whole English nation in his age."[70] Samuel Johnson characterized Shakespeare in similar terms, calling his drama "the mirrour of life" in which is presented "the whole system of life in motion."[71]

Some of the most prominent and influential twentieth-century Marxist theoreticians, especially Russian and Chinese, have made similar assertions regarding their canons, although the analogy should perhaps not be pressed too far. The first sentence of G. Plekhanov's last substantial publication declares that "Marxism is a complete theoretical system."[72] In the words of Leszek Kolakowski, "Plekhanov insisted that Marxism was a complete and integral body of theory embracing all the main questions of philosophy," as did Karl Kautsky, who "was fascinated by Marxism as a coherent theoretical

[67] Chang-tai Hung, *Going to the People: Chinese Intellectuals and Folk Literature, 1918– 1937* (Cambridge: Harvard University Press, 1985), pp. 72–73.

[68] Ku Chieh-kang, quoted ibid., p. 155.

[69] Frank Kermode, *Forms of Attention* (Chicago: University of Chicago Press, 1985), pp. 90 and 75.

[70] John Dryden, "Preface" to *Fables Ancient and Modern*, in *Selected Poetry and Prose of John Dryden*, ed. and annot. Earl Miner (New York: Random House, 1969), pp. 504 and 508.

[71] Samuel Johnson, "Preface to the Plays of William Shakespeare," in *Eighteenth-Century English Literature*, eds. Geoffrey Tillotson et al. (San Diego: Harcourt Brace Jovanovich, 1969), pp. 1068 and 1067.

[72] G. Plekhanov, *Fundamental Problems of Marxism*, p. 1, quoted in David McLellan, *Marxism after Marx: An Introduction* (New York: Harper and Row, 1979), p. 67.

system by which the whole of history could be comprehended."[73] Such ideas, which did much to shape the character of Soviet ideology, led the Italian Marxist Antonio Labriola to criticize Plekhanov and his cohorts for trying to make of Marxism "a new kind of universal wisdom (*Allweisheit*)," a characterization that, he said, "will make scientific socialism laughable before the whole world."[74] Labriola's apprehensions on this account might well have been confirmed by the writings of the "versatile dilettante" Paul Lafargue, who, says Kolakowski, held that Marx's works "could be used by anyone to unlock the secrets of all sciences, however little particular knowledge he might possess."[75] But the notion that new Marxist classics are comprehensive appeared in an even more exaggerated form during the Cultural Revolution with respect to Mao Tse-tung's works, which were extolled as "an eternal universal truth, an eternally valid guide for every human action."[76]

Modern Marxists, moreover, have adopted several other common commentarial assumptions and strategies, which should not be too surprising in view of R. H. Tawney's characterization of Marx as "the last of the Schoolmen."[77] Soviet Marxists, for example, have tended to assume that their tradition is monolithic or self-consistent, and French Marxists such as Jean Jaurès that it is moral, "the highest expression of man's eternal longing for freedom and justice."[78] In order to support such propositions, Marxists have employed strategies and arguments similar to those used by commentators in classical or scrip-

---

[73] Leszek Kolakowski, *Main Currents of Marxism: Its Origins, Growth, and Dissolution,* vol. 2: *The Golden Age,* trans. P. S. Falla (Oxford: Oxford University Press, 1982), pp. 340 and 35.

[74] Antonio Labriola, quoted in Russell Jacoby, *Dialectics of Defeat: Contours of Western Marxism* (Cambridge: Cambridge University Press, 1981), p. 44.

[75] Kolakowski, *Main Currents,* vol. 2, p. 142.

[76] Helmut Martin, *Cult and Canon: The Origins and Development of State Maoism* (Armonk, N.Y.: M. E. Sharpe, 1982), p. 29. In recent years, however, Russian and Chinese Marxists have drawn back from the notion that their canon is comprehensive and self-sufficient. Reformers in China, for example, have cited contradictions between Marx and Engels in arguing that Marxism and its classics were incomplete and in need of further development. See Peter R. Moody, Jr., *Chinese Politics after Mao: Development and Liberalization, 1976 to 1983* (New York: Praeger, 1983), p. 67. Soviet Marxist theorists, even before Gorbachev, divided Lenin's " 'single piece of steel' into separate philosophical disciplines . . . some of which may even be said to exist apart from dialectical and historical materialism." James P. Scanlan, *Marxism in the USSR: A Critical Survey of Current Soviet Thought* (Ithaca: Cornell University Press, 1985), p. 42.

[77] R. H. Tawney, quoted in Edward Shils, *Tradition* (Chicago: University of Chicago Press, 1981), p. 136.

[78] Scanlan, *Marxism,* pp. 329–330; the quotation on Jaurès is from Kolakowski, *Main Currents,* vol. 2, p. 35.

tural traditions. For example, when Soviet Marxists attempt to "philosophize in the grand manner," they have tended to draw their summary statements from "a few well-mined pages" of Friedrich Engels' *Anti-Dühring* and *Ludwig Feuerbach and the Outcome of Classical German Philosophy*.[79] They thus assert the profundity of their canon by focusing on its more philosophical parts or passages and, in some cases, even extract modern *mahāvākyas* and *mantras* from their canonical texts. Marxist theoreticians have also occasionally devised modal distinctions, one of the most famous of which is Mao Tse-tung's discrimination between antagonistic and nonantagonistic contradictions. Vulgar Marxist renderings of the relationships between base and superstructure, moreover, have a deep kinship with the allegorical schemas traditionally used for interpreting Holy Scripture, as Frederic Jameson has pointed out.[80] Finally, the general intellectual style prevalent in Marxist readings of their canonical texts, which George Steiner has called "exegetic, Talmudic, disputative to an almost pathological degree of semantic scruple and interpretative nicety,"[81] is reminiscent of traditional commentators' approaches to their classics or scriptures.

The Marxist classics are not the only modern canon in regard to which some traditional commentarial assumptions have reappeared. Modern critics have treated Freud's works as comprehensive, as primarily concerned with the reconciliation of apparent discrepancies and incongruities in such psychic phenomena as dreams, and even as possessing an analogue to (or perhaps parody of) an ethical substratum.[82] Even contemporary physicists, particularly elementary particle theorists, have assessed theories in their field by similar criteria. First, they have consistently sought a "concise and beautiful answer that encompasses the whole story," more specifically a grand unified field theory that would explain the four forces of nature: the electromagnetic force, the gravitational force, and the strong and weak nuclear forces.[83] Although it may be true that "the ground of physics is littered with the corpses of unified theories," as the Princeton physicist

[79] Scanlan, *Marxism*, p. 21.

[80] Frederic Jameson, *The Political Unconscious: Narrative as a Socially Symbolic Act* (Ithaca: Cornell University Press, 1981), p. 32.

[81] George Steiner, *On Difficulty and Other Essays*, p. 5, quoted in Jay, *Marxism and Totality*, p. 17.

[82] Kermode, *Forms of Attention*, p. 84; Rieff, "The Tactics of Interpretation," pp. 54–56.

[83] John Schwarz, quoted in Michio Kaku and Jennifer Trainer, *Beyond Einstein: The Cosmic Quest for the Theory of the Universe* (New York: Bantam Books, 1987), p. 194; Heinz R. Pagels, *The Cosmic Code: Quantum Physics as the Language of Nature* (New York: Bantam Books, 1983), p. 297.

Freeman Dyson has asserted, most physicists strive for completeness, for what Steven Weinberg has called "a truly unified view of nature."[84]

Second, elementary particle physicists have been drawn to theories that reveal or assume the existence of a coherent order in nature, of a "tapestry" instead of a "patchwork quilt," on the grounds that "the more elegant and simple your scheme is, the more success it seems to have."[85] Third, they have understandably been reluctant to accept theories that contain internal contradictions. For "if a theory is inconsistent, it will eventually make ridiculous predictions."[86] Theories that fail to eliminate or adequately explain the seeming superfluity or redundancy of certain elementary particles, such as the "muon," are also suspect. Thus: "To physicists, the existence of carbon-copy quarks means that the G.U.T. theory cannot be a fundamental theory of the universe."[87] Such a fundamental theory, in the estimation of most physicists, must also be clear and simple, and even evince a certain kind of symmetry.[88] It must, in the words of Albert Einstein, use "a minimum of primary concepts and relations."[89] Finally, modern physicists have occasionally addressed the question of whether or not the cosmos is moral in the sense that it corresponds with human expectations and concerns. The most famous statement on this issue is perhaps Einstein's remark that "the notion that statistical laws are final and that God draws a lot, is highly unsympathetic to me."[90]

. . . . .

Thus, traditional commentarial assumptions or presuppositions have persisted or reappeared in the modern world in fields ranging from literary criticism to Marxist ideology to elementary particle physics—perhaps an indication that some of them have a universal psychological or cultural basis. But what of the genre of the commentary itself? Here the continuities are perhaps less striking, although one modern

[84] Freeman Dyson, *Disturbing the Universe*, p. 62, quoted in Kaku and Trainer, *Beyond*, p. 16; Steven Weinberg, quoted in Pagels, *Cosmic Code*, p. 239.

[85] Sheldon Glashow, "Nobel Prize Acceptance Speech, Stockholm, 1979," quoted in Kaku and Trainer, *Beyond*, p. 75; John Schwarz, quoted ibid., p. 195.

[86] Kaku and Trainer, *Beyond*, p. 100.

[87] Ibid., p. 119.

[88] Ibid., p. 196; Pagels, *Cosmic Code*, pp. 216 and 221.

[89] Einstein, quoted in Pagels, *Cosmic Code*, p. 297.

[90] "Einstein to James Franck," quoted in Yehuda Elkana, "The Myth of Simplicity," in *Albert Einstein, Historical and Cultural Perspectives: The Centennial Symposium in Jerusalem*, eds. Gerald Holton and Yehuda Elkana (Princeton: Princeton University Press, 1982), p. 239.

literary theorist has argued that the novel is a new form of commentary that is "rooted in exegesis."[91] But whereas more standard commentarial forms dominated the higher intellectual world of most postclassical, premodern cultures, in modern times they have been increasingly confined within the rather narrow frame of reference works. Even those moderns who are firmly committed to a religious tradition or political ideology rarely present their ideas or interpretations of their tradition in the form of a direct commentary on a canonical text. Usually they prefer to write separate tracts, treatises, or essays.

This supersession of the commentary by other genres or modes of discourse may be traced at least as far back as the seventeenth century in both China and Europe. As Benjamin Elman has pointed out, Ch'ing classical scholars devised new genres—including "additions and corrections" (*pu-cheng*), "analysis of evidence" (*pien-cheng*), and "critical essays" (*pien*)—that were "distinguishable from the traditional forms of annotating and commenting on earlier texts."[92] A similar development took place in the European Renaissance, when "the treatise, the dialogue, and later the essay, and even the letter and speech, took the place of the question and the commentary on Aristotle."[93] Even seventeenth-century Jesuit scholars eventually dropped the commentary form in favor of the comprehensive treatise.[94]

The abandonment or supersession of commentarial forms in the intellectual culture of early-modern times has often gone unremarked. Yet this development is probably of greater significance in the intellectual transition between the medieval and modern worlds than most of the great ideas of the leading philosophers and scientists of this same age. For the form of the commentary influenced modes of thought, and did not just provide the format for their expression.

There may well be a universal commentarial mentality that prefers to frame its cogitations in the margins of a text. But such commentarial confinement is not necessarily a mark of pedantry or of a lack of originality. Great ideas and insights may be presented in commentarial forms and formats, just as great music may take the form of the fugue. The commentary itself may become a new classic, as has happened repeatedly in the history of canons. Indeed, many (or much)

---

[91] Harold Fisch, "The Hermeneutic Quest in Robinson Crusoe," in Hartman and Budick, eds., *Midrash and Literature*, p. 213.

[92] Elman, *From Philosophy to Philology*, pp. 204–205 and 45.

[93] Paul Oskar Kristeller, *Eight Philosophers of the Italian Renaissance* (Stanford: Stanford University Press, 1964), p. 24.

[94] J. L. Heilbron, *Elements of Early Modern Physics* (Berkeley: University of California Press, 1982), p. 102.

of the classics or scriptures were originally conceived as commentaries.

Nearly all kinds of commentary may, of course, stand accused of being products of the silver age, of having lost direct contact with the primordial life force that supposedly infused the classics. To gaze directly on this life force in its overwhelming and barbaric totality, however, would be a sight more powerful than most of us could bear. Hence the rarity of figures like Moses and Arjuna in world intellectual history. Hence also the necessity of commentaries as buffers in defense of sanity and civilization.[95] Had such buffers been better maintained in modern times, perhaps some of the barbarities of our present century, when the life (or death) force has on several occasions run amok, might have been deflected. As Thomas Carlyle once remarked, it is not the Goths and Vandals but *Homer* who has filled Europe with wars. But had Homer continued to be properly expurgated as he was by Alexandrian scholars, had modern Homeric critics not insisted on presenting a more primordial Homer even to schoolchildren, perhaps some of modern Europe's wars would not have been joined with such a high degree of enthusiasm and abandon.[96] Had Motoori Norinaga (1730–1801) and his successors, in their search for the original, irrationalist Japanese spirit,[97] not removed the Confucian commentarial veneer from the ancient Japanese historical classic the *Kojiki* (Record of Ancient Matters), perhaps modern Japan's wars would have been fought with less ignoble intensity. And had the notion that Confucius expressed his moral judgments on the

[95] Frank Kermode, drawing on Aby Warburg, makes a somewhat similar observation regarding reinterpretations in the history of art: "Artists make contact with these mnemic energies, and the history of art can be seen as a history of reinterpretations, updatings of these symbols, in the course of which they are purged of their original ecstasy and terror. In this way, he [Warburg] said, 'humanity's holdings in suffering become the possessions of the humane.'" Kermode, *Forms of Attention*, p. 21.

[96] For an account of the influence of Homer and the Greek historians on wars in Western history, including World War I, see Eric A. Havelock, "War as a Way of Life in Classical Greece" and "War and the Politics of Power," in *Classical Values and the Modern World*, ed. Etienne Gareau (Ottawa: University of Ottawa Press, 1972), pp. 20–21 and 76, respectively. Havelock remarks that "the English-educated subaltern in World War I was expected to lead his company to destruction in the face of machine gun fire, and did so with gallantry. . . . It is indisputable that the morale required for such suicidal prowess had been accumulated by a study of the classics" (Havelock, "War as a Way of Life," p. 20). I am indebted to David Keightley for this reference.

[97] Maruyama Masao comments that Norinaga "in interpreting the classics, especially the *Kojiki* and the *Nihon shoki* . . . abandoned all a priori categories and accepted in toto all sorts of illogical and immoral features as part of the ancients' consciousness." Maruyama, *Studies in the Intellectual History of Tokugawa Japan*, trans. Mikiso Hane (Princeton: Princeton University Press; Tokyo: University of Tokyo Press, 1974), p. 160.

men and events of his age through the language of the *Spring and Autumn Annals* not been debunked, perhaps some of the disloyal ministers and unfilial sons in modern Chinese history would have behaved more circumspectly.

> You [Moses] speak with us, and we will listen, but let God not speak with us, lest we die.
>
> [Exodus 20:19]

GLOSSARY OF CHINESE NAMES, TERMS, AND TITLES IN THE TEXT

(not including those which appear in the bibliography)

Ai　哀

Chan Jo-shui　湛若水

Chan-kuo ts'e　戰國策

Ch'an　禪

Chang Ju-yü　章如愚

Chang Tai　張岱

Chang Tsai　張載

chao　詔

Chao Ch'i　趙岐

Chao K'uang　趙匡

Chao P'eng-fei　趙鵬飛

Chao Shu-sheng　趙樞生

Chao T'ai-ch'ing　趙臺卿

Chao Yüeh-chih　晁說之

chen　貞

Chen Te-hsiu　真德秀

Ch'en Chen-sun　陳振孫

Ch'en Hsiang-tao　陳祥道

Ch'en Hung-hsü　陳弘緒

Ch'en Li　陳立

Ch'en Li-fu　陳立夫

Ch'en Shao　陳邵

Ch'en Shih-yüan　陳士元

Ch'en Tsung-chih　陳宗之

Ch'en Yüan　陳淵

Ch'en Yüeh　陳岳

Cheng Ch'iao　鄭樵

Cheng Hsüan　鄭玄

Cheng Ju-hsieh　鄭汝諧

cheng-ming　正名

Cheng Yü　鄭玉

cheng-yüeh　正月

Ch'eng Hao　程顥

Ch'eng Hsüan-ying　成玄英

Ch'eng I　程頤

chi-chu　集注

chi ta-ch'eng　集大成

ch'i　氣

Ch'i　齊

Chia Hsüan-weng　家鉉翁

Chia K'uei　賈逵

ch'ien　乾

Ch'ien Mu　錢穆

Ch'ien Ta-hsin　錢大昕

chih (knowledge)　識

chih (simplicity)　質

Chin P'ing-mei　金瓶梅

Chin-ssu lu　近思錄

Ch'in Chin-chün　秦近君

ching　經

"Ching-chieh"　經解

ching-hsüeh　經學

ching-shih chih hsüeh　經世之學

Ch'iu　求

Ch'iu Chün　丘濬

Chou Ju-teng　周汝登

Chou-li　周禮

Chou Tun-i　周敦頤

Chu Chen　朱震

Chu Sheng　朱升

chu-tzu　諸子

Chu-tzu yü-lei　朱子語類

chü-luan　據亂

chuan　傳

"Ch'üan-hsüeh"　勸學

Chuang-tzu　莊子

Ch'un-ch'iu　春秋

Ch'un-ch'iu fan-lu　春秋繁露

chung　忠

Chung-yung　中庸

chuntai　春態

daoxue　道學

Fa-yen 法言
Fang Hsiao-ju 方孝孺
Feng Hsiu 馮休
Feng Ts'ung-wu 馮從吾
fu 福
Fu Hsi 伏羲
Fu Ssu-nien 傅斯年
Han Fei-tzu 韓非子
Han Wu-ti 漢武帝
Han Yü 韓愈
Hao Ching 郝經
heng 亨
Ho Hsiu 何休
Ho Yen 何晏
hsi 檄
Hsi 羲
"Hsi-ming" 西銘
"Hsi-tz'u" 繫辭
Hsia 夏
"Hsiang-chuan" 象傳
Hsiao-hsüeh 小學
hsiao-k'ang 小康
hsien-che 賢者
hsin (mind) 心
hsin (trust) 信
hsin-hsüeh 心學
hsing 性
Hsü Ch'ien 許謙
Hsü Fu-kuan 徐復觀
"Hsü-kua" 序卦
Hsü Shen 許愼
Hsü Yu-wang 許有王
Hsüan 軒
Hsüeh Hsüan 薛瑄
Hsün Shuang 荀爽
Hu An-kuo 胡安國
Hu Ping 胡炳
Huai-nan-tzu 淮南子
Huan 桓
Huan T'an 桓譚
Huang Tsung-hsi 黃宗羲
"Hung-fan" 洪範
Hung-lou meng 紅樓夢

Hung Tz'u-k'uei 洪次夔
I-ching 易經
I-chuan 易傳
I-li 儀禮
i-li chih hsüeh 義理之學
I-li ching-chuan t'ung-chieh
　儀禮經傳通解
I-wei ch'ien-tso-tu 易緯乾鑿度
jen 仁
Kan Wen-ch'uan 千文傳
K'ang Yu-wei 康有爲
"Kao-yao mo" 皋陶謨
k'ao-chü chih hsüeh 考據之學
ko-wu 格物
Ku Chieh-kang 顧頡剛
Ku-liang 穀梁
Ku-liang chuan 穀梁傳
Ku Yen-wu 顧炎武
Kuan-tzu 管子
k'un 坤
Kung Tzu-chen 龔自珍
Kung-yang 公羊
Kung-yang chuan 公羊傳
K'ung Kuang-sen 孔廣森
K'ung-tzu chia-yü 孔子家語
K'ung Ying-ta 孔穎達
Kuo Hsiang 郭象
Kuo-yü 國語
Kuo Yung 郭雍
Lao P'eng 老彭
Lao-tzu 老子
li (principle) 理
li (profit) 利
Li Ao 李翱
Li-chi 禮記
li-hsüeh 理學
Li Kuang-ti 李光地
Li Kung 李塨
Li Ts'an 李粲
"Li-yün" 禮運
Liu Feng-lu 劉逢祿
Liu Hsiang 劉向
Liu Hsieh 劉勰

Liu Hsin　劉歆
Liu-i lun　六藝論
Lo Ch'in-shun　羅欽順
Lu　魯
Lu Ch'un　陸淳
Lu Hsiang-shan　陸象山
Lu Pao-ch'ien　陸寶千
Lu Te-ming　陸德明
Lu Yüan-chün　盧元駿
Lü-shih ch'un-ch'iu　呂氏春秋
Lü Ta-kuei　呂大圭
Lü Tsu-ch'ien　呂祖謙
Lun-yü　論語
Lun-yü lei-k'ao　論語類考
Ma Jung　馬融
Ma Wang Tui　馬王堆
Mao Tse-tung　毛澤東
Meng-tzu　孟子
ming　命
mo　謨
Mo-tzu　墨子
Mou Tsung-san　牟宗三
Ou-yang Hsiu　歐陽修
pa-cheng　八政
Pan Ku　班固
pien　辨
pien-cheng　辨證
p'ien　篇
p'ing t'ien-hsia　平天下
po　剝
Po-hu t'ung-i　白虎通議
po-shih　博士
pu-cheng　補正
san-chuan　三傳
san-shih　三世
Shan Meng-tzu　刪孟子
shan-yen　善言
sheng-jen　聖人
sheng-p'ing　升平
Shih-chi　史記
Shih Chieh　石介
Shih-ching　詩經
shu　恕

Shu-ching　書經
Shui-hu chuan　水滸傳
Shun　舜
shuo　說
"Shuo-kua"　說卦
Shuo-yüan　說苑
Ssu-k'u ch'üan-shu　四庫全書
Ssu-ma Ch'ien　司馬遷
Ssu-ma Kuang　司馬光
Ssu-ma T'an　司馬談
ssu-shu　四書
ssu-tuan　四端
Su Ch'e　蘇轍
Su Hsün　蘇洵
Sui-shu, ching-chi chih　隋書經籍志
Sun Ch'i-feng　孫奇逢
Sun Fu　孫復
Sun Shih　孫奭
Sung Hsiang-feng　宋翔鳳
"Ta-chuan"　大傳
"Ta-hsiang chuan"　大象傳
"Ta-hsü"　大序
Ta-hsüeh　大學
Ta-hsüeh yen-i　大學衍義
Ta-Tai Li-chi　大戴禮記
ta-t'ung　大同
"T'ai-chi t'u"　太極圖
t'ai-p'ing　太平
"T'ai-tsu"　太族
Tan Chu　啖助
T'ang　唐
T'ang Chün-i　唐君毅
Tao t'ung　道統
te　德
t'i　體
t'i-yung　體用
Tiao Pao　刁包
tien　典
t'ien　天
t'ien-tao　天道
t'ien-tao–jen-tao　天道人道
"T'ien-yün"　天運
Ting　定

Tou K'o-ch'in　竇克勤
"Tsa-kua"　雜卦
Ts'ai Shen　蔡沈
ts'e　策
Tseng-tzu　曾子
Tso-chuan　左傳
Tsou Hao　鄒浩
ts'u-chang chih hsüeh　詞章之學
Ts'ui Shu　崔述
Tsung-heng chia　縱橫家
Tuan Yü-ts'ai　段玉裁
Tung Chung-shu　董仲舒
T'ung-shu　通書
Tzu-hsia　子夏
Tzu-ssu　子思
Wang An-shih　王安石
"Wang-chih"　王制
Wang Ch'ung　王充
Wang Hsi　王晳
Wang Jo-hsü　王若虛
Wang K'e-k'uan　汪克寬
Wang Po　王柏
Wang Shen　王紳
Wang Shen-tzu　王申子
Wang Su　王肅
Wang Wei　王褘
wen　文
Wen　文
Wu　武
wu-ch'ang　五常

Wu Ch'eng　吳澄
wu-ching　五經
Wu-ching cheng-i　五經正義
Wu Kuei-fang　吳桂芳
wu-shih (five affairs)　五事
wu-shih (five beginnings)　五始
Wu T'ing-tung　吳廷棟
yang　陽
Yang Hsiung　楊雄
Yang Tsai　楊載
Yao　堯
"Yao-tien"　堯典
Yeh Meng-te　葉夢得
Yen Jo-chü　閻若璩
Yen-tzu　顏子
yin　陰
yin-yang　陰陽
Yu　由
Yü　禹
Yü Ju-yen　俞汝言
"Yü-kung"　禹貢
"Yü-pei"　玉杯
Yü Shu　喻樗
yüan (origin)　元
yüan (accordingly)　爰
yüeh　曰
"Yüeh-chi"　樂記
Yüeh-ching　樂經
yung　用
Zhou Zuoren　周作人

SELECTED BIBLIOGRAPHY

This bibliography includes only those primary and secondary sources which I found most useful in my comparative study of commentarial approaches to the classics and scriptures and which might be most helpful to those undertaking a similar study. I particularly regret that there is not enough space to include all the Chinese and Japanese sources cited in the notes.

SOURCES IN CHINESE AND JAPANESE

Chang Hsüeh-ch'eng 章學誠. *Wen-shih t'ung-i* 文史通義 (The Comprehensive Meaning of Literature and History). Taipei: Kuang-wen shu-chü, 1967 reprint.

Ch'en Ch'un 陳淳. *Pei-ch'i tzu-i* 北溪字義 (The Meanings of [Confucian Philosophical] Terms [According to Ch'en] Pei-ch'i). Beijing: Chung-hua shu-chü, 1983 reprint.

Ch'en Li 陳立. *Kung-yang i-shu* 公羊義疏 (Subcommentary on the Meanings of the *Kung-yang Commentary*). SPPY ed.

——— 陳澧. *Tung-shu tu-shu chi* 東塾讀書記 (Reading Notes of [Ch'en] Tung-shu). Taipei: Shang-wu yin-shu-kuan, 1970 reprint.

Chiang Po-ch'ien 蔣伯潛. *Shih-san ching kai-lun* 十三經概論 (General Discussions of the Thirteen Classics). Shanghai: Ku-chi ch'u-pan she, 1983.

Chin-ssu lu 近思錄 (Reflections on Things at Hand). Compiled by Chu Hsi 朱熹 and Lü Tsu-ch'ien 呂祖謙. Annotated by Chiang Yung 江永. Taipei: Kuang-wen shu-chü, 1972 reprint.

Ching-i k'ao 經義考 (Investigations of Meanings in the Classics). 8 vols. Compiled by Chu I-tsun 朱彝尊. SPPY ed.

Ching-yüan 經苑 (Garden of the Classics). 6 vols. Compiled by Ch'ien I-chi 錢儀吉. Taipei: Ta-t'ung shu-chü, 1970 reprint.

Ch'ing-ju hsüeh-an 清儒學案 (Scholarly Records of Ch'ing Confucians). 8 vols. Compiled by Hsü Shih-ch'ang 徐世昌. Taipei: Shih-chieh shu-chü, 1979 reprint.

Chou-I chi-chieh tsuan-shu 周易集解纂疏 (The *Chou Change* with Collected Explications and Commentaries). Compiled by Li Ting-tso 李鼎祚. Taipei: Kuang-wen shu-chü, 1971 reprint.

Chou Yü-t'ung 周予同. *Chou Yü-t'ung ching-hsüeh shih lun-chu hsüan-chi* 周予同經學史論著選集 (Selected Treatises by Chou Yü-t'ung on the History of Classical Studies). Compiled by Chu Wei-cheng 朱維錚. Shanghai: Jen-min ch'u-pan she, 1983.

Chu Hsi 朱熹. *Chou-I pen-i* 周易本義 (Basic Meaning of the *Chou Change*). Taipei: Hua-lien ch'u-pan she, 1971 reprint.

——— 朱熹. *Ssu-shu chi-chu* 四書集注 (The Four Books with Collected Commentaries). Taipei: Hsüeh-hai ch'u-pan she, 1974 reprint.

Ch'u Po-ssu 褚柏思. *Liu-ching tao lun* 六經道論 (A Discussion of the Way of the Six Classics). Taipei: K'ai-ming shu-tien, 1971.

Ch'un-ch'iu Kung-yang chuan chu-shu 春秋公羊傳注疏 (The *Kung-yang Commentary* on the *Spring and Autumn Annals* with Subcommentaries). Compiled by Juan Yüan 阮元. SPPY ed.

Chung-kuo tzu-hsüeh ming-chu chi-ch'eng, Ju-chia tzu pu 中國子學名著集成儒家子部 (A Collection of Distinguished Works of Chinese Philosophy, Section on Philosophers of the Confucian School). Compiled by Huang Chieh 黃杰 et al. Taipei: Chung-kuo tzu-hsüeh ming-chu chi-ch'eng pien yin-chi chin-hui, 1977.

Han-shu, I-wen-chih chu-shih hui-pien 漢書藝文志注釋彙編 (*Han History* "Treatise on Bibliography" with Collected Annotations). Compiled by Chen Kuo-ch'ing 陳國慶. Beijing: Chung-hua shu-chü, 1983.

Hiraoka Takeo 平岡武夫. *Keisho no seiritsu* 經書の成立 (The Formation of the Classics). Osaka: Zenkoku shobō, 1946.

Honda Shigeyuki 本田成之. *Chung-kuo ching-hsüeh shih* 中國經學史 (History of Chinese Classical Studies). Taipei: Ku-t'ing shu-wu, 1975 reprint.

Hsün-tzu chi-chieh 荀子集解 (*Hsün-tzu* with Collected Explications). Annotated by Wang Hsien-ch'ien 王先謙. Taipei: Shih-chieh shu-chü, 1974 reprint.

Huang-Ch'ing ching-chieh 皇清經解 (Explications of the Classics from the Brilliant Ch'ing Era). 21 vols. Compiled by Juan Yüan 阮元 et al. Taipei: Fu-hsin shu-chü, 1972 reprint.

Ku-chin t'u-shu chi-ch'eng 古今圖書集成 (Complete Collection of Illustrations and Books, Past and Present). 79 vols. Compiled by Ch'en Meng-lei 陳夢雷 et al. Taipei: Ting-wen shu-chü, 1977 reprint.

Ku-liang pu-chu 穀梁補注 (The *Ku-liang Commentary* with Supplementary Commentaries). Compiled by Chung Wen-cheng 鍾文烝. SPPY ed.

Ku-shih pien 古史辨 (Critiques on Ancient History). 7 vols. Compiled by Ku Chieh-kang 顧頡剛. Shanghai: Ku-chi ch'u-pan she, 1982 reprint.

Li Yüeh-kang 李曰剛 et al. *San-Li yen-chiu lun-chi* 三禮研究論集 (A Collection of Articles on the Study of the Three Ritual Classics). Taipei: Li-ming wen-hua shih-yeh, 1981.

Liao P'ing 廖平. *Chin-ku hsüeh k'ao* 今古學考 (Investigations of New and Old Text Studies). Ch'ang-an ch'u-pan she, 1974 reprint.

P'i Hsi-jui 皮錫瑞. *Ching-hsüeh li-shih* 經學歷史 (History of Classical Studies). Taipei: I-wen yin-shu-kuan, 1966 reprint.

——— 皮錫瑞. *Ching-hsüeh t'ung-lun* 經學通論 (Comprehensive Discussions of Classical Studies). Taipei: Ho-Lo t'u-shu ch'u-pan she, 1974 reprint.

Shao Yung 邵雍. *Huang-chi ching-shih shu* 皇極經世書 (Book of the Supreme Polarities Governing the World). SPPY ed.

Ssu-k'u ch'üan-shu tsung mu 四庫全書總目 (General Catalog to the Complete Library in Four Treasuries). 10 vols. Compiled by Chi Yün 紀昀 et al. Taipei: I-wen yin-shu-kuan, 1974 reprint.

Ssu-shu wu-ching, Sung-Yüan jen chu 四書五經宋元人注 (The Four Books and Five Classics with Sung and Yüan Commentaries). 3 vols. Beijing: Chung-kuo shu-tien, n.d.

Sun Ch'un-tsai 孫春在. *Ch'ing-mo ti Kung-yang ssu-hsiang* 清末的公羊思想 (The *Kung-yang* Thought of the Late-Ch'ing Era). Taipei: Shang-wu yin-shu-kuan, 1985.

Sung Ting-tsung 宋鼎宗. *Ch'un-ch'iu Sung-hsüeh fa-wei* 春秋宋學發微 (A Disclosure of the Subtleties of Sung Studies on the *Spring and Autumn Annals*). Taipei: Wen-shih-che ch'u-pan she. 1986.

Tai Chen 戴震. *Meng-tzu tzu-i shu-cheng* 孟子字義疏證 (Explications and Verifications on the Meanings of Terms in *Mencius*). Taipei: Shih-chieh shu-chü, 1966 reprint.

Ts'ai Shih-ming 蔡世明. *Ou-yang Hsiu ti sheng-p'ing yü hsüeh-shu* 歐陽修的生平與學術 (Ou-yang Hsiu's Life and Scholarship). Taipei: Wen-shih-che ch'u-pan she, 1980.

Tseng-pu Sung-Yüan hsüeh-an 增補宋元學案 (Scholarly Records of Sung and Yüan [Confucians] with Supplements). 6 vols. Compiled by Huang Tsung-hsi 黃宗羲 and Ch'üan Tsu-wang 全祖望. SPPY ed.

Wang Ching-chih 王靜芝 et al. *Ching-hsüeh yen-chiu lun-chi* 經學研究論集 (A Collection of Articles on Research in Classical Studies). Taipei: Li-ming wen-hua shih-yeh. 1981.

Wang Yang-ming 王陽明. *Ch'uan-hsi lu* 傳習錄 (Instructions for Practical Living). Annotated by Yeh Chün-tien 葉鈞點. Taipei: Shang-wu yin-shu-kuan, 1971 reprint.

Wang Ying-lin 王應麟. *Weng-chu K'un-hsüeh chi-wen* 翁注困學紀聞 (A Record of What I Have Learned in Difficult Studies, with Weng's Commentary). 4 vols. SPPY ed.

SOURCES IN WESTERN LANGUAGES

Ackroyd, P. R., and C. F. Evans, eds. *The Cambridge History of the Bible*. Vol. 1: *From the Beginnings to Jerome*. Cambridge: Cambridge University Press, 1970.

Arapura, John G. *Gnosis and the Question of Thought in Vedānta: Dialogue with the Foundations*. Dordrecht: Martinus Nijhoff, 1986.

Augustine, St. *On Christian Doctrine*. Translated by D. W. Robertson, Jr. Indianapolis: Bobbs-Merrill, Library of Liberal Arts, 1979.

Ayoub, Mahmoud. *The Qur'ān and Its Interpreters*. Vol. 1. Albany: State University of New York Press, 1984.

Baljon, J. M. S. *Modern Muslim Koran Interpretation (1880–1960)*. Leiden: E. J. Brill, 1968.

Bowker, John. *The Targums and Rabbinic Literature: An Introduction to Jewish Interpretations of Scripture*. Cambridge: Cambridge University Press, 1969.

Bruce, F. F., and E. G. Rupp, eds. *Holy Book and Holy Tradition*. Grand Rapids, Mich.: William B. Eerdmans, 1968.

Cassiodorus Senator. *An Introduction to Divine and Human Readings*. Translated with an introduction and notes by Leslie Webber Jones. New York: W. W. Norton, 1969.

Chan, Wing-tsit, ed. *Chu Hsi and Neo-Confucianism*. Honolulu: University Press of Hawaii, 1986.

——. *Neo-Confucian Terms Explained (The "Pei-hsi tzu-i") by Ch'en Ch'un, 1159–1223*. Translated, edited, and with an introduction by Wing-tsit Chan. New York: Columbia University Press. 1986.

Clarke, Howard. *Homer's Readers: A Historical Introduction to the Iliad and the Odyssey*. Newark: University of Delaware Press, 1981.

Cohen, Shaye J. D. *From the Maccabees to the Mishnah*. Philadelphia: Westminster Press, 1987.

Comparetti, Domenico. *Vergil in the Middle Ages*. Translated by E. F. M. Benecke. London: S. Sonnenschein; New York: Macmillan, 1895; New York: Alfred Hafner, 1929 reprint.

Coward, Harold. *Sacred Word and Sacred Text: Scripture in World Religions*. Maryknoll, N.Y.: Orbis Books, 1988.

Curtius, Ernst Robert. *European Literature and the Latin Middle Ages*. Translated by Willard R. Trask. Princeton: Princeton University Press, 1973.

Denny, Frederick, and Rodney L. Taylor, eds. *The Holy Book in Comparative Perspective*. Columbia: University of South Carolina Press, 1985.

Deutsch, Eliot, and J. A. B. van Buitenen, eds. *A Source Book of Advaita Vedānta*. Honolulu: University Press of Hawaii, 1971.

Eisenstein, Elizabeth L. *The Printing Press as an Agent of Change: Communications and Cultural Transformations in Early-Modern Europe*. 2 vols. in 1. Cambridge: Cambridge University Press, 1980.

Elman, Benjamin A. *From Philosophy to Philology: Intellectual and Social Aspects of Change in Late Imperial China*. Cambridge: Harvard University Press, 1984.

Farrar, Frederic W. *History of Interpretation*. New York: E. P. Dutton, 1886; Grand Rapids, Mich.: Baker Book House, 1961 reprint.

Faur, José. *Golden Doves with Silver Dots: Semiotics and Textuality in Rabbinic Tradition*. Bloomington: Indiana University Press, 1986.

Fitzgerald, James L. "The Great Epic of India as Religious Rhetoric: A Fresh Look at the *Mahābhārata*." *Journal of the American Academy of Religion* 51, no. 4 (December 1983): 611–630.

Fontaine, Jacques, and Charles Pietri, eds. *Le Monde latin antique et la Bible*. Paris: Editions Beauchesne, 1985.

Froehlich, Karlfried, trans. and ed. *Biblical Interpretation in the Early Church*. Philadelphia: Fortress Press, 1984.

Frye, Northrop. *The Great Code: The Bible and Literature*. San Diego: Harcourt Brace Jovanovich, Harvest/HBJ Books, 1983.

Gardner, Daniel K. *Chu Hsi and the Ta-hsüeh: Neo-Confucian Reflection on the Confucian Canon*. Cambridge: Harvard University Press, 1986.

Gätje, Helmut. *The Qur'ān and Its Exegesis: Selected Texts with Classical and Modern Interpretations*. Translated and edited by Alford T. Welch. Berkeley: University of California Press, 1976.

Gellrich, Jesse M. *The Idea of the Book in the Middle Ages: Language Theory, Mythology, and Fiction*. Ithaca: Cornell University Press, 1985.

Ghate, V. S. *The Vedānta: A Study of the Brahma-Sūtras with the Bhāṣyas of S'amkara, Rāmānuja, Nimbārka, Madhva, and Vallabha*. Government Oriental Series, class C, no. 1. Poona: Bhandarkar Oriental Research Institute, 1960.

al-Ghazālī. *The Jewels of the Qur'ān*. A translation, with an introduction and annotation, of al-Ghazālī's *Kitāb Jawāhir al-Qur'ān*. Kuala Lumpur: University of Malaysia Press, 1977.

Graham, William A. *Beyond the Written Word: Oral Aspects of Scripture in the History of Religion*. Cambridge: Cambridge University Press, 1987.

Handelman, Susan A. *The Slayers of Moses: The Emergence of Rabbinic Interpretation in Modern Literary Theory*. Albany: State University of New York Press, 1982.

Harbison, E. Harris. *The Christian Scholar in the Age of Reformation*. Grand Rapids, Mich.: William B. Eerdmans, 1983.

Hardie, Philip R. *Virgil's Aeneid: Cosmos and Imperium*. Oxford: Clarendon Press, 1986.

Hartman, Geoffrey H., and Sanford Budick, eds. *Midrash and Literature*. New Haven: Yale University Press, 1986.

Havelock, Eric Alfred. *Preface to Plato*. Harvard University Press, 1982.

Holtz, Barry, ed. *Back to the Sources: Reading the Classic Jewish Texts*. New York: Summit Books, 1984.

Iyengar, K. R. Srinivasa, ed. *Asian Variations in Ramayana: Papers Presented at the International Seminar on 'Variations in Ramayana in Asia; Their Cultural, Social and Anthropological Significance,' New Delhi, January 1981*. New Delhi: Sahitya Akademi, 1983.

Jansen, J. J. G. *The Interpretation of the Koran in Modern Egypt*. Leiden: E. J. Brill, 1974.

Josipovici, Gabriel. *The Book of God: A Response to the Bible*. New Haven: Yale University Press, 1988.

Kalton, Michael C. *To Become a Sage: The Ten Diagrams on Sage Learning by Yi T'oegye*. Translated, edited, and with commentaries by Michael C. Kalton. New York: Columbia University Press, 1988.

Kermode, Frank. *The Classic: Literary Images of Permanence and Change*. Cambridge: Harvard University Press, 1983.

————. *Forms of Attention*. Chicago: University of Chicago Press, 1985.

————. *The Genesis of Secrecy: On the Interpretation of Narrative*. Cambridge: Harvard University Press, 1982.

Kugel, James L., and Rowan A. Greer. *Early Biblical Interpretation*. Philadelphia: Westminster Press, 1986.

Lamberton, Robert. *Homer the Theologian: Neoplatonist Allegorical Reading and the Growth of the Epic Tradition*. Berkeley: University of California Press, 1986.

Lo Ch'in-shun. *Knowledge Painfully Acquired: The 'K'un-chih chi' by Lo Ch'in-shun*. Translated, edited, and with an introduction by Irene Bloom. New York: Columbia University Press, 1987.

Lopez, Donald S., Jr., ed. *Buddhist Hermeneutics*. Honolulu: University Press of Hawaii, 1988.

————. *The Heart Sūtra Explained: Indian and Tibetan Commentaries*. Albany: State University of New York Press, 1988.

McMullen, David. *State and Scholars in T'ang China*. Cambridge: Cambridge University Press, 1988.

Maccoby, Hyam. *Early Rabbinic Writings*. Cambridge: Cambridge University Press, 1988.

Malmqvist, Göran. "Studies on the Gongyang and Guuliang Commentaries, I." In *Bulletin of the Museum of Far Eastern Antiquities* no. 43 (1971), pp. 67–222.

Mondésert, Claude, ed. *Le Monde grec ancien et la Bible*. Paris: Editions Beauchesne, 1984.

Murphy, Roland E., ed. *Medieval Exegesis of Wisdom Literature: Essays by Beryl Smalley*. Atlanta: Scholars Press, 1986.

Murrin, Michael. *The Allegorical Epic: Essays in Its Rise and Decline*. Chicago: University of Chicago Press, 1980.

Murty, K. Satchidananda. *Revelation and Reason in Advaita Vedānta*. Waltair: Andhra Unversity; New York: Columbia University Press, 1959.

Myres, John L. *Homer and His Critics*. London: Routledge and Kegan Paul, 1958.

Nakamura, Hajime. *A History of Early Vedānta Philosophy*. Translated by Trevor Leggett, Sengaku Mayeda, Taitetz Unno, and others. Delhi: Motilal Banarsidass, 1983.

Neusner, Jacob. *Judaism, The Classical Statement: The Evidence of the Bavli*. Chicago: University of Chicago Press, 1986.

———. *Midrash in Context: Exegesis in Formative Judaism*. Philadelphia: Fortress Press, 1983.

Origen. *Origen* [Selections]. Translation and introduction by Rowan A. Greer. New York: Paulist Press, 1979.

Pfeiffer, Rudolf. *History of Classical Scholarship from the Beginnings to the End of the Hellenistic Age*. Oxford: Clarendon Press, 1968.

Porton, Gary G. *Understanding Rabbinic Midrash: Texts and Commentary*. Hoboken, N.J.: KTAV Publishing, 1985.

Potter, Karl. H., ed. *Encyclopedia of Indian Philosophies: Advaita Vedānta up to Śamkara and His Pupils*. Princeton: Princeton University Press, 1981.

Rahman, Fazlur. *Islam and Modernity: Transformation of an Intellectual Tradition*. Chicago: University of Chicago Press, 1982.

Ramban [Nachmanides]. *Commentary on the Torah: Genesis*. Translated and annotated by Rabbi Dr. Charles B. Chavel. New York: Shilo Publishing, 1971.

Rashi. *Commentaries on the Pentateuch*. Selected and translated by Chaim Pearl. New York: Viking Press, 1973.

Riché, Pierre, and Guy Lobrichon, eds., *Le Moyen Age et la Bible*. Paris: Editions Beauchesne, 1984.

Riegel, Jeffrey Kenneth. "The Four 'Tzu Ssu' Chapters of the *Li Chi*: An Analysis of the *Fang Chi, Chung Yung, Piao Chi*, and *Tzu I*." Ph.D. diss., Stanford University, 1978.

Rippin, Andrew, ed. *Approaches to the History of the Interpretation of the Qur'ān*. Oxford: Clarendon Press, 1988.

Ruthven, K. K. *Critical Assumptions*. Cambridge: Cambridge University Press, 1979.

Sadowski, Frank, ed. *The Church Fathers on the Bible*. New York: Alba House, 1987.

Safrai, Shmuel, ed. *The Literature of the Sages, First Part: Oral Tora, Halakha, Mishna, Tosefta, Talmud, External Tractates*. Assen/Maastricht: Van Gorcum; Philadelphia: Fortress Press, 1987.

Sanders, James A. *Canon as Paradigm: From Sacred Story to Sacred Text*. Philadelphia: Fortress Press, 1987.

Scholem, Gershom. *Kabbalah*. New York: New American Library, Meridian Books, 1978.

Sharma, Arvind. *The Hindu Gītā: Ancient and Classical Interpretations of the Bhagavadgītā*. London: Duckworth, 1986.

Shchutskii, Iulian K. *Researches on the I Ching*. Translated by William L.

MacDonald and Tsuyoshi Hasegawa with Hellmut Wilhelm. Princeton: Princeton University Press, 1979.

Simonsuuri, Kirsti. *Homer's Original Genius: Eighteenth-Century Notions of the Early Greek Epic (1688–1798)*. Cambridge: Cambridge University Press, 1979.

Smalley, Beryl. *The Study of the Bible in the Middle Ages*. 3rd ed., rev. Oxford: Basil Blackwell, 1983.

Smith, Wilfred Cantwell. "The True Meaning of Scripture: An Empirical Historian's Nonreductionist Interpretation of the Qur'ān." *International Journal of Middle East Studies* 11, no. 4 (July 1980): 487–505.

Spinoza, Benedict de. *Tractatus Theologico-Politicus*. Translated by R. H. M. Elwes. London: George Routledge and Sons, 1895.

Steinsaltz, Adin. *The Essential Talmud*. Translated by Chaya Galai. New York: Basic Books, 1976.

al-Tabarī. *The Commentary on the Qur'ān* by Abū Ja'far Muhammad B. Jarīr al-Tabarī, being an abridged translation of *Jāmi' al-bayān 'an ta'wīl āy al-Qur'ān*, with an introduction and notes by J. Cooper. Vol. 1. Oxford: Oxford University Press, 1987.

Todorov, Tzvetan. *Symbolism and Interpretation*. Translated by Catherine Porter. Ithaca: Cornell University Press, 1986.

Tu Wei-ming. *Centrality and Commonality: An Essay on Chung-yung*. Honolulu: University Press of Hawaii, 1976.

Twitchett, Denis, and Michael Loewe, eds. *The Cambridge History of China*. Vol. 1: *The Ch'in and Han Empires, 221 B.C.–A.D. 220*. Cambridge: Cambridge University Press, 1986.

Wansbrough, John. *Quranic Studies: Sources and Methods of Scriptural Interpretation*. Oxford: Oxford University Press, 1977.

Wilhelm, Hellmut. *Change: Eight Lectures on the I Ching*. Translated by Cary F. Baynes. Princeton: Princeton University Press, 1973.

Wolf, F. A. *Prolegomena to Homer, 1795*. Translated with introduction and notes by Anthony Grafton, Glenn W. Most, and James E. G. Zetzel. Princeton: Princeton University Press, 1985.

INDEX

Abravanel, Don Isaac, 154
accommodation (commentarial strategy), 169–170, 193
Adler, Joseph, 129n.220
Aeneid: coherence of, 113; commentaries on, 78; comprehensiveness of, 93–95; as divinatory manual, 103; moralization of, 125; word order in, 157. *See also* Vergil
Aeschylus, 63
Age of Prophecy (Jewish history), 39
Alexandrian scholars, 30, 78, 179, 222
allegory, 80, 122, 139, 169, 177, 193
alphabet, Hebrew, 57, 131, 144, 150
Ambrose, Saint, 32n.49
Analects, 17–18, 26, 52, 53; accommodation in, 169–170; addition of to canon, 50–51; in commentaries of Cheng Hsüan, 44; as commentary, 64, 70; contradictions in, 208; morality of, 129; omissions in, 183–186; organization of, 111n.123; profundity of, 213–214; superfluities in, 188–189
Anselm, Saint, 81
Apocrypha, 154
Aristotle, 91; commentaries on, 81, 146; consistency of, 116; as encyclopedist, 90; on Homer, 125
Aron, Raymond, 91, 135
Artaxerxes, 39
Arya Samaj, 98
Augustine, Saint, 98n.58, 117–118, 190, 194
Averroës, 126

Bacon, Roger, 96, 116
Barthes, Roland, 210
Bavli (Babylonian Talmud), 57, 90, 99n.58; coherence of, 108; comprehensiveness of, 95
Bernard of Clairvaux, Saint, 84
Bhagavad Gītā, 10, 58, 59, 60, 61; comprehensiveness of, 99; consistency of, 120, 173; key phrases in, 195; metaphors for, 53; obscurity in, 134
Bhave, Vinoba, 134
Bible: clarity of, 194; coherence of, 106;

comprehensiveness of, 96, 203–204; consistency in, 117–118, 162; essential passages in, 181; immorality in, 122; inspiration of, 87–88; miscellaneous character of, 21–22; obscurities in, 198n.246; order of books in, 109–110
Bible, Hebrew, 31, 144; lacunae in, 154
Blackwell, Thomas, 92
Bloom, Harold, 57
Bodde, Derk, 40
Boethius, 146
Boismard, Marie-Emile, 137
"Book" religions, 59
books, burning of (Ch'in dynasty), 40, 68, 177, 207
Borges, Jorge Luis, 72, 196
Bouvet, Joachim, 102–103
Brahman, 170, 180, 191; duality of, 173
Brandon, S.G.F., 38n.1
Brāhma Sūtra, 31, 60, 72, 84, 180; comprehensiveness of, 106; consistency of, 120
Brihadāranyaka Upanishad, 112
bsTan-dar-lha-ram pa (Buddhist commentator), 49
Buddha, 168; inconsistencies of, 170
Buddhism, 7n.10, 61; accommodation in, 170–171; Japanese, 194–195; Mahāyāna, 180–181; Mādhyamika school of, 170

calendar, 77, 147
Calvin, John, 86
canon, Confucian, 10–11; additions to, 49–50; arrangement of, 47, 151; closure of, 60, 68–69; coherence of, 113–115, 146–147, 207; comprehensiveness of, 100–106, 140–141; consistency of, 160–162, 207–209; cosmology of, 46, 161–163; diversity of, 21; essence of, 191–193; essential passages in, 183–186; explication of text in, 75–79; expurgation of, 29, 32, 178–179; immorality in, 177; incorporation of commentary into, 63–64; integration of, 4, 42–48; during latter Han dynasty, 43–44; moral function of, 45, 211–212;

Canon, Confucian (*cont.*)
  numerology in, 147–148; obscurities
  in, 198; oral transmission of, 43; order
  of books in, 115; order of study for,
  113–114; origin of, 4, 24, 34–35, 38;
  pedagogical function of, 45; as product of declining era, 25–26; profundity of, 212–214; recensions of, 153–
  154; reconstruction of, 40–42; as reflection of Confucius' nature, 48; reformations of, 50; satires on, 206
canonization: consequences of, 5–6; definition of, 38; of Islamic literature, 39;
  of later works, 54–61, 216–220; role of
  politics in, 38–40
canons: characteristics of, 89, 136; coherence of, 106–115; comprehensive
  nature of, 90–91, 136, 140–145, 202–
  206; consistency of, 115–121; discontinuity in, 136; imperfections in, 170;
  modern, 216–220; morality of, 121–
  129; superfluities in, 186–187. *See also*
  classics
Cassiodorus, 96, 132, 181
Chaitanya, 61
Chang Hsüeh-cheng, 152–153, 186
Chang Tai, 149
Chang-tai Hung, 216
Chang Tsai, 54, 82
Chan Jo-shui, 73
Chao Ch'i, 11, 18, 189
Chao K'uang, 198
Chao P'eng-fei, 71
Chao T'ai-ching, 150
Ch'ao Yüeh-chih, 49
Ch'en Chen-sun, 51, 74
Ch'en Ch'un, 164–165, 175; commentar-
  ies on Mencius, 83
Cheng Ch'iao, 24–25, 74
Cheng Hsüan, 11, 41, 43–44, 141, 161,
  208; on *Record of Rites*, 64, 162; on
  Rites of Chou, 176
Cheng Hsüan-ying, 69
Ch'eng I, 3, 151, 166; on *Analects*, 185–
  186; on *Annals*, 16–17, 134; on *Change*,
  81; on Four Books, 20n.69; on Men-
  cius, 83, 142; on *Record of Rites*, 207;
  on superfluities, 188; and textual lacu-
  nae, 143–144; use of modal distinc-
  tion, 174
Cheng Ju-hsieh, 185
Cheng Yü, 17

Ch'en Hsiang-tao, 140; on *Analects*, 160–
  161
Ch'en Hung-hsü, 73
Ch'en Li, 26, 105, 149, 189, 208–209
Ch'en Li-fu, 53, 154
Ch'en Shao, 29
Ch'en Shih-yüan, 77–78
Chen Te-hsiu, 77, 185
Ch'en Tsung-chih, 104
Ch'en Yüan, 192
Chia Hsüan-weng, 73–74
Chia K'uei, 44, 158n.72
Ch'ien Ta-hsin, 184, 191–192, 214
Chien Yüeh, 75
China: feudal culture of, 3; intellectual
  history of, 3–4; political upheavals in,
  37, 40
Ch'in Chin-chün, 77
Ch'in dynasty, 40
"ching," definition of, 50
Ching-i k'ao (Investigation of Meanings in
  the Classics), 20
Ch'iu Chün, 77, 183
Chou, Duke of, 66, 72, 104
Chou dynasty, 176; decline of, 25–26
Chou Ju-teng, 32, 140
Chou Tun-i, 16, 54–55
Chou Yü-t'ung, 3, 141
Chronicles, Book of, as commentary, 63,
  87
Chuang-tzu, 69
Chuang-tzu, 168
Chu Hsi, 5, 10–11, 151; on *Analects*, 18,
  160, 178, 188–189; on *Annals*, 131,
  178, 212; anthologies by, 55, 82; on
  Change, 14, 102, 213; commentaries on
  Mencius, 83; on comprehensiveness of
  canon, 100; criticism of Ch'eng I, 205;
  definition of humanity, 208–209; on
  Documents Classic, 207; on duality, 192;
  on Five Classics, 54; on Four Books,
  50–52, 83, 84, 115, 149; on *Great
  Learning*, 69, 153; metaphysics of,
  164–165; on morality, 124; on
  omissions of Confucius, 184–185; parallelism of, 167–168; on *Songs*, 28,
  141; and textual lacunae, 143–144;
  use of modal distinction, 174
Ch'un-ch'iu fan-lu, 81
Chung Wen-cheng, 134, 191; on the *Annals*, 143
Ch'u Po-ssu, 49

Chu Sheng, 100

Clarke, Howard, 92, 139

Classic of Change (I-ching), 4, 11, 12; coherence of, 151–152; comprehensiveness of, 100, 101, 141–142, 204–205; content of, 13–14; difficulties of, 12–13; divination in, 66–67, 124; duality of, 192; essence of, 191; in Han dynasty, 42; hierarchies in, 148; inconsistencies in, 161; modal distinctions in, 175; numerology in, 148–149; obscurity in, 134, 198; origin of, 24, 36; pairing of with *Annals*, 12–15, 17; pairing of with *Mencius*, 19; philosophy in, 101; position of in canon, 15–16; profundity of, 130

classics: as anthologies, 23–24; coherence of, 106–115, 163, 206–207; cohesiveness of, 145–146, 155–156; comprehensiveness of, 140–145, 202–206; consistency of, 139, 176, 208–211; divine inspiration of, 24; encyclopedic nature of, 33–35; essence of, 193, 194–195; essential passages in, 179–183; expurgation of, 178–179; heterogeneous nature of, 21–24; interrelationships among, 147–149; morality of, 128–129, 139, 177–179, 211–212; moralization of, 125–127; obscurities in, 133–135, 139, 189–190, 197–199; pedagogical uses of, 135; profundity of, 129–135, 139, 202; survival of, 85; triviality in, 131–133. *See also* canons

Classified Conversations of Master Chu (Chu-tzu yü-lei), 165

Classified Investigations on the Analects (Lun-yü lei-k'ao), 77

Cohen, Shaye J. D., 137

coherence (of canons), 106–115, 163, 206–207

Collected Commentaries on the Four Books (Ssu-shu chi-chu), 55

commentaries: canonization of, 84; definition of, 62, 64–65; and divination, 65–67; as encyclopedias, 77–79; genres supplanting, 221; hidden, 64; historians of, 8; language of, 139; mingling of with canon, 63–64, 68–71; necessity for, 71–75; oral transmission of, 68; similarities among, 5–6; and survival of the classics, 85; and transi-

tion to modern scholarship, 200–202, 214–216

commentators: Ch'ing, 147, 176, 205–206, 214–216; Hellenistic, 124–125; strategies of, 145, 146, 167, 176, 188; Sung, 74–75; T'ang, 49, 74–75. *See also* exegetes; Neo-Confucians

commentators, Confucian: cosmology of, 161–163; dualities employed by, 166–167; use of allegory, 169; use of modal distinction, 174–175

commentators, Han, 10, 13, 36, 42, 43–46, 74–75, 113; and reconstruction of classics, 40–42; on role of Confucius, 30

Complete Library in Four Treasuries (Ssu-k'u ch'üan-shu), 16

Comprehensive Book (T'ung-shu), 55

Comprehensive Discussions in White Tiger Pavilion, 46

comprehensiveness, of canonical literature, 89–100, 136, 140–145, 202–206

Confucianism: diversity of canon in, 100; in Korea, 121; monopolization of texts, 35–36; nonethnocentricism of, 21n.1; and Sung commentators, 11; triumph of, 90

Confucius, 18; on *Analects*, 32–33; as author of *Annals*, 73, 103, 143, 156, 159–160; as author of canon, 5, 12, 17n.58, 26, 36; as author of Five Classics, 147; as editor of canon, 24–25, 26–30, 36, 47, 113, 131; expurgation of classics, 27–28, 36; historiography of, 141; on human nature, 184; as moralist, 129; omissions in teachings of, 184–186; pedagogical techniques of, 68, 149; political science of, 141; portrayal of by Mencius, 32n.49; and *Songs*, 28, 33, 36–37, 105, 123; as transmitter of canon, 27, 28, 29; use of accommodation, 169

contradiction, in canons, 136

cosmogony, as commentarial strategy, 167

cosmology, in Confucian canon, 46, 161–163

Council of Jabne, 39

Coward, Harold, 201n.3

Cultural Revolution, 218

Cyprian, 129n.209

David (king of Israel), 31, 36
de Bary, William Theodore, 55
Demetrius (Alexandrian scholar), 78
De naturis rerum (Nequam), 78
Deportment and Rites (I-li), 23, 215; in latter Han commentaries, 44
Derrida, Jacques, 210
Descartes, René, 209–210
Deutsch, Eliot, 180, 193
De vita et poesi Homeri (Pseudo-Plutarch), 92
Dōgen, 181
"Diagram of the Great Ultimate" (T'ai-chi t'u), 55
Dilthey, Wilhelm, 210
Dimock, Edward, 63
divination, 4, 21, 65–68, 124; origin of canons in, 103
Doctrine of the Mean (Chung-yung), 17, 52, 53, 167, 183; arrangement of, 151; essential passages in, 180, 192; and Neo-Confucian commentators, 19
Documents Classic, 20; addition of to canon, 51; arrangement of, 47, 151; contradictions in, 208; destruction of, 40; duality of, 192; modal distinctions in, 175; numerology in, 150; origin of, 24; origin of political science in, 101; pairing of with Annals, 14; Sung commentators on, 149; versions of, 34, 35–36, 41
Dream of the Red Chamber (Hung-lou meng), 216
Dryden, John, 190, 217

Ecclesiasticus, Book of, 174
Einstein, Albert, 220
Eisenstein, Elizabeth, 70, 209
Elman, Benjamin, 54, 221
Elyot, Thomas, 94
"Encouragement of Learning" (Ch'üan-hsüeh), 45
Engels, Friedrich, 219
Epic of Gilgamesh, 9
Epicurus, 92
Erasmus, Desiderius, 92
Eusebius, 109
Eustathius, bishop of Thessalonica, 78, 125
exegetes: angels as, 31; assumptions of, 135–136, 139; Byzantine, 82; as

prophets, 87; typology of, 66. See also commentators; Neo-Confucians
exegetes, Christian biblical, 4, 6, 84, 87, 109, 114, 117, 122, 146; language of, 166n.99; moralization of, 129; on obscurities, 197; on triviality, 131–132
exegetes, Qur'ānic, 66, 110, 118, 157, 181–182; contemporary, 200; on superfluities, 187
exegetes, rabbinic, 82, 86, 107–108, 117, 131, 136n.243; on superfluities, 186–187. See also Judaism, rabbinic
Exodus, Book of, 146
Extended Meaning of the Great Learning (Ta-hsüeh yen-i), 77
Ezekiel, Book of, 117
Ezra, Book of, 108
Ezra (exegete), 86

Fang Hsiao-ju, 113, 186
fathers of the church, 84–85
Faur, José, 3
Felton, Henry, 112
Feng Ching, 152n.48
Feng Hsiu, 179
Feng Ts'ung-wu, 174
figures of speech, literalization of, 36
Finley, Moses, 9
Five Classics, 11, 16; admission of into canon; comprehensiveness of, 100; cosmology of, 163; and Neo-Confucian commentators, 53–54; numerology of, 49; origins of, 41; in seventeenth century, 54. See also Six Classics
forgers, 41
Four Books (ssu-shu), 12; addition to canon, 50–51, 53, 54, 121; coherence of, 113, 207; cosmology of, 163; enumeration of, 17–18; morality of, 129; pedagogical uses of, 52, 145; recension of, 154; relation to Five Classics, 51–54; relation to Six Classics, 18; unity of, 51–53
four-seven debate (Korea), 121
La Franciade (Ronsard), 93n.24
Freud, Sigmund, canonization of, 200, 219
Friedman, Richard Elliott, 108
Frye, Northrop, 22, 88, 93n.24
Fu Hsi, 32, 47, 130; numerology of, 152
Fulgentius, 157
Fu Ssu-nien, 35

Gadamer, Hans-Georg, 6
Gandhi, Mohandas K., 195
Gardner, Daniel, 115
Gellrich, Jesse, 128, 194
gematria (interpretive techniques), 130–131
Genesis, Book of, 96, 173–174
Gestalt psychology, 106
Ghose, Aurobindo, 111
al-Ghāzalī, 3, 66, 97, 187
Gikatilla (Kabbalist), 95
glosses, 75–79, 81; biblical, 80
Gnostics, 56
Goodspeed, E. J., 109
Gorak, Jan, 5
Gospels: numerology in, 150; recensions of, 154
Graham, William A., 4n.4, 21n.1, 201n.4
"Great Commentary" (to the *Change*), 101, 103, 115, 162, 174–175
Great Learning (Ta-hsüeh), 17, 52, 53, 113; addition of to canon, 50–51; arrangement of, 151; commentaries on, 77; essential passages in, 180, 181, 192; lacunae in, 153; and Neo-Confucian commentators, 19, 149
Greene, Thomas, 197
Gregory the Great, Saint, 84–85
Griffin, Jasper, 92

haggadah, 154
Hananiah ben Hezakiah, 117
Handelman, Susan, 8
Han dynasty, and establishment of canon, 38–39
Han Yü, 140, 189, 208; use of accommodation, 169
Hao Ching, 19, 83
Harbison, E. Harris, 183, 190
Havelock, Eric A., 125, 222n.96
Heart Sūtra, 181
Heraclides, 177
Heraclitus, 92, 124
hermeneutics. *See* commentators; exegetes
heroes, portrayal of, 31–32
hexagrams, 66–67, 147–149, 152, 161, 162, 167, 175, 191
Hillel, 194, 195
Hiraoka Takeo, 13
Ho Hsiu, 44, 156
Holtz, Barry, 62

Homer: canonization of, 39–40; coherence of, 112, 113n.132, 207; commentarial traditions on, 4, 8–9, 78, 85, 177; as commentator, 30; comprehensiveness of, 91–93, 141n.7, 202–203; consistency of, 116–117; essential passages in, 182; expurgation of, 30, 222; imitations of, 93; immorality in, 179; lacunae in, 154; during Middle Ages, 9; pedagogic uses of, 122, 124–125; Plato's characterization of, 172–173
Homeridae, 31, 87
Honda Shigeyuki, 4
Horace, 125
Ho Yen, 184
Hsü Ch'ien, 176
Hsüeh Hsüan, 55, 192
Hsü Fu-kuan, 81
Hsün Shuang, 162
Hsün-tzu, 34, 176
Hsü Shen, 44
Hsü Yu-wang, 131
Huai-nan-tzu ([Book of the] Master of Huai-nan), 25
Huang Tsung-hsi, 102
Hu An-kuo, 55, 104, 158
Hugh of St. Victor, 80, 109; use of modal distinction, 173
Hu Ping, 52
Hung Tz'u-k'uei, 147

Ibn Abi al-Fadl al-Mursî, 97
Ibn Khaldhûn, 197
Iliad, 4, 92; coherence of, 112; commentaries on, 78; expurgation of, 179; literary qualities of, 23
Imams, 56
implausibility, in canons, 136
Irenaeus, 150
Islam, 5; canonization of literature of, 39; legalistic nature of, 119; Sunni, 56
Itō Jinsai, 100, 213n.56

Jaffee, M. S., 187
Jansen, J.J.G., 200n.1
Jaurès, Jean, 218
Jerome, Saint, 132, 150
Jesuits, 60, 221
Jesus, 194; as commentator, 30; discourse of, 168; discrepancies in teachings of, 170
Jnāneshvari, 99

Joachim of Fiore, 56
Job, Book of, 96, 128–129
John Chrysostom, Saint, 133
John of Salisbury, 94
Johnson, David, 124
Jomier, Jacques, 200n.1
Josipovici, Gabriel, 110n.115
Juan Yüan, 33
Judaism, medieval, 60–61
Judaism, rabbinic, 4, 56, 86–87, 154, 195, 201; origins of, 7–8; and super-fluity, 139. *See also* exegetes, rabbinic
Justin Martyr, Saint, 118, 172

Kabbala, 57, 108, 203
Kamban, 127
K'ang Yu-wei, 16, 154, 176
Kan Wen-ch'uan, 148
Karaist movement (Judaism), 61
Karlgren, Bernhard, 130
kathenotheism (in Veda), 164n.93
Kautsky, Karl, 217
Keightley, David, 67
Kermode, Frank, 106, 135, 193, 197–198, 217
King, Martin Luther, Jr., 56
Kitagawa, Joseph M., 120n.163
Kūkai, 181
Kālidāsa, 63
Kolakowski, Leszek, 217
Kramers, R. P., 35, 41
Kristeller, Paul, 81
Ku Chieh-kang, 217
Ku-chin t'u-shu chi-ch'eng (Complete Collection of Illustrations and Books, Past and Present), 20
Ku-liang Commentary (Ku-liang chuan), 13, 74; addition of to canon, 49; chronology in, 158, 159; and divination, 67
K'ung Kuang-sen, 71, 104
Kung Tzu-chen, 147
K'ung-tzu shih-chia (House of Confucius), 36
Kung-yang Commentary (Kung-yang chuan), 13, 68, 148, 156, 188, 198; addition of to canon, 49; and divination, 67; numerology in, 147; omens in, 74
K'ung Ying-ta, 212
Kuo Hsiang, 69
Kuo-yü (Conversations of the States), 75
Kuo Yung, 152
Ku Yen-wu, 192, 205

Labriola, Antonio, 218
lacunae, in classics, 141, 143–144, 153
Lafargue, Paul, 218
Langton, Stephen, 70
Lao-tzu, 69
Lao-tzu, 168
Laplanche, François, 202
Ledéaut, Roger, 72
Legge, James, 156
Le Goff, Jacques, 168
Li Ao, 27
Liao P'ing, 142, 147
Li Kuang-ti, 191
Li Kung, 177, 189
literary criticism, contemporary, 200–201
Liu Feng-lu, 16, 147, 148; on *Analects*, 18, 32; on *Annals*, 159
Liu Hsüan, 44
Liu Hsiang, 43; on *Annals*, 25; and reconstruction of classics, 41
Liu Hsieh, 101
Liu Hsin, 15, 75
Liu-li (Discussions of the Six Arts), 41
Lo Ch'in-shun, 83, 184, 211
Lombard, Peter, 181
Lotus Sūtra, 181
Lü-shih ch'un-ch'iu, 35
Lü Ta-kuei, 123, 212
Lu Ch'un, 75, 205
Lu Hsiang-shan, 60
Lukács, George, 89
Lu Pao-ch'ien, 175
Lu Te-ming, 23
Luther, Martin, 63, 183, 190, 193–194, 210n.42
Lutheranism, 61
Lu Yüan-chün, 32–33
Luzatto, Samuel David, 86

Macrobius, 9, 94, 117
Mahābhārata, 9, 58–59, 63, 90, 98–99; comprehensiveness of, 91; creation of, 31; miscellaneous character of, 22; moralization of, 127–128; superfluities in, 188
mahāvākyas (key phrases), 195–196, 219
Maimonides, 107–108, 116, 135
Ma Jung, 43, 44
mantras, 195, 219
Mao Tse-tung, 218, 219

Marxism: canonical character of, 89, 91, 217–219; obscurity in, 135
Mascaro, Juan, 112
al-Mashriqi, 187
Matsui Rashu, 153
Matthew, Book of, 194
Maudūdī, Maulana Abūl Alā, 187
Mencius, 17–18, 25, 45, 53, 149; addition of to canon, 50–51; comprehensiveness of, 143; essence of, 192; expurgation of, 179; numerology in, 150; pairing of with *Classic of Change*, 19; recension of, 154
Mencius, 18, 34, 83; attitude of toward *Songs*, 37; on human nature, 176; immorality of, 178; on profit, 142; and transmission of Confucian way, 52
Meng-tzu tzu-i shu-cheng, 81
midrash, 5, 39, 62, 107, 117; in contemporary criticism, 201; origins of, 65
Midrash Tehillim, 155
Mirandola, Pico della, 209
Mishnah, 57, 107–108, 162; necessity for commentaries on, 73
Mī māmsā (commentarial tradition), 119, 133, 197
modal distinction, 171–176, 187, 193, 219
Mohism, 34, 90
Montaigne, Michel Eyquen de, 209
Morality, in canons, 121–129
Moses (patriarch), 31, 36, 57, 86, 186–187, 222; death of, 39
Motoori Norinaga, 222
Mou Tsung-san, 215
Muhammad, 97; as commentator on Qur'ān, 30–31
Music Classic (Yüeh-ching), 11n.32, 162, 189; reconstruction of, 40

Naitō Torajirō, 69
Nakai Riken, 153, 213n.56
Nehemiah, Book of, 108
Neo-Confucians, 10–12, 18, 53–54, 183, 211; challenges to canon, 60; cosmology of, 163; metaphysics of, 164–166; and order of the canon, 113; use of modal distinction, 174–175; Yüan, 53–54. *See also* commentators; exegetes
Neo-Confucians, Ming, 10, 53–54, 205; on *Change*, 102
Neo-Confucians, Sung, 10, 53–54, 145,

183, 185, 205, 209, 213; additions of to canon, 50–52; and canonization of Four Books, 12, 121; on *Change*, 102; dualities of, 166; exegesis of, 85; metaphysics of, 168; moralizations of, 123–124
Neo-Platonism, 91
Nequam, Alexander, 78
Neusner, Jacob, 31, 57, 82, 90, 98n.58, 119, 201n.2
New Culture Movement, 216
New Testament: as commentary, 63; essential passages in, 182
New Text school, 44, 141, 147, 148, 176, 208
Nicholas of Lyra, 192n.217
Nietzsche, Friedrich, 210
novelists, Ch'ing, 216
Numbers, Book of, 96, 130
Numenius, 117
numerology, 46, 49, 147–150

Odyssey, 62–63, 92, 141n.7; literary qualities of, 23; moralization of, 125
Old Testament: as commentary on Pentateuch, 63–64; exegesis of, 66; immorality in, 177; numerology in, 150; order of books in, 114; superfluities in, 188n.195
Old Text school, 44, 141, 208
Olivelle, Patrick, 59
Origen, 84, 109, 114, 169; on allegories, 177; on clarity of scripture, 190, 197; commentary on Book of Numbers, 130; on consistency of Scripture, 118
Ortelius, Abraham, 204
Ou-yang Hsiu, 12n.34, 71, 152n.48

Pan Ku, 15, 46, 145
Parmenides, 62–63
patristic literature, 82
Paul (apostle), 150
Pearson, Birger, 8n.20
Pelikan, Jaroslav, 82
Pentateuch: coherence of, 108; commentaries on, 86; comprehensiveness of, 95
Perrault, Charles, 206
Pertti, Nikkilä, 35n.63
Pesher (exegesis), 65
Peterson, Willard, 36n.68
Petronius Arbiter, 62

philology, in commentaries, 80
physics, and commentarial assumptions, 219–220
p'ien (precursor of book), 35
P'i Hsi-jui, 3, 29, 141, 176, 208
Plaks, Andrew, 216
Plato, 90–91, 92, 114; on Homer, 202–203
Plekhanov, G., 217–218
Poliziano, Angelo, 92
Pope, Alexander, 93, 203
Popul Vuh, 67; comprehensiveness of, 99–100
Porphyry, 173
po-shih (erudites), 42
Prashna Upanishad, 112
Prickett, Stephen, 198n.246
printing, invention of, 70; impact of on commentarial traditions, 201–202
Proclus (Neo-Platonist), 172
Psalms, Book of, 96
Pseudo-Plutarch, 92, 197
Purānas ("Ancient Lore"), 58
pyromancy, 67

Qur'ān: arrangement of, 155; coherence of, 110–111; comprehensiveness of, 96–98; consistency of, 118–119; essential passages in, 181–182; homogeneity of, 22–23; lacunae in, 144; legalistic nature of, 119; morality of, 121–122; necessity for commentaries on, 72; obscurities in, 134–135, 197, 198–199; personification of, 109; role of Muhammad in interpretation of, 31; sciences in, 97; Sunni additions to, 56; superfluities in, 133, 187–188; word order in, 157

Radhakrishnan, S., 99
Rahman, Afzalur, 97
Rahman, Fazlur, 134
Rajagopalachari, Chakravarti, 178
Rāma, 178
Rāmānuja (Vedantist), 116, 120
Rāmāyana, 9–10, 58, 63; immorality in, 132, 178; key phrases in, 195–196; moralization of, 126–128; oral commentary on, 79; profundity of, 133
Ramban, 95
Rashi, 86, 108, 162, 187

Razi, Imam, 79
"Record of Music." See *Music Classic* (Yüeh ching)
Record of Rites (Li-chi), 12, 19, 142, 215; as commentary, 64; composition of, 28–29; comprehensiveness of, 105; contents of, 23
Records of the Historian (Shih-chi), 41
Reflections on Things at Hand (Chin-ssu lu), 52, 55, 82–83
Reformation, Protestant, 60, 85
Ricoeur, Paul, 214
Riegel, Jeffrey Kenneth, 36–37, 39n.3, 151
Rig Veda, 112
Rites of Chou (Chou-li), 11n.32, 23, 208; discrepancies in, 176; in latter Han commentaries, 44; origin of, 24
Roland of Cremona, 80
Roy, Ram Mohun, 58
Ruthven, K. K., 106, 128

Sadducees, 57n.78
Safrai, Shmuel, 72
"sages" (*sheng-jen*), 71
Sa'id ben Jabayr, 72
Saint-Beuve, Charles-Augustin, 128
Salutati, Coluccio, 125
Saraswati, Dayananda, 59, 98
Satyricon (Petronius), 62
Schadewaldt, Wolfgang, 211
Scholem, Gershom, 3n.2
School Sayings of Confucius (K'ung-tzu chia-yü), 26; reconstruction of, 41
Schwartz, Benjamin, 141
sciences, in commentaries, 80–81
Scott, John A., 134
scribes, medieval, 137
Second Temple period (Jewish history), 8, 39
Sefer Yesira (Book of Creation), 72
Seneca, 203
Servius, 94
Shakespeare, William: canonical character of, 89, 217; obscurity in, 135
Shankara (Vedantist), 3, 5, 10, 72, 98, 106, 120, 180; on clarity of Veda, 190–191; as cultural hero, 84; simplifications of, 194; use of accommodation, 170; use of modal distinctions, 173
Shao Yung, 16, 47

Shchutskii, Iulian, 103, 124
Shih Chieh, 55
Shikitei Sanba, 206
Shui-hu chuan (novel), 126
Shuo-yüan (Garden of Discourses), 25, 41
Silvester, Bernard, 78
Simeon ben Zemah Duran, 8
Six Classics, 11, 25; comprehensiveness of, 101; essential passages in, 181, 193; expurgation of, 27–28; as macrocosm, 48; numerology of, 46, 49; relationship of to Four Books, 18; unity of, 75. *See also* Five Classics
Six Dynasties era, 76
Smalley, Beryl, 78, 80, 114
Sāma Veda, 112
Smith, Jonathan Z., 6, 89
smriti (literature of recollection), 59, 71, 84
Solomon, 36, 53
Songs Classic, 19, 36–37; comprehensiveness of, 105–106; destruction of, 40; duality of, 192; immorality in, 122–123, 177–178; origin of, 24; and origin of literature, 101; pairing of with *Annals*, 14–15, 45; as product of declining era, 25
speech-act theory (of canonical arrangement), 111
Spinoza, Benedict de, 203–204, 209, 213n.54
Spring and Autumn Annals (Ch'un-ch'iu), 11, 12, 223; Ch'ing commentators on, 147; chronological arrangement of, 47; composition of, 26, 36; comprehensiveness of, 100, 101, 103–105, 143, 204–205; content of, 13–14; cosmology of, 159; difficulties of, 12–13; divination in, 67; expurgation of, 29–30; hierarchies in, 148; inconsistencies in, 160, 161; lacunae in, 143; legal uses of, 42; links with *Songs*, 45; morality of, 123–124, 158–159, 211–212; necessity for commentaries on, 73; obscurities in, 71, 134, 198; origin of historiography in, 101; pairing of with *Classic of Change*, 12–15, 17; pairing of with *Documents Classic*, 14; position of in canon, 15–17; as product of declining era, 25; Sung commentaries on, 13, 83; superfluities in, 188; terminol-

ogy of, 158, 159; word order in, 156–158
sūrahs (Qur'ān), 110–111, 155
sruti (literature of revelation), 59, 71, 84
Ssu-ma Ch'ien, 41
Ssu-ma Kuang, 51
Ssu-ma T'an, 21
St. Matthew, gospel of: as commentary, 63
Staal, Frits, 180n.154
Steiner, George, 219
Steinsaltz, Adin, 155
sūtras, 134, 170; comprehensiveness of, 106; profundity of, 181; simplification of, 195; unity of, 49
Su Ch'e, 14, 73n.49, 143
Su Hsün, 135n.242, 152
Sun Ch'i-feng, 102
Sun Fu, 56
Sun Shih, 150
Sung Hsiang-feng, 157
Sung Ting-tsung, 13
superfluity, in canons, 131, 136, 139
Swift, Jonathan, 137–138, 203

al-Tabarī, 79, 110, 133, 155, 157; on obscurities, 199; on superfluities, 187
Tai Chen, 168
Tale of a Tub (Swift), 137–138, 203
Tale of Genji, 126
Talmud, 57, 61, 182; as commentary, 86
Tan Chu, 75
T'ang Chün-i, 215
Taoism, 69
Tao-t'ung (transmission of the Way), 83
Tedlock, Dennis, 67, 99
"Ten Wings," 36, 151n.47, 183; composition of, 12; comprehensiveness of, 101; divination in, 66; morality of, 124
Thapar, Romila, 7
theocentricity, 21n.1
Theodore of Mopsuestia, 172n.117
Tiao Pao, 134
Todorov, Tzvetan, 118, 136
Torah, 8, 62; additions to, 56–57; arrangement of, 155; coherence of, 107–108; consistency in, 117; essential passages in, 182; exegesis of, 119; necessity for commentaries on, 72; obscurity in, 135; Oral, 57, 187; superfluity in, 131

Tou K'o-ch'in, 55
tragedy, Greek, 126
"Treatise on Bibliography" (I-wen chih), 45, 46, 68n.23, 130, 152
"Tribute of Yü" (Yü-kung), 42
trigrams, 152
Trinity, doctrine of, 171–172
Ts'ai Shen, 149, 151, 160, 192; on *Documents Classic*, 161; use of modal distinction, 175
Tseng-tzu, 52, 140–141
Tso Commentary (Tso-chuan), 13, 15n.47, 73–75; addition of to canon, 49; morality of, 124; oral transmission of, 68; as supplement to *Annals*, 143
Ts'ui Shu, 215
Tuan Yü-ts'ai, 50
Tulsīdās, 10, 58, 127
Tung Chung-shu, 38, 39, 103, 124, 134
Tzu-hsia, 25
Tzu-kung, 213
Tzu-ssu, 52, 207

Upanishads, 7, 22, 35n.62, 84, 180; coherence in, 112; consistency of, 120; dualities in, 170–171; medieval, 59; metaphors for, 53

Vaisnaviya Tantrasara, 53
van Buitenen, J.A.B., 22, 180, 193
van der Loon, P., 124
Veda, 7; additions to, 57–60; arrangement of, 111; comprehensiveness of, 98; consistency of, 116, 119–120; lacunae in, 84; philology in, 80; purpose of, 133; sciences in, 98
Vedānta (commentarial tradition), 4, 7, 59–60, 72, 132, 180; accommodation in, 170–171; on harmony of the Veda, 116, 119; and resolution of contradictions, 139; simplifications of, 195; use of modal distinctions in, 173
Vedāntasāra, 112, 144
Vergil: coherence of, 113n.132; commentarial traditions on, 8–9; comprehensiveness of, 94–95; during Middle Ages, 9, 146. See also *Aeneid*
Vermes, Geza, 136–137, 195n.230
Vālmīki, 32n.49, 127
Voltaire, 121–122, 210
Vyasatirtha, 173

Vyāsa, 31, 36, 58; as compiler of *Mahābhārata*, 59

Wang An-shih, 212
Wang Ch'ung, 71, 150
Wang Hsi, 123
Wang Jo-hsü, 213–214
Wang K'e-k'uan, 104
Wang Po, 207
Wang Shen, 101
Wang Shen-tzu, 141
Wang Su, 41, 44
Wang Wei, 52
Wang Yang-ming, 29, 60, 175; metaphysics of, 164; on Six Classics, 48; on *Songs Classic*, 177; use of accommodation, 169
Wang Ying-lin, 15, 100
Way, 16, 17, 46; Confucian, 52, 60, 140–141, 166, 168; of earth, 101, 184; of heaven, 19n.67, 101, 115, 213; kingly, 25, 53, 71, 191; of man, 19n.67, 101, 115; of nature, 101; of the sages, 101, 198, 215
Wei Chao, 130
Weil, Simone, 125
Wen, King, 71, 104, 130, 152, 153
"Western Inscription" (Hsi-ming), 54–55
Whitman, Cedric H., 112
Wilhelm, Hellmut, 103, 142, 151n.47
William of Auvergne, 204
Wolf, F. A., 87, 139, 207, 211
"worthies" (*hsien-che*), 71
Wu, Emperor, 38, 39; role of in reconstruction of classics, 42
Wu Ch'eng, 23
Wu-ching-i (Correct Meanings of the Five Classics), 76–77
Wu Kuei-fang, 192
Wu T'ing-tung, 185

Xenophanes, 124
Xiloj, Andrés, 99

Yajur Veda, 112
Yang Hsiung, 27
Yang Tsai, 52
Yeh Meng-te, 74, 104
Yen Jo-chü, 41

Yen-tzu, 140

Yerushalmi (Palestinian Talmud), 57, 90, 119

yin-yang duality, 162–163, 166, 174–175, 192

Yi T'oegye, 82, 163

Yü Ju-yen, 212

Yohanah, Rabbi, 144

Youn Sa-soon, 121

Yü Shu, 193

Zenodotus, 179

Zhou Zuoren, 217

Zohar, 62